DRUG ABUSE TREATMENT
Through **COLLABORATION**

DRUG ABUSE TREATMENT *Through* COLLABORATION

PRACTICE *and* RESEARCH PARTNERSHIPS THAT WORK

edited by

JAMES L. SORENSEN,

RICHARD A. RAWSON, JOSEPH GUYDISH,

and JOAN E. ZWEBEN

AMERICAN PSYCHOLOGICAL ASSOCIATION

WASHINGTON, DC

Published by
American Psychological Association
750 First Street, NE
Washington, DC 20002
www.apa.org

To order
APA Order Department
P.O. Box 92984
Washington, DC 20090-2984
Tel: (800) 374-2721; Direct: (202) 336-5510
Fax: (202) 336-5502; TDD/TTY: (202) 336-6123
Online: www.apa.org/books/
E-mail: order@apa.org

In the U.K., Europe, Africa, and the Middle East, copies may be ordered from
American Psychological Association
3 Henrietta Street
Covent Garden, London
WC2E 8LU England

Typeset in Goudy by Page Grafx, Inc., St. Simons Island, GA

Printer: Data Reproductions, Auburn Hills, MI
Cover Designer: NiDesign, Baltimore, MD
Technical/Production Editor: Kristen R. Sullivan

The opinions and statements published are the responsibility of the authors, and such opinions and statements do not necessarily represent the policies of the American Psychological Association.

Library of Congress Cataloging-in-Publication Data
Drug abuse treatment through collaboration: practice and research partnerships that work / edited by James L. Sorensen ... [et al.].— 1st ed.
      p. cm.
   Includes bibliographical references and index.
   ISBN 1-55798-985-0 (alk. paper)
   1. Drug abuse—Treatment. I. Sorensen, James L.

RC564 .D7775 2003
616.86′06—dc21

2002034222

British Library Cataloguing-in-Publication Data
A CIP record is available from the British Library.

Printed in the United States of America
First Edition

CONTENTS

CONTRIBUTORS

M. Douglas Anglin, Department of Psychiatry and Biobehavioral Sciences, Drug Abuse Research Center, University of California, Los Angeles

Thomas E. Backer, Human Interaction Research Institute, Encino, CA

Steven Belenko, National Center on Addiction and Substance Abuse, Columbia University, New York

Vivian B. Brown, PROTOTYPES, Centers for Innovation in Health, Mental Health, and Social Services, Los Angeles, CA

Deni Carise, Treatment Research Institute, Philadelphia, PA

H. Westley Clark, Center for Substance Abuse Treatment, Rockville, MD

Frances Cotter, Substance Abuse and Mental Health Services Administration, Center for Substance Abuse Treatment, Rockville, MD

George De Leon, Center for Therapeutic Community Research at National Development and Research Institutes, New York

Elizabeth Piper Deschenes, Department of Criminal Justice, California State University, Long Beach

Don C. Des Jarlais, The Baron Edmond de Rothschild Chemical Dependency Institute, Beth Israel Medical Center, New York

Dennis M. Donovan, Alcohol and Drug Abuse Institute, Department of Psychiatry and Behavioral Sciences, University of Washington, Seattle

Alice A. Gleghorn, San Francisco Department of Public Health, Community Substance Abuse Services, San Francisco, CA

John S. Goldkamp, Crime and Justice Research Institute, Philadelphia, PA

Õzge Gûrel, Treatment Research Institute, Philadelphia, PA

Joseph Guydish, Department of Medicine and the Institute for Health Policy Studies, University of California, San Francisco

ix

Holly Hagan, Center for Drug Use and HIV Research, Institute for AIDS Research, National Development and Research Institutes, New York

Alan I. Leshner, American Association for the Advancement of Science, Washington, DC

Walter Ling, Department of Psychiatry and Biobehavioral Sciences, Integrated Substance Abuse Programs, David Geffen School of Medicine, University of California, Los Angeles

Arthur Margolin, Department of Psychiatry, Substance Abuse Center, Yale University School of Medicine, New Haven, CT

Dennis McCarty, Department of Public Health, Oregon Health Sciences University, Portland

A. Thomas McLellan, Treatment Research Institute and University of Pennsylvania, Philadelphia

Theresa Moyers, Department of Psychology, University of New Mexico, Albuquerque

Joseph Nowinski, Department of Psychology, University of Connecticut, Storrs

Roger H. Peters, Department of Mental Health, Law and Policy, Louis de la Parte Florida Mental Health Institute, University of South Florida, Tampa

David Purchase, North American Syringe Exchange Network, Tacoma, WA

Richard A. Rawson, Department of Psychiatry and Biobehavioral Sciences, Integrated Substance Abuse Programs, David Geffen School of Medicine, University of California, Los Angeles

James L. Sorensen, Department of Psychiatry, University of California, San Francisco; San Francisco General Hospital, San Francisco

Elisa Triffleman, The Public Health Institute, Berkeley, CA; Yale University School of Medicine, New Haven, CT

Joan E. Zweben, Fourteenth Street Clinic and East Bay Community Recovery Project, Oakland, CA

A CHALLENGE TO PRACTITIONERS: BRINGING EVIDENCE-BASED PRACTICES INTO CLINICAL SETTINGS

H. WESTLEY CLARK

As the director of the Center for Substance Abuse Treatment (CSAT), I am gratified by this opportunity to contribute to expanding our knowledge, sharing insights, and developing strategies for combating substance abuse through innovations in treatment. This book provides an excellent venue for the idea exchange that is so necessary—among researchers, health care providers, addiction treatment professionals, community coalition builders, and the general public alike—if we are to deliver effective addiction-related services.

It is crucial that scientists and practitioners—indeed, everyone with an interest in substance abuse—understand the vast changes that are taking place in treatment as we reap the fruits of research. Together, CSAT and the National Institute on Drug Abuse sponsored the 1998 Institute of Medicine study titled *Bridging the Gap Between Practice and Research*, which critically analyzed the importance of finding solutions that can bring down the barriers between research and clinical practice (Lamb, Greenlick, & McCarty, 1998).

Recent unprecedented growth in the support for substance abuse research has induced scientific advances—ever-more-frequent findings relating to neuroscience, pharmacology, clinical management, health services delivery, and other disciplines. Those responsible for bringing to people in need the hope that is treatment face numerous emerging challenges. At a time when practitioners are stretched to the limit to provide critically needed services to clients, they are now called on to integrate a continuous stream of evidence-based practices into their clinical settings.

CSAT recognizes the demands placed on treatment providers and exerts national leadership in efforts to enhance the quality of treatment services and make them available to individuals who need them, including those with co-occurring drug, alcohol, mental, and physical problems. CSAT supports a variety of activities aimed at fulfilling the congressional mandate that its mission reflects. The charge, in particular, is "to improve the lives of individuals and families affected by alcohol and drug abuse by ensuring access to clinically sound, cost-effective addiction treatment that reduces the health and social costs to our communities and the nation."

CSAT's initiatives and programs are based on research findings and the belief of experts in the addiction field that treatment and recovery work best in a community-based, coordinated system of comprehensive services. We build on partnerships with communities and private organizations to address these needs. This book makes a compelling contribution to this same interest. As editors James L. Sorensen, Richard A. Rawson, Joseph Guydish, and Joan E. Zweben insightfully note in chapter 1, the historical absence of substance abuse research-to-practice links suggests a lack of collaboration between cultures. Building lasting bridges between scientists and providers is perhaps the single most formidable challenge that faces the field of substance abuse. This volume includes as contributors esteemed scientists and practitioners; its organization gives even-handed treatment to each discipline in a wholly appropriate fashion. This pioneering compendium itemizes numerous effective ways to integrate science with clinical care in the treatment of drug dependence. As such, it should be of interest to anyone whose work brings him or her into contact with drug and alcohol users. It is especially useful as a training resource for individuals entering the substance abuse field.

Against this backdrop stands the National Treatment Plan Initiative and its call to fully integrate services and research. Published by CSAT in November 2000, *Changing the Conversation* recognizes the critical need for every segment of the treatment field to plan and work together to make culturally relevant, appropriate treatment happen for those addicted to alcohol and drugs. It also recommends the development of a treatment system based on the best scientific evidence, one that promotes consistent communication and collaboration among service providers, academic institutions, and researchers and establishes incentives and assistance for programs and staff in applying new standards and treatment methods.

For its part, CSAT partners with community-based entities and organizations to support science-based programs and services through a variety of initiatives. Prominent among them are its community-based Practice Improvement Collaboratives (PICs). The purpose of the PIC program is to improve the quality of treatment by increasing interaction and knowledge exchange among community stakeholders—treatment providers, organizations providing support services, researchers, and policymakers, including health plan managers and purchasers of substance abuse treatment.

Collaborative projects in diverse locations bring together practitioners in daily clinical practice and scientists who are identifying effective new treatment modalities. How exciting a time this is, given the many advances that the science is making; yet how difficult it is, with science moving so rapidly, to move these advances from research into clinical practice. The reasons for this paradox are myriad:

- So little is known about the process of the diffusion of new knowledge to the field.
- Inducing behavioral and organizational change (in any endeavor, including substance abuse) is a complex process.
- There is a lack of awareness among individuals who administer and pay for addiction treatment regarding the cost, time, staff, and administrative support needed to effectively integrate innovations into existing systems of care delivery.
- There are a finite amount of resources available to the field to upgrade outdated technological and management information systems that are key to putting into practice innovations in service delivery.

Nonetheless, there is every reason to be buoyed by the future of treatment.

As Alice A. Gleghorn and Frances Cotter skillfully discuss in chapter 13, CSAT is determined that PICs increase the capability of community treatment programs to adopt evidence-based clinical and service delivery practices. Providers need to be an integral part of the change process, identifying priority practice improvement needs and obtaining necessary training and administrative support to implement and sustain permanent change.

Currently, PICs are implementing a broad range of evidence-based practices, motivational interviewing, screening, and interventions for American Indian youth; cognitive–behavioral therapy for youth with depression and alcohol abuse; treatment for offenders who have co-occurring mental health and substance abuse disorders; and pharmacotherapy. PICs also have demonstrated that local coalitions have a unique capability to mobilize key players, engage policymakers, and leverage resources that go well beyond the initial projections. Evidence-based practices, as they are developed on the basis of scientific research, will provide little help to patients who experience drug and alcohol addiction if practitioners in the field do not adopt these new protocols and integrate them into their professional practice.

CSAT's Addiction Technology Transfer Centers (ATTCs) and Treatment Improvement Protocols (TIPs) likewise further the knowledge application and technology transfer necessary to create the new scientific understanding of addiction. Today, it can take 20 years between the discovery of an effective treatment or intervention and its adoption as part of community-based care. CSAT's ATTC network—which now serves all 50 states plus Washington, DC; Puerto Rico; the U.S. Virgin Islands; and the Pacific Trust Territories—has a clear role to play in reducing the time it takes to incorporate scientific advances into community care.

Drawing on current health services research from such sources as the National Institutes of Health as well as the Substance Abuse and Mental Health Services Administration's own program evaluations, ATTCs help upgrade standards of professional practice for treatment providers, prepare practitioners to function in managed care settings, and promote the inclusion of addiction treatment training in academic programs. ATTCs keep pace with the latest field and academic research and translate these findings into information practitioners can use, distributed through continuing education courses, specialized publications, curriculum enhancements, and other learning opportunities.

CSAT's TIPs are the best practice guidelines for the treatment of substance abuse. CSAT's Office of Evaluation, Scientific Analysis, and Synthesis draws on the experience and knowledge of clinical, research, and administrative experts to produce the TIPs, which are distributed to a growing number of facilities and individuals across the country. Treatment providers must begin to incorporate new methods and best practices into their programs. However, in so doing, they must remain cognizant of the fact that change, after all, is evolutionary.

As new research findings on better ways to treat patients come to the fore, professionals in the substance abuse treatment field must make certain that the research-to-practice gap does not become pronounced but instead disappears. At the end of the day, if real change is to occur, there must be a buy-in from treatment providers, administrators, and staff of local service delivery systems as well as from the recovery community—the families and friends of those who are served—from local colleges and universities, from the faith community, and from community outreach groups. The message substance abuse professionals convey—that treatment is powerful—must be accompanied, and continually confirmed, by the highest quality science that determines what treatments work best, under what conditions, and for whom.

The addiction field has to move past its earlier dichotomy between researchers and practitioners. By working together, researchers and practitioners can identify and further develop promising scientific protocols, use the most rigorous scientific standards to test them, and put into practice those that prove to be the most effective treatments.

To be sure, it will not be easy to achieve this new paradigm. As the federal government's leader in taking research data and translating it for use by practitioners, CSAT salutes the contributors to this work for articulating the pressing need for systemic change represented by ongoing research–practice collaboration.

REFERENCES

Center for Substance Abuse Treatment. (2000). *Improving substance abuse treatment: The national treatment plan initiative: Changing the conversation* (DHHS Publication No. SMA 00-3480). Rockville, MD: Author.

Lamb, S., Greenlick, M. R., & McCarty, D. (Eds.). (1998). *Bridging the gap between practice and research: Forging partnerships with community-based drug and alcohol treatment*. Washington, DC: National Academy Press.

BLENDING RESEARCH AND PRACTICE: DESIGNING TREATMENT STUDIES TO MEET REAL-WORLD NEEDS

ALAN I. LESHNER

A major priority for the National Institute on Drug Abuse (NIDA), especially since the 1990s, has been to bridge the disconnect that exists between what science has revealed about drug abuse and addiction and what the public perceives to be true about them. As the world's largest supporter of research on drug abuse and addiction, NIDA has a clear responsibility to disseminate its research findings to the widest variety of audiences possible, including researchers; the public; clinicians, counselors, and other practitioners; and civic officials and policymakers.

NIDA staff have been working particularly hard to bridge the specific disconnect between what science has taught us and how treatment and prevention are practiced. Although we are attempting to bridge this disconnect in all disciplines, the most focused example of our efforts is in the treatment arena. NIDA has launched a "Blending Research to Practice" initiative to ensure that, among other things, our research efforts are in fact disseminated, adapted, and adopted in a timely manner by treatment practitioners.

As the name of our initiative on this topic implies, we view this effort as a "blending" or partnering of disciplines. Our experience has been that *technology transfer* and *research-to-practice* are not the most appropriate terms to use to describe this particular concept. We have found that the most productive relationships to foster the incorporation of scientific principles into ongoing treatment involve true partnerships between researchers and practitioners. It is important not only that researchers and practitioners learn from each other during this process but also that the best results occur when practitioners serve as real partners in the conceptualization, design, and implementation of research protocols. These protocols will answer whether science-based treatments are useful in real-life settings and will determine how they can best be incorporated into ongoing practice. This is *blending*, not *technology transfer* or *research-to-practice*. All interactions are bidirectional.

Much preparation went into the launch of this initiative. First, we went through the findings from our treatment research portfolio and distilled the overarching principles that characterize effective drug addiction treatment. The result has been one of NIDA's most popular publications, the *Principles of Drug Addiction Treatment* guide (NIDA, 1999). To foster more widespread use of scientifically based treatment components, we included this publication along with our newly developed treatment manuals and other information about science-based drug abuse treatment strategies in the "NIDA Clinical Toolbox," which was shipped to the nearly 12,000 drug abuse treatment programs around the country.

It was while going through this assessment and development process that we realized there is as much researchers can learn from practitioners as the reverse; thus we began encouraging more bidirectional interactions and knowledge exchanges between the research community and the prevention and treatment communities. NIDA then declared as its foremost goal for the new millennium the improvement of drug abuse treatment nationwide using science as the vehicle. Several activities have been part of this endeavor, including the development of new and improved medications and behavioral therapies as well as the creation of a new mechanism to bring drug abuse researchers into the real world of the treatment clinic while simultaneously creating opportunities that allow practitioners to participate in treatment research. The principal instrument of this effort is NIDA's National Drug Abuse Treatment Clinical Trials Network (CTN). I highlight some overarching concepts that characterize this mechanism and provide one or two examples of the blending that I have already witnessed through the work of the CTN.

The CTN grew out of a set of recommendations in the 1998 Institute of Medicine (IOM) report, *Bridging the Gap Between Practice and Research*. One of the editors of this book, James L. Sorensen, had a major role in that effort. The IOM suggested that the drug addiction field should model a national treatment research infrastructure after the very successful clinical trials networks in cancer treatment, allergy and infectious disease, HIV/AIDS, epilepsy, and other medical fields (Lamb, Greenlick, & McCarty, 1998).

The CTN is a cooperative undertaking of NIDA, university drug abuse scientists, and community treatment providers in which researchers and practitioners work together to test research-based treatments in community settings. In less than 2 years, we have launched and established this relatively permanent national treatment research infrastructure. As of the fall of 2001, for example, NIDA was funding 14 nodes across the country and was supporting seven research protocols conducted at 52 sites with more than 3,600 patients.

A central operating principle for the CTN is that all its efforts are true partnerships between the researchers and the practitioners, and that has proven critical to its rapid development and apparent early successes. The full involvement of both scientists and practitioners in all aspects of the CTN's work is now its hallmark. For example, treatment protocols to be run in the CTN must both retain the science base of new treatments and ensure they are applicable in the clinic. As a result of this partnering, it is expected that when a CTN study demonstrates that a research-based therapy works in the clinic, the protocol for that treatment will be adopted quickly as a standard of care by community treatment providers. Likewise, it is anticipated that researchers will take the knowledge gained from working with practitioners back to their laboratories to inform the design of new treatment studies that meet the real-world needs of the clinic. The establishment of agreed-on working protocols is just one example of how the CTN is putting research into practice.

To further our efforts to bridge the existing gap between research and practice, NIDA plans to provide support to the Center for Substance Abuse Treatment's Addiction Technology Transfer Centers (ATTCs) to ensure that treatment systems can be in an even better position to serve the needs and interests of people with substance use disorders. It is expected that these ATTCs will take the findings from the protocols in NIDA's CTN and help disseminate this research-based knowledge so that addictions treatment and public health/mental health personnel, institutional and community corrections professionals, and individuals in other related disciplines can adapt and adopt the research to suit their needs. Because many of NIDA's clinical research nodes are near ATTCs, research can be readily disseminated and made applicable to individuals affiliated with or served by the CTN and the ATTC. We are quite excited by the impact that this collaborative effort will likely have on how communities receive and develop the skills, systems, and necessary support to implement new research findings.

I think readers of this book will learn some valuable lessons about what it takes to develop and implement successful treatment programs. After reading several of the chapters, I too received an even greater appreciation for the difficulties that researchers, practitioners, and policymakers face daily. There are many obstacles to be overcome, but this book offers rays of hope to those committed to making a difference.

Overall, I am quite encouraged by the willingness of both the individuals working at the research bench and those in the proverbial "trenches" to bridge this gap between research and practice; there also appears to be sincere interest in closing it as well. In time, this blending of clinical research and practice will be second nature to us all and will enable the field of drug abuse to realize the full potential of science-based treatments to reduce the tremendous personal and social costs of drug addiction.

REFERENCES

Lamb, S., Greenlick, M. R., & McCarty, D. (Eds.). (1998). *Bridging the gap between practice and research: Forging partnerships with community-based drug and alcohol treatment.* Washington, DC: National Academy Press.

National Institute on Drug Abuse. (1999). *Principles of drug addiction treatment.* Bethesda, MD: National Institutes of Health.

PREFACE

This volume personifies and recommends new collaborations. The idea for the book began with a discussion between James L. Sorensen and Richard A. Rawson about the problems in the field of substance abuse treatment. Researchers were ignoring clinical realities, treatment programs were ignoring research, and policymakers were looking at options that ignored the value of both research and treatment. In the language of the substance abuse treatment field, everyone was in denial, as suggested by the cartoon that opens this book. As clinical researchers, Sorensen and Rawson had a healthy respect for both clinicians and scientists; they enlisted a researcher (Joseph Guydish) and a clinical administrator (Joan E. Zweben) to coedit this book highlighting the efforts in the field that had the promise to meld "bench" and "trench" into a more effective force in reducing the problems of drug dependence.

We intend to reach clinicians and program directors who are coping with the problems of drug abuse as well as researchers and policymakers who are attempting to devise new treatments and service arrays for treatment of drug problems. Most of all, we intend to reach people just entering the field, with the hope that the message will have a renewable following. Our message, put simply, is that clinicians and researchers need to collaborate.

This book should be of interest to various professionals whose work brings them into contact with drug users. For example, psychologists, psychiatrists, social workers, nurses, parole officers, and substance abuse treatment counselors will find it useful in their work and of value in their formal education programs. The book should be of special interest to academics who are searching for promising areas to research in substance use and want to know about issues in conducting applied research. We hope it will be used in colleges and universities in courses in psychology, public health, social work, public administration, and nursing at the undergraduate and graduate levels.

This book is not a cookbook; neither is it intended to restrict readers to a narrow, theoretically bounded range of techniques. Rather, we intend to increase readers' understanding of treatment and research options and provide a range of alternatives for each, allowing practitioners and researchers to blend their own strengths with models that have come before.

Many individuals have contributed to the material presented in this book. Highest on this list are the authors and colleagues who provided the chapters. We also appreciate the contribution of our present and former students and protégés, who listened to us as we worked through the details of the collaborative processes that we recommend. Likewise, we are most grateful to our clients, whose experiences have provided invaluable insights that have shaped our thinking about what the field of substance abuse treatment really needs. Finally, and most important, we recognize and appreciate the support of our families, who tolerated the special obsession that this book became for us.

Much of the work in this volume was supported in part by grants and contracts from the federal government, particularly the National Institute on Drug Abuse and the Center for Substance Abuse Treatment. We asked the directors of these two programs to write the forewords to this volume because they lead the two largest and most important funding agencies in the United States supporting research and treatment, respectively.

We dedicate this volume to research and practice leaders now deceased; our effort in writing this book continues in the fine tradition of leaders in the field who also contributed to improving practice through research and improving research through practice.

DRUG ABUSE TREATMENT
Through COLLABORATION

1

INTRODUCTION: THE NEED FOR RESEARCH–PRACTICE COLLABORATION

JAMES L. SORENSEN, JOSEPH GUYDISH, RICHARD A. RAWSON, AND JOAN E. ZWEBEN

An outpatient treatment that provides rewards to cocaine abusers for abstaining from drugs proves to be startlingly effective with most patients. Why has this powerful technique not swept through the drug abuse treatment field? For many providers, cost is the bottom line. Despite the promise of the technique, the rewards average about $500 for each patient for a 12-week treatment and can be as high as $1,100 per patient. In a typical treatment program, the approach seems unaffordable. Other treatment providers object to rewarding patients for abstinence on principle, believing it is a bribe that

This volume reflects the support of numerous organizations and individuals. Organizations that provided support for this chapter include the National Institutes of Health (Grants P50DA09253, R01DA08753, R01DA11344, R01DA12221, R01DA14922, R01DA14470, R01DA11972, R01DA09419, P50DA12755, and Cooperative Agreements U10DA15815 and U10DA13045), the Substance Abuse and Mental Health Services Administration (Center for Substance Abuse Treatment Task Order 282-98-0026 and the Center for Substance Abuse Treatment TI12623), U.S. Department of Health and Human Services (Cooperative Agreement UD1TI11440 and UD1TI1295), and the Robert Wood Johnson Foundation (Grant 037367). We appreciate the editorial support of Karen Sharp, Nancy Killion, Sarayu Rao, and Pamela Zilavy.

will not have lasting value. This issue illustrates the gap between research and practice in drug abuse treatment. Sometimes clinical practice may be several years behind the current research findings. From another viewpoint, research may be so disconnected from practice that clinicians think research-developed treatments are too unrealistic or visionary.

A promising clinical technique developed outside the traditional scientific community may take years before it draws the attention of researchers. For example, therapeutic community treatments for drug abuse were developed in the 1960s by private organizations such as Synanon, which operated independent of research. When researchers finally documented the effectiveness of this approach, policymakers more readily embraced the treatment.

Bringing drug abuse treatment and research into accord is essential, because drug abuse is such an important problem. Drug abuse costs the United States nearly $100 billion a year—in reduced productivity, crimes and incarceration, and treatment for drug abusers and their family members (Holland & Mushinski, 1999). Considering this social cost, it is imperative that society treat drug abuse using approaches that are both clinically effective and cost effective. Thus, the gap between research and treatment is one of our society's most critical unresolved issues.

In 1998, the Institute of Medicine produced the report *Bridging the Gap Between Practice and Research* (Lamb, Greenlick, & McCarty, 1998), which described the enormous separation between the science and treatment of substance use disorders. One conclusion of this report was that scientific advances are not being incorporated sufficiently into drug abuse treatment in the United States. This research–practice gap is a significant problem in improving the health of Americans.

TREATMENT OF DRUG ABUSE

There are about 11,000 specialized drug abuse treatment programs in the United States, staffed by counselors from diverse backgrounds. Although 11,000 is a large number of programs, the number pales in proportion to the problem. The Office of National Drug Control Policy (2000) pointed out that approximately 5 million drug users needed immediate treatment in 1998, whereas only 2.1 million received it. The demand for drug treatment often exceeds the supply, so drug users sit on waiting lists (Gibson & Lovelle-Drache, 1991).

Treatment for drug problems is effective. The economic benefits of drug abuse treatment—including more employment, less crime, and less need for expensive medical care—have been known for decades. Yet drug abuse treatment is not nearly as effective as it could be. There are long waits for services in many communities. Policy leaders have difficulty "selling" these programs to the community and placing program facilities in neighborhoods. Innovators have been developing new treatment approaches. The criminal justice system has developed "drug courts," a new way to link the power of the criminal justice system with the constructive intervention of the treatment system. In one experiment, an interim methadone clinic was created to provide temporary methadone maintenance without counseling, and patients in this program reduced their drug use compared with patients left on a waiting list (Yancovitz, Des Jarlais, Peyser, & Drew, 1991). A "fast track" into treatment may be beneficial: One study found that individuals who were admitted rapidly to a program were less likely to drop out of treatment in the first 6 months (Bell, Caplehorn, & McNeil, 1994). Yet existing programs, although underfunded, are in a seller's market, with little reason to change their approach even when it becomes outdated. Research can have a vital role in determining the relative value of new treatment approaches.

RESEARCH ON DRUG ABUSE TREATMENT

Research has made important contributions to drug abuse treatment. Researchers developed nearly all the medications that are used in treatment, including opiate agonists (e.g., methadone and levo-alpha-acetylmethadol [LAAM]), opiate antagonists (naltrexone, naloxone), and medications used to help alleviate mental disorders. Likewise, researchers developed effective behavioral treatments, such as relapse prevention and motivational enhancement therapy. A recent booklet from the National Institute on Drug Abuse (NIDA) includes no fewer than a dozen examples of treatment approaches that were developed through research (NIDA, 1999; see Exhibit 1.1). Also,

EXHIBIT 1.1
Effective Treatment Approaches Developed Through Research

- Relapse prevention
- Supportive–expressive psychotherapy
- Individualized drug counseling
- Motivational enhancement therapy
- Behavioral therapy for adolescents
- Multidimensional family therapy for adolescents
- Multisystemic therapy
- Combined behavioral and nicotine replacement therapy for nicotine dependence addiction
- Community reinforcement approach plus vouchers
- Voucher-based reinforcement therapy for patients in methadone maintenance treatment
- Day treatment with abstinence contingencies and vouchers
- Matrix model of drug abuse treatment

Note. Adapted from *Principles of Drug Addiction Treatment*, National Institute on Drug Abuse, 1999 (NIH No. 99-4180). In the public domain.

in many cases research clearly influences practice: In the early 1980s, research indicated that higher methadone doses decreased heroin use and increased treatment retention (Hargreaves, 1983). In response, methadone doses rose considerably from 1988 to 1992 (D'Aunno, Folz-Murphy, & Lin, 1999).

Yet for the most part research is not integrated with treatment of drug abuse. The director of NIDA has set a policy goal for science to replace ideology as a guiding principle for drug abuse treatment. The time is long past due for both treatment and research professionals to ingrain into their protégés a deep respect for both science and practice in the treatment of drug dependence.

The gap between research and practice was illustrated in a 1998 Public Broadcasting System report (Moyers & O'Neill, 1998). Esteemed television journalist Bill Moyers produced a four-part documentary on the American perspective on substance abuse. The first 2 hours described tremendous advancements in addiction research during the 1980s and 1990s. Moyers interviewed scientists who were researching the genetic influences on development of substance use disorders; using sophisticated positron emission tomography technology, he showed how drug use changes the brain and how we can now see the areas of the brain that are involved when an addicted person experiences drug craving; he interviewed the director of NIDA, who described addiction as a "brain disease." This first segment left the impression that researchers are on the verge of a scientific revolution in helping people with addiction disorders. Much of the remainder of the series described the activities that are used throughout America as the mainstream addiction treatments. Moyers visited public clinics and well-appointed private treatment organizations, and he talked with doctors and counselors in many settings. Amazingly, the U.S. treatment system described in 1998 was indistinguishable from what was in place in 1975. The groundbreaking research in the 1990s has produced far too few benefits in the treatment of addictive disorders.

THE TREATMENT–RESEARCH DISCONNECTION

Both researchers and treaters of substance abuse have fonts of knowledge, yet often each operates as if the other's perspective were irrelevant. The gap between treatment and research is understandable. There has been a knowledge explosion about substance use. It has become nearly impossible for well-informed researchers or clinicians to keep up with their own field, much less another specialization. Policymakers have sounded many calls to transfer the information between the research and clinical areas of expertise (Brown, 1998; Johnson, 1993), yet there is little research on how to transfer these technologies. Among the many reasons for the gap is the public's hesitation to fund either research or treatment for addiction (Lamb et al., 1998).

For researchers, the most acceptable way to disseminate study results is through scientific journals. Counselors, however, seldom use the research literature for guidance (Sorensen & Guydish, 1991). Indeed, in a study of methods to disseminate a job seekers' workshop in drug abuse treatment, Sorensen, Hall, Loeb, and Allen (1988) found *no* adoption of the job seekers' workshop based on publication in the literature, compared with 4% adoption if they sent programs a brochure and training manual, 19% if staff went to a training session about the approach, and 28% when they went to programs and conducted training on site.

Have researchers failed to ask meaningful questions about treatment of drug abuse? From the perspective of treatment personnel, the answer may be "yes." On the other hand, researchers' viewpoint may be that treatment professionals have not been open to new ideas and that treatment approaches are driven not by data but by inertia. On the treatment side, there are wonderful intentions, but the lack of money, organization, professionalism, and training can create an anti-empirical orientation. On the research side, there are brilliant minds, but by avoiding the difficult-to-study issues research can be sterile and conformist, sacrificing relevance to scientific rigor. Many chapters in this book present practical ways that clinical leaders and researchers can promote the needed practice–research integration.

To some degree, the problem is a failure of communication between cultures. In a survey of substance abuse counselors in Massachusetts, 46% identified themselves as in recovery from alcohol or drug problems (Mulligan, McCarty, Potter, & Krakow, 1989). The ranks of counselors have been filled with significant numbers of paraprofessionals, whereas researchers come from a more academically trained background. This has led to two separate knowledge bases about treatment efficacy: one informed by personal experience, the other informed by scientific research. Brown (2000) contended that new government initiatives need to emphasize interpersonal communications and highlight what is important in technology transfer. In this way, research findings can influence treatment programs, and vice versa.

HOW TO USE THIS BOOK

In this book we aim to promote more effective linkage between practitioners and researchers. The book comes from our experience as both. The multidisciplinary cast of contributors probes such topics as what field-developed treatments have attracted researchers' attention, what research-developed treatments have been readily adopted into the field, and what examples illustrate ways that practitioners and researchers can collaborate.

Health professionals who work with drug users have many questions about how they can provide more effective treatment. Researchers are on the lookout for emerging treatments that show promise. Put simply, both groups want to know what works. What can clinicians and researchers do to promote more effective treatment and research? Readers of this book will learn of several treatments that show promise from a research viewpoint as well as promising clinical interventions that have not been well researched; they will gain information about specific interventions that could be adapted to their community; and they will gain a broader perspective about treatment, research, and policy. These issues are increasingly important, as there is an expanding emphasis on the application of research findings and research–practice integration.

Organization

The 18 chapters of this book are organized into four parts that cover the following broad topics: (a) examples of dissemination of knowledge from practice to research, (b) examples of dissemination of knowledge from research to practice, (c) examples of collaboration, and (d) implications. Because there is at least some reciprocity between research and practice in all topics, readers may find that as written not all chapters neatly fit the scheme. To provide insights into the various chapters and their place in the bigger picture, at the beginning of each part we provide introductions that discuss the context of each chapter. In developing the book, our philosophy was to provide positive examples—treatment or research approaches that worked—rather than to dwell on negative examples of the disconnection we are trying to remedy. Readers should not interpret the absence of a chapter about a treatment or research strategy as a lack of confidence in the technique. For example, there is not a chapter on the use of vouchers to reward abstinence, even though the book begins with a discussion of this highly effective, research-developed treatment method. Instead, the absence of a specific treatment or research approach in this book is more likely because the technique remains primarily on one side of the practice–research divide and does not yet provide a strong example of how to overcome the gap. When a negative example is presented, it is included as a contrast to a prototype that worked. Thus, Parts I, II, and III are filled with illustrations that people in the field can emulate.

Suggestions to Readers

Each reader will use this book differently. If you are interested in benefiting from treatment or research developments, Parts I and II will be most useful. If your questions concern how and where to integrate research and practice, Part III provides useful approaches. To understand the ingredients needed to link practice and research, we recommend Part IV.

It is in the best interest of people in the addiction field to learn as much about treatment and research as they can. People have the same kinds of problems, whether their starting point is research, treatment, or policy. The differences are a matter of degree. People who have a problem with drugs are in need of allies in their efforts to change, and a most effective ally can be the knowledgeable helping professional. By maximizing the linkage between research and practice, readers can help individuals overcome the devastating problems of drug abuse.

REFERENCES

Bell, J., Caplehorn, J. R. M., & McNeil, D. R. (1994). The effect of intake procedures on performance in methadone maintenance. *Addiction, 89*, 463–471.

Brown, B. (1998). Making a difference—Is journal publication enough? *Journal of Substance Abuse Treatment, 15*, 87–88.

Brown, B. S. (2000). From research to practice: The bridge is out and the water's rising. *Advances in Medical Sociology, 7*, 345–365.

D'Aunno, T., Folz-Murphy, N., & Lin, X. (1999). Changes in methadone treatment practices: Results from a panel study, 1988–1995. *American Journal of Drug and Alcohol Abuse, 25*, 681–699.

Gibson, D. R., & Lovelle-Drache, J. (1991). Individual counseling. In J. L. Sorensen, L. A. Wermuth, D. R. Gibson, K.-H. Choi, & S. L. Batki (Eds.), *Preventing AIDS in drug users and their sexual partners* (pp. 116–129). New York: Guilford Press.

Hargreaves, W. A. (1983). Methadone dosage and duration for maintenance treatment. *National Institute on Drug Abuse: Treatment Research Monographs, 83*, 19–79.

Holland, P., & Mushinski, M. (1999). Costs of alcohol and drug abuse in the United States, 1992. *Statistical Bulletin/Metropolitan Insurance Companies, 80*(4), 2–9.

Johnson, E. M. (1993). Technology transfer: Knowledge for helping. In L. Harris (Ed.), *Problems of drug dependence 1992: Proceedings of the 54th annual scientific meeting: College on the Problems of Drug Dependence, Inc.* (NIDA Research Monograph 132, NIH No. 93-3505, pp. 3–8). Washington, DC: U.S. Government Printing Office.

Lamb, S., Greenlick, M. R., & McCarty, D. (Eds.). (1998). *Bridging the gap between practice and research: Forging partnerships with community-based drug and alcohol treatment.* Washington, DC: National Academy Press.

Moyers, J. D., & O'Neill, J. D. (Executive Producers). (1998). *Moyers on addiction: Close to home* [Television series]. New York: Thirteen/WNET and Public Affairs Television, Inc.

Mulligan, D. H., McCarty, D., Potter, D., & Krakow, M. (1989). Counselors in public and private alcoholism and drug abuse treatment programs. *Alcoholism Treatment Quarterly, 6*(3–4), 75–89.

National Institute on Drug Abuse. (1999). *Principles of drug addiction treatment* (NIH No. 99-4180). Rockville, MD: Author.

Office of National Drug Control Policy. (2000). *ONDCP National Drug Control Strategy 2000.* Washington, DC: Author.

Sorensen, J. L., & Guydish, J. R. (1991). Adopting effective interventions. In J. L. Sorensen, L. A. Wermuth, D. R. Gibson, K.-H. Choi, & S. L. Batki (Eds.), *Preventing AIDS in drug users and their sexual partners* (pp. 153–167). New York: Guilford Press.

Sorensen, J. L., Hall, S. M., Loeb, P., & Allen, T. (1988). Dissemination of a job seekers' workshop to drug treatment programs. *Behavior Therapy, 19,* 143–155.

Yancovitz, S. R., Des Jarlais, D. C., Peyser, N. P., & Drew, E. (1991). A randomized trial of an interim methadone maintenance clinic. *American Journal of Public Health, 81,* 1185–1191.

I

DISSEMINATION FROM PRACTICE TO RESEARCH

INTRODUCTION: DISSEMINATION FROM PRACTICE TO RESEARCH

JOSEPH GUYDISH

In substance abuse, as in every clinical field, practice preceded research. When self-help programs and therapeutic communities (TCs) began, they were not research driven. Their originators were concerned with the absence of, and pressing need for, effective treatments to serve substance abusers. The chapters in Part I tell the story of practice–research collaboration from the viewpoint of treatments that started in clinical settings and then incorporated research to improve the intervention. It is encouraging that, although time-honored interventions such as TCs operated for some time before research supported them, recent interventions, such as needle exchange programs (NEPs) and drug courts, have deployed practice–research partnerships more quickly.

No one is better positioned to describe the practice–research partnership in TCs than George De Leon (chapter 2), who, because of his pioneering and long-standing work, is both the storyteller and a main actor. He describes how TCs emerged outside the scientific mainstream, the development of the TC research–practice partnership, and the value of this partnership in sustaining TC funding and supporting the evolution of treatment. De Leon describes two phases of *practice–research reciprocity*. This use of a phased model reflects TC treatment, in which participants move through graduated phases of responsibility and privilege, and will be familiar to TC practitioners. Phase I research addressed questions of the feasibility, effectiveness, and cost-effectiveness of TCs. Findings cast light on the high rates of early dropout from TCs and led to the observation—now incorporated throughout substance abuse treatment—that longer time in treatment is associated with better outcomes. TC treatments were refocused away from passively waiting for clients to "hit bottom" to actively intervening with individuals seeking treatment. Strategies emerging from this work include assessment of pretreatment motivation and matching of clients to TC formats and point toward innovations incorporating TC principles into nonresidential settings. Phase II (1990–present) witnessed increased support for TC research which, having demonstrated global effectiveness, was now concerned with extending treatment to diverse populations and clarifying the essential ingredients of TCs. Through this work, the TC approach has been extended to serve substance-abusing persons who are also mentally ill, those who are involved in the criminal justice system, those who are homeless, women with children, and those in methadone treatment. The TC research–practice reciprocity supported cross-fertilization among treatment providers, researchers, and funders that framed the evolution of the TC intervention. This synergy is the aim and the goal for practice–research collaboration in the substance abuse field as a whole.

Arthur Margolin (chapter 3) and Joseph Nowinski (chapter 4) discuss other treatment approaches that are widely used in practice but are insufficiently studied. Acupuncture, with roots in Chinese medicine, enjoys a long history, yet its adaptation to drug abuse treatment is recent. Acupuncture has broad appeal, because it appears to reduce craving and is a nonverbal approach that may be suited to clients who are less talkative or more ambivalent about treatment. In reporting on a series of acupuncture studies, Margolin elaborates the challenges of investigating treatments using clinical trials. These include the development of suitable control conditions, the need for staff who are well trained in multiple acupuncture protocols, and problems of placebo controls and blinding clinicians to different treatment conditions. In doing so, Margolin raises the bar for research in substance abuse treatment. Although the randomized-trial approach has steadily influenced research in the past 10 years, Margolin hints that randomized trials may not be sufficiently subtle when one is investigating Eastern-oriented approaches in which effectiveness depends on harmony within the client, the clinic, and the client–clinic interaction.

In discussing self-help approaches, Nowinski (chapter 4) opens a different window on the challenges of practice–research collaboration. He describes the range of self-help approaches, distinguishing among them on dimensions of philosophy, strategy, and organization. He discusses how to incorporate self-help strategies into substance abuse treatment, and these comments will be helpful to practitioners. He speaks only briefly to the issues of research, but this is not accidental. Self-help interventions often rely on volunteerism and anonymity as therapeutic tools. For these reasons, self-help approaches are relatively divorced from treatment, research, and policy initiatives. With few exceptions, self-help interventions remain apart from practice–research collaborative efforts and represent both a challenge to and an opportunity in the field.

The final chapters in this section add perspectives from public health (Holly Hagan, Don C. Des Jarlais, and David Purchase, chapter 5) and criminal justice (Elizabeth Piper Deschenes, Roger H. Peters, John S. Goldkamp, and Steven Belenko, chapter 6). When David Purchase started one of the first NEPs in the United States, needle exchange was illegal, controversial, and risky. In 1988, and for years after, the people who conducted NEPs and the injection drug users (IDUs) who used them were liable to arrest. Across the country, participants on both sides of the exchange table were prosecuted. Federal policy proscribed the use of federal funds to support NEP services or research. Purchase exchanged needles because the IDUs he had known as a treatment provider had incurred the new and lethal risk of HIV infection. He believed that giving IDUs access to clean needles could reduce that risk. Hagan et al. describe how Purchase first approached local authorities and asked for their cooperation. The health department assigned a researcher to work with the NEP to assess its effectiveness. The result was a partnership in which all participants, including exchange participants, had a sense of ownership. This collaboration led to two vital outcomes: (a) a feedback loop, in which data from NEP studies were continually reported to policymakers, showing that NEPs had benefits and no apparent negative effects, and (b) a legal test of whether the health department could, by declaring HIV infection a health emergency, circumvent state drug paraphernalia laws and conduct NEP services. These outcomes not only supported the NEP in Tacoma, Washington, but they also offered research findings, a partnership model, and a legal precedent to help develop NEPs in other communities. The development of NEPs, and the years of debate, thought, and study underlying that development, also affected the field of substance abuse treatment, drawing treatment professionals into the current philosophical framework of harm reduction.

Like NEPs, drug courts (Deschenes et al., chapter 6) emerged first as a grassroots effort. They developed out of judges' frustration with ineffective "revolving-door" court strategies. Unlike NEPs, however, drug courts benefited from federal support and have enjoyed wide appeal. The drug court movement, in addition to the approximately 650 drug courts operating nationally, is supported by a federal Drug Court Program Office, practice standards, and professional associations and training institutes. In a startling departure from the history of other interventions, federal funding for drug courts carried with it a research mandate that required jurisdictions to work with researchers, framing a practice–research partnership. The value of this strategy, in addition to rapid deployment of research, was to include research collaborators early, giving the field a platform for building evidence-based practices. The disadvantage was that research activities in any single drug court were underfunded, and evaluation focused on process rather than outcome measures. Deschenes et al. note that few drug court research reports have been published in scientific journals and that this body of work is inaccessible to the broader academic community. This offers a counterpoint to the complaint that articles in scientific journals do not reach clinicians and is a reminder that findings from practice–research efforts must be disseminated in venues that reach both the practice and scientific communities. As a consequence of a process evaluation focus, and of limited reporting in scientific journals, the scientific base supporting drug courts is relatively weak, and the field needs outcomes research.

2

THERAPEUTIC COMMUNITIES: RESEARCH–PRACTICE RECIPROCITY

GEORGE DE LEON

The therapeutic community (TC) has proved to be a powerful treatment approach for substance abuse and related problems in living. Fundamentally a self-help approach, the TC has evolved into a sophisticated human services modality, as is evident in the range of its services, the diversity of the population served, and the substantial body of supporting research. Currently, TC agencies in the United States serve thousands of individuals and families yearly. TC programs have been implemented in various other settings, both residential and nonresidential (e.g., hospitals, jails, schools, halfway houses, day treatment clinics, and ambulatory clinics). TCs offer a wide variety of services, including social, psychological, educational, medical, legal, and social/advocacy.

Some of the material in this chapter is drawn from George De Leon (in press), "The Research Context for Therapeutic Communities in the USA," and is adapted with permission from the copyright holder, Jessica Kingsley Publishers. The work involved in developing this chapter was supported in part by National Institute on Drug Abuse Grant P50-DA07700.

Much of what is known about the TC approach and its effectiveness is based on the long-term residential model, also termed the *traditional TC*. Traditional TCs are similar in planned duration of stay (12–15 months), structure, staffing pattern, perspective, and rehabilitative regime, although they differ in size (30–600 beds) and client demography. Staff are composed of TC-trained clinicians and other human services professionals. Primary clinical staff are usually former substance abusers who themselves were rehabilitated in TC programs. Other staff consist of professionals providing medical, mental health, vocational, educational, family counseling, fiscal, administrative, and legal services.

The TC views drug abuse as a deviant behavior, reflecting impeded personality development or chronic deficits in social, educational, and economic skills. Thus, the principal aim of the TC is a global change in lifestyle: abstinence from illicit substances; elimination of antisocial activity; and development of employability, prosocial attitudes, and values.

The quintessential feature of the TC approach may be termed *community as method* (De Leon, 1998, 2000). What distinguishes the TC from other treatment approaches (and other communities) is the purposive use of the peer community to facilitate social and psychological change in individuals. Thus, in a TC all activities are designed to produce therapeutic and educational change in individual participants, and all participants are mediators of these therapeutic and educational changes.

Although the TC emerged outside of the medical–scientific mainstream, its evolution has been advanced by the reciprocal contributions of both research and practice. This chapter illustrates this reciprocity across some 30 years of TC research. During this period, policy and practice issues shaped research agendas, which in turn influenced treatment practice and programming.

The main lines of TC research in the United States are organized into two eras, or phases: (a) the early phase (circa 1970–1989) and (b) the current phase (1990–present). For each phase, I summarize the key treatment and policy questions and research conclusions and offer examples of practice–research reciprocity. In the last section of this chapter I explore some of the insights for both research and practice learned from the evolution of science in the TC.

PHASE 1 (1970–1989)

Beginning in the 1960s, the heroin epidemic and its crime consequences launched an expansion of drug treatment resources and research activities. TCs had emerged as alternatives to conventional medical and mental health treatments for opioid abusers, but their doors were open to alcoholics and other substance abusers. The TC perspective of the disorder, the client, and recovery differed from that of other major treatment modalities (see De Leon, 2000, Part 2). The residents in TCs were usually the most severe substance abusers, with wide-ranging personality problems in addition to their drug use, and many displayed histories of antisocial behavior. Thus, treatment focused on the whole person and on changing lifestyles and identity rather than simply achieving abstinence. These broad goals could be achieved only through an intensive, 24-hour-a-day, 7-day-a-week treatment in a long-term residential setting.

The TC approach was not well understood but, more important, it was viewed as expensive, particularly compared with outpatient counseling and pharmacotherapy such as methadone maintenance. Furthermore, dropout was the rule, suggesting that the broad impact of the TC was limited when defined in terms of the number of clients completing treatment. These issues were fundamental to the survival of the TC as a bona fide health care modality that deserved continued public funding. They framed three key lines of inquiry in Phase 1: (a) the description of the social and psychological profiles of TC admissions, (b) documentation of the effectiveness of TC treatment, and (c) illumination of the phenomenon of retention in treatment. The main issues and conclusions in each line of inquiry are summarized next.

Who Comes for Treatment?

The broad issue underlying this line of inquiry was the validation of the TC perspective of the disorder and recovery, that is, that the individuals served required long-term residential treatment. Studies describing the social and psychological characteristics of admissions to TC programs documented that substance abuse among TC admissions is a disorder of the whole person (e.g., De Leon, 1984, 1985; Hubbard, Rachal, Craddock, & Cavanaugh, 1984; Simpson & Sells, 1982). In addition to their substance abuse, the drug abusers who enter TCs reveal a considerable degree of psychological disability, which is further confirmed in diagnostic studies. Despite the TCs' policy concerning psychiatric exclusion, the large majority of adult and adolescent admissions meet the criteria for coexisting substance abuse and other psychiatric disorders (De Leon, 1989, 1991; Jainchill, De Leon, & Pinkham, 1986).

Are TCs Effective?

The unique recovery goal of the TC is changing lifestyles and identities. Thus, it was essential to document the effectiveness of long-term residential TCs particularly as compared with other treatment modalities. A particular issue was the clarification of outcomes among individuals who do not complete treatment, as dropout occurs in the majority of admissions.

The main findings from outcome studies document that long-term residential TCs are effective in reducing drug abuse and antisocial behavior, particularly in opioid abusers (De Leon, 1984; De Leon & Jainchill, 1981–1982; Hubbard et al., 1989; Simpson & Sells, 1982). The extent of social and psychological improvement is directly related to retention in treatment. In the studies that have investigated psychological outcomes (e.g., depression, anxiety, self-concept), results uniformly showed significant improvement at follow-up (e.g., Biase, Sullivan, & Wheeler, 1986; De Leon, 1984; De Leon & Jainchill, 1981–1982; Holland, 1983).

What Is Known About Retention in TC Treatment?

Length of stay in treatment is the largest and most consistent predictor of positive posttreatment outcomes. However, as with other drug treatment modalities, most TC clients leave long-term treatment prematurely. Thus, understanding retention was, and remains, crucial for improving the impact and cost–benefit of TC treatment. Studies show that temporal overall levels of retention vary, but the temporal pattern of dropout is uniform across TC programs (and other modalities). Dropout is highest in the early days of treatment and characteristically declines thereafter. Thus, the probability of remaining in treatment increases with time in treatment itself (e.g., De Leon & Schwartz, 1984). For example, approximately 60% of all admissions to community-based, long-term TC residential programs remain 90 days; of these survivors, 60%–70% will complete 12 months of residence.[1]

There are no reliable client characteristics that predict retention, with the exception of severe criminality and severe psychopathology, that are correlated with earlier dropout. Studies point to the importance of dynamic factors in predicting retention in treatment, such as perceived legal pressure, motivation, and readiness for treatment (e.g., Condelli & De Leon, 1993; De Leon, 1988, De Leon, Melnick, Kressel, & Jainchill, 1994; Hubbard, Collins, Rachal, & Cavanaugh, 1988; Simpson & Joe, 1993).

The main conclusions from this research indicate that although retention is a legitimate concern, it should not be confused with treatment effectiveness. TCs are effective for individuals who remain long enough for treatment influences to occur. Obviously, a critical issue for TCs is maximizing holding power to benefit more clients.

---

[1]Retention (and outcome) comparisons with other modalities such as detoxification or 28 day rehab centers are invidious for various reasons. These modalities reflect wide differences in the clients served (e.g., social–psychological–health profiles, their sources of referral and treatment history), and the diversity of the treatment approaches (e.g., setting, source of funding, philosophy and goals of treatment).

Overall, Phase 1 research confirmed that TCs were serving the most difficult substance abusers. Moreover, findings consistently supported the validity of the TC perspective on addiction and recovery, namely, that substance abuse is a disorder of the whole person and that long-term treatment is needed to achieve the TC recovery goals of changing lifestyles. The Phase 1 research also contributed to changing practices in several ways.

First, TCs now focus on retention: TCs were (and to some extent still are) criticized for their high dropout rates, particularly early in treatment. Critics viewed this as evidence of the limited impact of this treatment approach. The TC view of dropout was complex: It made the individual primarily responsible for getting ready for treatment. TC staff defended this view on the basis of clinical experience, arguing that dropouts were simply not ready to change, that motivational and readiness factors changed only as a result of the negative life experiences associated with addiction. Dropouts had to have another "run" and "hit bottom," which would lead to death or readiness for change. Moreover, TC programs accepted high dropout rates as an inherent selection process that was necessary to sustain a healthy program. This view resulted in little systematic effort to modify the treatment approach to reduce dropout, much less enhance motivation.

Based largely on the Phase 1 research, staff no longer "blame the client" for early dropout, recognizing that motivational/readiness factors should be assessed and enhanced as part of the treatment plan. Many TCs currently incorporate strategies within the basic TC regimen to sustain motivation in treatment (e.g., family involvement, individual counseling and senior staff seminars, medications; see De Leon, Hawke, Jainchill, & Melnick, 2000).

Second, TCs also focus on assessment. Admission practices have become elaborated to address clients' psychological suitability for the TC as well as risk for early dropout, and an increasing number of programs monitor clinical progress and motivational changes. There is an increased awareness of the importance of client–treatment matching. Multisetting TC agencies attempt to assess which clients are appropriate for longer and shorter term TC residential treatment as well as for TC-oriented day care and outpatient treatment. Matching strategies have been primarily conducted by clinical assignment. However, as described in the subsequent discussion of Phase 2, researchers have developed client–treatment matching protocols as tools to assist in these assignments (e.g., Melnick, De Leon, & Thomas, 2001).

The shortening of residential treatment for some clients has encouraged the use of continuing care programs in nonresidential settings. This has reflected clinical and research experience that underscored the need for sufficient involvement in treatment, regardless of setting, to maximize effectiveness. To date, however, TC programs, and the drug treatment field in general, await convincing research documenting the impact of client–treatment matching on both retention and outcomes.

An indirect effect of Phase 1 research has been increased affirmation and morale. Research has confirmed the perspective of the TC and its advocates' clinical views with respect to outcomes and retention. This has generally strengthened perceptions of the credibility of the TC approach. As a result, TC clinical staff and program management articulate with confidence what they do and how well TCs work.

PHASE 2 (1990–PRESENT)

Phase 2 witnessed a considerable increase in federal support for TC research. This reflects not only the scientific gains in Phase 1 but also the persistence of the drug problem and the evolution of the TC itself. The fact that drug treatment works does not necessarily solve society's drug problem. Substance abuse and related problems remain pervasive in terms of the diversity of populations and drugs of abuse. In response to this, TCs have modified their practices and adapted the approach for special populations, settings, and funding requirements. Illustrations of these modifications and adaptations have been described elsewhere (De Leon, 1997, 2000, chapter 25).

Current applications include TC programs for adolescents (Jainchill, 1997), homeless substance abusers, mentally ill chemical abusers in community-based and institutional settings (Sacks, Sacks, & De Leon, 1999), inmates in correctional settings (Inciardi, Martin, Butzin, Hooper, & Harrison, 1997), women and children (Coletti et al., 1992; Stevens & Glider, 1994), and methadone-maintained clients (De Leon, Staines, Sacks, Brady, & Melchionda, 1997). Patient differences, as well as clinical requirements and funding realities, have encouraged the development of modified residential TCs with shorter planned durations of stay (3, 6, and 12 months) as well as TC-oriented day treatment and outpatient ambulatory models (e.g., Guydish et al., 1999).

Current modifications of the TC practices are those that can be incorporated into the TC model itself. Family services approaches include family therapy, counseling, and psychoeducation. Primary health care and medical services are offered for the growing number of residential patients with sexually transmitted and immune-compromising conditions, including HIV seropositivity, AIDS, syphilis, and Hepatitis C. Screening, treatment, and increased health education have become more sophisticated, both on site and through linkages with community and primary health care agencies. Aftercare services involve linkages with other service providers. Relapse prevention training (e.g., Lewis & Ross, 1994) has been incorporated into the TC day. Twelve-step components may be introduced at any stage in residential treatment but are considered mandatory in the re-entry stages of treatment and in the aftercare or continuance stages of recovery after the client has left the residential settings. Mental health services include psycho-pharmacological adjuncts and individual psychotherapy (see De Leon, 1997, for illustrative adaptations and modifications).

The evolution of the TC caused basic policy issues, such as the feasibility, effectiveness, and cost–benefits of its various adaptations, to resurface. In particular, managed care pressures to reduce the cost of treatment have challenged the necessity for long-term residential treatment. However, a second issue that emerged from the adaptations and modifications of the TC concerned the fidelity of the approach itself. The wide diversity of TC-oriented programs has raised a variety of theoretical and quality assurance questions. These issues associated with the diversity of clients served and the fidelity of the TC adaptations have directed two main lines of inquiry in Phase 2: (a) evaluation of the effectiveness of standard TCs serving the new generation of drug users as well as modified TCs for special populations and (b) conducting studies to clarify the essential elements of the TC approach. Federal funding of research on these questions has included support for studies conducted at the Center for Therapeutic Community Research on special populations and large-scale multimodality surveys such as the National Treatment Improvement Evaluation Study ("Preliminary report," 1996) and the Drug Abuse Treatment Outcome Study (Simpson & Curry, 1997). The following section summarizes the findings and conclusions of the main Phase 2 questions.

Are Contemporary TCs Effective and Cost-Effective for Treating the Current Diversity of Substance Abusers?

Studies have addressed the client admission profiles of both standard and modified TCs. These have focused on psychiatric comorbidity, retention characteristics, short- and long-term outcomes, and cost analyses. Special populations that have been studied are mentally ill chemical abusers, adolescents, the homeless population, criminal justice clients, and mothers with children, as well as methadone-maintained clients. The findings and conclusions regarding the admission profiles and the effectiveness of standard and modified TCs are briefly summarized in Exhibit 2.1.

The weight of the evidence from the Phase 2 studies indicates that current standard and modified TCs provide effective treatment for the current generation of substance abusers who reveal a wide range of social and psychological problems. Based on their unique self-help perspective, TCs provide a favorable cost–benefit alternative to traditional institutional-based treatments in mental health, hospital, correctional, and community-based settings.

What Is the TC Treatment Approach, and Why Does It Work?

TCs are complex programs that are considered difficult and costly to implement relative to other treatment modalities. Specification of the

EXHIBIT 2.1
Phase 2 Research: Effectiveness of Standard and Modified Therapeutic Communities (TCs)

Standard TCs

- National, multimodality survey studies uniformly show that community-based standard TC residential programs were serving the most severe substance abusers compared with other treatment modalities (Simpson & Curry, 1997). Client admission profiles indicate that contemporary TCs are serving individuals who reveal a considerable degree of social and psychological dysfunction in addition to their substance abuse.
- Long-term residential programs obtain positive outcomes in drug use, criminality, employment, and psychological adjustment that are comparable or superior to other modalities that treat less severe substance abusers ("Preliminary report," 1996; Simpson & Curry, 1997). Also, cost–benefits for long-term residential treatment exceeded those of other treatment modalities, particularly benefits associated with reduction in crime (Flynn, Kristiansen, Porto, & Hubbard, 1999).
- The planned duration of residential treatments is generally shorter than in earlier years; however, outcomes are still favorable among the clients who complete or stay longer in treatment. The differential effects of longer and shorter planned durations of residential stay remain to be clarified. In initial studies that have attempted to match clients to settings (residential–outpatient), evidence points to improved retention.

Modified TCs

- Drug use and criminality declined along with improvements in employment and psychological status for various special populations (De Leon, 1997; De Leon, Sacks, Staines, & McKendrick, 2000; Simpson, Wexler, & Inciardi, 1999). Again, improvements were correlated with length of stay in treatment (Inciardi et al., 1997; Jainchill, Hawke, De Leon, & Yagelka, 2000; Melnick, De Leon, & Thomas, 2001; Simpson, 1981). Aftercare—services beyond primary treatment in the residential TC—is a critical component of stable outcomes. Thus, regardless of planned duration of primary treatment, individuals must continue in the treatment process for some undetermined time beyond the residential phase.
- Aftercare models must be integrated with the primary treatment model in terms of philosophy, methods, and relationships to provide effective continuity of care (e.g., De Leon, Sacks, et al., 2000). Studies in progress on samples leaving prison-based modified TC treatment suggest the superiority of TC-oriented vs. non-TC-oriented aftercare (Sacks, Peters, et al., in press).
- Fiscal studies indicate that TC-oriented programs reveal favorable cost–benefit gains, particularly in reduction of expenditures associated with criminal activity in mental health services (e.g., French, Sacks, De Leon, Staines, & McKendrick, 1999; French, Sacks, McKendrick, & De Leon, 2000).

Note. From "The Research Context for Therapeutic Communities in the USA," by G. De Leon, in press, London: Jessica Kingsley Publishers. Copyright by Jessica Kingsley Publishers. Reprinted with permission.

"active ingredients" of the method and an understanding of the treatment process are critical to substantiate the validity of the TC approach, to justify its costs, and to improve the approach itself through research and training. Studies clarifying the treatment approach have mainly been conducted by the Center for Therapeutic Community Research at the National Development and Research Institutes, Inc. These have focused on elaborating the theory and method of the TC approach, developing instruments for assessing client motivation and readiness for treatment and clinical progress, defining and validating the essential elements of the TC model, identifying TC treatment environments that relate to risk for client dropout, and providing a conceptual formulation of the treatment process. The main findings and conclusions from these studies are briefly summarized in Exhibit 2.2.

Research–Practice Reciprocity

Phase 2 research has documented the fact that standard TCs continue to serve the most serious substance abusers as compared to outpatient and other residential modalities. More important, it has provided empirical

EXHIBIT 2.2
Phase 2 Research: Clarifying the Therapeutic Community (TC) Approach: Findings and Conclusions

Program diversity

Empirical studies have identified the essential elements of the TC program model. TC programs have been differentiated in terms of standard and modified types and with respect to environmental factors that relate to dropout (e.g., Jainchill, Yagelka, & Messina, 1999; Melnick & De Leon, 1999; Melnick, De Leon, Hiller, & Knight, 2000).

Motivation

The role of motivational and readiness factors in entry and retention in TC treatment has been assessed (e.g., De Leon, Melnick, & Hawke, 2000; Simpson & Joe, 1993), and initial studies have measured the contribution of these factors to the treatment process in the TC (Melnick, De Leon, Thomas, Wexler, & Kressel, 2001).

Clinical assessment

An array of related instruments has been developed to measure client progress in the TC assessed by the clients, staff, and peers (e.g., Kressel, Palij, & De Leon, 2001; Kressel, Palij, De Leon, & Rubin, 2000).

Theoretical framework

Research has contributed to the development of a comprehensive theoretical framework of the TC approach. This framework is used to guide clinical practice, program planning, and treatment improvement as well as empirical studies of treatment processes and client–treatment matching (De Leon, 2000).

Note. From "The Research Context for Therapeutic Communities in the USA" by G. De Leon, in press, London: Jessica Kingsley Publishers. Copyright by Jessica Kingsley Publishers. Reprinted with permission.

evidence for the feasibility and effectiveness of implementing modified TC programs into various institutional settings (e.g., mental hospitals, homeless shelters, prisons, methadone clinics). These scientific gains have advanced initiatives to extend TC-oriented programs further into mainstream human services.

The Phase 2 era witnessed how the reciprocity between practice and research unfolds. TC agencies initially responded to the diversity of clients entering treatment by modifying and adapting the model. Evaluation research followed practice in providing empirical data as to effectiveness and cost-effectiveness. In turn, these scientific gains have advanced initiatives to extend TC programs further into mainstream human services. An impressive illustration of these advances is the expansion of TC-oriented programs in the correctional system and, to a lesser extent, into community residences for people with mental illness and homeless shelter settings. Finally, research confirmation of the adaptation of the TC for special populations and settings encouraged the cross-fertilization of clinical practices among TC and traditional mental health, correctional, and human services professionals.

The second line of inquiry to clarify the essential elements of the treatment approach has had important practice and policy effects. The elaboration of the theoretical framework of the treatment approach and the supporting research have facilitated significant initiatives to improve TC treatment through quality assurance and clinical practice training. National standards for prison- and community-based TC treatment have been developed and promulgated. Efforts are underway to establish a process for program accreditation and staff training based on these standards and grounded in theory (e.g., Therapeutic Communities of America, Criminal Justice Committee, 1999, 2001).

SOME INSIGHTS AND ISSUES

In the fields of conventional medicine and mental health, research generally precedes the widespread implementation of evidenced-based treatments or clinical practices. For example, in addiction treatment randomized, controlled trials launched methadone detoxification and maintenance. Contingency contracting, cognitive–behavioral approaches, and motivational interviewing were borrowed from mainstream psychological treatment research, modified for addiction treatment, and evaluated under controlled designs.

In the evolution of the TC, however, research has generally followed practice, as has the formulation of its theoretical underpinnings. In turn, theory and research have informed changes in TC program management and clinical practice This unique reciprocity of research and practice in TCs over the years contains insights for both science and treatment.

Science Insights

Self-Selection

For drug treatment research in general, and TC studies in particular, the issue of selection has clouded the interpretation of treatment effectiveness. Length of stay in treatment has been identified as the most consistent predictor of posttreatment success. However, self-selection factors may influence those who seek, remain in, and complete treatment. In the past 10 years, field-effectiveness studies have confirmed a long-held clinical understanding that selection factors, such as motivation and readiness, contribute to treatment retention and outcomes (De Leon et al., 1994; Joe, Simpson, & Broome, 1998; Melnick, De Leon, Hawke, Jainchill, & Kressel, 1997). This body of work supports a perspective outlined in other writings in which self-selection is viewed as a prerequisite for treatment effectiveness (e.g., De Leon, 1998; De Leon, Melnick, & Hawke, 2000). Clients who are more highly motivated are more likely to use treatment differently than clients with less motivation to change themselves.

Such an interactional view of self-selection in the treatment process has important clinical and research implications. For example, "good" treatments and clinical practices are those that identify, increase, and sustain motivational factors for change. With respect to research, client motivational/readiness factors must be routinely measured and their contribution to retention and outcomes assessed in studies of treatment effectiveness. Moreover, comparative treatment designs must assure that motivational/readiness factors are equally distributed across treatment conditions.[2]

Practice, Research, and Theory

Since its inception, TC treatment was grounded in its own native theory, consisting of the TC's common practices, beliefs, and assumptions concerning self-help recovery. However, the cumulative knowledge base from the reciprocity between research and practice over the years has recently fostered the elaboration of a more formal theory of the TC. The latter reframes the TC—its essential elements, practices, beliefs, and assumptions—into a unique social–psychological treatment approach (see De Leon, 2000). The validity of this theoretical framework is currently being explored in studies that focus on improving treatment effectiveness through process oriented-research (e.g., De Leon, 2001; Kressel, 2000).

---

[2]A sample assessment tool to measure motivational/readiness for TC treatment is reflected in the CMRS scales (De Leon et al., 1994). The increasing use of these scales illustrates a useful dissemination of knowledge from research to practice.

Retention

Time in program has been the most consistent predictor of successful outcomes. However, TC clinicians have emphasized that time alone is a proxy for dosage of treatment: Individuals must remain in a program long enough for time-correlated interventions to work and for treatment benefits to occur. Thus, present cost pressures to reduce planned durations of residential treatment must consider client factors in relationship to treatment intensity.

Policy and Research Paradigms

Effectiveness studies, such as those conducted on TC treatment as it is practiced in the field, have established the benefits of TC treatment before efficacy studies, that is, those conducted in controlled conditions. The evidence from the field studies remains compelling based on the numbers of clients studied and the replication of findings across years, samples, and investigative teams. From a policy perspective, the field-effectiveness studies have provided the main empirical justification for continued federal funding for drug treatment expansion and for treatment services research. Moreover, the field-effectiveness studies constitute a knowledge base to guide efficacy studies of treatment improvement. This point is illustrated in the National Institute on Drug Abuse's (NIDA's) current emphasis on controlled studies of why and how TCs work rather than on whether they work.

A Research–Practice Utilization Model

A key insight emerging from the years of reciprocity between TC research and practice underscores the need for appropriate models of technology transfer. Successful reciprocity depends on how effectively programs use research to improve treatment. The experience in TCs indicates that involvement in research projects, the use of scientific information, and the value of research itself must be reinforced through its application to program needs.

However, the use of research in human services settings in general, and in TCs in particular, has typically been impeded by the communication difficulties and perceptual distortions that often exist between research and nonresearch people (De Leon, 1979, 1980). For example, program evaluations may be viewed as hidden threats to the funding or survival of treatment agencies. Data systems are viewed as remote substitutions for face-to-face interactions rather than as technological extensions that could facilitate human services. Service program staff often perceive "data people" as removed from the realities of delivering day-to-day treatment. Research activities (such as completing forms) are seen as uncompensated burdens that are not relevant to service delivery. Researchers may view program people as inflexible in their beliefs and lacking objectivity concerning the work. Often they find line workers recalcitrant to participating in research-dictated boundaries, such as random designs, or not open to learning research-relevant skills (such as record keeping) that will increase accountability. Researcher–clinician communication is often impeded by different vernaculars—an issue that is critical to translating the meaning and value of research for practice.

These issues have shaped an approach to maximize research use that has evolved over the years of reciprocity in TC programs. The premise of the approach is that use of research for clinical practice and programming is optimized when treatment programs themselves are completely involved in the purpose, design, and conduct of research. In Exhibit 2.3, key components of the approach that illustrate the theme of research–practice integration in relation to use are outlined.

EXHIBIT 2.3
Maximizing Utilization of Research for Practice

Assessment

Treatment agencies are more likely to use research for practice when they are ready to change their customary administrative or clinical practices. Thus, before research projects or findings are introduced into treatment settings, evaluations are essential to assess agency (organizational) readiness to engage and use research to change its practices.

Preparation

Treatment agencies (and practitioners) need to be prepared to engage in research efforts, and use findings for clinical practice. This involves planning sessions that represent a cross-fertilization of research, clinical, and administrative staff in the purpose, conduct, relevance, and impact of the research project. Clinical and administrative input are essential to define the questions and address the issues of design and data collection. Project personnel should be composed of agency-based research and externally based research teams, and funding should be sufficient to support agency participation in research.

Dissemination

A variety of strategies and products are used to advance research use. These include research–practice–management seminars in which all participants contribute to the interpretation of the findings, recommendations, and limits of a study. Appropriate written, audio, and video formats are developed for describing findings, conclusions, and implications. Research personnel are effectively used as educators in translating scientific findings into curricula for training in program management and clinical practices.

CLINICAL PRACTICE AND A NEW RESEARCH AGENDA

The evolution of the scientific knowledge base has gradually shifted the research question from whether TCs work to how they work. To a considerable extent, this shift reflects both policy and scientific issues. TCs "work" for serious substance abusers, for special populations, and in various settings. The weight of the outcome research accumulated over 30 years has established the field effectiveness of the TC as a global approach. However, to establish the TC as an evidenced-based treatment, researchers must isolate the components of the approach that are critical to its effectiveness. Identifying the active treatment ingredients of the TC approach remains a compelling question for improving treatment, funding policy as well as science. Reducing the costs of treatment—by limiting its planned duration, for example—can be rationally implemented only if the necessary and sufficient TC interventions are known.

These issues are shaping a current focus of research on the treatment process in therapeutic communities. Illuminating the treatment process in the TC, however, underscores the necessity for continued practice–research reciprocity. In contrast with evaluation of treatment outcomes, which involves minimal intrusion into the activities of the treatment program, studying the treatment process in the TC often requires research strategies that perturb the process itself. Program management and, in particular, clinical staff, must be completely supportive of research activities that can alter standard procedures, practices and, possibly, the treatment environment. Such support is particularly compelling considering the unique nature of the TC treatment approach.

The TC is a global treatment that consists of management and clinical practices that are embedded in the program's daily regimen of formal activities (e.g., planned meetings, groups, work assignments) and informal activities (unplanned, spontaneous peer–peer and peer–staff interactions). Each activity is potentially an intervention, and all activities are interrelated to produce individual change (De Leon, 2000, see chapter 24).

Research strategies that attempt to study the active ingredients of this global approach may be "deconstructive" or "enhancive." Deconstructive strategies attempt to isolate the necessity or sufficiency of a hypothesized ingredient (e.g., peer groups) by subtracting it from the treatment regimen. Enhancive strategies intensify a specific activity or practice (e.g., formal training of residents in the theory of peer roles) to improve their treatment impact.

The intrusive character of both strategies requires an extraordinary cooperation among researchers, program management, and clinical practitioners as to the goals, significance, and conduct of the research itself. Indeed, the success of this cooperation may generate innovative strategies for studying treatment process as well as improve treatment practices. Finally, the maturation of the reciprocity between research and practice in TCs is dramatically illustrated in two cooperative initiatives between NIDA and the Therapeutic Communities of America, the North American association of TCs. One initiative addresses the elaboration of a TC treatment process research agenda, as discussed previously. This has resulted in a recent NIDA request for research applications dedicated to understanding and improving TC treatment. The second initiative focuses on disseminating a NIDA project that is in preparation and that outlines TC principles and practices grounded in clinical theory and supported by research (NIDA, 2002). These products reflect the cross-fertilization of the TC treatment field workers (practitioners and program managers), researchers (program based and independent), and the federal funding agency. They also signify an evolutionary landmark in how reciprocity assures the success of both research and treatment objectives.

REFERENCES

Biase, D. V., Sullivan, A. P., & Wheeler, B. (1986). Daytop Miniversity—Phase 2 college training in a therapeutic community: Development of self-concept among drug free addicts. In G. De Leon & J. T. Ziegenfuss (Eds.), *Therapeutic communities for addictions* (pp. 121–130). Springfield, IL: Charles C Thomas.

Coletti, D. S., Hughes, P. H., Landress, H. J., Neri, R. L., Sicilian, D. M., Williams, K. M., et al. (1992). PAR village: Specialized intervention for cocaine abusing women and their children. *Journal of the Florida Medical Association, 79*, 701–705.

Condelli, W. S., & De Leon, G. (1993). Fixed and dynamic predictors of client retention in therapeutic communities. *Journal of Substance Abuse Treatment, 10*, 11–16.

De Leon, G. (1979). People and data systems. In *Management information systems in the drug field* (National Institute on Drug Abuse Treatment Research Monograph Series, DHEW Publication No. ADM-79-836, pp. 107–120). Rockville, MD: National Institute on Drug Abuse.

De Leon, G. (1980). *Therapeutic communities: Training self evaluation. Final report of project activities* (National Institute on Drug Abuse Grant No. 1H81-DAO). New York: National Development and Research Institute.

De Leon, G. (1984). *The therapeutic community: Study of effectiveness* (National Institute on Drug Abuse Treatment Research Monograph Series ADM-84-1286). Washington, DC: U.S. Government Printing Office.

De Leon, G. (1985). The therapeutic community: Status and evolution. *International Journal of Addictions, 20*, 823–844.

De Leon, G. (1988). Legal pressure in therapeutic communities. In C. G. Leukefeld & F. M. Tims (Eds.), *Compulsory treatment of drug abuse: Research and clinical practice* (NIDA Research Monograph 86, DHHS No. ADM-88-1578, pp. 160–177). Rockville, MD: National Institute on Drug Abuse.

De Leon, G. (1989). Psychopathology and substance abuse: What we are learning from research in therapeutic communities? *Journal of Psychoactive Drugs, 21,* 177–188.

De Leon, G. (1991). Retention in drug-free therapeutic communities. In R. W. Pickens, C. G. Leukefeld, & C. R. Schuster (Eds.), *Improving drug abuse treatment* (NIDA Research Monograph 106, pp. 218–244). Rockville, MD: National Institute on Drug Abuse.

De Leon, G. (Ed.). (1997). *Community as method: Therapeutic communities for special populations and special settings.* Westport, CT: Greenwood.

De Leon, G. (1998). Commentary: Reconsidering the self-selection factor in addiction treatment research. *Psychology of Addictive Behaviors, 12,* 71–77.

De Leon, G. (2000). *The therapeutic community: Theory, model, and method.* New York: Springer.

De Leon, G. (Principal Investigator). (2001). *Treatment process: Enhancing peer mentor performance.* Unpublished grant proposal, Center for Therapeutic Community Research, National Development and Research Institutes, New York.

De Leon, G. (in press). The research context for therapeutic communities in the USA. In J. Lees, N. Manning, D. Menzies, & N. Morant (Eds.), *Researching therapeutic communities.* London: Jessica Kingsley.

De Leon, G., Hawke, J., Jainchill, N., & Melnick, G. (2000). Therapeutic communities: Enhancing retention in treatment using "senior professor" staff. *Journal of Substance Abuse Treatment, 19,* 375–382.

De Leon, G., & Jainchill, N. (1981–1982). Male and female drug abusers: Social and psychological status 2 years after treatment in a therapeutic community. *American Journal of Drug and Alcohol Abuse, 8,* 465–497.

De Leon, G., Melnick, G., & Hawke, J. (2000). The motivation/readiness factor in drug treatment research: Implications for research and policy. In D. McBride, R. Stephens, & J. Levy (Eds.), *Emergent issues in drug treatment: Advances in medical sociology* (Vol. 7, pp. 103–129). Greenwich, CT: JAI Press.

De Leon, G., Melnick, G., Kressel, D., & Jainchill, N. (1994). Circumstances, motivation, readiness and suitability (the CMRS scales): Predicting retention in therapeutic community treatment. *American Journal of Drug and Alcohol Abuse, 20,* 495–515.

De Leon, G., Sacks, S., Staines, G., & McKendrick, K. (2000). Modified therapeutic community for homeless mentally ill chemical abusers: Treatment outcomes. *American Journal of Drug and Alcohol Abuse, 26,* 461–480.

De Leon, G., & Schwartz, S. (1984). The therapeutic community: What are the retention rates? *American Journal of Drug and Alcohol Abuse, 10,* 267–284.

De Leon, G., Staines, G. L., Sacks, S., Brady, R., & Melchionda, R. (1997). Passages: A modified therapeutic community model for methadone-maintained clients. In G. De Leon (Ed.), *Community as method: Therapeutic communities for special populations and special settings* (pp. 225–246). Westport, CT: Greenwood.

Flynn, P. M., Kristiansen, P. L., Porto, J. V., & Hubbard, R. L. (1999). Costs and benefits of treatment for cocaine addiction in DATOS. *Drug and Alcohol Dependence, 57,* 167–174.

French, M. T., Sacks, S., De Leon, G., Staines, G., & McKendrick, K. (1999). Modified therapeutic community for mentally ill chemical abusers: Outcomes and costs. *Evaluation and the Health Professions, 22,* 60–85.

French, M. T., Sacks, S., McKendrick, K., & De Leon, G. (2000). Services use and cost by MICAs: Differences by retention in a TC. *Journal of Substance Abuse, 11*(2), 1–15.

Guydish, J., Sorensen, J. L., Chan, M., Werdegar, D., Bostrom, A., & Acampora, A. (1999). A randomized clinical trial comparing day and residential drug abuse treatment: 18-month outcomes. *Journal of Consulting and Clinical Psychology, 67,* 428–434.

Holland, S. (1983). Evaluating community based treatment programs: A model for strengthening inferences about effectiveness. *International Journal of Therapeutic Communities, 4,* 285–306.

Hubbard, R. L., Collins, J. J., Rachal, J. V., & Cavanaugh, E. R. (1988). *The criminal justice client in drug abuse treatment* (NIDA Research Monograph No. 86). Research Triangle Park, NC: Research Triangle Institute.

Hubbard, R. L., Marsden, M. E., Rachal, J. V., Harwood, H. J., Cavanaugh, E. R., & Ginzburg, H. M. (1989). *Drug abuse treatment: A national study of effectiveness.* Chapel Hill: University of North Carolina Press.

Hubbard, R. L., Rachal, J. V., Craddock, S. G., & Cavanaugh, E. R. (1984). Treatment Outcome Prospective Study (TOPS): Client characteristics and behaviors before, during, and after treatment. In F. M. Tims & J. P. Ludford (Eds.), *Drug abuse treatment evaluation: Strategies, progress, and prospects* (NIDA Research Monograph No. 51, DHHS No. ADM-84-1329, pp. 42–68). Rockville, MD: National Institute on Drug Abuse.

Inciardi, J. A., Martin, S. S., Butzin, C. A., Hooper, R. M., & Harrison, L. D. (1997). An effective model of prison-based treatment for drug-involved offenders. *Journal of Drug Issues, 27,* 261–278.

Jainchill, N. (1997). Therapeutic communities for adolescents: The same and not the same. In G. De Leon (Ed.), *Community as method: Therapeutic communities for special populations and special settings* (pp. 161–178). Westport, CT: Greenwood.

Jainchill, N., De Leon, G., & Pinkham, L. (1986). Psychiatric diagnoses among substance abusers in therapeutic community treatment. *Journal of Psychoactive Drugs, 18,* 209–213.

Jainchill, N., Hawke, J., De Leon, G., & Yagelka, J. (2000). Adolescents in TCs: One-year posttreatment outcomes. *Journal of Psychoactive Drugs, 32,* 81–94.

Jainchill, N., Yagelka, J., & Messina, M. (1999). *Development of a Treatment Environmental Risk Index (TERI): Assessing risk for client dropout.* Unpublished manuscript, Center for Therapeutic Community Research, National Development and Research Institutes, New York.

Joe, G. W., Simpson, D. D., & Broome, K. M. (1998). Effects of readiness for drug abuse treatment on client retention and assessment of process. *Addiction, 93,* 1177–1190.

Kressel, D. (Principal Investigator). (2000). *A protocol to improve therapeutic community training.* New York: Center for Therapeutic Community Research, National Development and Research Institutes.

Kressel, D., Palij, M., & De Leon, G. (2001). *The predictive validity and clinical utility of instruments measuring client progress in therapeutic community treatment.* Unpublished manuscript, Center for Therapeutic Community Research, National Development and Research Institutes, New York.

Kressel, D., Palij, M., De Leon, G., & Rubin, G. (2000). Measuring clinical progress in therapeutic community treatment: The Client Assessment Inventory (CAI), Client Assessment Summary (CAS) and Staff Assessment Summary (SAS). *Journal of Substance Abuse Treatment, 19,* 267–272.

Lewis, B. F., & Ross, R. (1994). *Therapeutic community: Advances in research and application, NIDA Monograph 144* (NIH Publication No. 94-3633). Washington, DC: Superintendent of Documents, U.S. Government Printing Office.

Melnick, G., & De Leon, G. (1999). Clarifying the nature of therapeutic community treatment: The Survey of Essential Elements Questionnaire (SEEQ). *Journal of Substance Abuse Treatment, 16,* 307–313.

Melnick, G., De Leon, G., Hawke, J., Jainchill, N., & Kressel, D. (1997). Motivation and readiness for therapeutic community treatment among adolescent and adult substance abusers. *American Journal of Drug and Alcohol Abuse, 23,* 485–507.

Melnick, G., De Leon, G., Hiller, M. L., & Knight, K. (2000). Therapeutic communities: Diversity in treatment elements. *Journal of Drug Use and Misuse, 35,* 1819–1847.

Melnick, G., De Leon, G., & Thomas, G. (2001). A client–treatment matching protocol (CMP) for therapeutic communities: First report. *Journal of Substance Abuse Treatment, 21,* 119–128.

Melnick, G., De Leon, G., Thomas, G., Wexler, H. K., & Kressel, D. (2001). Treatment process in therapeutic communities: Motivation, progress and outcomes. *American Journal of Drug and Alcohol Abuse, 27,* 633–650.

National Institute on Drug Abuse. (2002). *Therapeutic community* (Research Report Series, NIH Publication No. 02-4877). Rockville, MD: U.S. Department of Health and Human Services, National Institutes of Health.

Preliminary report: The persistent effects of substance abuse treatment—One year later. (1996, September). Rockville, MD: U.S. Dept. of Health and Human Services, Substance Abuse and Mental Health Services Administration, Center for Substance Abuse Treatment.

Sacks, S., Peters, J., Sacks, J. Y., Wexler, H. K., Roebuck, C., & De Leon, G. (in press). Modified therapeutic community for MICA offenders: Description and interim findings. *Criminal Justice and Behavior.*

Sacks, S., Sacks, J. Y., & De Leon, G. (1999). Treatment for MICAs: Design and implementation of the modified TC. *Journal of Psychoactive Drugs, 32,* 19–30.

Simpson, D. D. (1981). Treatment for drug abuse: Follow-up outcomes and length of time spent. *Archives of General Psychiatry, 38,* 875–880.

Simpson, D. D., & Curry, S. J. (Eds.). (1997). Drug Abuse Treatment Outcome Study (DATOS) [Special issue]. *Psychology of Addictive Behaviors, 11*(4), 211–337.

Simpson, D. D., & Joe, G. W. (1993). Motivation as a predictor of early dropout from drug abuse treatment. *Psychotherapy, 30,* 357–368.

Simpson, D. D., & Sells, S. B. (1982). Effectiveness of treatment for drug abuse: An overview of the DARP research program. *Advances in Alcohol and Substance Abuse, 2,* 7–29.

Simpson, D. D., Wexler, H. K., & Inciardi, J. A. (Eds.). (1999). Drug treatment outcomes for correctional settings, Parts 1 and 2 [Special issue]. *Prison Journal, 79*(4).

Stevens, S., & Glider, P. (1994). Therapeutic communities: Substance abuse treatment for women. In F. M. Tims, G. De Leon, & N. Jainchill (Eds.), *Therapeutic community: Advances in research and application* (NIDA Research Monograph No. 144, NIH No. 94-3633, pp. 162–180). Rockville, MD: National Institute on Drug Abuse.

Therapeutic Communities of America, Criminal Justice Committee. (1999). *Therapeutic Communities in Correctional Settings: The Prison Based TC Standards Development Project, Phase II* (final report prepared for the White House Office of National Drug Policy [ONDCP]). Washington, DC: Author.

Therapeutic Communities of America, Criminal Justice Committee. (2001). *Therapeutic Community Standards Development Project, Phase III American Correctional Association Version* (final report prepared for the Center for Substance Abuse Treatment). Washington, DC: Author.

3

AURICULAR ACUPUNCTURE FOR THE TREATMENT OF COCAINE ADDICTION

ARTHUR MARGOLIN

Auricular acupuncture is provided as a part of numerous substance abuse programs worldwide, and its presence in these programs increases yearly. Yet acupuncture's acceptance among addiction clinicians is not matched by that of addiction researchers, who legitimately ask, What evidence supports the effectiveness of this intervention? This question, in turn, raises the further question of how this treatment modality is most appropriately investigated in a research context designed to maximize the quality of the evidence obtained. However, it is not clear how studies should be designed such that the experimental treatment reflects acupuncture's actual use in clinical settings. Given the vast conceptual territory spanned by acupuncture theory and practice in the United States—including the framework of traditional Chinese medicine and its current use in the West relative to current theories of addiction, as well as current biomedical precepts for determining

Preparation of this chapter was supported by Grant AT000451 from the National Center for Complementary and Alternative Medicine and Grant DA08513 from the National Institute on Drug Abuse.

effectiveness of interventions—acupuncture's use in the treatment of addictions raises a number of thorny methodological issues regarding the transition from practice to research (cf. Liao, Lee, & Ng, 1994). Given the lack of acceptance of acupuncture in the research community, this chapter focuses on these issues. I examine how investigators have approached them and how acupuncture research can be informed by the ways in which this treatment is provided within clinical settings.

BACKGROUND OF AURICULAR ACUPUNCTURE IN THE UNITED STATES

Acupuncture Within the Framework of Chinese Medicine

Acupuncture has been a fundamental component of medicine in China for at least 4,000 years, provided as a treatment by itself as well as in conjunction with herbal remedies and other forms of treatment (Birch & Felt, 1999). Although the corpus of Chinese medicine, as it has evolved and accreted over centuries, is highly variegated, one principle underlying its multifarious concepts is the interconnectedness, and therefore the dynamic mutual influence, of all nature (Unschuld, 1985). Traditionally, the basis of this dynamic is *qi* (pronounced "chee"), a fundamental concept within Chinese medicine that has no exact Western equivalent. Heuristically, an understanding of *qi* presumes knowledge of the proper evolving role of a thing, at whatever level, that is required for it to sustain a harmonious relationship to other evolving things, as the entire complex configures and reconfigures itself in an orderly fashion. Experientially, it is the palpable sense of a thing as it functions or malfunctions within this ongoing complex network of interconnections. For example, consider the life cycle of a leaf as it supports the growth and development of its parent tree throughout the change of seasons. In the summer, the healthy green leaf appropriately possesses "strong" *qi*. However, in the fall and winter it is appropriate for the leaf to lose *qi* and to turn brown, eventually falling to the ground. In this example, the rise and fall of *qi* is in keeping with natural, seasonal rhythms. However, *qi* can also rise and fall within the human body discordantly, in ways that are indicative of a systemic problem, in which case it can be manipulated to bring it back to harmonious and proper functioning. This is a fundamental operative principle of Chinese medicine.

Within the body, there are specific channels through which *qi* travels, sometimes referred to as *meridians*. These channels connect various "organ" systems. Where the meridians lie close to the surface of the body, the flow of *qi* can be influenced—either increased or decreased—by stimulating the pathway at prescribed points by the insertion of needles—hence acupuncture. It should be obvious from even this cursory description that acupuncture is a treatment system based on a conceptual framework that is in many respects divergent from that of Western biomedicine. Determining the degree to which and in what respects these differences should influence research of this treatment modality within Western treatment programs presents a significant challenge to investigators in this area.

Development of Acupuncture for the Addictions

The use of acupuncture for the treatment of drug addiction was discovered serendipitously in 1972 by Wen, a Hong Kong neurosurgeon conducting a series of studies on the analgesic properties of acupuncture. Individuals addicted to heroin who volunteered to be participants reported that their opiate withdrawal symptoms seemed to be lessened on the days they received the acupuncture treatments. Wen and Cheung (1973) undertook a series of uncontrolled studies on the use of acupuncture in the treatment of opiate addiction and reported promising results. Over the past 20 years, numerous studies have investigated acupuncture for the treatment of various addictions, including opiates, tobacco, and alcohol (for a review, see Brewington, Smith, & Lipton, 1994). Findings from these studies have not been particularly consistent; however, controlled research on acupuncture is in its infancy, and it would be premature to attempt to formulate any definitive conclusions based on evidence from studies conducted thus far.

Although auricular acupuncture has been used in the treatment of a number of addictive disorders, it is currently most frequently used for the treatment of cocaine addiction. This is due, in part, to the lack of a generally effective agent for the treatment for cocaine addiction, whereas there exist a number of pharmacological agents with some degree of efficacy for the treatment of addiction to other substances. Because the preponderance of recent clinical acupuncture research in the addictions has focused on cocaine addiction, in this chapter I focus on acupuncture for the treatment of this disorder.

Auricular Acupuncture and the National Acupuncture Detoxification Association Protocol

The 1999 National Household Survey on Drug Abuse reported 1.5 million current cocaine users and, of particular concern, noted a 37% increase in the number of new users from 1990 to 1998 (Substance Abuse and Mental Health Services Administration, 2000). Given the dearth of effective treatments for cocaine addiction, it is not surprising that clinical reports of promising results for auricular acupuncture have generated enthusiasm for this unconventional treatment modality. The type of acupuncture most often used to treat cocaine addiction is *auricular acupuncture*—insertion of needles into the outer ear. Currently, this form of acupuncture is used in more than

700 substance abuse treatment facilities in the United States and Europe. The acupuncture protocol currently used in addiction treatments has been codified by the National Acupuncture Detoxification Association (NADA). This protocol calls for the insertion of thin stainless steel needles into three to five points, or zones, within the auricle, or outer ear. As recommended by NADA, acupuncture is typically provided to patients in groups, while the individuals are seated in comfortable chairs. Treatment sessions last about 45 minutes. Acupuncture is not considered to be an effective treatment for cocaine addiction in and of itself but as an essentially nonverbal treatment that may, for example, engage "difficult" patients in the treatment process, perhaps before they are ready to enter into therapeutically meaningful verbal counseling with treatment staff. Acupuncture is thus always offered as part of a comprehensive treatment program, which typically includes some form of psychosocial therapy, such as individual drug or group counseling (Brumbaugh, 1995).

Questions Concerning Mechanism of Action

There are a number of physiological theories concerning auricular acupuncture's mechanism of action. These include modulation of neural circuits in the mesolimbic system affected by drugs of abuse (Katims, Ng, & Lowinson, 1992), stimulation of the vagus nerve in the auricle (Ulett, 1992), and release of endogenous opioids (Simmons & Oleson, 1993). It should be noted that no study to date has examined the biochemical correlates of auricular acupuncture administered without electrical stimulation; it is not known, for example, that the previously mentioned hypotheses would apply to this form of treatment. Thus, at present there is no accepted biochemical "marker" of an active auricular treatment, or one that would differentiate an active from a control treatment.

With respect to a possible psychological basis for acupuncture's putative effects in the addictions, research by my team at Yale University suggests that the NADA acupuncture protocol may reduce craving for cocaine compared with a needle insertion control (Avants, Margolin, Chang, Kosten, & Birch, 1995). This finding is also consistent with clinical observations (Smith et al., 1997). If this is the case, auricular acupuncture may facilitate initiation of cocaine abstinence in patients for whom craving is the primary trigger for continued cocaine use. Similar to a course of psychotropic pharmacotherapy, acupuncture may be of benefit in providing relatively rapid relief for patients, which may suggest that, also similar to pharmacotherapy, the time course and duration of acupuncture's treatment effects are likely to be different from those of a psychosocial intervention (cf. Elkin, Pilkonis, Docherty, & Sotsky, 1988). A reduction in cocaine craving together with a daily respite from cocaine-focused thoughts and behavior provided by acupuncture treatments may make patients more receptive to psychosocial treatments and may provide the foundation upon which more enduring effects of verbally mediated therapies can be constructed.

ISSUES INVOLVED IN INVESTIGATING AURICULAR ACUPUNCTURE IN RANDOMIZED CLINICAL TRIALS

Preliminary studies investigating the effectiveness of acupuncture for the treatment of cocaine addiction have reported positive results (Margolin, Avants, Chang, & Kosten, 1992). However, findings from controlled studies have been inconclusive: Some studies have reported positive treatment effects for acupuncture (e.g., Konefal, Duncan, & Clemence, 1994), whereas others, including two large-scale trials, have found no difference between the acupuncture and control groups (Bullock, Kiresuk, Pheley, Culliton, & Lenz, 1999; Margolin, Kleber, et al., 2002). As I discuss in the next section, the determination of acupuncture's effectiveness in the addictions is hampered by difficulties involved in investigating this treatment modality under controlled conditions (Margolin, Avants, & Kleber, 1998). For example, critical aspects of high-quality randomized clinical trials, such as use of appropriate control conditions, maintaining a blind, and controlling and checking on participant bias, are in a relatively nascent stage with respect to acupuncture research.

Acupuncture treatments typically involve patients reposing in a quiet setting under relaxing conditions. Because relaxation has been associated with a reduction in drug craving (Margolin, Avants, & Kosten, 1994), which may in turn reduce drug use and have other beneficial effects independent of any presumed acupuncture effects, some acupuncture studies have included a no-needle insertion, relaxation control condition (e.g., Avants, Margolin, Holford, & Kosten, 2000). In addition, to control for placebo effects attendant to the insertion of needles, some studies have used needle insertion into "sham" points, for example, points proximate to active points. However, it is possible that use of control points proximate to the NADA points in the concave center of the outer ear (concha) may be too active. Helix points— that is, points located on the outer rim of the ear—may be more suitable (Margolin, Chang, Avants, & Kosten, 1993). Thus, acupuncture studies may need to consider multiple control groups, all of them active treatments to some degree, to eliminate possible confounds that arise in the provision of this treatment.

Blinding

Blindness, or masking of the active and control treatments to participants, protects against multiple sources of bias. However, it is nearly impossible to conduct acupuncture research under double-blind conditions, that is, in which neither the participants nor the acupuncturist knows which treatment is active or inactive. To be unaware of which treatment condition is which, the treatment provider would have to be inexperienced in delivering acupuncture treatments. This is clearly not feasible, because to enhance the internal validity of the study, and to increase acceptance of findings within the acupuncture community, the acupuncturists in clinical trials should be competent and experienced in providing acupuncture treatments to substance abusers. Indeed, it may well be considered unethical to have acupuncture-naïve individuals provide treatments to patients.

Participant Bias

Participant bias in a single-blind study may enhance the placebo power of the hypothesized active treatment and diminish that of the control groups. Vincent and Richardson (1995) suggested conceptualizing placebo power in acupuncture studies as a function of two primary factors: (a) the treatment provider–patient relationship and (b) treatment credibility. In acupuncture studies, these factors can be assessed using two instruments originally developed for psychotherapy studies, which are also conducted under unblinded conditions: the Working Alliance Inventory (Horvath & Greenberg, 1989) and the Treatment Credibility Scale (Borkovec & Nau, 1972). The former was developed to evaluate the relationship between the patient and the treatment provider, and the latter was originally developed to evaluate the credibility of different psychotherapies and has been modified to be used in acupuncture research (Vincent, 1990).

FACTORS THAT MAY CONTRIBUTE TO OUTCOME WITHIN A RESEARCH SETTING: EXAMPLES FROM RESEARCH AT YALE MEDICAL SCHOOL

As noted earlier, acupuncture by itself is not expected to constitute an effective intervention for cocaine addiction but is intended to be offered in conjunction with psychosocial treatments. However, the synergism, or lack thereof, between acupuncture and various psychosocial contexts has been the subject of little systematic research. To give the reader a sense of the complexity of this issue, and its bearing on assessments of acupuncture's efficacy, I next briefly present findings from three related studies conducted by my research team at Yale Medical School. These studies result in part from a serendipitous sequence of events. After 82 participants were enrolled into a randomized trial of acupuncture, and after completion of that study, the research design was adopted for a multisite study, the Cocaine Alternative Treatment Study (CATS), in which the next 83 participants took part. After completion of CATS, 30 patients were subsequently entered into a third, exploratory study. The three studies were closely related in design, yet they had a number of differences, as I describe in the following sections, that permitted exploration of various aspects of the treatment context that may influence outcome in acupuncture studies. Study 1 investigated the effectiveness of acupuncture when it is provided in conjunction with a comprehensive methadone maintenance program (MMP), which included individual counseling, and a weekly coping skills training group (CST). Study 2 investigated the effectiveness of acupuncture when provided in an MMP without CST but with financial incentives for attendance at the assigned study intervention. Study 3 explored the effectiveness of acupuncture with neither CST nor financial incentives.

Study 1: Auricular Acupuncture + CST

Design

Eighty-two cocaine-dependent, methadone-maintained patients were randomly assigned to one of three treatment groups: auricular acupuncture, control acupuncture, or relaxation group. Treatment lasted 8 weeks. In addition, all patients received daily methadone, individual counseling, and a weekly CST group. The primary outcome was cocaine use as assessed by thrice-weekly urine toxicology screens.

Treatment Conditions

In the active-treatment group, needles were inserted into the auricle bilaterally at four zones: "sympathetic," "lung," "liver," and "shen men." All of these zones are located within, or near, the ear concha. In the needle insertion control condition four needles were inserted into zones on the ear helix bilaterally at three zones not used for the treatment of addictive disorders. The relaxation control groups viewed videos of nature scenes on a large-screen television. In all three conditions, treatment was delivered for 40 minutes each weekday (Monday through Friday) for 8 weeks, following receipt of daily methadone dose. No financial incentives were provided for attendance. Patients assigned to the two needle insertion conditions were blind to whether they were receiving the NADA protocol.

Results

Sixty-three percent of the 82 randomized patients completed the 8-week trial; 46% completed auricular acupuncture; 63% completed the needle insertion control, and 81% completed the relaxation control. There was a significant difference in the time patients in the three groups were retained in treatment, with patients assigned to acupuncture completing fewer treatment weeks than patients assigned to either of the two control conditions [auricular acupuncture = 5.2 (+3.0) weeks, needle insertion control = 6.7 (+2.5) weeks, relaxation control = 7.0 (+2.3) weeks].

Longitudinal analyses of the urine data (i.e., the 24 urine toxicology screens) showed that patients assigned to acupuncture did better in treatment than patients who received relaxation or the needle insertion control, insofar as they were more likely to provide a cocaine-negative urine screen while in the study (acupuncture–relaxation comparison: odds ratio = 3.41, 95% confidence interval = 1.33–8.72; acupuncture–needle control comparison: odds ratio = 2.40, 95% confidence interval = 1.00–5.75).

The findings from this study suggested efficacy for acupuncture over two control treatments in a difficult-to-treat patient population when acupuncture is provided in conjunction with a comprehensive drug treatment program (for further details of this study, see Avants, Margolin, et al., 2000). However, it left open the contribution of the psychosocial component of the treatment program to outcome, which was explored in the next series of studies.

Study 2: Acupuncture Without CST, With Financial Incentives for Attendance

Design

In this study, in which participants were enrolled as part of CATS, the weekly manual-guided CST group intervention previously provided to all participants in Study 1 was eliminated to facilitate consistency in the treatment context across the three methadone maintenance sites participating in the multisite study. In addition, financial incentives were provided for treatment attendance in an attempt to increase retention (participants were paid $2 per session, plus a bonus of $10 weekly for attending a minimum of 3 sessions per week). This study enrolled 83 cocaine-dependent methadone-maintained patients. As in Study 1, patients were randomized to three groups: NADA protocol, control acupuncture in helix sites, or relaxation group.

Results

To explore the potential effect of eliminating the group psychosocial treatment and of adding financial incentives for attendance on outcome, an overall analysis was conducted on the samples from Study 1 and Study 2. The analyzable sample size for the purpose of this comparison was therefore $n = 165$ (Study 1: $n = 82$, Study 2: $n = 83$). The analysis [a 2 (research protocol) × 3 (treatment condition) factorial analysis of variance] showed that there was a significant improvement in retention in the NADA auricular acupuncture condition in Study 2 relative to Study 1 but poorer retention in the control conditions. In contrast to the findings from Study 1, patients assigned to auricular acupuncture did not do better in treatment compared with patients assigned to the two control conditions—there were no differences in outcome among the three groups (see Table 3.1).

In an attempt to understand the discrepant findings between Studies 1 and 2, several possibilities were considered. At pretreatment, the participants in the two studies were equivalent on all measured variables, including sociodemographic characteristics, severity of addiction, and severity of psychiatric and other addiction-related problems as measured by the Addiction Severity Index (McLellan, Luborsky, Woody, & O'Brien, 1980), suggesting that the different findings did not result from enrolling patient samples with different characteristics. However, comparisons between patients retained in Study 1 and those retained in Study 2 showed that patients retained in Study 1, without financial incentives, attended significantly more treatment sessions, were marginally less ambivalent about treatment, and viewed treatment as significantly more credible for health problems. It is noteworthy that in Study 1, in which treatments were provided in a context of an MMP with CST and with no financial incentives for attendance, patients assigned to the NADA acupuncture protocol provided significantly more cocaine-negative urines than patients assigned to either control condition, whereas in Study 2, in which treatments were provided in the context of an MMP without CST but with financial incentives for attendance, there were no significant differences in cocaine use between the acupuncture and control groups. Thus, patients retained by providing financial incentives may have been less intrinsically motivated for treatment, thought of treatment as less

TABLE 3.1
Comparisons Between Patients in Studies 1 and 2

| Characteristic | Study 1: MMP with CST, no financial incentives | | | | | | Study 2: MMP with financial incentives, no CST | | | | | |
| | NADA acu | | Needle control | | Relaxation | | NADA acu | | Needle control | | Relaxation | |
	M	SD	M	SD	M	SD	M	SD	M	SD	M	SD
Weeks retained	5.2	3.0	6.7	2.5	7.1	2.3	6.8	2.2	6.2	2.9	5.9	3.0
Cocaine-free urines (ITT)	6.4	7.3	4.5	3.8	3.7	5.6	4.1	5.9	3.1	5.2	6.2	6.9
Cocaine-free urines (TC)	11.3	7.6	6.3	7.3	4.3	6.0	5.1	6.5	3.3	5.9	8.6	7.1

Note. MMP = methadone-maintenance program; CST = coping skills therapy; NADA = National Acupuncture Detoxification Association; acu = acupuncture; ITT = intent-to-treat sample (n = 165); TC = treatment completer sample (n = 108).

credible, and were more likely to attend only the minimum number of treatments that were required to receive the financial bonus (Margolin, Avants, & Holford, 2002).

Study 3: Exploratory Study Eliminating Financial Incentives for Attendance

Design

In an effort to explore the influence of providing financial incentives for attendance, an exploratory study was conducted in which 30 cocaine-dependent, methadone-maintained patients were randomly assigned to the three treatment conditions of Studies 1 and 2 and received neither financial incentives nor the manual-guided CST.

Results

Treatment retention was relatively poor and did not differ by condition. There was also no difference in cocaine use during treatment (cocaine-free urines provided by the intention-to-treat sample: NADA acupuncture, $M = 4.4$, $SD = 7.7$; needle insertion control, $M = 1.8$, $SD = 4.0$; relaxation control, $M = 3.4$, $SD = 6.3$). These data, although preliminary and limited by a small sample size, may nonetheless be interpreted as suggesting that, although the financial incentives may have improved retention in Study 2, it may have been the manual-guided CST group intervention that interacted with the treatment conditions in Study 1 in a manner that influenced positive treatment outcome. The relatively poor outcome for the NADA protocol in the absence of a psychosocial intervention is thus consistent with assertions in the clinical literature suggesting that acupuncture is an adjunctive treatment modality that needs to be provided in conjunction with a psychosocial intervention to be effective.

Study 4: Post Hoc Exploratory Comparison of Methadone Maintenance, CST Only, Acupuncture Only, and Acupuncture + CST

Design

To further explore the possible synergistic effect of CST and acupuncture as suggested by Study 1, a comparison was conducted of the NADA acupuncture protocol, with and without CST (from Studies 1 and 2), to patients who had received CST only or standard methadone maintenance only. These patients functioned as so-called "historical controls" (Pocock, 1976). The data sets of Studies 1 and 2 were merged with the data sets of two clinical trials in progress in the same MMP, one of which included the CST-alone condition ($n = 48$), the other of which included the standard methadone maintenance (methadone maintenance alone) condition ($n = 19$). Only patients who met *Diagnostic and Statistical Manual of Mental Disorders* (American Psychiatric Association, 1987) criteria for cocaine dependence and who had completed 8 weeks of the assigned treatment modality were included in these analyses to examine the effect of each intervention among patients who received an equivalent "dose" of treatment in each condition.

Results

The percentage of patients in each condition who provided cocaine-free urine screens in the 8th week of treatment were as follows: Patients who received acupuncture plus CST had the highest rate of abstinence: 57%, compared with 40% in the CST-only condition, 15% in the acupuncture-only condition, and 10% in the standard methadone maintenance only condition. These findings are summarized in Table 3.2.

Taken together, these preliminary analyses provide a further basis for hypothesizing an interaction between acupuncture and a psychosocial treatment, and they further underscore the importance of treatment context in the evaluation of acupuncture, a point I discuss further in the next section. Consistent with other findings in the addiction literature, these analyses also point to the importance of motivation as a factor determining treatment outcome. The provision of financial incentives may have produced a confusing motivational context for patients insofar as payments were linked to attendance rather than outcome (i.e., clean urines). It appears that the financial incentives, intended to increase retention and to prevent a high dropout rate in the control groups, may in fact have served to retain unmotivated patients in the acupuncture group. Patients who are motivated to participate in a research study primarily for cash payments (perhaps to buy illicit drugs) may have little or no desire for abstinence and hence may make it unlikely that the beneficial effect of acupuncture over and above the control conditions, if it exists, will be detected.

TABLE 3.2
Summary of Provisional Findings Based on Studies 1–4

Study 1: Without incentives, with CST	Study 2: With incentives, without CST	Study 3: Without incentives, without CST	Study 4: Without incentives, MM, acu, CST, acu + CST
Acu + CST > controls	Acu only = controls	Acu only = controls	Acu + CST > CST > acu > MM

Note. CST = coping skills training; MM = methadone maintenance; acu = acupuncture.

Conducting acupuncture research is a complex endeavor that presents unique problems and issues in addition to those that generally attend any investigation of a procedure under controlled conditions. Acupuncture research is still in a formative stage, and there are thus myriad outstanding issues that need to be addressed and elucidated. Some of the issues that may warrant consideration follow.

1. Controlling for Needle Insertion: Pros and Cons

Although clinical trials conducted in research clinics that use multiple controls may have credibility in the research community, their standing with counselors and other treatment providers in the field, and hence their impact on which treatments are actually provided, may be less than hoped for. Research studies have often been criticized by the acupuncture community as "unfair" tests of acupuncture because of the "artificial" conditions under which they are conducted. For example, as discussed previously, controls for needle insertion perform a crucial function of excluding alternative hypotheses that treatment outcomes resulted principally from nonspecific factors associated with treatment administration. However, although use of this control condition may enhance the internal validity of the study, it may also limit its external validity by influencing other aspects of the research design in a way that considerably deviates from clinical practice. There are several reasons for this. First, in community-based settings the NADA auricular acupuncture protocol is almost always provided by counselors who, although certified in their respective states to perform auricular acupuncture treatments in substance abuse treatment settings, are not licensed acupuncturists. The NADA training procedures instruct counselors on the insertion of needles into five specific regions of the auricle, and state regulations typically preclude NADA-trained individuals who are not licensed acupuncturists to insert needles into any other points, which would of course include helix control points. Second, it is not known whether nonprofessional acupuncturists have the skill necessary to reliably provide control needle insertion treatments and to differentiate them from the NADA protocol. A finding of no difference between two needle insertion groups could be ascribed to lack of skill on the part of counselors providing acupuncture treatments. Last, NADA-trained substance abuse counselors may be reluctant to provide cocaine-abusing patients with a sham, and presumably ineffective, treatment; if counselors favored the group receiving the NADA protocol, the validity of the research design would obviously be undermined. Given the complexities of using a needle insertion control group when testing acupuncture in real-world settings, it is nevertheless important to determine the efficacy of the NADA protocol as it is actually delivered in these settings, without use of a needle insertion control, and to compare it to other credible interventions, such as CST, that can also be delivered by substance abuse counselors.

2. Choice of Appropriate Research Design

The preponderance of addiction acupuncture studies conducted to date have randomized patients to active or control treatments, with all patients either receiving, or not receiving, an adjunctive psychosocial treatment. As discussed previously, the contribution of concurrent psychosocial treatments to outcomes with auricular acupuncture is an important issue that warrants further investigation. However, a design in which all patients either receive or do not receive an ancillary treatment does not allow an investigation of the interaction between acupuncture and a psychosocial treatment; neither does it permit an evaluation of acupuncture's contribution to outcome over and above the psychosocial treatments. One way to address these issues would be to use a factorial design, configured to the particular clinical context in which the study will be conducted. For example, for studies conducted in a methadone clinic, in which all patients receive standard care—which consists of methadone plus individual counseling—a 2 (acupuncture or no acupuncture) × 2 (psychosocial group treatment or no psychosocial group treatment) factorial design allows for multiple relevant comparisons: acupuncture only, psychosocial group only, acupuncture + psychosocial group, standard care. Among other issues, this would address the contribution of acupuncture to outcome over and above both standard care and a psychosocial treatment as well as combined effects of psychosocial group and acupuncture. These are important issues to address, with potentially important policy implications, even though not using a needle insertion control would not allow investigation of other important issues, such as whether it is needle insertion alone, or needle insertion into specific points, that constitutes the effective basis of treatment.

3. Matching Patients to Treatment

There is no reason to suppose that acupuncture will have universal appeal to all cocaine-abusing patients. In fact, the data presented earlier showed a relatively greater dropout rate in the acupuncture group, suggesting the importance of determining the subset of patients for whom this treatment is indicated. Auricular acupuncture is a nonverbal treatment administered by a treatment provider and is passively received by the patient. It is thus considerably different from a psychosocial intervention, such as CST, that aims to help patients identify and reduce their skill deficits through role play and practice in a group setting (see Monti, Abrams, Kadden, & Cooney, 1989).

To investigate which treatment modality is most efficacious for which subgroups of MMP patients, a decision must be made regarding which patient characteristics to study. On the basis of previous research, the following four patient characteristics may be relevant to consider, especially in studies that allow for the direct comparison of acupuncture to a psychosocial treatment.

1. *Personal treatment preference.* Contrary to clinical intuition, there is evidence in the literature that providing patients with their preferred treatment modality does not necessarily produce better clinical outcomes (Avants et al., 1999). However, the unconventional nature of acupuncture may provoke more than usual interest, or aversion, in patients. Therefore, it may be of value to determine patients' treatment preference prior to randomization and to conduct retrospective analysis to determine whether patients who were randomly assigned to their preferred treatment modality (matched) achieved greater benefit from treatment than those who were not (mismatched).

2. *Cognitive impairment.* A substantial percentage of cocaine- and opioid-dependent patients self-report symptoms of cognitive impairment in the range of patients with known neuropsychological deficits (Avants, Margolin, McMahon, & Kosten, 1997). Cognitive deficits such as impaired concentration and memory difficulties have the potential to impede acquisition and retention of skills taught in CST groups. For patients with such deficits, a nonverbally mediated intervention, such as acupuncture, may be a better match.

3. *Social anxiety.* Previous research at Yale University indicated that socially anxious methadone-maintained patients achieved greater benefit from a once-weekly CST group intervention than from a more socially demanding day treatment program (Avants, Margolin, Kosten, Rounsaville, & Schottenfeld, 1998). However, a psychosocial intervention such as CST has not been compared to an intervention, such as acupuncture, that has even fewer social demands. Acupuncture may thus be an even better match for socially anxious patients than the more socially demanding CST.

4. *Coping style.* Previous research at Yale University that investigated coping in this patient population has suggested that reduced avoidant coping is related to abstinence in this patient population (Avants, Warburton, & Margolin, 2000). Thus, an intervention such as CST, in which approach coping skills (e.g., problem solving, logical analysis, positive reappraisal, seeking guidance and support) are emphasized may be of greater benefit to patients with an approach coping style than would acupuncture, which does not address coping skills and which may be a better match for patients with an avoidant coping style.

CLOSING THOUGHTS: ROLE OF TREATMENT CONTEXT

"Treatment context" has at least two relevant senses for addiction research: (a) patient–practitioner interactions and (b) the inclusion of a given treatment within a broader set of treatments offered concurrently. In the typical randomized clinical trial, treatment context is typically noted in regard to site and type of setting but is not usually otherwise specified. From an Eastern perspective, the treatment context would also include the prevailing attitude toward patients among staff, whether the setting is respectful and caring, whether it is in any degree coercive, and the way in which these various characteristics are palpably expressed. In addition, the acupuncturist's pattern of harmony, or disharmony, as it interacts with that of the patient within a given treatment session, may also be relevant. To Western researchers this may seem to be a far fetched or unfathomably complex issue to study. Yet it should be noted that the psychotherapy research literature has a long-standing interest in the alignment or misalignment of patient and therapist characteristics and the impact of this relationship on treatment outcome (Horvath & Symonds, 1991). More broadly, in biological research, the local, "microclimate" of an organism, created in large part by the interaction of the organism with relevant aspects of its environment, is regarded as crucial to whether it does, or does not, flourish (Lewontin, 2000). From the perspective of Chinese medicine, it may be counterproductive to attempt to rectify disharmony within patients amid a disharmonious treatment context; this may be especially true among addicted patients whose lives are usually pervasively chaotic. However, at present, there are no reliable estimates concerning what aspects of the treatment context significantly influence treatment outcome, let alone what relevant subsets of the environment count as microclimates for which patients.

Another sense of context concerns the total set of treatments within which the treatment being evaluated is a member. Over a decade of research on cocaine addiction strongly suggests that it is not a disorder for which there is a "magic bullet" or, in the case of acupuncture, a "magic lance." As noted previously, in clinical settings acupuncture is almost always offered as an adjunct to psychosocial services, not as a stand-alone treatment. This raises the issue of what configuration of treatments should be provided concurrent with the NADA protocol to optimize its effectiveness. At present, the answer to this question is not known, although studies such as the ones just discussed point to the potentially crucial effect that concurrent treatments may have on outcome. It must be admitted that this lacuna contributes to the complexity of interpreting even positive findings from randomized clinical trials of acupuncture, insofar as it would be desirable to parcel out the contribution of treatment context and other factors from acupuncture's effects. Interpretation of negative findings may also not be clear cut—for example, was the failure to find a treatment effect representative of the true effect, or is it due to an inappropriate treatment context, in a Western sense, in an Eastern sense, or both? As a first approach to this problem it would be helpful for acupuncture researchers to record characteristics of treatment programs in which research is conducted, including staff attitude and characteristics of the physical site. Observational studies have been useful in suggesting the potential utility of acupuncture when added to existing treatment programs (Shwartz, Saitz, Mulvey, & Brannigan, 1999), and these need to be followed up by controlled studies. Statistical approaches, such as structural equation modeling, that permit multiple influences on outcome to be considered simultaneously, may also be used. Such approaches may allow for the design of clinical trials of acupuncture in the future with more finely honed hypotheses and with greater sensitivity to the potential influence of contextual factors.

REFERENCES

American Psychiatric Association. (1987). *Diagnostic and statistical manual of mental disorders* (3rd ed., rev.). Washington, DC: Author.

Avants, S. K., Margolin, A., Chang, P., Kosten, T. R., & Birch, S. (1995). Acupuncture for the treatment of cocaine addiction: Investigation of a needle puncture control. *Journal of Substance Abuse Treatment, 12,* 195–205.

Avants, S. K., Margolin, A., Holford, T. R., & Kosten, T. R. (2000). A randomized controlled trial of auricular acupuncture for cocaine dependence. *Archives of Internal Medicine, 160,* 2305–2312.

Avants, S. K., Margolin, A., Kosten, T. R., Rounsaville, B. J., & Schottenfeld, R. S. (1998). When is less treatment better? Role of social anxiety on matching methadone patients to psychosocial treatments. *Journal of Consulting and Clinical Psychology, 66,* 924–931.

Avants, S. K., Margolin, A., Kosten, T. R., Sindelar, J. L., Rounsaville, B. J., Schottenfeld, R., et al. (1999). Day treatment vs. enhanced standard methadone services for opioid-dependent patients: A comparison of clinical efficacy and cost. *American Journal of Psychiatry, 156,* 27–33.

Avants, S. K., Margolin, A., McMahon, T. J., & Kosten, T. R. (1997). Association between self-report of cognitive impairment, HIV status, and cocaine use in a sample of cocaine-dependent methadone-maintained patients. *Addictive Behaviors, 22,* 599–611.

Avants, S. K., Warburton, L. A., & Margolin, A. (2000). The influence of coping and depression on abstinence from illicit drug use in methadone-maintained patients. *American Journal of Drug and Alcohol Abuse, 26,* 399–416.

Birch, S. J., & Felt, R. L. (1999). *Understanding acupuncture.* Edinburgh, Scotland: Churchill Livingstone.

Borkovec, T. D., & Nau, S. D. (1972). Credibility of analogue therapy rationales. *Journal of Behavioral Therapeutics and Experimental Psychiatry, 3,* 257–260.

Brewington, V., Smith, M., & Lipton, D. (1994). Acupuncture as a detoxification treatment: An analysis of controlled research. *Journal of Substance Abuse Treatment, 11,* 289–307.

Brumbaugh, A. G. (1995). *Transformation and recovery: A guide for the design and development of acupuncture-based chemical dependence treatment programs.* Santa Barbara, CA: Stillpoint Press.

Bullock, M. L., Kiresuk, T. J., Pheley, A. M., Culliton, P. D., & Lenz, S. K. (1999). Auricular acupuncture in the treatment of cocaine abuse: A study of efficacy and dosing. *Journal of Substance Abuse Treatment, 16,* 31–38.

Elkin, I., Pilkonis, P. A., Docherty, J. P., & Sotsky, S. M. (1988). Conceptual and methodological issues in comparative studies of psychotherapy and pharmacotherapy: II. Nature and timing of treatment effects. *American Journal of Psychiatry, 145,* 1070–1076.

Horvath, A. O., & Greenberg, L. S. (1989). Development and validation of the Working Alliance Inventory. *Journal of Consulting and Clinical Psychology, 36,* 223–233.

Horvath, A. O., & Symonds, B. D. (1991). Relation between working alliance and outcome in psychotherapy: A meta-analysis. *Journal of Counseling Psychology, 38,* 139–149.

Katims, J. J., Ng, L. K. Y., & Lowinson, J. (1992). Acupuncture and transcutaneous electrical nerve stimulation: Afferent nerve stimulation (ANS) in the treatment of addiction. In P. R. J. H. Lowinson & R. B. Millman (Eds.), *Substance abuse: A comprehensive textbook* (pp. 574–583). Baltimore, MD: Williams & Wilkins.

Konefal, J., Duncan, R., & Clemence, C. (1994). The impact of the addition of an acupuncture treatment program to an existing Metro–Dade County outpatient substance abuse treatment facility. *Journal of Addictive Diseases, 13*(3), 71–99.

Lewontin, R. C. (2000). *The triple helix: Gene, organism, and environment.* Cambridge, MA: Harvard University Press.

Liao, S. J., Lee, M. H. M., & Ng, L. K. Y. (1994). *Principles and practice of contemporary acupuncture.* New York: Marcel Dekker.

Margolin, A., Avants, S. K., Chang, P., & Kosten, T. R. (1992). Auricular acupuncture for the treatment of cocaine dependence in methadone-maintained patients. *American Journal on Addictions, 2,* 194–200.

Margolin, A., Avants, S. K., & Holford, T. R. (2002). Interpreting conflicting findings from clinical trials of auricular acupuncture for cocaine addiction: Does treatment context influence outcome? *Journal of Alternative and Complementary Medicine, 8,* 111–121.

Margolin, A., Avants, S. K., & Kleber, H. (1998). Investigating alternative medicine therapies in randomized controlled trials. *Journal of the American Medical Association, 280,* 1626–1628.

Margolin, A., Avants, S. K., & Kosten, T. R. (1994). Cue-elicited cocaine craving and autogenic relaxation: Association with treatment outcome. *Journal of Substance Abuse Treatment, 11,* 549–552.

Margolin, A., Chang, P., Avants, S. K., & Kosten, T. R. (1993). Effects of sham and real auricular needling: Implications for trials of acupuncture for cocaine addiction. *American Journal of Chinese Medicine, 21,* 103–111.

Margolin, A., Kleber, H. D., Avants, S. K., Konefal, J., Gawin, F., Stark, E., et al. (2002). Acupuncture for the treatment of cocaine addiction: A randomized controlled trial. *Journal of the American Medical Association, 287,* 55–63.

McLellan, A. T., Luborsky, L., Woody, G. E., & O'Brien, C. P. (1980). An improved diagnostic instrument for substance abuse patients: The Addiction Severity Index. *Journal of Nervous and Mental Disease, 168,* 26–33.

Monti, P. M., Abrams, D. B., Kadden, R. M., & Cooney, N. L. (1989). *Treating alcohol dependence.* New York: Guilford Press.

Pocock, S. J. (1976). The combination of randomized and historical controls in clinical trials. *Journal of Chronic Diseases, 29,* 175–188.

Shwartz, M., Saitz, R., Mulvey, K., & Brannigan, P. (1999). The value of acupuncture detoxification programs in a substance abuse treatment system. *Journal of Substance Abuse Treatment, 17,* 305–312.

Simmons, M. S., & Oleson, T. D. (1993). Auricular electrical stimulation and dental pain threshold. *Anesthetis Progress, 40*(1), 15–19.

Smith, M. O., Brewington, V., Culliton, P. D., Lorenz, K. Y., Ng, W. H., & Lowinson, J. H. (1997). Acupuncture. In J. Lowinson, P. Ruiz, & R. B. Millman (Eds.), *Substance abuse: A comprehensive textbook* (pp. 484–491). Baltimore, MD: Williams & Wilkins.

Substance Abuse and Mental Health Services Administration. (2000). *National Household Survey on Drug Abuse: Population estimates, 1999.* Washington, DC: U.S. Government Printing Office.

Ulett, G. A. (1992). *Beyond yin and yang.* St. Louis, MO: Warren H. Green.

Unschuld, P. U. (1985). *Medicine in China.* San Francisco: University of California Press.

Vincent, C. (1990). Credibility assessments in trials of acupuncture. *Complementary Medical Research, 4,* 8–11.

Vincent, C., & Richardson, P. H. (1995). Placebo controls for acupuncture studies. *Journal of the Royal Society of Medicine, 88,* 199–202.

Wen, H. L., & Cheung, S. Y. C. (1973). Treatment of drug addiction by acupuncture and electrical stimulation. *Asian Journal of Medicine, 9,* 138–141.

4

SELF-HELP GROUPS

JOSEPH NOWINSKI

In this chapter I provide an overview of self-help groups for people with alcohol and drug problems. I review the content, structure, and goals of several self-help groups, and I explore the ways in which self-help can be integrated into a comprehensive treatment plan. Finally, I examine some of the research that is now beginning to appear relative to the effectiveness of self-help in promoting and sustaining sobriety.

CURRENT STATUS OF THE SELF-HELP MOVEMENT

Following the growing popularity of Alcoholics Anonymous (AA; 1952, 1976), a number of similar 12-step fellowships have emerged, including Al-Anon (1966) and Narcotics Anonymous (1987). Meanwhile, individuals who wish to embrace a more fundamentalist Christian philosophy may now turn to organizations such as the Calix Society (n.d.) and Overcomers Outreach (1985, 1988). AA, however, remains by far the most ubiquitous self-help organization, with approximately 97,000 registered groups (AA, 1999) and more than 1.7 million members worldwide (AA, 1990a). In 1988, it was estimated that there were approximately 125,000 separate chapters of various 12-step groups in the United States and abroad (Madara & Meese, 1988). The 12-step movement now extends well beyond the issues of alcoholism and drug addiction and includes 12-step fellowships for "emotional addiction" (Emotions Anonymous, 1978), "food addiction" (Overeaters Anonymous, 1980), and "sex addiction" (Augustine Fellowship, 1986), to name a few.

In recent years, a number of secular self-help organizations have appeared. These groups ostensibly reject any notion of spirituality or reliance on a "higher power" for recovery. Included here are programs such as Women for Sobriety (WFS; 1993a) and Secular Organizations for Sobriety (SOS; n.d.). There also are several programs that rely on trained professionals for their implementation and that therefore are not truly self-help groups. These include SMART (Self-Management and Recovery Training) Recovery (1996) and Rational Recovery (Trimpey, 1992). These groups, as well as the various 12-step groups, all aim to help individuals overcome alcohol or drug problems. They differ significantly, however, with respect to philosophy, strategies for change, and organization.

One important distinction among self-help groups concerns the issue of spirituality. Some groups, such as AA, advocate some form of spiritual belief and consider such a belief to be vital to recovery. AA defines this belief in a higher power in a way that opens the door to a wide range of personal beliefs: "You can, if you wish, make AA itself your 'higher power.' In this respect they are certainly a power greater than you, who have not even come close to a solution" (AA, 1952, p. 27).

AA is sometimes mistaken for a religious sect, which it clearly is not. AA does not align itself with any denomination; neither does it espouse any particular religious dogma. Nevertheless, 12-step fellowships such as AA differ from secular self-help groups in that spirituality is integral to their philosophy. Secular self-help groups, such as SOS, deliberately disavow anything spiritual: "SOS is not a spin-off of any religious or secular group. There is no hidden agenda, as SOS is concerned with achieving and maintaining sobriety (abstinence), not religiosity" (SOS, n.d., p. 2).

Still other self-help groups, such as WFS, do not reject spirituality so much as they make no specific mention of it in their programs. WFS summarizes its philosophy in this way: "The WFS program is based upon metaphysical philosophy. The Fifth Statement, 'I am what I think,' is the entire basis for the program" (Kirkpatrick, 1982, p. 2).

In its literature, however, WFS states that it sees no inherent incompatibility with using both WFS and AA as aids to sustaining women's recovery. For every program described in this chapter, with the exception of Moderation Management (MM; 1996), the goal is *abstinence* from the use of alcohol or drugs. MM, as its name implies, seeks to teach skills needed to *control* drinking. The classification scheme is summarized in Table 4.1, which lists a number of the more popular self-help programs.

TABLE 4.1
Classification of Self-Help Organizations

Fellowships		Guided self-help groups
Spiritual	Secular	
Alcoholics Anonymous	Secular Organizations for	SMART Recovery
Narcotics Anonymous	Sobriety	Rational Recovery
Cocaine Anonymous	Women for Sobriety	Moderation Management[a]
Calix Society		
Overcomers Outreach		

[a]States that its goal is to help individuals reduce drinking; all others state that abstinence is the goal.

SPIRITUAL FELLOWSHIPS

Alcoholics Anonymous

The modern self-help movement for addictive behaviors had its origins in AA, which in turn was influenced by the Oxford Group movement, an international, nondenominational evangelical organization whose stated goal was to promote what it considered to be fundamental Christian precepts (Kurtz, 1988). The Oxford Group meetings impressed AA cofounder Bill Wilson with their atmosphere of kindness and acceptance and with their emphasis on spiritual renewal and fellowship as keys to personal transformation.

AA evolved from the Oxford movement, incorporating its emphasis on the power of fellowship and faith over self-determination as well as its beliefs in the virtues of taking one's "moral inventory" on an ongoing basis, of making amends to others, of publicly confessing one's faults and flaws, and of altruistic service to others. What differentiated AA from the Oxford movement was its less dogmatic, more pluralistic view of the concept of God, which AA reframed as a "higher power." This opened AA to a greater diversity of spiritual beliefs.

One national survey found that 3.1% of the adult population indicated they had been to an AA meeting at least once, and 1.5% indicated they had been to one in the past year (Room & Greenfield, 1991). These prevalence data were roughly three times greater than AA's own estimates of its prevalence (AA, 1990a). Because of its size, its organization, and the scope of its influence on society, AA has been described as a full-blown social movement, akin to the women's liberation and civil rights movements (Room, 1993).

The 12-step program of AA is presented in Exhibit 4.1. Narcotics Anonymous, Al-Anon, and other 12-step programs all advocate following these same steps as a program of recovery, the ultimate goal of which is a

EXHIBIT 4.1
The Twelve Steps of Alcoholics Anonymous

Step 1. We admitted we were powerless over alcohol—that our lives had become unmanageable.

Step 2. Came to believe that a Power greater than ourselves could restore us to sanity.

Step 3. Made a decision to turn our will and our lives over to the care of God *as we understood him.*

Step 4. Made a searching and fearless moral inventory of ourselves.

Step 5. Admitted to God, to ourselves, and to another human being the exact nature of our wrongs.

Step 6. Were entirely ready to have God remove all these defects of character.

Step 7. Humbly asked Him to remove our shortcomings.

Step 8. Made a list of all persons we had harmed and became willing to make amends to them all.

Step 9. Made direct amends to such people whenever possible, except when to do so would injure them or others.

Step 10. Continued to take personal inventory and when we were wrong admitted it.

Step 11. Sought through prayer and meditation to improve our conscious contact with God *as we understood him*, praying only for knowledge of his will for us and the power to carry that out.

Step 12. Having had a spiritual awakening as the result of these steps, we tried to carry this message to alcoholics and to practice these principles in all our affairs.

Note. From *Alcoholics Anonymous: The Story of How Many Thousands of Men and Women Have Recovered From Alcoholism* (3rd ed.) by Alcoholics Anonymous, 1976. Copyright 1976 by Alcoholics Anonymous World Services, Inc. (A.A.W.S.). Reprinted with permission. Permission to reprint the Twelve Steps does not mean that AAWS has reviewed or approved the contents of this publication, or that AAWS necessarily agrees with the views herein. AA is a program of recovery from alcoholism only; use of the Twelve Steps in connection with programs and activities that are patterned after AA but that address other problems, or in any other non-AA context, does not imply otherwise.

"spiritual awakening" (AA, 1952, p. 106). This is significant, because the 12-step program identifies itself as something more than a means of staying sober. This reflects the belief of the founders of AA that addiction is a part of a larger spiritual crisis and thus their view of recovery as a gradual process of spiritual renewal.

According to AA, the process of recovery and renewal begins with admitting that one's efforts to control drinking have failed and that as a result life has become unmanageable (Step 1). Within the 12-step culture this is also commonly referred to as *acceptance*. Acceptance is primarily a cognitive process, as defined by the psychiatrist Harry Tiebout (1953):

> Acceptance appears to be a state of mind in which the individual accepts rather than rejects or resists: he is able to take things in, to go along with, to cooperate, to be receptive. Contrariwise, he is not argumentative, quarrelsome, irritable, or contentious. (p. 3)

When working with clients who are involved in a 12-step program, practitioners should understand that the opposite of acceptance is what is meant by the term *denial*. The first step asks that the alcoholic stop resisting and face the facts: that personal efforts to control drinking have failed and that life has become unmanageable. Acceptance opens the door to change.

The second and third steps of the 12-step program are often linked together through the concept of *surrender*, conceptualized as a readiness to change:

> After an act of surrender, the individual reports a sense of unity, of ended struggles, of no longer divided inner counsel. He knows the meaning of inner wholeness and, what is more, he knows from immediate experience the feeling of being wholehearted about anything. (Tiebout, 1953, p. 9)

Unlike acceptance, which is primarily cognitive in nature, surrender is more akin to a spiritual phenomenon. Like resistance to acceptance, however, resistance to the idea of surrender is also part of what is meant by *denial* in the context of 12-step groups. On a practical level, newcomers to AA sooner or later are asked to "surrender" to the program. Practitioners should understand that this means embracing the 12-step program and following the traditions and the counsel of fellow AA members and one's sponsor.

AA meetings vary in format. *Open meetings* may be attended by people who do not necessarily acknowledge that they have an alcohol (or drug) problem as well as by those who are willing to admit that they have a drinking (or drug) problem. Open meetings are therefore appropriate for patients who are undecided about whether they have a problem with alcohol. In contrast, *closed meetings* are to be attended only by people who acknowledge a problem and have the requisite desire to stop drinking that is cited in AA literature as the sole requirement for membership (AA, 1952, p. 139). Each meeting has a chairperson, who is elected by the membership, and a secretary. These posts typically change periodically, although, in keeping with the AA tradition of decentralization, there is no set standard.

Meetings are governed by established rules of etiquette, which by custom are communicated orally to newcomers. Most important of these is the rule of anonymity: Members typically identify themselves by first name only, and they are strongly encouraged to regard everything that is said in an AA meeting as confidential. Additional rules of etiquette include not interrupting or questioning a speaker, respecting one's right not to speak, and avoiding dual relationships with members of the group. That is not to say that AA members do not socialize with one another; on the contrary, socializing before and after meetings is strongly encouraged. However, dating a member of one's "home group" is generally discouraged, as is any romantic involvement during one's first year of sobriety. Other types of 12-step meetings include the following.

Speaker Meeting

At speaker meetings, which are highly recommended for newcomers as well as for individuals who are undecided about whether they have a drinking or drug problem, group members and, on occasion, guest speakers take turns relating their personal stories. The format of these stories is as follows: *How things were, what happened,* and *how things are now.* Thus, these are tales of addiction and recovery. Storytelling facilitates bonding to the group, and to the fellowship of AA, by establishing a sense of shared experience. Storytelling also helps members to maintain their memories of the consequences that are associated with substance abuse and addiction. AA believes that any tendency to forget the unpleasant past is dangerous. One suggested method for staying sober is "remembering your last drunk" (AA, 1975).

Discussion Meeting

The format of a discussion meeting is to select a topic (e.g., gratitude, self-centeredness, resentments) and to take turns sharing thoughts about it. Typically, either the chairperson selects the topic or the members do so in rotation. Sometimes the topic is a reading from an AA publication.

Step Meeting

In step meetings, the format is to read one of the 12 steps and for members to share how they as individuals are "working" that step, that is, how they are attempting to implement it in their daily lives. Through attending step meetings, newcomers have an opportunity to learn how others have interpreted the steps and how they relate to lifestyle and attitude changes that are associated with recovery versus merely staying sober. Some step meetings limit themselves to the first 3 steps, whereas others include all 12 steps as topics for discussion.

Narcotics Anonymous and Cocaine Anonymous

Narcotics Anonymous and Cocaine Anonymous are fellowships that are open to people who wish to recover from drug addiction through the 12-step model. Narcotics Anonymous has published its own version of the "AA Big Book," (*Alcoholics Anonymous*; AA, 1976), titled *Narcotics Anonymous* (1987). It includes the identical 12-step program as AA, merely substituting the word *narcotics* for *alcohol*, as well as stories of recovery that are similar in theme to those that make up the second half of *Alcoholics Anonymous*. Their inherent compatibility means that it is possible and appropriate for people who are polysubstance abusers to make use of several 12-step programs concurrently.

Secular fellowships eschew any mention of God or spirituality in their programs. One such organization is WFS, which describes itself as "an organization whose purpose is to help all women recover from problem drinking through the discovery of self, gained by sharing experiences, hopes and encouragement with other women in similar circumstances" (WFS, n.d., p. 2). WFS sees itself and AA as complementary but nevertheless strongly advocates that women involved in AA also attend WFS because it believes that women have special needs that cannot be satisfactorily met through AA: "The problems of most women are tied to the male–female relationship, and these problems cannot be talked about or thoroughly explored in a mixed group" (Kirkpatrick, 1982, p. 2).

This criticism notwithstanding, AA has seen its greatest rate of growth in recent years among women (AA, 1990b), including women-only groups. This degree of acceptance of AA on the part of women led one reviewer to conclude that "I now believe that AA, a fellowship originally designed by and composed primarily of men, appears equally or more effective for women than for men" (Beckman, 1993, p. 246). Like AA, WFS advocates abstinence from alcohol and drugs. It seeks to help women achieve this through group support. WFS (1993a) described its meetings as "a conversation in the round." Groups are run by a moderator who is not a trained professional but rather a woman in recovery who is versed in the WFS philosophy. The moderator opens the meeting by reading aloud the *Thirteen Statements* of WFS (1993b). These statements (see Exhibit 4.2) form the basis of the WFS New Life Acceptance Program (WFS, 1993b).

EXHIBIT 4.2
The Women for Sobriety New Life Acceptance Program

---

1. I have a life-threatening problem that once had me.
2. Negative thoughts destroy only myself.
3. Happiness is a habit I will develop.
4. Problems bother me only to the degree I permit them to.
5. I am what I think.
6. Life can be ordinary or it can be great.
7. Love can change the course of my world.
8. The fundamental object of life is emotional and spiritual growth.
9. The past is gone forever.
10. All love given returns.
11. Enthusiasm is my daily exercise.
12. I am a competent woman and have much to give life.
13. I am responsible for myself and my actions.

Note. Copyright 1993 by Women for Sobriety, Inc. Reprinted with permission.

The New Life Acceptance Program identifies problems of self-esteem and self-acceptance as lying at the core of substance abuse problems in women. Recovery involves a process of gaining self-acceptance through active involvement in WFS. This view is affirmed in WFS literature that states "Guilt, depression, low (or no) self-esteem are the problems of today's woman and dependence upon alcohol temporarily masks her real needs, which are for a feeling of self-realization and self-worth" (WFS, n.d., p. 2). As strategies for change, WFS favors positive reinforcement through support, approval, and encouragement; positive thinking as emphasized in its New Life Acceptance program; and taking care of one's physical health.

GUIDED SELF-HELP GROUPS

As opposed to true self-help, some programs offer professionally guided help. Because they rely on the use of trained leaders, these programs are more centralized than the self-help fellowships described earlier.

SMART Recovery

SMART Recovery is "an abstinence-based, not-for-profit organization with a sensible self-help program for people having problems with drinking and using" (SMART Recovery, 1996, p. 2). In its conceptualization of alcoholism and addiction SMART, much like WFS, emphasizes that people drink or use drugs as a means of coping, even though this use of alcohol or drugs ultimately creates further problems. Accordingly, the SMART Recovery program emphasizes building alternative coping skills as the key to recovery.

SMART issues a standard meeting outline that begins with a general welcome, with special attention paid to newcomers. Members are asked next to share something positive that they have learned or done as a result of attending meetings. Members are then polled to see who if anyone may need some extra time to deal with concerns or problems. The bulk of the 1.5-hour meeting time is devoted to a discussion of one of SMART Recovery's main themes using one of the structured exercises developed by SMART Recovery. These themes relate to key areas of awareness and change and include building motivation, coping with urges, problem solving, and lifestyle changes (SMART Recovery, 1996).

SMART Recovery makes extensive use of cognitive–behavioral theory and technique as set forth in rational–emotive therapy (Ellis & Harper, 1975). Meetings end with each member being asked to say something about what he or she intends to do in the coming week to support his or her recovery. After the end of the formal meeting, members are encouraged to socialize and exchange phone numbers. Like other guided self-help programs,

SMART Recovery uses trained professionals to run meetings; these individuals, however, are not paid for their services.

Moderation Management

MM (Kishline, 1996) is the sole program for substance abusers that openly advocates moderation as opposed to abstinence as its long-term goal (MM, 1996). This program, which emphasizes progressive changes in lifestyle to support moderation, does, however, recommend an initial 30-day period of abstinence, presumably as a litmus test for moderation.

MM indicates that it "is not for alcoholics or chronic drinkers" but rather "is intended for problem drinkers who have experienced *mild to moderate* levels of alcohol-related problems' (MM, 1996, p. 1). According to MM, only through accurate self-assessment can one decide the difference between "mild to moderate" versus "severe" consequences of substance abuse. AA (1976) suggested such a test period as an aid to self-diagnosis for those who are in doubt:

> We do not like to pronounce any individual as alcoholic, but you can quickly diagnose yourself. Step over to the nearest barroom and try some controlled drinking. Try to drink and stop abruptly. Try it more than once. It will not take long for you to decide, if you are honest with yourself about it. (p. 31)

MM advocates a similar test, stating that it is for individuals who do *not* quickly find themselves returning to their pre-abstinence level of drinking following a period of abstinence. The MM program, like that of SMART Recovery, is based on a cognitive–behavioral model of addiction. The MM nine-step program for moderation (see Exhibit 4.3) includes many strategies

EXHIBIT 4.3
The Moderation Management (MM) Nine-Step Program

---

1. Attend MM meetings and learn about the program of Moderation Management.
2. Abstain from alcoholic beverages for 30 days and complete steps 3 through 6 during this time.
3. Examine how drinking has affected your life.
4. Write down your priorities.
5. Take a look at how much, how often, and under what circumstances you used to drink.
6. Learn the MM guidelines and limits for moderate drinking.
7. Set moderate drinking limits and start weekly "small steps" toward positive lifestyle changes.
8. Review your progress and update your goals.
9. Continue to make positive lifestyle changes, attend meetings for ongoing encouragement and support, and help newcomers to the group.

Note. From *Moderation Management: For People Who Want to Reduce Their Drinking* by Moderation Management, 1996. Copyright 1996 by Moderation Management. Reprinted with permission.

for change that are drawn from the cognitive–behavioral literature. MM also recommends a number of self-help books, all of which offer many cognitive–behavioral strategies for moderation. The primary difference between MM and SMART Recovery appears to be not so much in their techniques but in their respective goals.

EFFECTIVENESS OF SELF-HELP

Research on the effectiveness of self-help groups is limited but growing. There are no controlled studies, however, of self-help, and for good reason: The very nature of self-help does not lend itself to this research paradigm. It is not feasible, for example, to control treatment "dosage" in programs where the sole factor determining involvement is the individual's interest and motivation. Some people may choose to attend 1 AA meeting per week, for example, whereas others choose to follow the AA dictum of attending 90 meetings in 90 days. Similarly, it is not possible to control the types of meetings people attend, when and if a person will select a sponsor, whether a person will tell his or her story at a meeting, and so on. Finally, it is not possible to control whether individuals seek help in addition to going to AA. According to AA's General Service Office, 62% of active members indicate that they have sought such help (AA, 1999).

A second obstacle to meaningful research on self-help has been a lack of good instrumentation. In the absence of standard, reliable measures of AA participation it is difficult to compare results from different studies or to measure variables other than attendance per se. This limitation has fortunately recently been addressed. The Alcoholics Anonymous Affiliation Scale (Humphreys, Kaskutas, & Weisner, 1998) and the Alcoholics Anonymous Involvement Scale (Tonigan, Connors, & Miller, 1996) are both psychometrically sound measures of involvement in AA. These scales may make it possible to begin to study the dynamics of how AA helps.

Studies of the effectiveness of self-help to date have been mainly correlational in nature. In this area, the body of research is growing. The best-studied of the self-help groups is AA. AA itself conducts triennial surveys of its membership. Most other self-help groups do not engage even in this level of "research," relying instead on anecdotal reports about their effectiveness. According to its most recent survey (AA, 1999), 47% of active AA members had been sober for more than 5 years, and another 26% reported being sober between 1 and 5 years. An earlier member survey (AA, 1990b) reported that 40% of AA newcomers who remained active in the fellowship for 1 year stayed sober for a second year.

There is also some evidence to support the idea that more active participation in AA promotes recovery. A meta-analysis of studies of AA concluded that "AA members who 'work the program' are more likely to have a better status with respect to their drinking behavior" (Emrick, Tonigan, Montgomery, & Little, 1993, p. 55). In this regard, *working the program* entails the following: attending meetings regularly, getting a sponsor, leading a meeting, and doing service work. Additional studies, which are beginning to appear after the publication of treatment outcome data from Project MATCH (Project MATCH Research Group, 1997), further support the correlation between sustained sobriety and AA affiliation and involvement (Fiorentine, 1999; Humphreys, Moos, & Cohen, 1997; Morgenstern, Labouvie, McCrady, Kahler, & Frey, 1997).

Although the evidence suggests that individuals who actively work the AA program have a promising outcome with respect to drinking, according to AA surveys, 60% of individuals cease their involvement in AA within a year (AA, 1990b). Thus, only a minority of those who try AA on their own initiative stay with it. These data also suggest that the extra clinical effort required by the active facilitation approach may be worthwhile. In Project MATCH, trained therapists used Twelve-Step Facilitation (TSF), a manual-based treatment approach whose goal is promoting active involvement in AA and helping clients work through resistances to such involvement (Nowinski & Baker, 1998; Nowinski, Baker, & Carroll, 1995). The type of involvement that is the goal of TSF is precisely that which has been found to correlate with sobriety: getting a sponsor, networking, and so on. Posttreatment outcome data for TSF were favorable and have been presented in detail elsewhere (Project MATCH Research Group, 1997). A 3-year follow-up of Project MATCH patients found that continued participation in self-help remained a powerful predictor of recovery, especially for those whose pretreatment social network included significant others who either drank or had a tolerant attitude toward drinking (Longabaugh, Wirtz, Zweben, & Stout, 1998). This in turn raises a challenging question for future research: To what extent can practitioners enhance the effectiveness of self-help if they make it a primary goal of an active therapeutic intervention as opposed to being an ancillary goal, as it has tended to be in the past?

INTEGRATING SELF-HELP INTO CLINICAL PRACTICE

Although an understanding of the factors that account for why AA helps may be limited, a growing body of literature supports the general conclusion that going to AA meetings improves the prognosis for alcoholics. Therefore, it makes sense that clinicians should incorporate participation in a self-help group into their treatment plans for clients with alcohol problems. Practitioners can approach this issue of integrating self-help into a comprehensive treatment plan, however, in one of two ways. The first of these approaches could be called *passive facilitation*. In this approach, the therapist recognizes the usefulness of a self-help program in promoting recovery and may recommend attendance at meetings. Following up on this therapeutic recommendation, however, is typically limited to asking the patient if he or she has gone to any meetings.

In contrast, in *active facilitation* the therapist makes active involvement in one or more self-help groups an integral part of the treatment plan (Nowinski, 1996; Nowinski & Baker, 1998; Nowinski et al., 1995). In this approach, the patient's adherence with the recommendation that he or she use a self-help group becomes a discrete treatment goal. The therapist intentionally and consistently uses interventions (e.g., education, shaping, role playing) in an effort to achieve that goal. This is consistent with the findings cited earlier: that AA involvement is correlated with sobriety and that more vigorous participation in the various components of AA (e.g., sponsorship) is correlated with better outcomes.

To be an effective active facilitator, a therapist must be much more knowledgeable about the self-help group to which he or she is referring patients than is necessary under a passive approach. The therapist must have a good understanding of the philosophy, goals, and structure of the self-help group to understand the specific nature of any patient resistance that may arise.

In addition to a clear understanding of the workings of the self-help group that is being integrated into the treatment plan, an active facilitator is aware of the process that is associated with active involvement in mutual help and devotes a good amount of therapeutic time and effort to guiding that involvement. Resistance to involvement is identified by the active facilitator as something to be worked through with the patient. This process, whose goal is greater participation in the group, typically proceeds through several stages, described next.

Attendance

Active involvement in a self-help group obviously begins with being there. It is not surprising that resistance often is most evident at this initial point. It is helpful if the therapist is familiar with the format and the ground rules of the group to which the client is being referred. Knowing in advance what to expect when one walks into a meeting—be it an AA meeting, a SMART Recovery meeting, or a WFS meeting—puts the therapist in a position to anticipate issues and help the client overcome anticipatory anxiety. Role playing around potential issues (e.g., "Let's practice how you would introduce yourself") would be another way to desensitize anxiety.

Identification

A further step in the affiliation process is taken when the newcomer begins to *identify* with other members of the group. "Identify, don't compare" is advice often given to AA newcomers. Therapists can expect to encounter resistance to this, and the more this resistance can be worked through, the more the client can begin to bond with the self-help group. Client resistance at this stage typically takes the form of drawing contrasts between oneself and others in the group. By emphasizing differences (as opposed to similarities), resistant patients feel justified in not bonding with the group.

Networking

Networking—in which members are encouraged to build support networks by establishing long-term relationships with other members—is a part of all self-help groups. AA advocates networking in part through "telephone therapy" (AA, 1975) and sponsorship. SOS encourages networking as a means of establishing a "social safety net" in advance of the actual need for one (SOS, n.d.).

Rituals and Traditions

Ritual and tradition are additional means of facilitating deeper involvement in a group, and it is not surprising that self-help groups often incorporate rituals and tradition into their programs. WFS, for example, begins each meeting by reading the Thirteen Statements of its New Life Program, then asks members to "stroke" themselves, and ends each meeting by joining hands and reciting the WFS motto: "We are capable and competent, caring and compassionate, always willing to help another, bonded together in overcoming our addictions" (WFS, 1993a, p. 1). SMART Recovery meetings incorporate a ritual wherein members share successes from the preceding week.

CONCLUSION

Research on the relationship between self-help and clinical outcomes is limited, and most such studies concern AA rather than other self-help approaches. The available literature suggests that active and sustained engagement in AA is associated with better treatment outcomes. The challenges for researchers are to develop strategies to study self-help approaches more thoroughly, given the constraints of anonymity and the inability to control factors such as dosage and motivation. One approach, as used in Project MATCH, is to implement and test manual-based self-help interventions. The challenges for practice are to better integrate self-help approaches into treatment, by incorporating active facilitation of self-help into treatment plans and by supporting patients in their attendance, identification, and networking in the context of self-help interventions.

REFERENCES

Al-Anon. (1966). *Al-Anon family groups*. New York: Author.

Alcoholics Anonymous. (1952). *Twelve steps and twelve traditions*. New York: Author.

Alcoholics Anonymous. (1975). *Living sober: Some methods A.A. members have used for not drinking*. New York: Author.

Alcoholics Anonymous. (1976). *Alcoholics Anonymous: The story of how many thousands of men and women have recovered from alcoholism* (3rd ed.). New York: Author.

Alcoholics Anonymous. (1990a). *Alcoholics Anonymous 1989 membership survey*. New York: Author.

Alcoholics Anonymous. (1990b). *Comments on AA's triennial surveys*. New York: Author.

Alcoholics Anonymous. (1999). *Alcoholics Anonymous 1998 membership survey*. New York: Author.

Augustine Fellowship. (1986). *Sex and love addicts anonymous*. Boston: Author.

Beckman, L. J. (1993). Alcoholics Anonymous and gender issues. In B. S. McCrady & W. R. Miller (Eds.), *Research on Alcoholics Anonymous: Opportunities and alternatives* (pp. 233–248). New Brunswick, NJ: Rutgers University Press.

Calix Society. (n.d.). *Calix: What and why*. Minneapolis, MN: Author.

Ellis, A., & Harper, R. (1975). *A new guide to rational living*. North Hollywood, CA: Wilshire.

Emotions Anonymous. (1978). *Emotions Anonymous*. St. Paul, MN: Author.

Emrick, C. D., Tonigan, J. S., Montgomery, H., & Little, L. (1993). Alcoholics Anonymous: What is currently known? In B. S. McCrady & W. R. Miller (Eds.), *Research on Alcoholics Anonymous: Opportunities and alternatives* (pp. 41–76). New Brunswick, NJ: Rutgers University Press.

Fiorentine, R. (1999). After drug treatment: Are 12-step programs effective in maintaining abstinence? *American Journal of Drug and Alcohol Abuse, 25*, 93–116.

Humphreys, K., Kaskutas, L. A., & Weisner, C. (1998). The Alcoholics Anonymous Affiliation Scale: Development, reliability, and norms for diverse treated and untreated populations. *Alcoholism: Clinical and Experimental Research, 22*, 974–978.

Humphreys, K., Moos, R. H., & Cohen, C. (1997). Social and community resources and long-term recovery from treated and untreated alcoholism. *Journal of Studies on Alcoholism, 58*, 231–238.

Kirkpatrick, J. (1982, Summer). A self-help program for women alcoholics. *Alcohol and Research World*, pp. 1–2.

Kishline, A. (1996). *Moderate drinking: The Moderation Management guide for people who want to reduce their drinking*. New York: Crown.

Kurtz, E. (1988). *A.A.: The story*. New York: Harper/Hazelden.

Longabaugh, R., Wirtz, P., Zweben, A., & Stout, R. (1998). Network support for drinking: Alcoholics Anonymous and long-term matching effects. *Addiction, 93*, 1313–1333.

Madara, E., & Meese, A. (Eds.). (1988). *The self-help sourcebook: Finding and forming mutual-aid self-help groups* (2nd ed.). Denville, NJ: Self-Help Clearinghouse.

Moderation Management. (1996). *Moderation management: For people who want to reduce their drinking.* Ann Arbor, MI: Author.

Morgenstern, J., Labouvie, E., McCrady, B. S., Kahler, C. W., & Frey, R. M. (1997). Affiliation with Alcoholics Anonymous following treatment: A study of its therapeutic effects and mechanisms of action. *Journal of Consulting and Clinical Psychology, 65*, 768–777.

Narcotics Anonymous. (1987). *Narcotics Anonymous* (4th ed.). Van Nuys, CA: Author.

Nowinski, J. (1996). Facilitating 12-step recovery from substance abuse and addiction. In F. Rotgers, D. S. Keller, & J. Morgenstern (Eds.), *Treating substance abuse: Theory and technique* (pp. 117–138). New York: Guilford Press.

Nowinski, J., & Baker, S. (1998). *The twelve-step facilitation handbook: A systematic approach to early recovery from alcoholism and addiction.* San Francisco: Jossey-Bass.

Nowinski, J., Baker, S., & Carroll, K. (1995). *Twelve-step facilitation manual: A clinical research guide for therapists treating individuals with alcohol abuse and dependence* (NIAAA Project MATCH Monograph, Vol. 1, DHHS No. ADM-92-1893). Washington, DC: U.S. Government Printing Office.

Overcomers Outreach. (1985). *FREED (Fellowship in recovery, Reconciliation to God, Education about chemicals and addiction, Edification through faith in Christ, Dedicated service to others).* Anaheim, CA: Author.

Overcomers Outreach. (1988). *The 12 steps . . . with their corresponding scriptures!* Anaheim, CA: Author.

Overeaters Anonymous. (1980). *Overeaters Anonymous.* Torrance, CA: Author.

Project MATCH Research Group. (1997). Project MATCH: Post-treatment drinking outcomes. *Journal of Studies on Alcoholism, 58*, 7–29.

Room, R. (1993). Alcoholics Anonymous as a social movement. In B. S. McCrady & W. R. Miller (Eds.), *Research on Alcoholics Anonymous: Opportunities and alternatives* (pp. 167–187). New Brunswick, NJ: Rutgers University Press.

Room, R., & Greenfield, T. (1991). *Alcoholics Anonymous, other 12-step movements, and psychotherapy in the U.S. population, 1990* (Working Paper F281). Berkeley, CA: Alcohol Research Group.

Secular Organizations for Sobriety. (n.d.). *Secular Organizations for Sobriety: A self-empowerment approach to recovery.* Buffalo, NY: Author.

SMART Recovery. (1996). *SMART Recovery: Self-management and recovery training, member's manual.* Beachwood, OH: Author.

Tiebout, H. M. (1953). Surrender versus compliance in therapy with special reference to alcoholism. *Quarterly Journal of Studies on Alcohol, 14*, 58–68.

Tonigan, J. S., Connors, G. J., & Miller, W. R. (1996). Alcoholics Anonymous Involvement Scale: Reliability and norms. *Psychology of Addictive Behaviors, 10,* 75–80.

Trimpey, J. (1992). *Rational recovery: The new cure for substance addiction.* New York: Pocket Books.

Women for Sobriety. (1993a). *Welcome to WFS and the new life program.* Quakertown, PA: Author.

Women for Sobriety. (1993b). *WFS: Who we are.* Quakertown, PA: Author.

Women for Sobriety. (n.d.). *Women and addiction: A way to recovery.* Quakertown, PA: Author.

5

THE TACOMA SYRINGE EXCHANGE STUDIES: PUBLIC HEALTH PRACTICE INFLUENCES RESEARCH

HOLLY HAGAN, DON C. DES JARLAIS, AND DAVID PURCHASE

The harm reduction approach to health problems in injection drug users (IDUs) has had a profound and lasting effect on the relationship between research and public health practice, and the history of needle exchange research provides several excellent examples of successful collaboration between the two. Harm reduction embraces the idea that drug users are motivated and capable of developing, adopting, and maintaining disease control and risk reduction measures (Des Jarlais, Friedman, & Ward, 1993). In a very early example, the Junkiebonden of Amsterdam developed needle exchange as a method to reduce hepatitis B transmission in the 1980s in collaboration with the health department (Buning, Coutinho, van Brussel, van Santen, & van Zadelhoff, 1986). This act represented a shift in the relationship between an affected population and public health experts, including researchers. Harm reduction and needle exchange have tended to

The Tacoma syringe exchange research referred to in this chapter was supported by Grant 001553-12-RGR from the American Foundation for AIDS Research.

place IDUs and activists in a lead role and to link research more directly to the actions and points of view of these new leaders (Brettle, 1991; Marlatt, 1996). Overall, this constitutes a change from the previously held view of drug users as "subjects"—core transmitters of disease and a locus of infection in the community (Ginzburg, 1988)—to the recognition of their importance as participants in disease control efforts (Loxley, 2000).

The activist and participant identities of many individuals involved in setting up and running needle exchanges in many ways precluded the possibility of acquiescing to public health experts. Having taken personal risk of arrest for operating an illegal public health activity, needle exchange practitioners were loathe to accept second-citizen status when it came to formulating research questions and developing operational guidelines for needle exchange (Sorge, 1990). Many resisted the adoption of needle exchange regulations such as requiring proof of identity, registering users, setting limits on the number of needles exchanged, or prohibiting the sale or transfer of syringes to other users (Des Jarlais, Paone, Friedman, Peyser, & Newman, 1995; Kochems et al., 1996). In some cases, research activities were viewed by needle exchange practitioners as an agent of institutionalized public health. Other needle exchange practitioners believed that empirical evidence of the safety and effectiveness of the programs was needed and that the debate over needle exchange could be fought and possibly won with research findings. However, this view of the usefulness of research was not universal among exchange operators, and a small number of programs steadfastly resisted collaborations with research or public health experts.

In this chapter we discuss the Tacoma Syringe Exchange studies as an example of how an individual activist did collaborate with both researchers and public health officials to develop and test a needle exchange program. Other exchange programs (e.g., in Los Angeles; Santa Cruz, New Mexico; and San Francisco) entered into similar collaborations with researchers (Guydish et al., 1991; Ochoa, Edney-Meschery, & Moss, 1999; Weiker, Edgington, & Kipke, 1999). The Tacoma case is useful as an illustration of how such collaboration could allow for independence and flexibility in the conduct of the public health program, generate sophisticated research, and permit the coexisting structure of public health departments and experts to contribute to the success and functioning of the exchange program.

A SHORT HISTORY OF THE TACOMA SYRINGE EXCHANGE

Tacoma is a working-class city on Puget Sound, Washington, just 35 miles south of Seattle. A center for manufacturing, Tacoma had a heroin-using population whose existence was widely acknowledged. Its visible drug market area was located so that it was almost the first thing a visitor might see on exiting the freeway to the city center. Running along the waterfront through downtown, Pacific Avenue was where drug users would congregate and mill around during the day and night, copping drugs, using, and socializing. And it was there on Pacific Avenue where, in August 1988, David Purchase placed a small wooden TV tray on the sidewalk and officially started the Tacoma Syringe Exchange. A report on the program published in the *International Working Group on AIDS and IV Drug Use* newsletter (Bischof et al., 1988) stated,

> On August 9, Dave Purchase, with a folding table, tupperware bowl, homemade sign and $125 worth of new sterile needles began the first[1] needle exchange in the United States. . . . In the first three days of operation Purchase exchanged 180 needles, and since then he has exchanged approximately 25 per hour. The exchange is in operation Tuesday–Thursday from 2–4 p.m.

Leading up to that day in August, Purchase laid the groundwork for the exchange by meeting with local politicians and police and informing them—without asking permission—that a syringe exchange was going to begin operating (Sherman & Purchase, 2001). Considerable help in arranging meetings came from a childhood friend, County Councilman Dennis Flannigan. Purchase had been the director of a drug treatment program and had a long history of working with drug injectors in Tacoma. He was dismayed by the drug treatment community's response to HIV/AIDS—to argue more strongly on behalf of abstinence—and the Amsterdam needle exchange program seemed a reasonable and compassionate approach to help drug users avoid HIV infection. At the time the plan for needle exchange was forming in his mind, Purchase was recovering from a serious injury and was not affiliated with any agency or institution. As a result, he didn't feel concerned about the agency liability consequences of what he intended to do, and he could live with the risk of arrest. Purchase paid a visit to the mayor of Tacoma, the director of the health department, the chief of police, and the county executive, all of whom supported the idea of needle exchange. These visits were intended to allow them time to prepare for any public reaction or media attention to the program.

Financial support for the exchange came from donations and from Purchase's personal resources. Although this gave him a degree of freedom, it limited the scope and size of the exchange operation and left him with insufficient numbers of syringes and condoms to meet demand. So far, the plan had worked to get the program up and running and to build some momentum for a stage of expansion, but a new strategy was needed to build the exchange

---

[1]Needle exchange work was carried out by the National AIDS Brigade in Boston as early as 1986, but it never became a "needle exchange program" in the sense of having regular hours and location and continuing to operate. Thus, the Tacoma program is the longest running exchange program in the United States.

program into an operation that would really serve the county's IDUs. A case study of the Tacoma needle exchange by Sherman and Purchase (2001) provides a more detailed history of the program.

LINKING UP WITH THE HEALTH DEPARTMENT

Purchase found several allies in the health department, in particular, Terry Reid, who was the manager of the county's only methadone maintenance program. Reid not only shared Purchase's knowledge of the local IDU population but also was a health department insider and could represent the needle exchange to health department management. Reid had also thought through the "bridge to treatment" possibilities presented by the exchange and developed a system for exchange workers to make referrals to methadone treatment. This aspect of the exchange—that it could reach injectors who would not otherwise enter treatment—was to become a key element in creating community acceptance of the program. Support within the health department was also important because the health department was the county's fiscal agency for state HIV prevention funding. With a ban against use of federal money to support needle exchange operations and research, local funding was crucial to the survival of the program (Rovner, 1998; Vlahov & Junge, 1998). In addition, the health department could provide in-kind support such as outreach staff, access to drug treatment, and research expertise.

Shortly after the exchange opened, in September 1988, Holly Hagan was hired by the health department as an AIDS epidemiologist; her first assignment was to conduct a survey to assess the impact of the needle exchange. Reid introduced Hagan to Purchase, who immediately agreed to allow clients of the exchange to be surveyed. A "handshake agreement" between Hagan and Purchase guaranteed that collaboration was established. In Purchase's words, "We're partners"; no further contractual arrangements were needed. This phrase ("we're partners") was to be repeated over the next 6 years, as the debate and local data suggested new directions for research on the program.

The first survey of the Tacoma needle exchange was carried out in September 1988 and included 30 needle exchange users interviewed over 3 days. The survey was designed to last no more than 5–10 minutes and asked clients about their drug use behavior before and after beginning to use the exchange. The methodology was crude—"quick and dirty" was an apt description—but met the objective of obtaining some very preliminary descriptive data to present to local policymakers who would soon decide the fate of the program. Eighty-seven percent of participants in this first survey reported that they were not sharing syringes or always used bleach or boiling to sterilize the syringe in the previous 30 days, while using the exchange. More than half of survey participants were women (57%), and all but 1 participant reported the same or less frequent numbers of injections since beginning to use the exchange. This was a convenience sample of users, and the proportion of women was probably due to selection bias by the interviewer, but it provided a description of who was using the exchange and the prevalence of injection risk behavior in that group.

In late October 1988, Reid and Hagan traveled to the National AIDS Update in San Francisco to learn more about the epidemiology and prevention of HIV. They attended a panel discussion moderated by Don Des Jarlais of the New York State Division of Substance Abuse Services. Des Jarlais spoke about the need for needle exchange programs to prevent HIV transmission in this population, and Reid and Hagan were familiar with articles he had written on this topic (Des Jarlais & Hopkins, 1985; Des Jarlais & Woods, 1988). After the panel discussion, Reid and Hagan introduced themselves, asking Des Jarlais, "We have a needle exchange in Tacoma; would you like to do a study with us?" Just as with Purchase, Des Jarlais needed no further urging and immediately agreed to participate in the research. He traveled to Tacoma the following week to discuss the research plan. It was Des Jarlais who paid out of pocket for research incentives and who donated time and personal resources to visit the exchange program and participate in the development of the research plan. He also arranged for Purchase to travel to Montreal, Quebec, Canada, for the International AIDS Conference in 1989, to discuss the program with other activists and scientists who were interested in needle exchanges.

EARLY RESEARCH

The new survey used a systematic sampling of exchange users (every third individual exchanging syringes) and included 66 participants enrolled September to October 1988. The survey instrument asked about risk behavior during the 30 days before the respondent first used the exchange and about the most recent 30 days while he or she had been using the program (Hagan et al., 1988). Systematic sampling yielded a slightly higher proportion of men (57%) than in the previous survey (43%). Participants reported a statistically significant reduction in injection risk behavior after beginning to use the exchange. Although a comparison group was still lacking, these data were urgently needed for a presentation to the county board of health in January 1989. Preparations for this meeting involved Purchase and health department managers and epidemiologists. The purpose of the meeting was to brief board members on what was known about needle exchange, to help them decide on local funding for the exchange program. With this in mind, the goal of the research was to present a profile of exchange users, report on risk behavior, and demonstrate to policymakers that the health department was involved and monitoring the program. These data would also represent a set of preliminary studies for an application to the American Foundation for AIDS Research to continue the study.

The Board of Health meeting on January 4, 1989, was unusual in many respects. There were several news teams filming the meeting, and the room was packed. Exchange survey data were presented, along with reports on its linkage to drug treatment and a statement from the chief of police citing the exchange program's benefits in terms of public safety in reducing accidental needlesticks. Three options were presented to the board: (a) no funding, (b) funding to maintain the current level of service, and (c) a level of support (approximately $40,000/year) that would permit expansion of hours and services. The board voted 4–1 in favor of the third option. Although board members later said the data were not very compelling, they were reassured that the proposal included ongoing study of the exchange by health department staff.

Now that the future of the program was somewhat secure, the research plan could also take a long view and prepare for a larger scale effort to address broader questions. Funding was needed to support the cost of participant incentives, interviewer time, and blood testing. All other costs were supported by the health department and by the donation of Des Jarlais's time to the project. A proposal was written to the American Foundation for AIDS Research, with the specific aims of monitoring behavior change and HIV seroprevalence in exchange users. This proposal was written in collaboration with the director of the exchange program, and all research activities were reviewed by him to make sure that they were acceptable and did not interfere with the operations of the program. To wit, needle exchange staff were not to be distracted from their work or used to complete research activities, and there was to be a clear separation between research staff, who could pay IDUs to participate in a survey, and exchange staff, who did not handle money on the street. This was to protect exchange staff from being harassed for money and protect their safety while interacting with participants carrying used syringes. Otherwise, the director of the program welcomed any new ideas on how to learn more about the program. He was particularly interested to know more about the small proportion of exchange users who still shared syringes and about HIV seroprevalence in program participants.

In October 1989, the city of Tacoma withheld its share of funding for the exchange (the county and the city had each agreed to pay half the cost) on the basis of an opinion issued by the Washington state attorney general that the program violated state drug paraphernalia laws. By this time, the survey data showed declining injection risk behavior among exchange participants, there was no indication that the exchange was recruiting new injectors or causing participants to inject more often (Hagan, Des Jarlais, Purchase, Reid, & Friedman, 1991; Hagan et al., 1988), and nothing had happened to indicate that the exchange was causing a public safety or public opinion problem. In fact, a poll carried out by the local newspaper indicated that two thirds of adults supported the continuation of the program. Support for the program was strong within the health department and among the majority of local policymakers, so it was decided that the health department would sue the city to recover the withheld funds, using research to show the public health benefits of the program and existing laws to show that the program was a legal public health activity.

Legal arguments in favor of needle exchange included that public officials (such as the police or the health officer) were exempt from drug paraphernalia laws and that Purchase was acting as a deputy of the health officer. The health officer also has broad powers in a public health emergency, including the power to institute a quarantine, and HIV was such an emergency. Moreover, it could be argued that it had been the intent of the Washington state legislature to include provision of needle exchange in the state AIDS omnibus bill, under the category of needle sterilization programs. The legal brief submitted to the court included affidavits from the health officer, citing data from the Tacoma needle exchange survey, and from the police chief, stating that needle exchange could reduce police officers' risk of accidental needlestick with HIV-contaminated syringes. There were also affidavits from IDUs, describing how the exchange helped them to protect themselves from HIV infection, and from other, less fortunate users who had acquired HIV before the exchange began and were exchanging syringes to prevent transmitting the infection to other IDUs. The owner of a maintenance company that picked up trash in the vicinity of the exchange called the health department and volunteered to submit an affidavit stating that, since the exchange had opened, the number of discarded syringes picked up by his crew had dropped from two per day to two per week. After reviewing briefs submitted by both sides, in February 1990, a Pierce County Superior Court judge declared that the program was legal (*Allen v. City of Tacoma*, 1990). In his order granting the plaintiff's motion for summary judgment, he noted that the Tacoma study data were consistent with research from European programs in showing that the exchange was associated with reduced risk behavior and did not appear to increase drug use.

By this time, a partnership between the needle exchange and the health department had formed to promote acceptance of needle exchange in the community by crafting a consistent message for the media and the public. The formula for this message was to describe the apparent benefits of the program (access to a difficult-to-reach population, more frequent contact with public health workers who could help them get into drug treatment) and the lack of indications of negative effects (users tended to be older, long-term drug users, with very few young or new injectors). As part of this partnership, research data were shared between the health department and the needle exchange. Authorship on publications summarizing research findings and exchange operations included the director of the exchange program, health department collaborators, and research staff (Des Jarlais, Hagan, Purchase,

Reid, & Friedman, 1989; Hagan et al., 1993; Hagan, Des Jarlais, Purchase, Friedman, et al, 1991; Hagan, Des Jarlais, Purchase, Reid, & Friedman, 1989; Hagan, Des Jarlais, Purchase, Reid, & Friedman, 1991; Hagan et al., 1988; Purchase, Hagan, Des Jarlais, & Reid, 1989). Presentations describing the program, and data describing users, could be delivered by the needle exchange director, health department managers, or the researchers; these included presentations to boards of health in other local areas, testifying to U.S. congressional committees, and presenting data at public health and scientific conferences (Des Jarlais et al., 1989; Hagan, Des Jarlais, Purchase, Friedman et al., 1991; Hagan et al., 1989; Purchase et al., 1989). Copies of presentations (those that did not reveal research hypotheses or suggest desired responses to survey questions) were also handed out at the needle exchange to participants. Exchange users saw these presentations as representing their own accomplishment ("We did it").

This sentiment—ownership of the exchange, a feeling of protectiveness toward the program, participation in the research as being part of "the cause"—in many ways enhanced the conduct of the research. Participants usually agreed to participate (80%–90%); in most cases refusal was temporary as they would return as soon as withdrawal symptoms were relieved. The vast majority of exchange users were also extremely cooperative, careful to follow the rules of research just as they observed the very few rules governing the exchange program. The most important rule of the exchange was to keep drug dealing away from the program, as it attracted police attention and police presence, causing users to scatter and stay away from the program for several hours. (Periodically, in the second and third years of the exchange operation, police observed the exchange with binoculars from half a block away. Users were aware of this, and those with outstanding warrants would send someone to the exchange on their behalf.) The research prohibited participants from enrolling more than once; participants could do follow-up interviews every 3 months but were not allowed to pretend they had not been interviewed before as a way to earn honoraria ($10) more often. This happened very few times (fewer than 10), and it was embarrassing for those who were caught (the presence of the research staff at the exchange meant that they were likely to run into the person they had deceived). Interviewers also felt that the exchange was a very safe setting and that interviewing injectors at other locations was less desirable. Thus, cooperation from exchange participants was, for the most part, highly advantageous to the conduct of the research. However, one drawback was that participants' eagerness to be helpful to the exchange program might cause the accuracy of self-reported risk behavior to suffer somewhat. As long as the research relied primarily on risk behavior interviews, this bias could potentially be present.

The partnership between the needle exchange and the health department included the appointment of Des Jarlais as a commissioner on the U.S. National Commission on AIDS, and this increased national attention paid to the program. Tacoma research data were highlighted in the commission's 1991 Report on "The Twin Epidemics of Substance Use and HIV" (National Commission on AIDS, 1991). This report led U.S. Rep. Charles Rangle (D-NY) to ask the U.S. General Accounting Office (GAO) to critically examine the basis for the commission's recommendation in favor of needle exchange. GAO staff traveled to two needle exchange programs—in Tacoma and in New Haven, Connecticut—to observe needle exchange operations. They also reviewed 20 published studies and 21 abstracts evaluating exchange programs and in 1993 issued a report concluding that needle exchange programs held promise as an AIDS prevention strategy (GAO, 1993). The quality of the Tacoma data was rated as "acceptable" by the GAO, along with data from European and Australian programs. However, the report also showed that virtually all the existing data supporting needle exchange were based on self-report and may be subject to social desirability bias. Clearly the research needed to change direction if it were to continue to make new contributions and be perceived as reliable.

Other data supported the validity of the Tacoma evaluation data. Research from New York showed a strong association between self-reported risk behavior and HIV incidence in IDUs (Marmor, Des Jarlais, Friedman, Lyden, & el-Sadr, 1984). In addition, direct observation of exchange programs in Tacoma, Amsterdam, and elsewhere clearly indicated that IDUs were motivated to obtain sterile injection equipment by coming to the exchange in substantial numbers, and studies in New York had also shown that IDUs were seeking sterile syringes on the illicit market (Des Jarlais, Friedman, & Hopkins, 1985). Thus, with the knowledge that IDUs would change their behavior to reduce risk of HIV, the research objective was more precisely defined as quantifying the degree of behavior change associated with participation in the Tacoma needle exchange and assessing the relationship between behavior change and HIV transmission in exchange users and in the community. This led to the use of biological outcomes in several other studies, including a follow-up prospective study of exchange users that showed very low incidence of HIV (0/665 person-years of observation; Hagan, Des Jarlais, Friedman, Purchase, & Reid, 1992) and a community case study that examined five cities in North America and Europe (including Tacoma) where low HIV incidence and prevalence had been maintained for a period of at least 5 years (Des Jarlais, Hagan, et al., 1995).

Tacoma–Pierce County has been one of the Centers for Disease Control (CDC) sentinel hepatitis surveillance counties since the 1970s (Alter, Hadler, & Judson, 1990). As such, case ascertainment and collection of risk behavior data are of higher quality than in most other counties in the United States. The Tacoma–Pierce County health department was the official site for the local sentinel counties study, and all activities were carried out by the health department communicable disease control section. A research plan was developed to carry out a case control study of hepatitis B and C in relation to needle exchange using the sentinel counties surveillance system to obtain cases. Questions on exchange use were added to the case interview instrument. Because the needle exchange research and the sentinel counties study were both conducted within the health department, negotiations with the CDC to use the sentinel counties' data in this manner were smoothed. Control participants included IDUs in other health department clinics, including HIV counseling and testing, methadone treatment, and the sexually transmitted disease clinic. This study was also supported by the American Foundation for AIDS Research and was one of the first to show an association between needle exchange and lower risk of a blood-borne viral infection (Hagan, Des Jarlais, Friedman, Purchase, & Alter, 1995). It was also the first time the research activities were not centered at the exchange program.

THE RESEARCH LOOP

Throughout 1988 to 1993, research questions were generated by activities at the exchange. Syringes collected during the first few weeks of the program had been stored "in case there was a reason to test them later." These stored syringes regularly came up in discussions of research, and the publication of articles describing a methodology for retrieving residual blood from syringes (Chitwood et al., 1990; Wolk et al., 1988) led to testing of more recent samples. One hundred percent of syringes exchanged in a 1-week period were collected, and 4% were anti-HIV positive (Hagan, Des Jarlais, Purchase, Friedman et al., 1991). This was consistent with estimates of HIV seroprevalence based on testing exchange participants (Hagan et al., 1993). Discussions of study results between researchers and exchange staff were frequent and informal, particularly when interviews were conducted at the needle exchange, and on many occasions interpretations generated by these discussions ended up in publications.

Communication between the exchange practitioners and researchers also tended to reinforce current practice. Needle exchange was a relatively new public health activity, and there was no instruction book to consult. Operating procedures were based on trial and error, consultation between exchange programs, good judgment, and reinforcement or reprioritization suggested by study findings. The data indicated that the program was attracting the intended segment of the IDU population (frequent injectors, those with a recent history of frequent syringe sharing, injectors of color; Hagan, Des Jarlais, Purchase, Reid, & Friedman, 1991; Hagan et al., 1993), that it was helping people get into treatment (43% of all referrals to methadone originated at the exchange, making it the largest single source of methadone referral in the county; Hagan et al., 1993), and that participants' risk behavior declined after beginning to use the exchange. Moreover, the incidence of drug-related hepatitis B in the community had declined after the exchange opened (Hagan, Des Jarlais, Purchase, Reid, Friedman, & Bell, 1991), participation in the exchange was associated with reduced risk of hepatitis B and C (Hagan et al., 1995), and there had been no HIV seroconversions observed in exchange users (Hagan et al., 1992). This multiple-arm research strategy could reasonably be defended as showing consistency across different methodologies. Scientific evidence to support continuation of the program was stronger than before. Together, these studies reinforced exchange operations and supported new measures (expansion to new sites and the inception of a mobile exchange–delivery service).

Research findings also suggested new directions for the exchange—"So, you're seeing more HIV infection in this group of IDUs, or risk behavior in those IDUs, thus we need to pay more attention to them." Evidence of gaps in the program—that is, residual risk behavior and population segments underrepresented in the exchange clientele—were the impetus behind the mobile exchange delivery. These data were also presented to the health department management, and the Community HIV Prevention Prioritization Committee, to support increased funding of exchange operations. Because most of the HIV prevention programming for IDUs in the region was centered at the exchange (the only exceptions being methadone treatment and a limited program offering HIV testing to IDUs), it was logical that the majority of HIV prevention funding earmarked for IDUs would be channeled to the exchange. The program grew, and its services, sites, and hours of operation were expanded. Screening for HIV, tuberculosis, and hepatitis; vaccination against hepatitis B; outreach education; drug treatment recruitment; and even voter registration were available at the needle exchange site. Public health practitioners recognized the importance of the program and the opportunity it presented to achieve multiple public health objectives for an important and underserved population. The strategy of collaboration among the three sets of interested parties (exchange practitioners, public health program managers, and researchers) made for a highly successful model needle exchange program.

CONCLUSION

Many needle exchange programs in the United States and abroad have been championed by public health researchers who are pleased to study a new public health intervention to address the needs of a neglected population. The history of the Tacoma needle exchange program's collaboration with research is unique only in its breadth and duration. This collaboration stressed ongoing, frequent discussions of research findings and modifications to program operations and long-term planning to build a scientifically strong foundation of research. An emphasis on studying the safety and efficacy of the program led to the examination of a large number of potential outcomes among drug users and in the community, and this in turn helped build a scientifically strong foundation of public health research.

REFERENCES

Allen v. City of Tacoma, No. 89-2-09067-3 (Wash. Super. Ct., Pierce County, May 9, 1990).

Alter, M. J., Hadler, S. C., & Judson, F. N. (1990). Risk factors for acute non-A, non-B hepatitis in the United States and association with hepatitis C virus infection. *Journal of the American Medical Association, 263*, 1218–1222.

Bischof, D., Des Jarlais, D. C., Lamb, S., Oliver, K., Serrano, Y., & Woods, J. (1988). Needle exchanges. *International Working Group on AIDS and IV Drug Use, 3*(2), 1, 12.

Brettle, R. P. (1991). HIV and harm reduction for injection drug users. *AIDS, 5*, 125–136.

Buning, E. C., Coutinho, R. A., van Brussel, G. H., van Santen, G. W., & van Zadelhoff, A. W. (1986). Preventing AIDS in drug addicts in Amsterdam. *The Lancet, 1*, 1435.

Chitwood, D. D., McCoy, C. B., Inciardi, J. A., McBride, D. C., Comerford, M., Trapido, E., et al. (1990). HIV seropositivity of needles from shooting galleries in south Florida. *American Journal of Public Health, 80*, 150–152.

Des Jarlais, D. C., Friedman, S. R., & Hopkins, W. (1985). Risk reduction for the acquired immunodeficiency syndrome among intravenous drug users. *Annals of Internal Medicine, 103*, 755–759.

Des Jarlais, D. C., Friedman, S. R., & Ward, T. P. (1993). Harm reduction: A public health response to the AIDS epidemic among injecting drug users. *Annual Review of Public Health, 14*, 413–450.

Des Jarlais, D. C., Hagan, H., Friedman, S. R., Friedmann, P., Goldberg, D., Frischer, M., et al. (1995). Maintaining low HIV seroprevalence in populations of injecting drug users. *Journal of the American Medical Association, 274*, 1226–1231.

Des Jarlais, D. C., Hagan, H., Purchase, D., Reid, T. R., & Friedman, S. R. (1989, July). *Safer injection among participants in the first North American syringe exchange program*. Paper presented at the Fifth International Conference on AIDS, Montreal, Quebec, Canada.

Des Jarlais, D. C., & Hopkins, W. (1985). "Free" needles for intravenous drug users at risk for AIDS: Current developments in New York City. *New England Journal of Medicine, 313*, 1476.

Des Jarlais, D. C., Paone, D., Friedman, S. R., Peyser, N., & Newman, R. G. (1995). Regulating controversial programs for unpopular people: Methadone maintenance and syringe exchange programs. *American Journal of Public Health, 85*, 1577–1584.

Des Jarlais, D. C., & Woods, J. S. (1988, May). Needle exchanges. *International Working Group on AIDS and IV Drug Use, 3*(1), 1, 5.

Ginzburg, H. M. (1988). Acquired immune deficiency syndrome (AIDS) and drug abuse. In R. P. Galea, B. F. Lewis, & L. A. Baker (Eds.), *AIDS and IV drug abusers* (pp. 61–74). Owings Mills, MD: National Health.

Guydish, J., Clark, G., Garcia, D., Downing, M., Case, P., & Sorensen, J. L. (1991). Evaluating needle exchange: Do distributed needles come back? *American Journal of Public Health, 81*, 617–619.

Hagan, H., Des Jarlais, D. C., Friedman, S. R., Purchase, D., & Alter, M. J. (1995). Reduced risk of hepatitis B and hepatitis C among injecting drug users participating in the Tacoma syringe exchange program. *American Journal of Public Health, 85*, 1531–1537.

Hagan, H., Des Jarlais, D. C., Friedman, S. R., Purchase, D., & Reid, T. R. (1992, June). *Multiple outcome measures of the impact of the Tacoma syringe exchange.* Paper presented at the Eighth International Conference on AIDS, Amsterdam.

Hagan, H., Des Jarlais, D. C., Purchase, D., Friedman, S. R., Damrow, T., Ip, R., et al. (1991, November). *Syringe HIV seroprevalence in relation to seroprevalence among syringe exchange users, and accidental HIV transmission.* Paper presented at the 119th annual meeting of the American Public Health Association, Atlanta, GA.

Hagan, H., Des Jarlais, D. C., Purchase, D., Friedman, S. R., Reid, T. R., & Bell, T. A. (1993). An interview study of participants in the Tacoma syringe exchange. *Addiction, 88*, 1691–1697.

Hagan, H., Des Jarlais, D. C., Purchase, D., Reid, T. R., & Friedman, S. R. (1989, July). *Drug use trends in participants in the Tacoma syringe exchange.* Paper presented at the fifth International Conference on AIDS, Montreal, Quebec, Canada.

Hagan, H., Des Jarlais, D. C., Purchase, D., Reid, T. R., & Friedman, S. R. (1991). The Tacoma syringe exchange. In S. R. Friedman & D. S. Lipton (Eds.), *Cocaine, AIDS, and intravenous drug use* (pp. 81–88). Binghamton, NY: Haworth Press.

Hagan, H., Des Jarlais, D. C., Purchase, D., Reid, T., Friedman, S. R., & Bell, T. A. (1991). The incidence of HBV infection and syringe exchange programs. *Journal of the American Medical Association, 266*, 1646–1647.

Hagan, H., Reid, T., Purchase, D., Jensen, H., Woods, J., Friedman, S. R., et al. (1988). Needle exchange in Tacoma, Washington—Initial results. *Newsletter of the International Working Group on AIDS and IV Drug Use, 3*(3–4), 4–5.

Kochems, L. M., Paone, D., Des Jarlais, D. C., Ness, I., Clark, J., & Friedman, S. R. (1996). The transition from underground to legal syringe exchange: The New York City experience. *AIDS Education and Prevention, 8*, 471–489.

Loxley, W. (2000). Doing the possible: Harm reduction, injecting drug use and blood borne viral infections in Australia. *International Journal of Drug Policy, 1*, 407–416.

Marlatt, G. A. (1996). Harm reduction: Come as you are. *Addictive Behavior, 21*, 779–788.

Marmor, M., Des Jarlais, D. C., Friedman, S. R., Lyden, M., & el-Sadr, W. (1984). The epidemic of acquired immunodeficiency syndrome (AIDS) and suggestions for its control in drug abusers. *Journal of Substance Abuse Treatment, 1,* 237–247.

National Commission on AIDS. (1991). *The twin epidemics of substance abuse and HIV.* Washington, DC: U.S. Government Printing Office.

Ochoa, K., Edney-Meschery, H., & Moss, A. (1999). Understanding heroin overdose. *Harm Reduction Communication, 9,* 10–12.

Purchase, D., Hagan, H., Des Jarlais, D. C., & Reid, T. (1989, July). *Historical account of the Tacoma syringe exchange.* Paper presented at the fifth International Conference on AIDS, Montreal, Quebec, Canada.

Rovner, J. (1998). USA continues federal ban on needle-exchange funding. *The Lancet, 351,* 1333.

Sherman, S. G., & Purchase, D. (2001). Point Defiance: A case study of the United States' first public needle exchange in Tacoma, Washington. *International Journal of Drug Policy, 12,* 45–57.

Sorge, R. (1990). A thousand points . . . Needle exchange around the country. *Health PAC Bulletin, 20,* 16–22.

U.S. General Accounting Office. (1993). *Needle exchange programs—Research suggests promise as an AIDS prevention strategy* (Report to the Chairman, Select Committee on Narcotics Abuse and Control, House of Representatives). Washington, DC: U.S. Government Printing Office.

Vlahov, D., & Junge, B. (1998). The role of needle exchange programs in HIV prevention. *Public Health Reports, 113*(Suppl. 1), 75–80.

Weiker, R. L., Edgington, R., & Kipke, M. D. (1999). A collaborative evaluation of a needle exchange program for youth. *Health Education and Behavior, 26,* 213–224.

Wolk, J., Wodak, A., Morlet, A., Guinan, J. J., Wilson, E., Gold, J., et al. (1988). Syringe HIV seroprevalence and behavioural and demographic characteristics of intravenous drug users in Sydney, Australia, 1987. *AIDS, 2,* 373–377.

6

DRUG COURTS

ELIZABETH PIPER DESCHENES, ROGER H. PETERS,
JOHN S. GOLDKAMP, AND STEVEN BELENKO

Substance-involved offenders have been identified by many federal agencies as a high-priority target population in developing new areas of program services and research. One reason for this is that despite the high prevalence rates of substance use disorders in criminal justice settings (Belenko, 1990; Peters, Greenbaum, Edens, Carter, & Ortiz, 1998; Robins & Regier, 1991), only 10%–13% of offenders receive any form of drug treatment (Belenko, 1998a; Simpson, Knight, & Pevoto, 1996). Another reason is the steady increase in the number of individuals placed in jails or prisons and under criminal justice supervision in the community (Beck et al., 2000; Mumola & Beck, 1997) who are extremely likely to reoffend and return to jail and prison without treatment (Wexler, Lipton, & Johnson, 1988).

We thank several individuals who contributed to the information contained in this chapter, including Marilyn Roberts and Jill Christine Beres from the Drug Court Program Office, Stacey Rodgers from the National Association of Drug Court Professionals, Michael Wilkosz from the National Drug Court Institute, Peter Delany from the National Institute on Drug Abuse, and Janice Munsterman from the National Institute of Justice. We also acknowledge the contributions of many colleagues who shared accounts of their research experiences.

In the past 20 years, there has been renewed interest in developing treatment alternatives to incarceration and in expanding the availability of treatment in criminal justice settings (Inciardi, McBride, & Rivers, 1996), and these efforts have been supported by federal block grant programs. In addition, many states have recognized the need to develop a coordinated strategy for rehabilitating drug-involved offenders. Current research and innovations in clinical practice have supported the development of offender substance abuse treatment programs in criminal justice settings (Gendreau, 1996; Peters & Hills, 1997; Peters & Steinberg, 2000; Wanberg & Milkman, 1998; Wexler, Falkin, Lipton, & Rosenblum, 1992).

Despite the recent availability of research and clinical information regarding treatment of substance-involved offenders, the practice and policy communities have not readily embraced this new knowledge. Neither have many community treatment or criminal justice agency coordinators used this knowledge to modify existing justice settings to stay abreast of contemporary research or to adopt new technologies (Gendreau, 1995), and there are fewer resources and opportunities for staff development and training compared with those available in community treatment settings.

The gap between knowledge and practice related to effective offender treatment strategies has not been well bridged by researchers, who are often daunted by the challenges of access to offender populations and by difficulties in locating offenders after their release from secure settings and who are often unfamiliar with the diverse set of criminal justice system agencies (Lamb, Greenlick, & McCarty, 1998). As a result of these different factors, practitioners, researchers, and administrators working in the criminal justice system or the treatment of substance abusing offenders are often isolated from their peers and are not well positioned to implement evidence-based and innovative practices. The consequences of inadequately coordinated knowledge development and application in this area include poor retention rates for offenders in many community treatment programs, poor morale and high turnover among counselors and other practitioners who work with this population, high rates of relapse and criminal recidivism (Gerstein & Harwood, 1990), and cynicism regarding the effectiveness of offender treatment services.

The emergence of drug courts that integrate treatment into the criminal justice system offers significant promise for developing better coordinated knowledge and exchange among practice, research, and policy communities to enhance substance abuse treatment and reform criminal justice. In this chapter we examine the development of drug courts; the role of federal, state, and local governments in expanding the programs and providing research funding; and the models of initial and continuing research, focusing on the issue of collaboration between researchers and practitioners in evaluating drug courts. We also provide recommendations regarding future areas for research.

The focus of drug courts is to reduce drug-related crime by placing drug offenders in treatment (Drug Strategies, 1999). Compared with traditional practices in criminal courts, drug courts represent a dramatic innovation in substance and method. They are motivated by the rehabilitative ideal that treatment of addicts will improve the chances that they will engage in law-abiding behavior and will reduce crime. Their method is based on non-adversarial proceedings in the courtroom and an emphasis on treatment in a structured approach that fosters accountability, using a collection of incentives and sanctions to encourage successful progress (Hora, Schma, & Rosenthal, 1999). There is ongoing court supervision and leveraged involvement in treatment that is coordinated by a multidisciplinary team focused on the twin goals of public safety and rehabilitation from substance use disorders.

Although most, if not all, drug courts are voluntary, in the sense that the criminal defendant or convicted offender is not required to participate, once the candidate decides to participate, the stakes are high—both in terms of possible positive outcomes (such as dismissal of charges and restored health) and in terms of negative outcomes (the high probability of conviction and sentences to confinement). The strict rules and strong enforcement by the drug court judge appeal to treatment providers, who normally do not have such "coercive" influences to bring to bear on addicts who are in treatment to support their retention. Most substance abuse treatment interventions are premised on the belief that treatment can be successful if the participant can somehow stay in treatment and that the longer he or she is in treatment, the greater his or her chance of achieving a successful outcome, that is, of a lower probability of relapse. If the drug courts increase retention of criminally involved substance abusers in treatment, and if treatment is effective, then successful outcomes are more likely with this difficult-to-treat criminal justice population.

EMERGENCE AND DEVELOPMENT OF TREATMENT DRUG COURTS

Drug courts emerged in response to system overcrowding and the perceived ineffectiveness of a "revolving door" criminal justice system (Terry, 1999) as well as frustration with the lack of coordinated treatment access and delays in getting offenders into treatment (H. Haas, 1993; Goldkamp, White, & Robinson, 2001b). At the time drug courts were developed, there were few alternatives and a lack of better ideas as to how to deal with drug offenders. In an attempt to treat the underlying problems of addiction, these courts incorporated treatment principles into the criminal justice system, which some have labeled a form of therapeutic jurisprudence (Hora et al., 1999).

Drug courts are a form of coercive treatment that research evidence suggests is more effective for addicts than voluntary treatment (Satel, 2001).

Early Pioneers

The emergence of drug courts, which can be traced to the drug court in Miami, Florida, in 1989, is a grassroots movement that began in local jurisdictions and spread across the United States (Goldkamp, 1999b). In putting together the key elements of the Miami drug court, Dade County judicial leaders, the state attorney, and the public defender "unwittingly paved the way for the national drug court movement" (Goldkamp, 1999b, p. 23). The movement grew through an informal network of committed judicial leaders and officials who shared lessons and borrowed and adapted procedures designed in drug court sites. Passage of the Omnibus Crime Control Act by Congress in 1994, which created the Drug Court Program Office (DCPO) and made available federal funding to support the establishment of drug courts, helped transform the vibrant but small movement from 30 to 50 jurisdictions into a national phenomenon.

The spread of the knowledge of the success and popularity of the early drug courts among the judicial community was a major factor in their rapid growth. Local judges who participated in national and state judicial conferences and observed the drug courts in Miami, Florida; Oakland, California; Portland, Oregon; and Las Vegas, Nevada, were important leaders in the movement in that they brought the concept of the drug court back to their jurisdictions. The collective experience of judicial professionals—and, in some cases, chief probation officers or defense attorneys—led the path toward innovation. In many jurisdictions, however, the lack of support of key political figures became a major barrier to program implementation.

Expansion of Drug Courts

The federal government has played a significant role in the growth and development of drug courts. As of January 2002 there were almost 1,000 drug courts nationwide and another 453 courts in the planning process (*OJP Drug Court Clearinghouse*, 2002). In the state of California alone there are 122 drug courts. During the first 10 years of drug courts' existence the model was adapted in a variety of different settings, in rural locations as well as urban ones, including American Indian and Alaskan Native villages. In addition to diversification of the original model to include diversion and plea- and sentence-based courts, drug courts sparked a great deal of related innovation in other types of courts. One could argue that drug courts were responsible for the development of a range of "problem-solving" courts, including juvenile drug courts, community courts, domestic violence courts, family drug courts, mental health courts, and others (Goldkamp, 2000).

Since 1995, DCPO has provided funding for program planning, implementation, and expansion of existing drug courts, starting with $11.9 million in 1995 and increasing to nearly $50 million for fiscal year 2001. Almost $175 million has been awarded to approximately 700 communities, and as a result more than 450 have implemented a drug court (DCPO, 2001; U.S. General Accounting Office [GAO], 2002). The Drug Court Training and Technical Assistance Project, which began in 1995, has evolved over the years in response to the changes and trends observed in the field. In the past 2 years there have been more than 50 training workshops and 3,500 incidences of technical assistance, with more than 120 monitoring visits to drug courts.

The National Association of Drug Court Professionals (NADCP), which was formed in 1994 by members of the 12 original drug courts, now has more than 2,000 members worldwide. The mission of this organization has been to promote the establishment and funding of drug courts (Drug Strategies, 1999). In addition, NADCP helps provide technical assistance for the collection of information and support of association members.

Standards for Drug Courts

As drug courts proliferated in the early 1990s, NADCP recognized the need to develop benchmarks to assist the drug court field in defining core elements of treatment-based drug courts. A consensus-building process was established, beginning with the development of critical elements and followed by the appointment of a Drug Courts Standards Committee. After several planning sessions and a field review, the result was "Defining Drug Courts: The Key Components" (U.S. Department of Justice, 1997), a document that has been widely adopted by statewide drug court associations and individual drug courts in developing standards and guidelines for the development of comprehensive drug courts.

RESEARCH AND EVALUATION

Compared with the wealth of resources for drug court planning and implementation, support for evaluation research that examines the contributions of drug courts has been longer in coming. State and local governments have played a small role in funding research and disseminating results. Notwithstanding a recent statement that "Drug court practitioners increasingly recognize the value of outcome evaluations for improving their programs and securing continued funding" (Drug Strategies, 1999, p. 41), the partnership with researchers has generally been forced on drug court practitioners by the federal government's demands for program evaluation. Despite the fact that the body of research is now growing, there is still a gap between drug courts in practice and research about their impact. This gap is partly normal in the sense that drug courts are fairly new, and it takes time for both the innovation to set in and for research to capture its effects. Even given emerging research findings relating specifically to drug courts, it is fair to say that research has made little impact on practice at this stage.

Role of the Federal, State, and Local Governments

Several organizations are advocates and/or funders of research on drug courts. They include the National Institute of Justice, the Drug Court Clearinghouse and Technical Assistance Project, the National Drug Court Institute (NDCI), the National Institute on Drug Abuse (NIDA), and the Center for Substance Abuse Treatment (CSAT). NADCP provides support for evaluation by including monitoring and evaluation as one of the 10 key components of drug courts (U.S. Department of Justice, 1997). In 1995, DCPO mandated that drug courts receiving federal funds for implementation conduct a process evaluation and encouraged outcome evaluations. DCPO also supports the National Drug Court Evaluation Program, which is funded through the U.S. Department of Justice. A recent GAO (2002) report concluded that better data collection and evaluation efforts are needed to measure the impact of drug court programs to inform the public, Congress, and other stakeholders.

Federal funding to support drug court research has been limited and generally insufficient for comprehensive or rigorous evaluation designs. The Office of Justice Programs has the smallest federal budget compared with other agencies. In the past 10-year period, approximately $5 million was expended, with a total of 11 grants supporting process or impact evaluations of drug courts. Research awards by NIDA are often restricted to projects with strong scientific merit, and only 14 awards were made between 1994 and 2001. CSAT funded 2 multiyear drug court evaluations. Both included follow-up interview data on relapse and other measures. Excluding the 5 studies that involve multiple sites, only 17 individual drug courts are represented in the 27 projects funded by the National Institute of Justice, NIDA, or CSAT.

At the state level, most of the money goes into program development and implementation, not research. In several states where drug courts have been implemented in multiple jurisdictions, the legislature has required program evaluations. Since 1990, the State Justice Institute has supported a limited number of research studies on drug offenders and drug courts.

The majority of evaluations have been funded at the local level, either through the awards given to drug courts by DCPO or various agencies such as the administrative office of the courts, countywide criminal justice organizations, or treatment providers. These types of awards typically do not support the large-scale evaluation efforts necessary for an impact evaluation but can support smaller process evaluations. There are several problems with local-level funding beyond that of limited resources; these may include lack of objectivity or scientific merit, inexperienced researchers, and political influence. On the other hand, contracted research can provide very specific results and answers to questions when the research has been well designed and implemented and there are support and involvement on the part of key stakeholders.

Dissemination Strategies for Research Findings and "Best Practices"

Clearinghouses and Technical Assistance

With funding from DCPO, staff at American University's Justice Programs Office maintain a clearinghouse of drug court operational materials, evaluations, and funding information. The Justice Programs Office aids in the development of state-of-the-art materials on drug court activities and conducts annual surveys of drug courts. Information is disseminated through various publications and on the Internet. Jurisdictions in need of technical assistance can contact American University for referrals to a network of experienced practitioners and consultants.

Because of the multidisciplinary nature of drug courts, published research appears in a range of professional journals representing various disciplines (i.e., criminology/criminal justice, judicial/legal, substance use and treatment, and public health). Drug court professionals and administrators and policymakers may read journals only in their area of expertise and as a result may not be aware of the majority of the literature in this area. Thus, there is a greater need in the drug court field to develop research digests or summaries of the research literature and to disseminate information regarding available literature to a broad range of drug court professionals. NDCI has attempted to fulfill this role.

NDCI was established in 1998 with the primary goals of promoting research and disseminating research findings (Drug Strategies, 1999). As of September 2002, there were three published resource guides, six fact sheets, and six monographs, covering various topics such as implementing drug courts, issues of confidentiality, and judicial ethics. The *NDCI Review*, which is published twice a year and distributed free to a mailing list and all members of NADCP, typically includes three or four articles and a research update. These scholarly articles, which are summarized and written in lay terms for practitioners, represent only a limited amount of the research being conducted on drug courts.

Training Conferences, Workshops, and Mentor Courts

National training conferences designed to promote both education and research have been conducted for the past 9 years. The first, which was held in Miami, Florida, in December 1993, was attended by almost 500 people. At the time, there were only about 25 drug courts in operation, most of them based on diversion (Goldkamp, 1999b). In this first national conference there was only one session on research. In comparison, there were 3,000 attendees at the conference in June 2001, which included panel sessions covering the fundamentals of evaluation, data management systems, using evaluations to impact policymakers, selecting an evaluator, measuring drug court costs and benefits, and current drug court evaluation results. With the growth of family and juvenile drug courts there is now a separate conference for these courts, which in its second year drew an audience of 4,000.

For the past 4 years, DCPO has encouraged jurisdictions that are planning drug courts to send their planning teams and evaluators to a series of introductory, skills-based, and operational workshops. NDCI has also convened a series of regional evaluation workshops to provide technical assistance to teams of local drug court administrators and researchers. One of the by-products of these workshops is the promotion of greater interchange and collaboration between practitioners and researchers. In addition, the workshops have created an expanding network of academics and professional researchers for consultation and technical assistance.

Through a cooperative agreement with DCPO, NADCP developed a network of mentor courts to educate and train drug court practitioners who are planning or implementing drug courts in their own jurisdictions. Operational since 1996, the network expanded from the original 7 sites to 30 in 2002.

DRUG COURT RESEARCH APPROACHES

Research on drug courts has generally followed the expansion of drug courts, with few exceptions. The initial research studies on drug courts were conducted by researchers in the criminal justice field who had established ties with the local infrastructure and collaborated in the design of the evaluation (Goldkamp, 1999b) and, in one instance, resulted in establishing a pilot drug court because of the evaluation (Deschenes & Greenwood, 1994; Deschenes & Petersen, 1999). In other instances, drug court planners have contacted researchers for advice on data collection and evaluation (Cosden, Peerson, & Crothers, 1997; Finigan, 1998; Gottfredson, Coblentz, & Harmon, 1996; Harrell, Cavanagh, & Roman, 2000; Logan, Williams, Leukefeld, & Minton, 2000; Schiff & Terry, 1997; Shichor & Sechrest, 2001; Torres & Deschenes, 1997). When the federal government (DCPO) began requiring process evaluations as a condition for receipt of funding for drug court program implementation, less experienced criminal justice researchers and practitioners began to conduct these evaluations. More recent research collaborations with the courts have been initiated by researchers (Goldkamp, White, & Robinson, 2001a, 2001b, 2001c, 2001d).

Much of the initial research efforts focused on a limited number of issues. Given that the primary impetus was to reduce the burden of drug offenders on the criminal justice system, research tended to emphasize the program outcomes of recidivism and graduation status. In addition, the earliest studies described the structure of the new drug courts in terms of the target population and collaborative approach of program personnel. There was limited discussion of the impact of drug courts on relapse and the structure of the treatment program. This deficiency may be due in part to the fact that the pioneers of the drug court movement were judges and the majority of researchers outside of the court setting were trained in criminal justice research.

Advances in Drug Court Research

In the past few years there has been a gradual shift in the culture of drug courts and a greater willingness to participate in evaluation research. Judges and lawyers appear to be more amenable to listening to the opinions of researchers, particularly when researchers provide evidence that can be used to support their cause. For example, when there is a need to find continued funding for the drug courts many judges will focus on the research results that provide evidence of lower recidivism and lower criminal justice system costs. There is some evidence that treatment providers are increasing their collaboration with researchers, particularly for projects that receive funding from NIDA.

Drug courts are well suited for *action research*, which focuses on finding a solution to a local problem in a local setting. Methodologists and theorists have described action research (Kemmis & McTaggart, 1988; Lewin, 1951; Stringer, 1999; Whyte, 1991) as a dynamic and interactive process of change whereby social science research informs and shapes social action. In drug courts, action research involves creating a partnership among the team members, the key stakeholders, and the evaluator. In developing this collaboration it is imperative that both parties determine the goals of the evaluation, outlining reasonable expectations, needed resources, and the uses of the evaluation (Porter, 2000). Regular meetings between the researcher and the program coordinator are useful to check for clarity and accuracy of information and to discuss the data collection and early findings. In fostering a positive working relationship researchers should consider what is important to the courts to contextualize the research findings.

Recent research approaches have expanded to include more in-depth longitudinal evaluations and more sophisticated quantitative techniques as well as qualitative approaches, experimental designs with random assignment, and statewide evaluations. In-depth longitudinal evaluations of two of the oldest drug courts (those in Las Vegas and Portland) are based on a collaborative, team-oriented approach. The research has been guided by a drug court typology (Goldkamp, 1999a) and has looked at the relative impact of the two courts within the context of drug courts (Goldkamp et al., 2001d) during the 1990s. The research has attempted to assess the drug court model by examining the ingredients thought to be responsible for positive effects (Goldkamp et al., 2001c). The actions of a single drug court judge and the influence of shifting policies (e.g., a new prosecutor in Las Vegas) have played an important part in the impact of these courts over time (Goldkamp et al., 2001b, 2001d).

Other research uses more advanced quantitative techniques. Studies in Florida recently examined the effects of time in treatment, or treatment "dosage" in drug courts, and found that the duration of participants' drug court involvement is correlated with positive outcomes during follow-up (Peters, Haas, & Hunt, 2001). Other related investigations (Peters, Haas, & Murrin, 1999; Peters & Murrin, 2000) have identified key predictors of retention and arrest in drug courts (e.g., age, drug of choice, prior criminal involvement) and have begun to examine gender differences in the development of substance abuse problems among drug court participants (Haas & Peters, 2001).

Qualitative research methods, such as focus groups with program staff and surveys of participants, have led to changes in the drug courts (Deschenes et al., 1999) and informed research results (Goldkamp et al., 2001a). After a survey of participants indicated a need for additional educational or vocational training, the treatment program in one jurisdiction began to offer various specialty courses, including anger management, assertiveness training, self-esteem through journaling and creativity (art therapy), financial management, life trauma recovery, and relapse prevention (Deschenes, Emami, Klein, & Moreno, 2000). Discussion among participants in six different cities pointed to the variation in drug and crime problems by neighborhood, which suggests the need to strengthen neighborhood resources (Goldkamp, 2000). Research using focus groups of drug court participants has indicated that they are afraid of losing their jobs and that they fear walking into the courtroom and being reprimanded by the judge in front of their peers as well as facing jail or other sanctions (Goldkamp, 2000; Harrell & Smith, 1996).

A number of states have adopted a statewide strategy in evaluating drug courts. In California, Florida, New Mexico, New York, and Ohio (to name a few), the administrative offices of the courts have been active in promoting drug courts, encouraging research, and seeking increased funding from the legislature. Many states are developing or implementing computerized databases (management information systems [MISs]) to systematically gather data, which helps promote program evaluation. In New Mexico, the Institute for Social Research, which developed the drug court MIS and assisted with data entry, provides management information to the 15 drug courts (P. Guerin, personal communication, February 7, 2001). The nature of cooperation and collaboration between the researchers and the courts depends on the personality and culture of each individual court in New Mexico. Despite geographical distances between the research team and the courts, periodic communication with the courts has helped foster their "buy-in" for the statewide evaluation.

Challenges in Research and Evaluation

Researchers face myriad challenges in evaluating drug courts. Some of these are easily resolved, whereas others are more difficult. The first challenge is obtaining the cooperation of multiple stakeholders to gain access to data or permission to conduct surveys or interviews with participants. In addition, some practitioners may be concerned with issues of confidentiality. In some instances it is advantageous for various parties to sign an agreement, or *memorandum of understanding*, which lays out the requirements and stipulates that the researchers will follow federal and state regulations regarding human participants protection. Because drug courts involve several agencies, another challenge has been the introduction of a computerized MIS that tracks individuals and monitors program operations. The lack of computerized data often creates more difficulties for researchers. Finally, the quality of the data in terms of reliability and validity can be a major issue. Data may not have been entered consistently, causing a problem with missing data, or the information needed, such as jail time or arrests after program completion, may not be available for all participants. These problems often make it difficult to conduct impact evaluations.

MEASURING THE IMPACT OF RESEARCH

Compared with the rapid growth of drug courts, research development has been slow, despite federal funding and DCPO requirements. The second *Drug Court Publications Resource Guide* (Tauber, Snavely, & Wilkosz, 2000) listed 89 evaluations representing 28 different states and 55 jurisdictions; an additional 11 reports were added to the third edition (Freeman-Wilson & Wilkosz, 2001). It is apparent from these numbers that many courts have not yet completed even the mandatory process evaluations. Less than one quarter of the reports have been published or are currently under review for publication. Thus, there is limited exposure of these evaluations to the larger academic or practitioner audience.

The four published reviews of existing drug court research assert that there is still very little known about the effectiveness of drug courts (Belenko 1998b, 1999, 2001; GAO, 1997). Most drug court research has focused on local process evaluations (Belenko, 1999); a small but growing number of studies have focused on outcomes and impact, including attempts to assess cost implications (Belenko, 2001). A handful of studies have looked at the operation and the impact of drug courts over time and across jurisdictions. Few studies have been able to measure the comparative impact of the drug courts on relapse among substance abusers, largely because of the difficulty of obtaining drug use data for comparison groups that do not remain under close supervision of the criminal justice system. Small studies have, understandably, been shaped more in response to the interests of officials and policymakers who are more often interested in basic questions about drug court success in terms of recidivism than in response to interests of researchers who specialize in substance abuse treatment. On the local level, researchers may not be prepared to provide administrators with the type of information they believe is important. Administrators and court officials may find researchers overly academic and their discussions of methods and measurement abstruse and unresponsive.

The most frequently reported program outcomes in process evaluations are rates of retention and graduation (Belenko, 1999, 2001). Unfortunately, the lack of consistency in measures across jurisdictions makes it difficult to calculate and compare rates. Some evaluations have examined the predictors of retention or graduation, and others have looked at time in treatment, but there is still little known in this area. Very few evaluations have reported drug test results, although the number that report the proportion of positive urine tests has been increasing. Half of the 37 evaluations reviewed by Belenko in 2001 included interviews with participants, staff, or both.

Only 12 of the impact evaluations reviewed by Belenko in 1999 included comparison groups and measures of postprogram outcomes after drug court participation. The primary outcome examined is recidivism, but the jurisdictions vary in the type of measurement included, making comparisons across jurisdictions difficult. Moreover, the variation in eligibility criteria, drug court structure, and type of comparison group leads to difficulties in making comparisons across programs. Other outcomes reported in these studies include pre–post comparison of scores on the Addiction Severity Index (McLellan, Luborsky, Woody, & O'Brien, 1980) and self-reported drug use. A limited number of evaluations analyzed rates of rearrest during program separate from rates of rearrest postprogram. Belenko's 2001 review included three evaluations with recidivism rates measured for drug court participants during program participation and six evaluations with postprogram recidivism rates. Only one evaluation included data on drug use at 12 months after admission.

Cost analyses examining the economic benefits and avoided costs of the drug court have been included in five of the evaluation reports reviewed by Belenko in 1999 and another five in 2001. Wide variation in the type of information and methodology makes it difficult to compare or synthesize the results. Some evaluations included the operational costs of the drug court, whereas others included more complete enumeration of economic benefits. In many cases the actual costs were estimated on the basis of various types of proxy measures. Efforts are currently underway to develop a protocol for gathering comprehensive outcome and cost-avoidance information for adult drug courts in California, which would use data from in-depth studies of several existing courts in different sites to validate proxy measures (North-west Professional Consortium, Inc., & Administrative Office of the Courts, Judicial Council of California, 2002).

RECOMMENDATIONS FOR FUTURE RESEARCH PARTNERSHIPS

Poor planning, implementation, and evaluation often lead to the failure of criminal justice interventions (Welsh & Harris, 1999). Better programs can be created and improved only through planned change, which involves systematic and scientific research. In examining the intervention of the drug court it is possible to see the strengths and weaknesses of the implementation of this program and how sound evaluation research could provide a means for dialogue between practitioners and researchers. Researchers have played a key role in describing the nature of the problem, its causes, and possible solutions and have helped drive the creation of drug courts. The goals and objectives of the drug courts have been varied and at times not well specified. Documenting these goals and objectives either in the process or outcome evaluation aids in building a sound knowledge base and a social strategy. The fact that DCPO requires these goals and objectives be clearly stated in proposals has strengthened program implementation.

Using research to determine best practices is a fundamental component in developing a model program or policy. In the late 1980s, criminal justice researchers began to document the advantages and disadvantages of intensive supervision and drug testing, while substance abuse researchers were providing evidence that "treatment works." In implementing the early drug courts, many of the pioneers had to rely on what they believed would work, because there was little research to provide evidence of what type of elements were necessary. Specifying the 10 key components of drug courts, and using this model to train drug court judges and other professionals, have been essential ingredients in successful program implementation. Yet these key components were not based on research, which makes them difficult to evaluate. We have not yet reached the stage of determining the impact of these various components on the success of drug courts. A theoretical model of drug courts and a typology (see, e.g., Goldkamp, 1999a, or Longshore et al., 2001) are needed to improve research efforts.

For the drug court to become entrenched public policy there must be more than simply a grassroots movement for change. Thus, how research is conducted and disseminated, and how findings are communicated, are crucial to the implementation of various policies. The extent to which research translates into practice and practice informs research is in many ways determined by the people who control the funding and provide the training. DCPO and NADCP have taken a critical role in training the drug court teams and key stakeholders in how to develop action plans for monitoring program implementation and outcomes and for initiating their programs. Although the DCPO requirement that drug courts conduct a process evaluation has led to an increase in the number of jurisdictions with evaluations, this sometimes meant that fewer impact evaluations have been funded. The 2002 GAO report included several recommendations to improve the data collection and evaluation efforts, which focus on improving response rates of DCPO grantees and consolidating efforts to analyze and report on the data. As drug court programs progress beyond the first several years of implementation, there is a greater need for outcome evaluation findings. The 2002 GAO report further recommended that federal funding be accelerated to implement a methodologically sound national impact evaluation.

Effective partnerships among researchers, judges, and program coordinators need to be established to ensure that drug court evaluation designs are rigorous and scientifically defensible. The most desirable research designs, such as random assignment of participants to either a drug court or to other levels of services (e.g., drug education), require significant negotiation with key judicial and administrative staff to address potential ethical and legal dilemmas related to unequal services received by people supervised by the courts. Similar coordination is needed to obtain comprehensive evaluation data from treatment, court, probation, and other criminal justice records and to ensure that informed consent for follow-up research is obtained from participants. Partnerships are also needed to identify costs incurred or averted by drug courts (e.g., costs related to arrests, new crimes committed, incarceration in jail, employment, health care use) that are related to follow-up outcomes affected by program participation. The resulting benefit–cost data may be among the most persuasive in justifying continuation or expansion of drug courts. Linkages between drug court researchers and practitioners are also needed to ensure that outcome research is translated into languages and formats that are appropriate and useful for administrators, policymakers, and funders.

REFERENCES

Beck, A. J., Bonczar, T. P., Ditton, P. M., Gilliard, D. K., Glaze, L. E., Harlow, C. W., et al. (2000). *Correctional populations in the United States, 1997*. Washington, DC: U.S. Department of Justice, Bureau of Justice Statistics.

Belenko, S. (1990). The impact of drug offenders on the criminal justice system. In R. Weisheit (Ed.), *Drugs, crime and criminal justice system* (pp. 27–78). Cincinnati, OH: Anderson.

Belenko, S. (1998a). *Behind bars: Substance abuse and America's prison population.*

New York: National Center on Addiction and Substance Abuse, Columbia University.

Belenko, S. (1998b). Research on drug courts: A critical review. *National Drug Court Institute Review, 1*(1), 1–44.

Belenko, S. (1999). Research on drug courts: A critical review 1999 update. *National Drug Court Institute Review, 2*(2), 1–58.

Belenko, S. (2001). *Research on drug courts: A critical review 2001 update.* New York: National Center on Addiction and Substance Abuse, Columbia University.

Cosden, M., Peerson, S., & Crothers, L. (1997). *Year 1 evaluation of the Santa Barbara County substance abuse treatment courts.* Santa Barbara: University of California. Unpublished report.

Deschenes, E. P., Emami, V., Klein, Z., & Moreno, K. (2000). *Drug court program change and development.* Long Beach: California State University Department of Criminal Justice.

Deschenes, E. P., & Greenwood, P. W. (1994). Maricopa County's drug court: An innovative program for first-time drug offenders on probation. *Justice System Journal, 17*, 99–115.

Deschenes, E. P., Imam, I., Foster, T. L., Diaz, L., Moreno, V., Patascil, L., & Ward, D. (1999). *Evaluation of Orange County drug courts.* Richmond, CA: Center for Applied Local Research.

Deschenes, E. P., & Petersen, R. (1999). Experimenting with the drug court model: Implementation and change in Maricopa County, Arizona. In W. C. Terry, III (Ed.), *The early drug courts* (pp. 139–165). Thousand Oaks, CA: Sage.

Drug Court Programs Office. (2001). *Drug Court grant program fiscal year 2001.* Washington, DC: U.S. Department of Justice.

Drug Strategies. (1999). *Drug courts: A revolution in criminal justice.* Washington, DC: Drug Strategies.

Finigan, M. (1998). *An outcome program evaluation of the Multnomah County S.T.O.P. drug diversion program.* Portland, OR: Northwest Professional Consortium.

Freeman-Wilson, K., & Wilkosz, M. (2001). *Drug court publications resource guide* (3rd ed.). Washington, DC: National Drug Court Institute, U.S. Department of Justice, Office of Justice Programs.

Gendreau, P. (1995). Technology transfer in the criminal justice field: Implications for substance abuse. In T. E. Backer & S. L. David (Eds.), *Reviewing the behavioral science knowledge base on technology transfer* (NIH No. 95-4035, pp. 198–209). Rockville, MD: National Institutes of Health.

Gendreau, P. (1996). Principles of effective intervention with offenders. In A. Harland (Ed.), *Choosing correctional options that work* (pp. 117–130). Newbury Park, CA: Sage.

Gerstein, D. R., & Harwood, H. J. (Eds.). (1990). *Treating drug problems: Volume 1.* Washington, DC: National Academy Press.

Goldkamp, J. S. (1999a). Challenges for research and innovation: When is a drug court not a drug court? In W. C. Terry, III (Ed.), *The early drug courts* (pp. 166–177). Thousand Oaks, CA: Sage.

Goldkamp, J. S. (1999b). The origin of the treatment drug court in Miami. In W. C. Terry, III (Ed.), *The early drug courts* (pp. 19–42). Thousand Oaks, CA: Sage.

Goldkamp, J. S. (2000). The drug court response: Issues and implications for justice change. *Albany Law Review, 63,* 923–961.

Goldkamp, J. S., White, M. D., & Robinson, J. B. (2001a). *An honest chance: Perspectives of drug court participants—Findings from focus groups in Brooklyn, Miami, Seattle, Las Vegas and San Bernardino.* Washington, DC: Drug Court Programs Office, Office of Justice Programs, U.S. Department of Justice.

Goldkamp, J. S., White, M. D., & Robinson, J. B. (2001b). Context and change: The evolution of pioneering drug courts in Portland and Las Vegas (1991–1998). *Journal of Law and Policy, 23*(2), 141–170.

Goldkamp, J. S., White, M. D., & Robinson, J. B. (2001c). Do drug courts work? Getting inside the drug court black box. *Journal of Drug Issues, 31,* 27–72.

Goldkamp, J. S., White, M. D., & Robinson, J. B. (2001d). *From whether to how drug courts work: Retrospective evaluation of drug courts in Clark County (Las Vegas) and Multnomah County (Portland).* Final report to the National Institute of Justice. Philadelphia: Crime and Justice Research Institute.

Gottfredson, D. C., Coblentz, K., & Harmon, M. A. (1996). *A short-term outcome evaluation of the Baltimore City drug treatment court program.* College Park: University of Maryland, Department of Criminology and Criminal Justice.

Haas, A. L., & Peters, R. H. (2001). Development of substance abuse problems among drug-involved offenders: Evidence for the telescoping effect. *Journal of Substance Abuse, 12,* 241–253.

Haas, H. (1993). *S.T.O.P., an early drug intervention and case management program, August 1991–January 1993.* Portland, OR: Multnomah County Circuit Court.

Harrell, A., Cavanagh, S., & Roman, J. (2000). *Evaluation of the DC Superior Court drug intervention program.* Washington, DC: U.S. Department of Justice.

Harrell, A., & Smith, B. (1996). *Evaluation of the District of Columbia Superior Court drug intervention program: Focus group interviews.* Washington, DC: National Institute of Justice.

Hora, P. F., Schma, W. G., & Rosenthal, J. T. A. (1999). Therapeutic jurisprudence and the drug treatment court movement: Revolutionizing the criminal justice system's response to drug abuse and crime in America. *Notre Dame Law Review, 74,* 439–538.

Inciardi, J. A., McBride, D. C., & Rivers, J. E. (1996). *Drug control and the courts.* Thousand Oaks, CA: Sage.

Kemmis, S., & McTaggart, R. (1988). *The action research planner* (3rd ed.). Geelong, Australia: Deakin University Press.

Lamb, S., Greenlick, M. R., & McCarty, D. (1998). *Bridging the gap between practice and research: Forging partnerships with community-based drug and alcohol treatment.* Washington, DC: National Academy of Sciences.

Lewin, K. (1951). *Field theory in social science.* New York: Harper & Row.

Logan, T. K., Williams, K., Leukefeld, C. G., & Minton, L. (2000). A process evaluation of a drug court: Methodology and findings. *International Journal of Offender Therapy and Comparative Criminology, 44*(3), 369–394.

Longshore, D., Turner, S., Wenzel, S., Morral, A., Harrell, A., McBride, D., et al. (2001). Drug courts: A conceptual framework. *Journal of Drug Issues 31*, 7–26.

McLellan, A. T., Luborsky, L., Woody, G. E., & O'Brien, C. P. (1980). An improved diagnostic instrument for substance abuse patients: The Addiction Severity Index. *Journal of Nervous and Mental Disease, 168*, 26–33.

Mumola, C. J., & Beck, A. J. (1997). *Prisoners in 1996*. Washington, DC: U.S. Department of Justice, Bureau of Justice Statistics.

Northwest Professional Consortium, Inc., & Administrative Office of the Courts, Judicial Council of California (2002). *California drug courts: An evaluation of costs and benefits, Phase 1 Final Report*. Unpublished report.

OJP Drug Court Clearinghouse and Technical Assistance Project at American University: Summary of drug court activity by state and county. (2002, January 17). Retrieved May 1, 2002, from http://www.american.edu/academic.depts/spa/justice/publication/drgchart2k.pdf

Peters, R. H., Greenbaum, P. E., Edens, J. F., Carter, C. R., & Ortiz, M. M. (1998). Prevalence of *DSM–IV* substance abuse and dependence disorders among prison inmates. *American Journal of Drug and Alcohol Abuse, 24*, 573–587.

Peters, R. H., Haas, A. L., & Hunt, W. M. (2001). Treatment dosage effects in drug courts. *Journal of Offender Rehabilitation, 33*(4), 63–72.

Peters, R. H., Haas, A. L., & Murrin, M. R. (1999). Predictors of retention and arrest in drug courts. *National Drug Court Institute Review, 2*(1), 33–60.

Peters, R. H., & Hills, H. A. (1997). *Intervention strategies for offenders with co-occurring disorders: What works?* Delmar, NY: National GAINS Center.

Peters, R. H., & Murrin, M. R. (2000). Effectiveness of treatment-based drug courts in reducing criminal recidivism. *Criminal Justice and Behavior, 27*, 72–96.

Peters, R. H., & Steinberg, M. L. (2000). Substance abuse treatment services in U.S. prisons. In D. Shewan & J. Davies (Eds.), *Drugs and prisons* (pp. 89–116). London: Harwood Academic.

Porter, R. (2000, June). *Action research*. Paper presented at the sixth annual conference of the National Association of Drug Court Professionals, San Francisco.

Robins, L. N., & Regier, D. A. (1991). *Psychiatric disorders in America: The Epidemiological Catchment Area Study*. New York: Free Press.

Satel, S. L. (2001). Drug treatment: The case for coercion. *National Drug Court Institute Review, 3*(1), 1–56.

Schiff, M., & Terry, W. C., III (1997). Predicting graduation from Broward County's dedicated drug treatment court. *Justice System Journal, 19*, 291–310.

Shichor, D., & Sechrest, D. K. (2001). Determinants of graduation from a day treatment drug court in California: A preliminary study. *Journal of Drug Issues, 31*, 129–148.

Simpson, D. D., Knight, K., & Pevoto, C. (1996). *Research summary: Focus on drug treatment in criminal justice settings*. Fort Worth: Institute of Behavioral Research, Texas Christian University.

Stringer, E. T. (1999). *Action research* (2nd ed.). Thousand Oaks, CA: Sage.

Tauber, J., Snavely, K. R., & Wilkosz, M. P. (2000). *Drug court publications resource guide* (2nd ed.). Washington, DC: National Drug Court Institute, U.S. Department of Justice Office of Justice Programs.

Terry, W. C., III. (1999). Judicial change and dedicated treatment courts: Case studies in innovation. In W. C. Terry, III (Ed.), *The early drug courts* (pp. 1–18). Thousand Oaks, CA: Sage.

Torres, S., & Deschenes, E. P. (1997). Changing the system and making it work: The process of implementing drug courts in Los Angeles County. *Justice System Journal, 19,* 267–290.

U.S. Department of Justice. (1997). *Defining drug courts: The key components*. Washington, DC: U.S. Government Printing Office.

U.S. General Accounting Office. (1997). *Drug courts: Overview of growth, characteristics, and results*. Washington, DC: U.S. Government Printing Office.

U.S. General Accounting Office. (2002). *Drug courts: Better DOJ data collection and evaluation efforts needed to measure impact of drug court programs*. Washington, DC: U.S. Government Printing Office.

Wanberg, K. W., & Milkman, H. B. (1998). *Criminal conduct and substance abuse treatment: Strategies for self-improvement and change: The participant's workbook*. Arvada, CO: Center for Addictions Research and Evaluation.

Welsh, W. N., & Harris, P. W. (1999). *Criminal justice policy & planning*. Cincinnati, OH: Anderson.

Wexler, H. K., Falkin, G. P., Lipton, D. S., & Rosenblum, A. B. (1992). Outcome evaluation of a prison therapeutic community for substance abuse treatment. In C. G. Leukefeld & F. M. Tims (Eds.), *Drug abuse treatment in prison and jails* (pp. 156–175). Washington, DC: U.S. Department of Health and Human Services.

Wexler, H. K., Lipton, D. S., & Johnson, B. D. (1988). *A criminal justice system strategy for treating cocaine–heroin abusing offenders in custody*. Washington, DC: U.S. Department of Justice, National Institute of Justice.

Whyte, W. F. (Ed.). (1991). *Participatory action research*. Newbury Park, CA: Sage.

II

DISSEMINATION FROM RESEARCH TO PRACTICE

INTRODUCTION: DISSEMINATION FROM RESEARCH TO PRACTICE

JOAN E. ZWEBEN

The chapters in this part tell the story of treatment interventions that were first developed in the research community and then transferred to clinical practice; they include both pharmacotherapy and behaviorally oriented approaches. The interventions also occupy different places in the history of drug abuse treatment, with methadone/levo-alpha-acetylmethadol (LAAM) dating to the 1960s, relapse prevention in the 1970s, and motivational interviewing in the 1990s.

Walter Ling, Richard A. Rawson, and M. Douglas Anglin (chapter 7) offer one of the most dramatic stories in substance abuse treatment history. Methadone and LAAM were developed and researched in the same time period, and both are pharmacologically similar treatments for heroin dependence. However, whereas methadone experienced relative success moving into practice, LAAM experienced relative failure. Ling et al. ascribe the success of methadone in part to the efforts of a "champion," Jerome Jaffe, a clinician and scientist who rose to policy leadership during President Richard Nixon's administration. At the same time, they ascribe the failure of LAAM to regulatory pressures that restricted its adoption. The way that regulatory policies hindered LAAM are now in full view, as both the National Institute on Drug Abuse and the Center for Substance Abuse Treatment roll out buprenorphine as an alternative opiate agonist therapy.

In describing the movement of relapse prevention into clinical practice, Dennis M. Donovan (chapter 8) identifies the key task of translation. Clinicians, who often are in recovery themselves, rely on their experiences, and less on academic publications, in implementing treatment. The early academic work of Alan Marlatt was indirectly supported by the independent clinical work of Terence Gorski, then directly supported by collaboration with Dennis Daley, who translated Marlatt's model into practice terms, complete with manuals and workbooks.

Theresa Moyers discusses motivational interviewing (chapter 9), which was developed more recently than relapse prevention. This approach has gained favor with clinicians and outreach workers, in part because it provides nonthreatening techniques for helping patients to change. Moyers reviews the elements and growth of the motivational interviewing technique and comments on the characteristics that facilitated its adoption by professionals in the field of substance abuse treatment.

7

PHARMACOLOGY, PRACTICE, AND POLITICS: A TALE OF TWO OPIATE PHARMACOTHERAPIES

WALTER LING, RICHARD A. RAWSON, AND M. DOUGLAS ANGLIN

The development and implementation of methadone maintenance for opioid dependence are undoubtedly the most important achievements in the treatment of substance abuse disorders over the past 50 years. Methadone maintenance has significantly reduced the morbidity and mortality associated with heroin addiction and related diseases contracted from poor injection hygiene, including HIV. Conversely, levo-alpha-acetylmethadol (LAAM), which underwent a far more exhaustive safety and efficacy evaluation before its general release has, by virtually all measures, failed to fulfill its promise. That investment in these two pharmacotherapies has resulted in such different outcomes is remarkable, not because one is effective and the other is not but rather because both medications share many of the same advantages and disadvantages. In fact, extensive research suggests that LAAM offers some significant advantages over methadone, yet methadone remains the primary

We acknowledge support from National Institute on Drug Abuse Grants DA 11972, DA 12755, DA 13045, and DA 10422 and several grants from the Robert Wood Johnson Foundation Substance Abuse Research Policy Program. We also thank Brian Perrochet, Sandy Dow, and Pilou Thirakul for assistance with manuscript preparation.

treatment modality for heroin addiction in the United States, as well as many other countries, whereas LAAM has not been well accepted.

In this chapter we review the contrasting stories of methadone and LAAM, recounting the evolution of medication-based treatment for opiate dependence with a focus on the development and practical implementation of the two medications. Lessons learned from the distinctly different histories of methadone and LAAM should provide valuable insight into the struggle that surrounds the transfer of research-based treatment strategies into widespread practical application. Although some of the issues we discuss are specific to pharmacotherapy development, the transfer of science-based knowledge into practical application generally occurs within an environment that is encumbered with comparable pitfalls and obstacles. Measures similar to those aiding the adoption of methadone maintenance may be useful in avoiding or dealing with these obstacles, however, and we describe some of these as well.

The observations and suggestions we discuss for improving the dissemination of research findings into practice are based on the lessons we have learned from our involvement in the development and implementation of both methadone and LAAM since the early 1970s. Covering the gamut from research to practice, these activities have included medication development trials, provision of LAAM and methadone in outpatient clinic systems in southern California, and extensive evaluation research on methadone/LAAM maintenance programs.

OVERVIEW

Methadone and its derivative, LAAM, were products of German efforts during World War II to synthesize a replacement for opiate analgesics (e.g., morphine), which had become unavailable to Germans as a result of Allied interruption of traditional supply routes. After the war, the need for such replacements was eliminated, but because methadone had proven to be an effective analgesic it continued to be extensively used in medical practice. In contrast, LAAM's early development as an analgesic was abandoned when undue toxicity was observed with the level of repeated dosing necessary to sustain analgesia. Neither drug was used for treatment of opiate dependence, because the age of opiate maintenance pharmacotherapy had not yet arrived, even though the properties that made these agents potentially useful for such purposes had already been demonstrated.

Methadone

Methadone was initially used in the 1950s as an adjunct to the detoxification of heroin addicts at federal narcotics hospitals in Lexington,

Kentucky, and Fort Worth, Texas. Detoxification was generally a short-term process, and temporarily abstinent individuals were released into the community with little after care. Relapse was common, as was the resultant return to crime and other antisocial activities. At that time, treatment of heroin addiction was considered best accomplished by correcting the underlying psychopathology of the addict; unfortunately, addicts were rarely able to achieve abstinence long enough to be rehabilitated.

This unproductive situation changed in the early 1960s, when Dole and Nyswander (1965) first recognized methadone's potential as a medication for dealing with heroin addiction in a different manner. They found orally administered methadone to be effective, with a considerably longer half-life than heroin, and it appeared that addicts could be given long-term "maintenance" with a once-daily methadone-dosing regimen. This longer half-life would eliminate between-dose cravings and would free addicts to become engaged in social and vocational rehabilitation. The genius of methadone maintenance was not that it provided a cure in the sense that was understood at the time but rather that the addicts' need for an opiate could be medically supervised and maintained while they underwent rehabilitation. As such, it did not result in complete abstinence from all opiates, but it did assist patients in reducing or eliminating their illicit drug use. Moreover, it helped prevent crime associated with procuring illicit drugs, and it allowed patients to live more productive and prosocial lives, all at greatly reduced cost to themselves and to society (Anglin & McGlothlin, 1985; Gerstein & Lewis, 1990).

During the 1960s and early 1970s, following Dole and Nyswander's (1965) seminal work, a growing number of physicians became interested in methadone maintenance treatment. The major impetus for the expansion of methadone maintenance, however, came from a somewhat unexpected source. This period was a time of social tolerance, liberation, and the "flower children." Drug experimentation was considered socially acceptable in some circles, and heroin, amphetamine, and marijuana use was on the rise. The Vietnam War was being waged. Veterans were returning home admitting to heroin use overseas, and their mothers were writing their congressmen wanting to know what the government was doing to help. Clinicians and politicians alike were beginning to feel a need to address these problems. Crime thought to be related to drug use was on the rise (Anglin & Perrochet, 1998).

President Richard Nixon, a staunch conservative, recognized the political significance of the issues at hand and felt a pragmatic need to respond in a manner consistent with societal expectations and concerns about the returning Vietnam veterans' heroin addiction and the resultant social disruption. He fortunately selected Jerome Jaffe, a psychiatrist who had worked at the Lexington Hospital in the late 1950s, as the nation's first "drug czar." Jaffe already had considerable knowledge about methadone treatment—and

LAAM, too, for that matter. Unlike the inpatient-based methadone treatment approach investigated by Dole and Nyswander (1965) and others, Jaffe had prescribed methadone for his heroin-addicted patients from his office-based practice in New York City, supervising their progress on an outpatient basis. In the early 1970s, with the power now vested in him as director of the newly formed White House Special Action Office for Drug Abuse Prevention (SAODAP), he introduced and expanded maintenance treatment of heroin addicts in the United States. Methadone was established as the standard treatment for opiate dependence, and a treatment system was implemented that would overcome social and political resistance in a manner that had not been seen before and has not since been duplicated. In fact, more than 300 methadone clinics were established over a period of 3 years, with the number of heroin addicts in treatment increasing from several thousand in 1970 to some 60,000 two years later (Rettig & Yarmolinsky, 1995).

Methadone treatment has subsequently followed a mixed course, sustained and bettered by factors largely unrelated to its properties as a safe and effective medication. This history is a reflection of how success or failure of medical implementation is subject to nonmedical societal and political judgments and forces. The basic tension between what methadone can achieve in the medical arena versus what its availability means to society at large continues to this day. As a medication, 30 years of experience has continued to support methadone's safety and efficacy, but as a treatment delivered within the context of American society, methadone maintenance has not substantially evolved in a manner consistent with results of extensive research. Thirty years ago, the system of methadone treatment delivery in the United States was viewed by the rest of the world as a model. In the ensuing years, other countries have largely evolved more pragmatic and rational approaches based on findings of research conducted predominantly in the United States, whereas the treatment delivery system in the United States proper has continued to be driven ideologically and characterized by societal ambivalence about the nature of heroin addiction and the addicts, believing that they are at once both sick people and sinners deserving of some help, but not too much. Treatment has remained unnecessarily restrictive, punitive, and highly regulated. Advocates of methadone maintenance treatment have mainly concerned themselves with its preservation as a business rather than a treatment. Only recently has there been some movement to modify the basic approach to methadone treatment, but substance abuse professionals now find themselves playing "catch-up" with much of the rest of the world.

LAAM

The course of LAAM development and implementation was very different from that of methadone. As we alluded to previously, early work by Fraser and Isbell (1952; Fraser, Nash, Vanhorn, & Isbell, 1954) had shown that LAAM reduces opiate abstinence symptoms in former heroin addicts maintained on morphine and blocks the effects of subsequently administered opiates. Research with LAAM was halted, however, when it became apparent that with the repeated dosing required to maintain acute analgesia, LAAM produced such toxic effects as respiratory depression, mental confusion, nausea, vomiting, and even coma in several postsurgical patients.

Although the success of methadone maintenance in the 1960s led to a renewed scientific and medical interest in LAAM, methadone's limitations were also becoming apparent. As a medication, methadone was long-acting enough, requiring only once-daily doses. Still, the regulations under which methadone was prescribed and dispensed were stringent. To satisfy the concerns of a conservative criminal justice system, addicts were required to attend clinics daily for extended periods, which effectively interfered with many of the activities needed for social rehabilitation, such as seeking employment. This demand also left them in the bind of having to earn take-home doses while leaving them little time or opportunity to do so. Thus, a medication with a longer half-life that would allow for less frequent clinic attendance would seem like a windfall, and LAAM seemed to fit the bill.

A number of studies conducted in the mid-1960s had established LAAM's viability for treatment of heroin addicts within the existing outpatient-methadone clinic system. In fact, before his appointment as drug czar, Jaffe was already experienced with using LAAM to treat addicts in methadone clinics in Chicago. At the time of his White House appointment, methadone and LAAM were both candidates for use in expanding treatment of heroin addicts. However, although methadone had been in use medically for many years, LAAM was still in its early stages of clinical development. Moreover, under government urgency, the formal approval processes usually required in the United States were suspended, and methadone was being used to treat heroin addiction under a special investigational approval, with the federal government serving as its sponsor. The notion was that methadone would be made available to meet addicts' immediate treatment needs, while the government fostered proper development of LAAM, which was expected to replace or supplement methadone once it was approved. To this end, it was the federal government that provided the encouragement and much of the funds needed for LAAM development at that time.

During the 1970s, the SAODAP gave LAAM top priority, and several large-scale clinical trials were conducted. Most noteworthy were the Veterans Affairs Cooperative Study (Ling, Charuvastra, Kaim, & Klett, 1976), the SAODAP Cooperative Study (Ling, Klett, & Gillis, 1978), and the Goldstein Cohort Study (Judson & Goldstein, 1979), which together firmly established LAAM's clinical safety and efficacy. After the National Institute on Drug Abuse (NIDA) was established in 1975, it was decided that LAAM treatment in clinical trials would be extended up to 80 weeks and include women of non-childbearing potential (Judson & Goldstein, 1983;

Ling, Blakis, Holmes, Klett, & Carter, 1980; Resnick, Washton, Garwood, & Perzel, 1981; Trueblood, Judson, & Goldstein, 1978). The subsequently conducted Whysner study (Whysner, Thomas, Ling, & Charuvastra, 1980), involving several different protocols, was designed to accumulate additional clinical experience. By 1980, it appeared that sufficient clinical data had been collected, and LAAM was thought to be ready for approval. However, an initial new drug application submission in February 1980 was considered insufficient for review because of lack of an adequate chemistry section, and a revised submission in 1981 was deemed unacceptable for review because of inappropriate data tabulation.

With national attention and resources being diverted to the cocaine epidemic in the 1980s, LAAM development was again placed on hold, except for one small fee-for-service study conducted in methadone clinics in California (Tennant, Rawson, Pumphrey, & Seecof, 1986). It was not until the early 1990s, under the auspices of NIDA's newly established Medications Development Division, that LAAM development efforts resurfaced. By this time, sufficient data concerning its safety and efficacy had been collected, but the demographics of drug users had changed, and the Food and Drug Administration (FDA) wanted a more contemporary group of patients, including larger numbers of women, to be tested. The Labeling Assessment Study (Fudala, Vocci, Montgomery, & Trachtenberg, 1997) and a small pharmacokinetic study (Beckson et al., 1995) provided the additional information needed and led to LAAM's approval in June 1993.

Finally, in August 1993, after years of extensive clinical evaluation, LAAM was made available for use in narcotic treatment programs (NTPs) in the United States. Expectations that LAAM would attract large numbers of previously untreated addicts into therapy were, however, unfulfilled. Because each state had its own review process for opiate agonists, regulatory hurdles at the state level hampered LAAM's full implementation, and although research had proved LAAM to be safe and effective, the treatment community was slow to adopt it. In fact, 3 years after its approval only 810 patients were receiving LAAM maintenance in only 62 of 750 licensed NTPs (Rawson, Hasson, Huber, McCann, & Ling, 1998). As of January 1, 2001—almost 8 years after approval—it is estimated that fewer than 2% of the 180,000 patients (approximately 3,500) receiving opiate agonist therapy in the United States were being treated with LAAM (Rawson & Hasson, 2000). It is clear that nearly 50 years of research and development had resulted in very different outcomes for methadone and LAAM.

DIFFERENT COURSES

Methadone

Methadone maintenance in the United States was essentially implemented while confirmatory research was being conducted. A unique set of circumstances in the United States during the late 1960s and early 1970s—including increased drug use and drug-related crime, an unpopular war, and a Presidential re-election campaign—had opened a window of opportunity for change. These factors, the leadership and political power of Jaffe and SAODAP, and the availability of federal funding to establish clinics, combined to make methadone maintenance a national presence in the treatment of opiate dependence. Thus, the implementation of methadone treatment represents not so much a planned "research to practice" effort as a reactive *limited* clinical research to practice effort to meet perceived social and political needs.

Gaining widespread general acceptance of methadone has not been easy. For more than 30 years, methadone treatment has existed primarily outside the parameters of mainstream health care services. It has been vigorously opposed by politicians, law enforcement leaders and, frequently, by other substance abuse treatment proponents, and it remains one of the most highly regulated services in medicine. Some 250 clinics had been established in the United States by 1972 to deliver methadone, but that number barely tripled over the ensuing 25 years, and even today methadone remains unavailable in eight states (Lamb, Greenlick, & McCarty, 1998).

Nevertheless, despite the opposition, the methadone treatment system has managed to expand rather steadily, albeit slowly, over the past 30 some years. Despite the withdrawal of much funding and conversion to client pay service, methadone's ability to reduce heroin use and heroin-related crime and, more recently, its effectiveness in reducing the spread of HIV, has provided the impetus for continued expansion. Thus, methadone treatment in the United States was borne of opportunity and leadership but, despite strong hostility and resistance, it has endured, simply because it works.

LAAM

In contrast to methadone, LAAM was extensively evaluated before its regulatory approval and attempted dissemination. In fact, by the time LAAM received FDA approval in 1993, methadone had already been in use as an opiate substitution therapy for more than 30 years. Yet, despite solid scientific evidence of its efficacy and its apparent advantages over methadone, LAAM's approval received only a tepid response by NTP providers.

Once approved at the federal level, LAAM still had to undergo a state-by-state approval process. Because no other drug had undergone this process since methadone's initiation in the early 1970s, many states were unfamiliar with their own preapproval regulatory procedures, which in most states were poorly defined. In some states as many as eight separate agencies required review, and some required special legislation and a governor's signature. Moreover, lacking the financial backing of a major pharmaceutical company to aggressively move LAAM through the regulatory maze of state approvals, supplies simply sat on the manufacturer's shelves. In fact, of the 10 states with the largest potential markets for LAAM, only Texas approved it within 24 months of its FDA approval (Rawson et al., 1998).

Another hindrance for LAAM was the lack of an advocate, or champion, a person or agency with the power and credibility to guide it through this extended approval process and to promote it to the relevant policymakers and practitioners. Jaffe's early involvement in methadone, and his reputation among the policymaking and treatment communities, did not ensure a continuity of influence for LAAM. Once he left SAODAP, his efforts to move LAAM expeditiously into application were not sustained. LAAM was in all respects an "orphan" drug, and the absence of a powerful advocate who could move the bureaucratic process forward was an important missing element.

To make matters worse, treatment providers themselves posed obstacles to LAAM's full implementation. Many were not enthusiastic about adopting a new medication. Some were suspicious that because LAAM was promoted by NIDA as an alternative to methadone, it was intended to replace rather than augment methadone treatment. The genesis of this belief is unclear, but it may have been that methadone had been publicly maligned for so long that any change in the status quo was considered a threat to eliminate it altogether. Some providers considered the cost of LAAM too prohibitive, although, in reality, the weekly per patient cost is only about 50% higher than for methadone (Rawson et al., 1998). However, because the cost of medication is less than 5% of an NTP's total operating cost, it is likely that the thrice-weekly dosing and elimination of take-home medication and procedures probably offset LAAM's slightly increased cost. In fact, cost seemed to be only an excuse for the providers' lack of enthusiasm for LAAM and for their belief that it did not offer sufficient benefits to justify the expense of adding new operating procedures at clinics. Also, take-home LAAM was not an approved option in the federal regulations, and patients were therefore required to attend a clinic indefinitely for three-times-a-week dosing, regardless of their treatment progress. Therefore, LAAM's thrice-weekly schedule, although an incentive during early phases of treatment, could be a disincentive for patients in longer term treatment, because many NTPs allowed patients to earn twice- or even once-weekly visit schedules with methadone.

Finally, LAAM was introduced with only a modest marketing effort. The BioDevelopment Corporation (BDC), the company that initially owned the rights to LAAM, was a start-up company with limited resources and experience in medication promotion. When BDC was purchased by Roxanne Pharmaceuticals, a much larger and resource-rich company, 18 months of BDC's patent exclusivity had expired, and numerous regulatory hurdles still had to be overcome. Although NIDA had sponsored the development of LAAM, once LAAM had been approved and the rights transferred to a private company, governmental agencies (NIDA and the Center for Substance Abuse Treatment) were restricted from promotional efforts for fear of impropriety. LAAM was thus introduced without the benefit of any major advertising or promotional programs. Instead, it received a rather quiet introduction into a very complex regulatory environment that had not been traversed for more than 20 years.

Clearly, the acceptance of methadone was based on pressing need, lack of alternatives, and political presence, which together hastened its implementation and widespread application. In contrast, the formal and long-suffering path of regulatory approval that LAAM was required to complete at both the federal and state levels prolonged its review and approval process. It is difficult to speculate, in retrospect, what the provider response to LAAM would have been if it had been more promptly available after its FDA approval and promoted through educational efforts, and if incentives had been provided for its use. It is certain, though, that any initial enthusiasm and interest that met LAAM's FDA approval had long dissipated by the time the state approval processes had been negotiated.

LESSONS LEARNED AND RECOMMENDATIONS FOR THE FUTURE

A variety of lessons can be learned from the contrasting stories of methadone and LAAM:

- Despite scientific support for their safety and efficacy, and their documented benefit over previous treatments, new pharmacotherapies in the treatment of addiction will not automatically be adopted by the provider system.
- Powerful advocacy or a well-financed marketing campaign (or both) are essential components to moving a new pharmacotherapy into application. Restraints against federal agencies in providing leadership in this regard need to be reduced.
- As it exists, the regulatory process governing the delivery of opiate agonist therapy creates a substantial deterrent to the implementation of new medications. Interest by the pharmaceutical industry in developing new medications for use in this system is likely to be minimal in light of the extreme delays and regulatory hurdles encountered by the manufacturers of LAAM. Given the multilayered regulatory process, an obstacle at any one level can stop treatment implementation. The levels that influenced the use of LAAM included, but were not limited to, legislative and executive branch approvals; drug development and pharmacy regulations; federal and state law enforcement agencies; federal, state, county, and local governmental substance abuse administrative agencies; service delivery licensing and credentialing agencies; policies of treatment financing agencies, including insurance companies, Medicaid,

and MediCare, and federal, state, and local financing agencies; trade groups; and local zoning boards. A streamlined process needs to be developed.

- To be rapidly adopted, a new addiction pharmacotherapy must have some substantial, unique properties or benefits to providers and patients.
- The same economic principles that govern other health service businesses in the United States govern the substance abuse service delivery system. New treatments are not adopted solely on the basis of their efficacy. The service delivery system responds to market forces as much, if not more than, it responds to scientific imperatives.
- Without adequate market support, government can move treatments with public health significance into application, but there needs to be a champion with the political influence and power to overcome institutional resistance to change.
- The attitudes of pharmacotherapy service delivery staff and decision makers are as much influenced by their ideologies as are the proponents of other specific substance abuse treatment philosophies, including drug-free approaches. That a treatment is delivered by a team with physicians and nurses does not make the challenge of addressing ideological bias any less important.

CONCLUSION

The successful adoption of a new treatment into mainstream use requires that it fill an important unmet clinical need or be more cost effective than existing treatments. It must have sound scientific support and demonstrate clinical, operational, or financial superiority over existing treatments. A new treatment should also economically benefit the service delivery system. A sponsor who has knowledge of the regulatory environment and knows how to influence that environment is a plus. Moreover, a new therapy should have adequate financial and expert resources to mount a marketing and training campaign that addresses the interests of patients, service providers, and policymakers. Last, it should have a business plan that anticipates and is prepared to address the ideological and often illogical biases of practitioners.

That methadone is currently the most widely used agonist treatment for opiate dependence whereas LAAM is barely used is, in part, the result of some specific situational and idiosyncratic circumstances. When the Nixon White House recognized that the crime associated with heroin addiction was an issue of political significance, it could have simply intensified the criminal justice response to addiction. However, because there was immense concern that a large number of Vietnam soldiers might return home with heroin addiction problems, a criminal justice solution did not appear to be politically palatable. The fact that a "30ish-something" clinician–researcher was available who had the necessary technical knowledge and experience to provide visionary leadership was quintessential. That this same individual and the team he or she built to support his or her efforts had the energy and influence necessary to override the objections of the bureaucracy and the Drug Enforcement Administration was also extraordinary. The selection of methadone as the first agent to be implemented was more a function of its status as an FDA-approved analgesic than its clinical superiority over LAAM. That LAAM was not rapidly approved early in the 1970s, as anticipated, was more a function of the inexperience of the substance abuse leadership than the scientific complexity of the approval process. In many ways, the nature of the heroin addiction treatment system in the United States is more a function of timing, politics, and circumstance than it is a result of a rational, scientifically supported plan.

It is difficult to speculate how much relevance the issues that influenced the development and implementation of methadone and LAAM will have for future approaches to addiction treatment. The lack of enthusiastic application that was encountered by LAAM has not been unique among substance abuse pharmacotherapies. The initial optimistic prospects that were anticipated for the use of naltrexone (both for opiate addiction in the 1980s and, more recently, for the treatment of alcoholism) have had similarly disappointing outcomes. Currently, the treatment system anxiously anticipates the approval and implementation of buprenorphine/naloxone as a revolutionary breakthrough and paradigm change in the treatment of opiate dependence. Buprenorphine/naloxone certainly has many properties that suggest that it may have a more successful application than LAAM. However, supporters of this new pharmacotherapy might well want to temper their optimism with caution. Moving from the world of the National Institutes of Health, government regulatory and approval agencies, and university-based research and into the unpredictable currents of the multilayered U.S. health care system, holds many surprises, and few guidelines exist to overcome even the expected obstacles and resistance, let alone the unforeseen ones. The long-awaited approval of buprenorphine, which has yet to be realized, and the absence of any tangible signs of enthusiastic embraces at the level of the health care system, suggest that many lessons have yet to be learned.

REFERENCES

Anglin, M. D., & McGlothlin, W. H. (1985). Methadone maintenance in California: A decade's experiences. In L. Brill & C. Winick (Eds.), *The yearbook of substance use and abuse* (Vol. 3, pp. 219–280). New York: Human Sciences Press.

Anglin, M. D., & Perrochet, B. (1998). Drug use and crime: A historical review of research conducted by the UCLA Drug Abuse Research Center. *Substance Use and Misuse, 33*, 1871–1914.

Beckson, M., Ling, W., Vocci, F., Pickworth, W., Fudala, P., Wilkins, J., et al. (1995). Pharmacokinetic studies of LAAM: Clinical correlates. In L. S. Harris (Ed.), *Problems of drug dependence* (NIDA Research Monograph No. 153, p. 255). Rockville, MD: U.S. Department of Health and Human Services.

Dole, V. P., & Nyswander M. A. (1965). A medical treatment for diacetylmorphine (heroin) addiction. *Journal of the American Medical Association, 193*, 646.

Fraser, H. F., & Isbell, H. (1952). Actions and addiction liabilities of alpha-acetyl-methadols in man. *Journal of Pharmacology and Experimental Therapeutics, 105*, 458–465.

Fraser, H. F., Nash, T. L., Vanhorn, G. D., & Isbell, H. (1954). Use of miotic effect in evaluating analgesic drugs in man. *Archives Internationales de Pharmacodynamie et de Therapie, 98*, 443–451.

Fudala, P. J., Vocci, F., Montgomery, A., & Trachtenberg, A. I. (1997). Levomethadyl acetate (LAAM) for the treatment of opioid dependence: A multisite, open-label study of LAAM safety and an evaluation of the product labeling and treatment regulations. *Journal of Maintenance in the Addictions, 1*(2), 9–39.

Gerstein, D. R., & Lewis, L. S. (1990). Treating drug problems. *New England Journal of Medicine, 323*(20), 844–848.

Judson, B. A., & Goldstein, A. (1979). Levo-alpha-acetylmethadol (LAAM) in treatment of heroin addicts: I. Dosage schedule for induction and stabilization. *Drug and Alcohol Dependence, 4*, 461–466.

Judson, B. A., & Goldstein, A. (1983). Episodes of heroin use during maintenance treatment with stable dosage of levo-alpha-acetylmethadol. *Drug and Alcohol Dependence, 11*, 271–278.

Lamb, S., Greenlick, M. R., & McCarty, D. (1998). *Bridging the gap between practice and research: Forging partnerships with community-based drug and alcohol treatment.* Washington, DC: National Academy Press.

Ling, W., Blakis, E. D., Holmes, E. D., Klett, C. J., & Carter, W. E. (1980). Restabilization on methadone after methadyl acetate (LAAM) maintenance. *Archives of General Psychiatry, 37*, 194–196.

Ling, W., Charuvastra, V. C., Kaim, S. C., & Klett, C. J. (1976). Methadyl acetate and methadone maintenance treatments for heroin addicts. *Archives of General Psychiatry, 33*, 709–720.

Ling, W., Klett, C. J., & Gillis, R. D. (1978). A cooperative clinical study of methadyl acetate: II. Friday-only regimen. *Archives of General Psychiatry, 35*, 345–353.

Rawson, R. A., & Hasson, A. L. (2000, June). *LAAM at 8 years post-approval: What lessons have been learned?* Paper presented at the annual meeting of the College on Problems of Drug Dependence, San Juan, Puerto Rico.

Rawson, R. A., Hasson, A. L., Huber, A. M., McCann, M. J., & Ling, W. (1998). A 3-year progress report on the implementation of LAAM in the United States. *Addiction, 93*, 533–540.

Resnick, R. B., Washton, A. M., Garwood, J., & Perzel, J. (1981). LAAM instead of take-home methadone. In L. S. Harris (Ed.), *Problems of drug dependence* (NIDA Research Monograph No. 41, pp. 473–475). Rockville, MD: National Institute on Drug Abuse.

Rettig, R. A., & Yarmolinsky, A. (1995). *Federal regulation of methadone treatment.* Washington, DC: National Academy Press.

Tennant, F. S., Rawson, R. A., Pumphrey, E., & Seecof, R. (1986). Clinical experiences with 959 opioid-dependent patients treated with levo-alpha-acetylmethadol (LAAM). *Journal of Substance Abuse Treatment, 3,* 195–202.

Trueblood, B., Judson, B. A., & Goldstein, A. (1978). Acceptability of methadyl acetate (LAAM) as compared with methadone in a treatment program for heroin addicts. *Drug and Alcohol Dependence, 3,* 125–132.

Whysner, J. A., Thomas, D. B., Ling, W., & Charuvastra, C. (1980). On the relative efficacy of LAAM and methadone. In L. S. Harris (Ed.), *Problems on drug dependence: Proceedings of the 41st annual scientific meeting of the Committee on Problems of Drug Dependence* (NIDA Research Monograph No. 27, pp. 429–434). Rockville, MD: National Institute on Drug Abuse.

8

RELAPSE PREVENTION IN SUBSTANCE ABUSE TREATMENT

DENNIS M. DONOVAN

Substance abuse has been described as a "chronic relapsing condition" (Connors, Maisto, & Donovan, 1996). Although relapse is neither a necessary nor sufficient criterion for a diagnosis of a substance use disorder, it is one that clearly captures the difficulties clients have after they stop using alcohol or drugs. Relapse is a common outcome following the initiation of abstinence, whether the abstinence was initially achieved with or without formal treatment. The rates of relapse associated with alcohol, cocaine, heroin, and other drugs of abuse are quite high, with some estimates suggesting that 60% or more of individuals relapse after stopping their substance use (McLellan, Lewis, O'Brien, & Kleber, 2000). These rates appear to be relatively comparable across alcohol and other drugs (Cummings, Gordon, & Marlatt, 1980), suggesting that there may be commonalities across substances with respect to the dynamics of relapse.

The preparation of this chapter was supported in part by Grant 1-U10-DA13714 from the National Institute on Drug Abuse and Grant 5-U10-AA11799 from the National Institute on Alcohol Abuse and Alcoholism. The opinions presented in this chapter are those of the author.

The high rates of relapse have concerned and frustrated clinicians, program administrators, and policymakers as well as individuals seeking to stay off alcohol or other drugs. A large segment of substance abuse professionals views abstinence as the primary, if not exclusive, goal for individuals seeking to change their substance use patterns. Within this context, relapse—failure to remain abstinent or drug free—has typically been viewed in the past as evidence of treatment failure (McLellan et al., 2000).

RELAPSE PREVENTION: EVOLUTION OF A CLINICAL APPROACH FROM HUMBLE RESEARCH ORIGINS

Although there had been an awareness of the high rates of relapse after treatment of substance use disorders for quite some time, it was not until the 1970s that researchers began to systematically focus on the nature and process of relapse (Connors et al., 1996). One of the first researchers to begin examining the relapse process was Alan Marlatt. Allen, Lowman, and Miller (1996) noted that "the work of Marlatt and colleagues in differentiating internal and external stimuli associated with relapse, and offering conceptually rich explanations of the relapse process, has had a remarkable influence on the field of alcoholism treatment" (p. S3). Since Marlatt's early work (Cummings et al., 1980; Marlatt & George, 1984; Marlatt & Gordon, 1985), the application of relapse prevention techniques has expanded to include drug abuse and a variety of other addictive behaviors. An important aspect of this early work was a shift from viewing relapse as a single event that defined failure to a more contemporary view of relapse as a multifaceted process in the natural course of recovery.

Although Marlatt's approach has had a profound impact on the field, it has evolved from relatively humble research origins (Marlatt, 1996; Marlatt & George, 1984; Marlatt & Gordon, 1985). His initial interest in relapse developed from an unpublished study, conducted in the mid-1970s, in which he attempted to determine the relative effectiveness of adding aversion therapy to standard inpatient treatment of alcoholism (see Marlatt, 1996, for a more thorough description of this study). Overall, the relapse rate for the participants was quite high: Nearly three quarters of the participants (73.8%) had consumed at least one drink during the first 90 days after their discharge from inpatient treatment. Compared with the standard inpatient-only condition, aversion therapy produced significantly greater decreases in relapse and drinking at the 3-month follow-up; however, no differences were found in drinking outcomes between the treatment and control conditions at the 15-month follow-up.

Marlatt concluded that aversion therapy was not sufficient by itself to maintain long-term abstinence and that something extra was needed to maintain the beneficial effects of aversion therapy found at the initial

3-month follow-up. Consistent with other tenets of behavior therapy, he thought that it might be useful to supplement the aversive conditioning by training patients to respond to alcohol-related cues with other behaviors, particularly ones incompatible with drinking. To do this, it was necessary to know what cues were related to the person's return to drinking, particularly the cues that occurred immediately before he or she resumed drinking as well as the consequences experienced afterward. This would allow the identification of triggers associated with relapse. Through subsequent training, these cues might come to serve as signals to that individual to leave the situation or engage in some other activity that is incompatible with drinking.

These cues, or triggers, could be identified by a thorough behavioral analysis of the antecedents and consequences of the slip. Participants who had relapsed were asked during their follow-up assessments to describe in great detail the circumstances surrounding their first drinking episode. This included information about the physical location, time of day, presence or absence of other people, type of beverage consumed, and a description of the external (environmental) or internal (subjective) events occurring in that general time period, along with the patients' perceptions of their feelings and emotions on the day of the first drink. They were also asked about how they felt after taking an initial drink.

These descriptions were subsequently sorted into categories on the basis of their similarity with one another (Cummings et al., 1980). The resultant categories have come to be known as a *relapse taxonomy*, or a listing of common high-risk relapse situations. The primary categories include (a) intrapersonal situations, such as coping with negative emotions, particularly anger, frustration, depression, and loneliness; (b) coping with negative physical or physiological states, such as withdrawal distress related to stopping alcohol or drug use or to pain, injury, or illness; (c) testing personal control (e.g., testing one's willpower or seeing if treatment "really worked"); and (d) giving in to the urge to drink either in the presence or the absence of substance-related cues. The taxonomy also includes a number of high-risk interpersonal situations, including (a) coping with interpersonal conflicts, particularly those that result in anger and frustration; (b) either direct or indirect social pressure to use; and (c) enhancement of positive emotions.

DEVELOPMENT OF A THEORETICAL MODEL OF RELAPSE

Few, if any, studies up to that point had documented the determinants of relapse, the magnitude of relapse episodes, or the patient's cognitive and affective reactions to relapse (Marlatt, 1996). Based on this early study, Marlatt outlined a preliminary intervention model that focused primarily on teaching patients to recognize and cope effectively with high-risk situations as a means of preventing relapse (Marlatt, 1978).

The Immediate Situation

Marlatt's model focuses on two levels of the individual's circumstances as they relate to potential relapse. The first focuses on the immediate high-risk situation and the individual's response to it. The model suggests that situations associated with prior substance use may represent a potential risk to an individual's continued abstinence. If the person has appropriate interpersonal and emotional skills available to cope with the situation—by avoiding, leaving, or successfully confronting it—then the risk of relapse is reduced. This also results in an increased sense of self-efficacy, a belief that one can cope effectively with similar situations in the future; this further decreases the risk of relapse.

On the other hand, if the individual does not have an adequate coping response available in a high-risk situation, then he or she experiences a decrease in self-efficacy, resulting in a sense of helplessness, passivity, and decreased self-control. In this situation, the individual's cognitive expectancies about the positive benefits of alcohol or drug use (e.g., the belief that a drink would help) increase, and the chances of relapse likewise increase significantly. The model predicts that if the person does drink or use drugs, he or she will experience an *abstinence violation effect*, a relatively predictable set of cognitive and emotional after effects of the use. In particular, the individual may often attribute responsibility for the slip to internal factors, viewing it as evidence that he or she is an addict who is incapable of staying clean and sober. This attribution often is accompanied by a sense of helplessness, depression, resignation, guilt, self-recrimination, and loss of control. To the extent that the person experiences these feelings and thoughts after an initial drink or use of drugs (lapse), the likelihood of continued use (relapse) is quite high.

The Broader Context

The second level of Marlatt's model involves the broader psychosocial context in which the individual interacts and in which the more immediate high-risk situations are embedded. Many addicts say that "I just found myself in" some sort of high-risk relapse situation, but this does not happen by chance. Although the more immediate precipitants of an actual high-risk situation play a major role in relapse, other, more distal factors also contribute. Among these is the general level of stress, or hassles, in the person's life. A component of this stress is conceptualized as the balance between *wants* versus *shoulds*. The model suggests that an imbalance between these—for example, when an individual's sense of obligations (*shoulds*) is greater than his or her wants—reduces the chances that the individual will do things that he or she enjoys and that help reduce stress, which often causes a buildup of frustration and resentment. Under these circumstances, the perceived benefits of using alcohol or drugs are heightened, and the desire to do so increases. This imbalance also may lead to what are described as *seemingly irrelevant decisions*: decisions a person makes that, although they appear to the person to have little relationship to the possibility of drinking alcohol or using drugs, may ultimately lead him or her into a high-risk situation, at which point the more proximal precipitants become more prominent and exert their influence. Examples of such decisions, often viewed as rationalizations for substance use behavior, might include a person going into a tavern where he used to drink to pay off his bar tab, or another person going to a party with friends with whom she used to use drugs because she was feeling lonely and depressed. Although on the face of it the individual might not see these activities as being problematic, in reality such decisions bring him or her into a high-risk setting.

Marlatt developed a set of interventions to address both the proximal and distal contributors to the relapse process. *Relapse prevention*, a generic term that refers to a wide range of cognitive and behavioral strategies, has two primary goals: (a) to prevent an initial lapse back to drinking or drug use and (b) to prevent an initial lapse, if it does occur, from becoming more serious by minimizing the physical, psychological, and social consequences of the return to use. Exhibit 8.1 lists a number of the types of interventions and problem-focused interventions used in relapse prevention programs.

TRANSITION FROM RESEARCH TO PRACTICE

Marlatt's model of relapse and intervention initially was accepted primarily by academicians and clinical researchers but was less well known

EXHIBIT 8.1
Relapse Prevention Techniques

1. Educate oneself about the relapse process.
2. Identify high-risk situations.
3. Identify personal "warning signs."
4. Develop and practice behavioral and cognitive coping strategies.
   - Coping with cravings and urges
   - Managing thoughts about alcohol/drugs
   - Drink/drug refusal skills
   - Problem solving
   - Coping with negative emotions such as anger, depression, anxiety, loneliness, and boredom.
5. Rethink decisions and goals—short-term vs. long-term consequences.
6. Plan for emergencies and coping with lapses.
7. Reframe relapse and the abstinence violation effect.
8. Develop a balanced lifestyle—*woulds* and *shoulds* vs. *wants*.
9. Develop peer groups supportive of a clean and sober life.

and not as readily embraced by the larger substance abuse treatment community. A number of factors likely contributed to this. One is that the early formulations of the model were published in academically oriented books and journals that are less often read by counselors in community-based treatment programs. Also, this work was being conducted during an era when there was considerable conflict between the views held by proponents of behavioral models and disease models concerning the etiology, maintenance, therapeutic goals, interventions, and course of recovery of alcohol and drug dependence. Academic researchers of that era were more inclined to adopt the behavioral conceptualization of substance abuse, whereas counseling staff, many of whom were themselves in recovery, were more inclined to adopt a disease orientation and a 12-step approach to recovery. These differences served as a barrier to the early clinical application of Marlatt's relapse prevention in community-based programs.

At least three important elements appear to have contributed to the initial acceptance and subsequent application of relapse prevention in community-based programs. First, the focus on relapse as a process and on interventions that might prevent or manage relapses was welcomed by clinicians as targeting the most pervasive and persistent problem in their day-to-day work. It made sense and had both appeal and practical applicability. In many ways, this new approach to relapse represented a paradigm shift, providing both clinicians and clients hope. As el-Guebaly and Hodgins (1998) concluded at the end of their review on craving, relapse, and interventions, "A clinician's familiarity with these strategies should contribute significantly to the transformation of the sense of failure engendered by a patient's relapse into a constructive challenge and opportunity" (p. 29).

The second element related to the more widespread acceptance of relapse prevention was the work of Terrance Gorski (1986, 2000; Gorski & Miller, 1979, 1986), who was developing a model of relapse and intervention at about the same time as Marlatt. The two worked contemporaneously and independently, and their models of relapse share many commonalities. A major difference, however, was the frame of reference in which each model was developed. Whereas Marlatt's model was developed within an academic research context, Gorski's evolved more from the perspective of a recovering counselor working primarily "in the trenches" with substance abusers. The latter point—Gorski's recovery status—helped reduce counselors' suspicion of Gorski's model of relapse that had accompanied Marlatt's academic model. The distinction between Marlatt's and Gorski's models led to the use of differing languages to describe their constructs: one that of a theoretician, the other that of a recovering counselor. In addition, Gorski presented many of the concepts of the relapse process in terms of a disease or medical model of alcoholism. These two features, the clinical orientation and the disease formulation, were much more familiar to, and more easily accepted by, the substance abuse counseling field. While Marlatt disseminated information through academic journals and professional academic meetings, Gorski published literature specifically targeting counselors. Gorski also developed a training program in which counselors who were trained in his model could be certified as relapse prevention specialists; they could also use the training to meet their continuing education requirements.

A third early influence in moving relapse prevention into community-based treatment programs was the work of Dennis Daley (1986, 1988, 1989a, 1989b), who attempted to translate Marlatt's constructs and model into layman's terms while still maintaining the cognitive–behavioral focus and orientation. Daley and Marlatt have subsequently worked together to further develop what Daley described as a "psychoeducational approach" (Daley & Marlatt, 1992, 1997; Daley & Salloum, 1999; Marlatt, Barrett, & Daley, 1999). A major contribution of Daley's work has been the development of relapse prevention workbooks and guidelines. Materials are available for the client, the counselor, and family members. These manuals provide session-by-session guidelines for addressing components of Marlatt's model, such as understanding the relapse process, identifying and handling personalized high-risk situations, managing anger and other negative emotions, learning to use leisure time without drinking or using drugs, learning to deal with social pressure to use, handling cravings, and how to deal with a slip if one occurs. The development of these easy-to-use materials provided clinicians the opportunity to use the concepts of relapse prevention in their work.

ADAPTING THE MODEL TO CLINICAL SETTINGS

Marlatt (1996, p. S47) stated that "teaching people about high-risk situations and how to cope with them more effectively is the essence of relapse prevention." It is this set of principles that has guided the application of relapse prevention in clinical settings. A number of different approaches to preventing and managing relapse have been developed, most of which derive from and share common features with Marlatt's model (see Connors et al., 1996; Daley, 1988; Donovan & Chaney, 1985; and Rawson, Obert, McCann, & Marinelli-Casey, 1993a, for more information about these other models). Furthermore, aspects of the relapse prevention model have been modified in a variety of ways to fit the specific needs of clinicians and clients.

Although originally targeted toward maintaining the therapeutic gains achieved in inpatient treatment, cognitive–behavioral interventions based on relapse prevention have been used as an independent, free-standing treatment, a component integrated into outpatient treatments, a major component of inpatient rehabilitation, and as aftercare or continuing care following more intensive outpatient or inpatient treatment (e.g., Daley & Salloum, 1999; Marlatt et al., 1999). It has also been used with a wide range of substance abusers, including those dependent on alcohol, cocaine, opiates, marijuana, and methamphetamine (Marlatt et al., 1999). The generalizability of the model to drugs other than alcohol, for which it was originally developed, seems appropriate given the similarities found across substances in the rates and temporal patterns of relapse, relapse precipitants, and predictors of relapse (Cummings et al., 1980; Hunt, Barnett, & Branch, 1972; McLellan et al., 1994). However, it is important that clinical programs take into account the unique features of the drugs that are being targeted for intervention as well as the specific subculture of individuals using them (Carroll, Rounsaville, & Keller, 1991; Rawson, Obert, McCann, & Ling, 1993).

To adapt to the practical time and fiscal constraints of clinical practice, there has been an emphasis on developing measures, both self-report and semistructured interviews, that can be used to assess elements of the relapse prevention model, such as high-risk situations and self-efficacy, in a more time-efficient manner than through a thorough behavioral analysis (Donovan, 1988, 1996a, 1998). Furthermore, relapse prevention materials derived from Marlatt's original focus on individual counseling have been adapted for use with group, couples, and family therapy formats (e.g., Monti, Abrams, Kadden, & Cooney, 1989; O'Farrell, Choquette, & Cutter, 1998). A number of workbooks (e.g., Daley, 1988; Monti et al., 1989) were instrumental in the early phases of this adaptation, providing session-by-session outlines of group topics and intervention targets in psychoeducational relapse prevention groups. Relapse prevention techniques have also been used in conjunction with pharmacological treatments (e.g., O'Malley, O'Connor, Farren, & Rounsaville, 1998; Schmitz, Stotts, Rhoades, Grabowski, 2001).

AN EXAMPLE OF RELAPSE PREVENTION IN PRACTICE

An example of the application of relapse prevention in clinical practice is the work of Rawson and his colleagues on the Matrix model of treatment for cocaine dependence (Rawson, Obert, McCann, & Ling, 1991; Rawson, Obert, McCann, & Ling, 1993; Rawson, Obert, McCann, & Marinelli-Casey, 1993a, 1993b; Rawson, Obert, McCann, Smith, & Ling, 1990; Rawson et al., 1995). This approach blends cognitive–behavioral and neurobiological components in its conceptualization of addiction and recovery in cocaine dependence, its integration of relapse prevention as a component of a more comprehensive treatment program, and the iterative process between program development and outcome evaluation in directing subsequent refinements of the interventions. The interaction between clinicians and clinical researchers working collaboratively in community treatment settings to tailor the relapse prevention of the Matrix model represents the "bridging of the gap" that has been called for by a number of investigators and clinicians (e.g., Sorensen & Midkiff, 2000).

The Matrix model, described as a "neurobehavioral" approach, is of interest because it has integrated relapse prevention into a more comprehensive outpatient program that has been adapted to the unique nature of the biochemical and biological readjustments and the stages of recovery from cocaine addiction. The program was shaped through an iterative process of treatment delivery and program evaluation, with a goal of developing an empirically supported treatment that is responsive to the unique needs of treatment-seeking cocaine addicts seen in clinics. Much of the material included in the program was developed through thorough behavioral analyses of the problems experienced by these clients as they moved through a period of abstinence from cocaine. Developers of these materials also have translated concepts that originated in theoretical models into the language and frame of reference of cocaine addicts. An example of this is found in the description of the stages clients go through in the recovery process. Rather than using more abstract, theoretical terms, as are found in other models of stages of change (e.g., DiClemente & Prochaska, 1998), the phases of recovery in the Matrix model are much more descriptive of clients' experiences. The five stages of recovery, each tied to the time since the individual last used cocaine, are (a) Withdrawal, (b) Honeymoon, (c) The Wall, (d) Adjustment, and (e) Resolution. Furthermore, the model also lists the behavioral, emotional, cognitive, and relationship issues or problems clients can expect in each of these five stages. The Wall is the stage in which clients are thought to be most vulnerable to relapse. Examples of the issues they encounter in each of these domains include the following: (a) behavioral—sluggishness/ lack of energy, insomnia, discontinuing treatment, resumed use of alcohol and marijuana; (b) emotional—depression, anxiety, boredom, irritability; (c) cognitive—euphoric recall of cocaine use, increased frequency of cocaine-related thoughts and craving, cognitive rehearsal of relapse; and (d) relationship—mutual blaming, irritability, devaluation of progress, threatened separation. These materials have been collated into a structured treatment manual that guides each session.

Clients begin attending the weekly 90-minute relapse prevention group in the second month of this 6-month program, after stabilization. Rawson et al. (1995) described this group as a central component of the Matrix treatment package. The group is co-led by a professional counselor and a recovering addict. The recovering cotherapist provides a positive role model for clients and is able to share information about what he or she did to prevent or manage relapse during his or her course of recovery. Group sessions follow a specific format and address a set of problems previously identified by addicts in treatment. The group addresses topics such as dealing with cocaine dreams, identifying warning signs of potential relapse in one's thinking and behavior, keeping distant from relapse, sexual readjustment, guilt and shame, disinhibiting drugs and alcohol, and relapse justification. A set of 40 relapse prevention exercises has been developed and adapted to use with cocaine abusers (Rawson et al., 1995). The group provides a setting in which clients can share information on precipitants of past relapses, relapse prevention techniques they have successfully used, and identifying and anticipating warning signs of impending relapse.

Another important component in the relapse prevention process is the *relapse analysis*. This analysis is conducted with the client's therapist in an individual session immediately after a slip or relapse has occurred. The first step in this session is to let the client talk in his or her own terms about the relapse and what went into it. Next, a structured exercise is used to guide the client and therapist in a systematic review of the cognitive, behavioral, and environmental factors that led up to the slip and the reaction of the client and individuals in his or her support network after the slip. To remove the fear and mystique of relapse, the client is encouraged to view the slip as a part of a larger process rather than an isolated event; to acknowledge his feelings about him- or herself and the relapse itself; and to reframe the self-depre-cating, negative, personalized attributions associated with the abstinence violation effect. The main goal of this process is to help prevent relapse from occurring in the future and to allow the development of a workable plan for continued progress toward becoming drug free. After analyzing the relapse, the client and therapist discuss changes that may be needed in the treatment plan to restabilize the client's status and situation and to prevent a recurrence of such a relapse.

OUTCOME EVALUATION OF RELAPSE PREVENTION APPROACHES

An important aspect of the development of relapse prevention is that attempts have been made to test the efficacy or effectiveness of this approach. Rawson et al. (1995) examined the effectiveness of the Matrix model across three levels of evaluation during the development and refinement of the intervention. An initial pilot study followed cocaine abusers who had self-se-lected either no formal treatment, 28-day inpatient treatment, or outpatient treatment in the Matrix model. The results suggested that few of the no-treatment participants actually engaged in self-help groups, and few sought formal treatment after their initial evaluation. Those in the outpatient Ma-trix treatment attended an average of 21.6 out of a possible 26 weeks; they also reported significantly lower rates of cocaine use than participants in the other two conditions.

An open trial of the Matrix outpatient treatment was conducted next to evaluate whether outcomes were related to differences in client charac-teristics. The participants were clients enrolled in two different sites of the Matrix Center; these sites differed significantly on a number of demographic variables, such as education, income, and socioeconomic status. Although participants at both sites had comparable outcomes with respect to self-report or urinalysis results of drug use (88% were negative on these measures), there were substantial differences in treatment retention. Nearly half of the participants (48%) at the more socially advantaged site completed the 6-month treatment, compared with only 22% at the other site. Overall, the mean length of participation, averaged across the two clinic sites, was 18.2 weeks of the scheduled 24-week program. The average length of time in treatment at the more advantaged site was over 5 months (21 weeks), whereas that of the less advantaged site averaged just over 3 months (13.2 weeks). Most notable is that there was considerably greater attrition in the first 2 weeks of treatment among participants at the less socially advantaged site (20% vs. 8%). The results again suggested that most individuals appear to engage in this type of treatment and achieve relatively good outcomes, but differences may occur when dealing with particular subgroups of clients. Such differences may require adaptations of the intervention to accommodate the needs of specific subgroups of clients.

The next level in the evaluation of the Matrix model involved a randomized clinical trial in which clients were assigned to either the Matrix outpatient intervention or referred to available substance abuse treatments in the community. Those assigned to the latter condition were provided with a detailed overview of the publicly and privately funded inpatient and outpatient treatment programs in their geographic area. They were given a referral appointment time to receive an evaluation at one of the programs in their community. Forty percent of those referred to community resources became involved in some form of formal inpatient or outpatient treatment. Both groups demonstrated marked, statistically significant reductions in drug use (based on urinalysis and self-report), psychosocial functioning as assessed by the Addiction Severity Index (McLellan et al., 1992), and depression. The two groups did not differ from one another on these measures. However, participants in the Matrix program rated their treatment as significantly more helpful than those who received treatment in the community. Furthermore, a significant relationship was found between the amount of treatment received and the number of cocaine negative urinalysis results for the Matrix participants, whereas no such relationship was found for participants in the community programs.

The results from this series of evaluations of the Matrix model are informative. They provide evidence that clients are able to engage and be retained in outpatient treatment of cocaine dependence and that rates of retention and time in treatment vary based on the characteristics of the population. Outcomes were best among individuals who completed the entire treatment, but even among those who did not complete it a greater length of time in the Matrix model treatment was associated with better outcomes. However, when considering some drug-related and psychosocial outcomes, individuals in community-based treatments may fare as well as those in the

Matrix model. These results parallel the findings of recent reviews of controlled clinical trials of relapse prevention interventions across a number of different addictive behaviors (Carroll, 1996; Irvin, Bowers, Dunn, & Wang, 1999). Although relapse prevention is clearly more effective than no treatment, this relative superiority is less distinct when compared against discussion groups or other types of active therapies.

WHAT GOES AROUND COMES AROUND: FROM PRACTICE BACK TO RESEARCH

Although clinicians have embraced relapse prevention as a general therapeutic orientation and as an important component to be integrated into more comprehensive programs, the findings from evaluations such as the ones conducted by Rawson et al. (1995) and those reviewed by Carroll (1996) suggest that there is room for continued improvement of this approach. Just as Rawson et al. (1995) used the results from each stage of the evaluation process to modify and refine the Matrix intervention, so too should the equivocal results from clinical trials spur researchers to look more carefully at the theoretical model and its components to determine whether modifications and refinements also need to be made in the model itself.

An example of this process is the recent series of investigations funded by the National Institute on Alcohol Abuse and Alcoholism to determine the reliability and validity of Marlatt's original taxonomy of high-risk situations (see the special supplement issue of the journal *Addiction*, 1996, on the Relapse Precipitants Replication Project [Lowman, Allen, & Miller, 1996]). The construct of high-risk situations has served as an important heuristic framework that has had a tremendous influence in substance abuse treatment. The assumption underlying the relapse taxonomy, as originally developed, is that it adequately and reliably captures the interpersonal and intrapersonal situations that precipitate relapse. However, the results of studies included in this multisite project have challenged this assumption.

As an example, some situations may have been classified as the most important factor in a relapse (e.g., a negative emotional state such as depression) as the result of a number of methodological decisions that prevented "craving" from being rated as the most proximal factor (Longabaugh, Rubin, Stout, Zywiak, & Lowman, 1996). A number of researchers have suggested that because of these methodological issues Marlatt's model underestimates the role of craving in relapse (Heather, 1989). Similarly, in contrast to what is often suggested to clients in treatment, the most recent lapse, about which clients are asked, appears to not be predictive of situations in which a subsequent lapse might occur (Maisto, Connors, & Zywiak, 1996). From a clinical perspective, it is clear that there are multiple factors that contribute to relapse, and these factors are likely to interact differently with respect to their timing and sequencing across different situations for the same person or across different individuals. However, Marlatt's original relapse taxonomy allowed only one factor—the most proximal—to be considered as the high-risk relapse precipitant (Maisto et al., 1996). The work on replicating and validating the relapse taxonomy is an important step in the clinical ap-plication–clinical research interaction and iteration process. A number of other aspects of Marlatt's model also are open to further exploration. One area in need of further evaluation, from both a theoretical and a practical perspective, is the abstinence violation effect (Hodgins, el-Guebaly, & Armstrong, 1995). Another area to be further explored is the appropriate assessment model to capture the stages of development in the progression toward relapse (Donovan, 1996b). There is also the need to continue work-ing toward the development of assessment instruments that are valid and fit within the context and constraints of clinical practice. It is of interest to see that there has been recent work to evaluate a measure of Gorski's "warning signs." Although these warning signs are discussed extensively in Gorski's writing (Gorski & Miller, 1986), and counselors have used the concept of the warning signs extensively in their work, until recently there had been no evaluation of the utility or validity this construct. However, Miller and Harris (2000) looked at a questionnaire consisting of these signs: The Assess-ment of Warning-Signs of Relapse (AWARE) Scale has been found to have excellent internal consistency and to predict subsequent slips and relapses. The general area of assessment is apparently yet another one in which bidi-rectional movement between research and practice has occurred with regard to relapse prevention approaches.

CONCLUSION

Relapse prevention is an approach that has evolved through continued interaction between researchers and practitioners in their attempts to under-stand, prevent, and intervene in the relapse process. Rawson et al. (1993b) suggested that the development and refinement of this model "was the major nonpharmacological substance abuse treatment advancement of the 1980s" (p. 93). Its popularity and wide use are due in large part to its flexibility, applicability, and its capability of being used effectively across a wide range of addictive behaviors and populations. The interventions and techniques subsumed under the umbrella of relapse prevention make practical sense to clinicians and clients alike. It addresses one of the main features of substance abuse and in so doing provides a sense of hope to recovering clients that they in fact can exert control over the likelihood of relapse by better under-standing the precipitants or situations that put them at risk; by developing coping skills that allow them to avoid, escape, or deal effectively with these situations; and by providing a frame of reference that suggests that they can minimize the harm associated with relapse if it does occur. As Marlatt (1996) noted in reflecting on the development of the relapse model and the results of the studies that attempted to replicate his original taxonomy,

> The "good news" about research findings on relapse precipitants is that the assessment of a patient's high-risk situations for relapse gives both the patient and the therapist a "handle" on how to cope with relapse risks or actual relapses. Rather than viewing relapse as an indicator of treatment failure (or as a reason for discharging alcoholics from treatment), it can be dealt with in a pragmatic manner as an error, a lapse, a slip or temporary setback, and not an inevitable collapse on the road to recovery. (p. S47)

Clearly relapse prevention has moved well beyond its humble research origins, and yet further work remains. Rawson et al. (1993b) indicated that continued empirical testing of these techniques and models, and the interaction between clinicians and researchers, is essential to the further development, refinement, and effectiveness of this approach.

REFERENCES

Allen, J. P., Lowman, C., & Miller, W. R. (1996). Perspectives on precipitants of relapse. *Addiction, 91*(Suppl.), 3–4.

Carroll, K. M. (1996). Relapse prevention as a psychosocial treatment: A review of controlled clinical trials. *Experimental and Clinical Psychopharmacology, 4,* 46–54.

Carroll, K. M., Rounsaville, B. J., & Keller, D. S. (1991). Relapse prevention strategies for the treatment of cocaine abuse. *American Journal of Drug and Alcohol Abuse, 17,* 249–265.

Connors, G. J., Maisto, S. A., & Donovan, D. M. (1996). Conceptualizations of relapse: A summary of psychological and psychobiological models. *Addiction, 91*(Suppl.), 5–13.

Cummings, C., Gordon, J. R., & Marlatt, G. A. (1980). Relapse: Strategies of prevention and prediction. In W. R. Miller (Ed.), *The addictive behaviors* (pp. 291–321). Elmsford, NY: Pergamon Press.

Daley, D. C. (1986). *Relapse prevention workbook for recovering alcoholics and drug dependent persons.* Holmes Beach, FL: Learning Publications.

Daley, D. C. (1988). *Relapse prevention: Treatment alternatives and counseling aids.* Bradenton, FL: Human Services Press.

Daley, D. C. (1989a). Five perspectives on relapse in chemical dependency. *Journal of Chemical Dependency Treatment, 2,* 3–26.

Daley, D. C. (1989b). *Relapse: Conceptual, research and clinical perspectives.* New York: Haworth.

Daley, D. C., & Marlatt, G. A. (1992). Relapse prevention: Cognitive and behavioral interventions. In J. H. Lowinson, P. Ruiz, R. B. Millman, & J. G. Langrod (Eds.), *Substance abuse: A comprehensive textbook* (pp. 533–542). Baltimore: Williams & Wilkins.

Daley, D. C., & Marlatt, G. A. (1997). Relapse prevention. In J. H. Lowinson, P. Ruiz, R. B. Millman, & J. G. Langrod (Eds.), *Substance abuse: A comprehensive textbook* (pp. 458–467). Baltimore: Williams & Wilkins.

Daley, D. C., & Salloum, I. (1999). Relapse prevention. In P. J. Ott, R. E. Tarter, & R. T. Ammerman (Eds.), *Sourcebook on substance abuse: Etiology, epidemiology, assessment, and treatment* (pp. 255–263). Boston: Allyn & Bacon.

DiClemente, C. C., & Prochaska, J. O. (1998). Toward a comprehensive, transtheoretical model of change: Stages of change and addictive behaviors. In W. R. Miller & N. Heather (Eds.), *Treating addictive behaviors* (pp. 3–24). New York: Plenum.

Donovan, D. M. (1988). Assessment of addictive behaviors: Implications of an emerging biopsychosocial model. In D. M. Donovan & G. A. Marlatt (Eds.), *Assessment of addictive behaviors* (pp. 3–48). New York: Guilford Press.

Donovan, D. M. (1996a). Assessment issues and domains in the prediction of relapse. *Addiction, 91*(Suppl. 12), S29–S36.

Donovan, D. M. (1996b). Marlatt's classification of relapse precipitants: Is the emperor still wearing clothes? *Addiction, 91*(Suppl.), S131–S137.

Donovan, D. M. (1998). Assessment and interviewing strategies in addictive behaviors. In B. S. McCrady & E. E. Epstein (Eds.), *Addictions: A comprehensive guidebook for practitioners* (pp. 187–215). New York: Oxford University Press.

Donovan, D. M., & Chaney, E. F. (1985). Alcoholic relapse prevention and intervention: Models and methods. In G. A. Marlatt & J. R. Gordon (Eds.), *Relapse prevention: Maintenance strategies in the treatment of addictive behaviors* (pp. 351–416). New York: Guilford Press.

el-Guebaly, N., & Hodgins, D. (1998). Substance-related cravings and relapses: Clinical implications. *Canadian Journal of Psychiatry, 43,* 29–36.

Gorski, T. T. (1986). Relapse prevention planning: A new recovery tool. *Alcohol Health and Research World, 11,* 6–11, 63.

Gorski, T. T. (2000). CENAPS model of relapse prevention therapy (CMRPT). In J. J. Boren, L. S. Onken, & K. M. Carroll (Eds.), *Approaches to drug abuse counseling* (pp. 21–34). Bethesda, MD: National Institute on Drug Abuse.

Gorski, T. T., & Miller, M. (1979). *Counseling for relapse prevention.* Hazel Crest, IL: Alcoholism Systems Associates.

Gorski, T. T., & Miller, M. (1986). *Staying sober: A guide for relapse prevention.* Independence, MO: Independence Press.

Heather, N. (1989). Does the Marlatt model underestimate the importance of conditioned craving in the relapse process? In M. Gossop (Ed.), *Relapse and addictive behaviour* (pp. 180–208). New York: Tavistock/Routledge.

Hodgins, D., el-Guebaly, N., & Armstrong, S. (1995). Prospective and retrospective reports of mood states before relapse to substance use. *Journal of Consulting and Clinical Psychology, 63,* 400–407.

Hunt, W., Barnett, L., & Branch, L. (1972). Relapse rates in addiction programs. *Journal of Clinical Psychology, 27*, 455–456.

Irvin, J. E., Bowers, C. A., Dunn, M. E., & Wang, M. C. (1999). Efficacy of relapse prevention: A meta-analytic review. *Journal of Consulting and Clinical Psychology, 67*, 563–570.

Longabaugh, R., Rubin, A., Stout, R. L., Zywiak, W. H., & Lowman, C. (1996). The reliability of Marlatt's taxonomy for classifying relapses. *Addiction, 91*(Suppl.), S73–S88.

Lowman, C., Allen, J. P., & Miller, W. R. (Eds.). (1996). Perspectives on precipitants of relapse. *Addiction, 91*(Suppl.).

Maisto, S. A., Connors, G. J., & Zywiak, W. H. (1996). Construct validation analyses on the Marlatt typology of relapse precipitants. *Addiction, 91*(Suppl.), S89–S97.

Marlatt, G. A. (1978). Craving for alcohol, loss of control, and relapse: A cognitive–behavioral analysis. In P. E. Nathan, G. A. Marlatt, & T. Loberg (Eds.), *Alcoholism: New directions in research and treatment* (pp. 271–314). New York: Plenum.

Marlatt, G. A. (1996). Taxonomy of high-risk situations for alcohol relapse: Evolution and development of a cognitive–behavioral model. *Addiction, 91*(Suppl.), S37–S49.

Marlatt, G. A., Barrett, K., & Daley, D. C. (1999). Relapse prevention. In M. Galanter & H. D. Kleber (Eds.), *Textbook of substance abuse treatment* (pp. 353–366). Washington, DC: American Psychiatric Press.

Marlatt, G. A., & George, W. H. (1984). Relapse prevention: Introduction and overview of the model. *British Journal of Addictions, 79*, 261–273.

Marlatt, G. A., & Gordon, J. R. (Eds.). (1985). *Relapse prevention: Maintenance strategies in the treatment of addictive behaviors.* New York: Guilford Press.

McLellan, A. T., Alterman, A. I., Metzger, D. S., Grissom, G. R., Woody, G. E., Luborsky, L., et al. (1994). Similarity of outcome predictors across opiate, cocaine, and alcohol treatments: Role of treatment services. *Journal of Consulting and Clinical Psychology, 62*, 1141–1158.

McLellan, A. T., Kushner, H., Metzger, D., Peters, R., Smith, I., Grissom, G., et al. (1992). The fifth edition of the Addiction Severity Index. *Journal of Substance Abuse Treatment, 9*, 199–213.

McLellan, A. T., Lewis, D. C., O'Brien, C. P., & Kleber, H. D. (2000). Drug dependence, a chronic medical illness: Implications for treatment, insurance, and outcomes evaluation. *Journal of the American Medical Association, 284*, 1689–1695.

Miller, W. R., & Harris, R. J. (2000). Simple scale of Gorski's warning signs for relapse. *Journal of Studies on Alcohol, 61*, 759–765.

Monti, P. M., Abrams, D. B., Kadden, R. M., & Cooney, N. L. (1989). *Treating alcohol dependence: A coping skills training guide.* New York: Guilford Press.

O'Farrell, T. J., Choquette, K. A., & Cutter, H. S. G. (1998). Couples relapse prevention sessions after behavioral marital therapy for male alcoholics: Outcomes during the three years after starting treatment. *Journal of Studies on Alcohol, 59*, 357–370.

O'Malley, S. S., O'Connor, P. G., Farren, C., & Rounsaville, B. J. (1998). Comparison of naltrexone in combination with either CB therapy or medical model counseling. *Journal of Addictive Diseases, 17*, 160.

Rawson, R. A., Obert, J. L., McCann, M. J., & Ling, W. (1991). Psychological approaches for the treatment of cocaine dependence—A neurobehavioral approach. *Journal of Addictive Disease, 11*, 97–119.

Rawson, R. A., Obert, J. L., McCann, M. J., & Ling, W. (1993). *Neurobehavioral treatment for cocaine dependency: A preliminary evaluation* (NIDA Research Monograph 135, pp. 92–115). Rockville, MD: National Institute on Drug Abuse.

Rawson, R. A., Obert, J. L., McCann, M. J., & Marinelli-Casey, P. (1993a). Relapse prevention models for substance abuse treatment. *Psychotherapy, 30*, 284–298.

Rawson, R. A., Obert, J. L., McCann, M. J., & Marinelli-Casey, P. (1993b). Relapse prevention strategies in outpatient substance abuse treatment. *Psychology of Addictive Behaviors, 7*, 85–95.

Rawson, R. A., Obert, J. L., McCann, M. J., Smith, D. P., & Ling, W. (1990). Neurobehavioral treatment for cocaine dependency. *Journal of Psychoactive Drugs, 22*, 159–171.

Rawson, R. A., Shoptaw, S. J., Obert, J. L., McCann, M. J., Hasson, A. L., Marinelli-Casey, P., et al. (1995). An intensive outpatient approach for cocaine abuse treatment: The Matrix model. *Journal of Substance Abuse Treatment, 12*, 117–127.

Schmitz, J. M., Stotts, A. L., Rhoades, H. M., & Grabowski, J. (2001). Naltrexone and relapse prevention treatment for cocaine-dependent patients. *Addictive Behaviors, 26*, 167–180.

Sorensen, J. L., & Midkiff, E. E. (2000). Bridging the gap between research and drug abuse treatment. *Journal of Psychoactive Drugs, 32*, 379–382.

9

MOTIVATIONAL INTERVIEWING

THERESA MOYERS

This chapter focuses on introducing readers to an evidence-based method of substance abuse treatment: motivational interviewing (MI). Theoretical assumptions of MI are discussed, as is current research indicating how it can be useful with drug and alcohol abusers, including evidence of limitations in applicability. Some obstacles to implementing MI within current treatment systems also are investigated.

UNDERLYING ASSUMPTIONS OF MI

Miller and Rollnick (2002) defined MI as a "person-centered, directive, method of communication for enhancing intrinsic motivation to change by exploring and resolving ambivalence" (p. 25). Several important assumptions underlie this definition. First, the method borrows heavily from client-centered therapy (Rogers, 1957), particularly in the emphasis placed on accurate empathy as a critical ingredient for successful therapy. Indeed, Rollnick and Miller (1995) stressed that the style or spirit of MI is more important in defining it than are the specific techniques. A genuine, egalitarian, and empathic therapeutic style is indispensable. Unlike a strictly

Rogerian approach, however, therapists using MI are directive—they have specific goals with regard to the client behaviors they wish to influence. MI is typically used in settings where maladaptive client behaviors (e.g., substance abuse or neglect of physical health) clearly indicate the direction of the therapist's efforts, rather than for more diffuse problems for which the desirable outcomes are less obvious.

It is also clear from this definition that the treatment provider's goal is to enlarge the existing motivation within a person rather than attempting to transplant or inject it from an external source. It is presumed that there are usually personal costs to a self-destructive behavior such as addiction, which the skillful interviewer can enlarge to provide momentum for change. Like other methods, however, MI will not convince individuals to change if they are determined to avoid it.

Finally, this definition indicates the theoretical mechanism of action for MI: the resolution of ambivalence that is the stumbling block of the change process (Prochaska & DiClemente, 1986). Specifically, Miller and Rollnick (2002) have emphasized the importance of two critical therapist behaviors: (a) reducing defensiveness and hostility and (b) increasing the frequency and intensity of client speech indicating the possibility of change. Other therapeutic goals, such as insight regarding immature defenses, confronting denial, or practicing behaviors that are inconsistent with drug abuse, are accorded little theoretical importance in this process of resolving ambivalence. The interviewer is permitted to assume that the client is likely to already have the expertise to determine how change should occur and will focus instead on the question of why change should occur. For some clients, of course, further therapeutic assistance will be needed even when ambivalence is no longer a threat to change, but the evidence from brief interventions offers the possibility that such intensive treatment is sometimes superfluous to success (Bien, Miller, & Tonigan, 1993; Heather, 1995; Miller & Wilbourne, 2002).

GOAL OF THERAPISTS' BEHAVIOR WHEN USING MI

The four foundational principles of MI provide a destination for therapist efforts. Each is based on a specific body of literature indicating usefulness in the treatment of addictive behaviors. These four principles can be thought of as the goal or end point of the therapeutic endeavor. These four principles, written in the form of prescriptions for therapists, are (a) Express Empathy, (b) Develop Discrepancy, (c) Roll With Resistance, and (d) Support Self-Efficacy.

Because empathy has consistently been linked with improved outcomes for clients in addictions treatment (Miller, Taylor, & West, 1980; Valle, 1981), it is a specific goal of therapists when using MI. Similarly, evidence indicates that client resistance, in the form of arguing, blaming, confronting, and minimizing, is associated with worse outcome (Miller, Benefield, & Tonigan, 1993); therefore, interviewers take pains to reduce these behaviors during interactions with clients by avoiding arguments, foregoing labels, and explicitly viewing resistance as a normal part of the change process rather than a pathological symptom of addiction. Confrontation is generally inconsistent with an MI approach. Because client self-efficacy is a predictor of outcomes (Burling, Reilly, Moltzen, & Ziff, 1989; Project MATCH Research Group, 1997), therapists purposefully direct the conversation toward client strengths even when failures have been a prominent part of the clients' addiction career. Interviewers will also attempt to enhance the discomfort that comes with a felt sense of discrepancy between what is most important in the person's value system and the self-destructive behavior that is occurring. The client's values are assumed to remain an important source of motivation, despite full-blown and lengthy substance abuse (Wagner & Sanchez, 2002).

HOW IS IT DONE? MOVING TOWARD A DESTINATION

Just as various means of transportation might lead to the same destination when taking a trip, so too might a therapist select any number of strategies to move in the direction of one of the foundational principles. Providers might decide to ask evocative, open-ended questions in a gentle fashion to provoke discrepancy or enhance self-efficacy. Active listening through the use of complex reflections is also a common characteristic of MI and is particularly important to convey empathy. An accepting and optimistic attitude on the part of the treatment provider often translates into affirmations of the client, especially about any strengths that might contribute to a possible behavior change. Careful summaries can be useful in conveying a grasp of important connections among the points the client is making. Another important strategy in using MI well is arranging the conversation in such a way that the client, rather than the therapist, is the one to offer comments about the need for change. This might be accomplished with a review of the pros and cons of the behavior in question; a values clarification exercise; or having clients rate, on an imaginary ruler, the importance they place on change and the confidence they have that they can accomplish it. Providers can also use reflections skillfully to negotiate direction from the verbal stream provided by the client. Here is one example of how this might look:

> *Client:* So I see I need to cut down using cocaine, but it's not as big a deal as everyone seems to think. My husband nags me about it all the time, but it's not like he says.
>
> *Interviewer:* Well, let me ask you this: What are the good things about using cocaine?

Client: What?

Interviewer: I'm curious what's good about it.

Client: You mean like . . . ?

Interviewer: What are the benefits in using it?

Client: (pause) There is nothing like the high I get from a snort.

Interviewer: (making a list) One good thing is the feeling that comes when you're high. Tell me more about that.

Client: Total euphoria. I feel like I can accomplish anything I put my mind to. I'm Superwoman. Nothing bothers me, not even my whiny kids.

Interviewer: A feeling of total power and exhilaration, then.

Client: Yeah, but when I come down I pay for it. It's a real downer, and it lasts forever. Then I just want to get high again, and the whole thing is a vicious cycle. And my kids are still whining.

Interviewer: So in the short run, it's a big payoff, but in the long term the cost is too much.

Client: Yeah, I've been thinking that I should cut it way back.

Interviewer: You might want to change, but you're not sure.

Client: No, I know I need to do something.

Interviewer: You've already thought about changes you might make.

Here the interviewer has chosen not to argue with the client's decision to blame others for the conflict surrounding her use of cocaine. Instead, she asks the client about the benefits of using cocaine, knowing that this is likely to elicit change talk if the client is genuinely ambivalent. She uses reflections and open questions to encourage self-examination, avoiding any confrontation when the client expresses satisfaction with her cocaine use and persisting in her questions about the benefits. When change talk does occur, the interviewer reflects it and encourages the client to think more about the plans she has already considered. The interviewer assumes that internal motivation to change is present and uses the conversation to increase the opportunities for the client to verbalize it. In effect, the interviewer is helping the client talk herself into changing.

STUDIES SUPPORTING THE USE OF MI IN THE TREATMENT OF DRUG ABUSE

Although there is strong evidence to support the use of MI with problem drinkers, both as a stand-alone treatment and as an enrichment to traditional treatment (Bien, Miller, & Boroughs, 1993; Brown & Miller, 1993; Handmaker & Miller, 1999; Heather, Rollnick, Bell, & Richmond, 1996; Project MATCH Research Group, 1998), the evidence for drug abuse treatment is less substantive and can be described as promising but inconclusive. The first study to investigate MI with drug users (Van Bilsen & Van Ernst, 1986) described a methadone treatment program that fostered a humanistic approach incorporating MI. One interesting feature of this study was the decision to allow clients to set treatment goals for themselves as opposed to adhering to a treatment goal of abstinence from heroin. Although this was not intended as a treatment outcome study, the authors reported that the MI was easily accepted by the program's clients. More recently, Saunders, Wilkinson, and Phillips (1995) conducted a randomized clinical trial in which drug users attending a methadone clinic were randomly assigned to either MI or an educational control procedure. Six months later, clients in the MI condition showed a greater likelihood of endorsing complete abstinence as a treatment goal, fewer opiate-related problems, and longer periods of abstinence than participants in the control condition. Booth, Kwiatkowski, Iguchi, Pinto, and John (1998) conducted a randomized, controlled study to investigate the impact of MI with injecting drug users. The goal of investigating the therapeutic utility of MI was somewhat compromised by the study's additional aim of investigating the importance of removing barriers to treatment entry, such as scheduling, transportation, and fees. The MI intervention was compared to a risk reduction approach for the control group, and both groups received the benefit of additional assistance in overcoming concrete treatment barriers. The results indicated no difference between MI and the risk reduction condition in regard to the number of clients who requested treatment; however, there was pronounced favorable effect on treatment entry as a result of removing barriers. Other studies addressing behaviors ancillary to substance use, such as treatment compliance and HIV-risk reduction, have similarly shown encouraging results (Carey et al., 1997; Daley & Zuckoff, 1998; Swanson, Pantalon, & Cohen, 1999).

A carefully controlled and rigorous study conducted by Stephens, Roffman, and Curtin (2000) compared a relatively pure version of motivational enhancement therapy (MI combined with personalized feedback) with a longer and more intensive treatment based on Marlatt and Gordon's (1985) relapse prevention model for participants with marijuana dependence. Stephens et al. found no difference between the brief, motivational intervention (two sessions) and the relapse prevention intervention (14 sessions) in any of the outcome measures. Clients in both conditions substantially reduced their marijuana use. Because of its quality, this study provides strong evidence that MI can be successfully adapted to the treatment of drug abuse with outcomes as favorable as those of longer, more intensive treatment.

A methodologically sound study conducted by Ershoff et al. (1999) investigated the smoking habits of pregnant women who received either a self-help book, the book plus a computerized learning program administered over the telephone, or the book and telephone counseling from nurses using MI methods. There were no differences among the groups in the number of smokers who were completely abstinent from nicotine in the 34th week of pregnancy. Conclusions about the effectiveness of MI are difficult to draw from this study, because it is not clear whether telephone contact is an appropriate format for a therapeutic method that relies so heavily on empathy, egalitarianism, and acceptance. Certainly this study indicates that telephone contact should be viewed with caution as a way of conducting MI.

Schneider, Casey, and Kohn (2000) used MI in a well-controlled study with clients referred for substance abuse counseling in an employee assistance program. Clients referred specifically for drug use (as opposed to alcohol abuse or polysubstance abuse) constituted 19% of the sample; however, outcome analyses did not examine this group independently. On a variety of substance abuse indicators, both the motivational and confrontational groups showed improvement in the follow-up period, indicating equal effectiveness of these two approaches. This study supports the idea that MI is compatible with employee assistance program settings and offers outcomes comparable to those of traditional interventions for voluntary participants with substance abuse problems in the workplace.

A study conducted by Longshore, Grills, and Annon (1999) addressed the issue of whether MI can be adapted to minority consumers of substance abuse treatment. This study was not a direct test of the impact of MI, because the intervention was a blend of several treatment approaches plus innovative elements designed to be congruent with the values of African American clients in this setting. Outcome measures were limited to clients' self-reports of their engagement in the treatment process and self-reports of intent to change; nevertheless, clients in the experimental condition scored more favorably on these measures than did clients in the control condition. At a 1-year follow up (Longshore & Grills, 2000), clients in the experimental condition were less likely than control participants to report current drug use. This study provides some support for the notion that MI can be successfully integrated into blended treatments that are acceptable to African American clients, although the design does not permit conclusions regarding any specific benefit of MI in outcomes. Most recently, two large, randomized controlled trials employing motivational interviewing in the treatment of drug abuse have shown no difference in drug use between clients receiving motivational interviewing and those in control groups (Donovan, Rosengren, Downey, Cox, & Sloan, 2001; Miller, Yahne, & Tonigan, in press). Both trials had sufficient numbers of patients to detect an effect of the method had there been one, and both were carefully implemented, particularly with regard to the fidelity of the motivational intervention. The clinical populations in both studies had multiple psychosocial problems in addition to substance use, including legal and vocational complications. It is possible that motivational interviewing is less likely to be effective when severe bio-psychosocial stressors are present, or that it must be supplemented with other interventions to directly impact drug use in such circumstances.

These studies provide a somewhat mixed picture of the usefulness of MI with drugs of abuse other than alcohol, although the results certainly encourage more empirical investigation. In a comprehensive review of randomized clinical trials of MI, Burke, Arkowitz, and Dunn (2002) directly addressed the disparity between the evidence for MI in addressing alcohol and drug problems. They reviewed separately the available randomized clinical trials for drugs of abuse and found that these studies yielded a much lower cumulative evidence score (–12) compared with alcohol (12). These findings should be viewed as tentative, because interventions for drugs of abuse other than alcohol were grouped with other types of interventions (HIV risk, smoking, and psychiatric treatment). Nevertheless, the current empirical evidence, although it strongly supports the use of MI for alcohol abuse disorders, is equivocal for other drugs of abuse.

DISSEMINATION OF MI: INDIVIDUAL AND SYSTEMIC COMPLEXITIES

Very little research to date has investigated the dissemination of MI, although several empirical studies are in progress. Miller and Mount (2001) investigated the use of a 2-day workshop in teaching MI to probation and community corrections officers, using paper-and-pencil tests as well as audiotaped work samples to evaluate the effectiveness of the training. It is interesting that on self-report measures the probation officers reported substantial increases in their understanding of MI and proficiency in using it. Paper-and-pencil measures of MI skills also yielded optimistic results, because most participants also showed increases in key skills (e.g., the number of reflections used to respond to client resistance statements). However, an examination of posttraining audiotaped work samples indicated only a modest increase in behaviors consistent with MI. Furthermore, behaviors contrary to the goals of MI (e.g., confrontation, warning) showed no decrease at all. When client outcomes were examined, no effect of training was apparent. Miller and Mount concluded that a one-shot training workshop is unlikely to influence practitioner behavior to the extent that client outcomes are affected. They further pointed out the hazards in accepting providers' self-reports as a reliable indicator of skill acquisition in this method. Finally, they pointed out that the successful acquisition of MI may depend on learning what *not* to do.

Another concern in disseminating MI involves the beliefs and theoretical orientations of potential users. Providers who are attempting to use MI for substance abuse clients may struggle with a variety of concerns, depending on their theoretical orientation and conceptualization of substance use (Moyers & Yahne, 1998). When providers have been trained to use confrontation as a therapeutic technique, it can be difficult to change to a clinical style that specifically disallows direct disagreement in favor of less forceful methods. Providers may experience some loss of authenticity when attempting this style, if confrontation has been an important part of their theoretical approach.

It is also not unusual for a clinician to feel a sense of distress about an open discussion of a client's goal, which may include no change at all. Motivational interviewers are explicitly encouraged to ask about the benefits of not changing, and this can seem dangerous to providers who assume that clients will view this as permission to continue a maladaptive behavior. The notion that clients are free to choose not to change may seem untenable, especially if providers have been successful using persuasion or even outright coercion with clients in the past. This balance between investment in and detachment from client outcomes may seem frustrating for providers who are very committed to a specific goal, such as entry into a treatment program.

The dilemma of balancing client choice and external accountability is especially acute when clients have entered the treatment setting as a result of pressure from the criminal justice system. Here, the use of MI can present a challenge, especially when every decision about the client's treatment has already been mandated by the legal system. To the extent that clinicians have less flexibility in their clinical approach because of external mandates, the use of MI will become more challenging and perhaps impossible. Client choice and clinician flexibility are essential for the proper use of this method. This is not to say that MI cannot be effective with coerced clients, for the outcome data indicate modest positive outcomes for MI in this population (Ginsburg, Mann, Rotgers, & Weekes, 2002). Talented providers can, and should, compensate by swiftly moving the clinical focus to the areas where the client does have choices. In such circumstances there is some indication that clients who are angry and resistant at the onset of treatment (as coerced clients surely often are) may benefit especially well from the use of MI (Project MATCH Research Group, 2001).

Another concern in implementing MI within a larger system is related to the question of who should receive it and what the proper dose is (e.g., how long should it go on). It is clear that not all clients require MI, because not all clients are reluctant to change. It is even the case that for the same client some topics are appropriate targets for MI (e.g., the client has not decided to abstain from heroin), whereas others are not (e.g., the client has already decided to use a clean needle for every injection). How does the provider decide which clients should receive MI and how much MI to try?

The most efficient strategy is to use MI only when client ambivalence or reluctance is probable. In settings where clients are highly likely to be angry or ambivalent, MI might make sense as an initial strategy for all clients. In other settings, ambivalence may be less problematic, and MI might be used on an as-needed basis. In some situations—for example, follow-up meetings with clients who have sustained abstinence for some period of time—MI is unlikely to be needed, at least for the initial target behavior. Finally, it is unlikely that one session of MI will completely and efficiently resolve all of a client's ambivalence about changing addictive behavior. Rather, the clinician must view MI as a tool to use when ambivalence is present, probably episodically throughout the course of treatment. Empirical evidence supports the use of two to four sessions of MI, either by itself or as a prelude to more traditional programs (Bien et al., 1995; Brown & Miller, 1993; Project MATCH Research Group, 1998). In general, MI does not proceed beyond five sessions or so without some client movement toward change. At some point, the gentle investigation of ambivalence to change becomes in itself coercive if the client is genuinely content with the status quo. Interviewers may choose to honor the client's decision, while expressing concern and inviting the client to return if his or her circumstances change.

A final barrier in implementing MI in larger systems is the issue of time investment. Providers may feel they do not have the time to ponder with clients, to explore values deeply, or to practice careful strategies for deflecting client resistance. This urgency is multiplied when systems mandate that lengthy assessments must be completed within the first visit or two. Providers complain that they cannot simultaneously be responsible for information gathering and for motivating clients, and they are correct. Again, using MI well requires that the clinician have some ability to exercise judgment about when assessments are completed and how best to respond to hostility or ambivalence, especially during the first few visits. If the provider truly has no discretion in this regard (e.g., the rule is ironclad), then the best to hope for is a "motivationally informed" assessment. However, treatment systems can and should make allowances for individualizing treatment, including the assessment, provided that (a) a minimum amount of critical information is gathered promptly and (b) the clinical indicators for delaying are documented. Where this approach is possible, more useful results from MI are likely. An added benefit may be that the rate of client dropout and uncompleted assessments will decline when MI is used before assessment.

CONCLUSION

MI is an empirically validated treatment for substance abuse. Many of the theoretical assumptions underlying MI may contradict or challenge the current conceptual models for drug treatment in the United States. It is likely that some providers will accept such underlying problems without difficulty, whereas others may struggle to implement this method. Although there is strong evidence to support the effectiveness of MI with alcohol abusers, there is a scarcity of research to indicate its usefulness with drug users, and more research is needed in this area.

REFERENCES

Bien, T. H., Miller, W. R., & Boroughs, J. M. (1993). Motivational interviewing with alcohol outpatients. *Behavioural and Cognitive Psychotherapy, 21*, 347–356.

Bien, T. H., Miller, W. R., & Tonigan, J. S. (1993). Brief interventions for alcohol problems: A review. *Addiction, 88*, 315–336.

Booth, R. E., Kwiatkowski, C., Iguchi, M. Y., Pinto, F., & John, D. (1998). Facilitating treatment entry among out-of-treatment injection drug users. *Public Health Reports, 113*(Suppl. 1), 116–128.

Brown, J. M., & Miller, W. R. (1993). Impact of motivational interviewing on participation and outcome in residential alcoholism treatment. *Psychology of Addictive Behaviors, 7*, 211–218.

Burke, B. L., Arkowitz, H., & Dunn, C. (2002). The efficacy of motivational interviewing and its adaptations: What we know so far. In W. R. Miller & S. Rollnick (Eds.), *Motivational interviewing: Preparing people for change* (2nd ed., pp. 217–250). New York: Guilford Press.

Burling, T. A., Reilly, P. M., Moltzen, J. O., & Ziff, D. C. (1989). Self-efficacy and relapse among inpatient drug and alcohol abusers: A predictor of outcome. *Journal of Studies on Alcohol, 50*, 354–360.

Carey, M. P., Maisto, S. A., Kalichman, S. C., Forsythe, A. D., Wright, E. M., & Johnson, B. T. (1997). Enhancing motivation to reduce the risk of HIV infection for economically disadvantaged urban women. *Journal of Consulting and Clinical Psychology, 65*, 531–541.

Daley, D. C., & Zuckoff, A. (1998). Improving compliance with the initial outpatient session among discharged inpatient dual diagnosis clients. *Social Work, 43*, 470–473.

Donovan, D. M., Rosengren, D. B., Downey, L., Cox, G. B., & Sloan, K. L. (2001). Attrition prevention with individuals awaiting publicly funded drug treatment. *Addiction, 96*(8), 1149–1160.

Ershoff, D. H., Quinn, V. P., Boyd, N. R., Stern, J., Gregory, M., & Wirtschafter, D. (1999). The Kaiser Permanente prenatal smoking-cessation trial: When more isn't better, what is enough? *American Journal of Preventive Medicine, 17*, 161–168.

Ginsburg, J. I. D., Mann, R. E., Rotgers, F., & Weekes, J. R. (2002). Motivational interviewing with criminal justice populations. In W. R. Miller & S. Rollnick (Eds.), *Motivational interviewing: Preparing people to change* (pp. 333–346). New York: Guilford Press.

Handmaker, N., & Miller, W. R. (1999). Findings of a pilot study of motivational interviewing with pregnant drinkers. *Journal of Studies on Alcohol, 60*, 285–287.

Heather, N. (1995). Brief intervention strategies. In W. R. Miller & R. Hester (Eds.),

Handbook of alcoholism treatment approaches: Effective alternatives (pp. 105–122). Boston: Allyn & Bacon.

Heather, N., Rollnick, S., Bell, A., & Richmond, R. (1996). Effects of brief counseling among male heavy drinkers identified on general hospital wards. *Drug and Alcohol Review, 15,* 29–38.

Longshore, D., & Grills, C. (2000). Motivating illegal drug use recovery: Evidence for a culturally congruent intervention. *Journal of Black Psychology, 26,* 288–301.

Longshore, D., Grills, C., & Annon, K. (1999). Effects of a culturally congruent intervention on cognitive factors related to drug use recovery. *Substance Use and Misuse, 34,* 1223–1241.

Marlatt, G. A., & Gordon, J. R. (1985). *Relapse prevention: Maintenance strategies in the treatment of addictive behaviors.* New York: Guilford Press.

Miller, W. R., Benefield, R. G., & Tonigan, J. S. (1993). Enhancing motivation for change in problem drinking: A controlled comparison of two therapist styles. *Journal of Consulting and Clinical Psychology, 61,* 455–461.

Miller, W. R., & Mount, K. A. (2001). A small study of training in motivational interviewing: Does one workshop change clinician and client behavior? *Behavioural and Cognitive Psychotherapy, 29,* 457–471.

Miller, W. R., & Rollnick, S. (2002). *Motivational interviewing: Preparing people to change* (2nd ed.). New York: Guilford Press.

Miller, W. R., Taylor, C. A., & West, J. C. (1980). Focused versus broad-spectrum behavior therapy for problem drinking. *Journal of Consulting and Clinical Psychology, 48,* 590–601.

Miller, W. R., & Wilbourne, P. L. (2002). Mesa Grande: A methodological analysis of clinical trials of treatments for alcohol use disorders. *Addiction, 97,* 265–277.

Miller, W. R., Yahne, C. E., & Tonigan, J. S. (in press). Motivational interviewing in drug abuse services: A randomized clinical trial. *Journal of Consulting and Clinical Psychology.*

Moyers, T. B., & Yahne, C. E. (1998). Motivational interviewing in substance abuse treatment: Negotiating roadblocks. *Journal of Substance Misuse, 3,* 30–33.

Prochaska, J. O., & DiClemente, C. C. (1986). Toward a comprehensive model of change. In W. R. Miller & N. Heather (Eds.), *Treating addictive behavior: Processes of change* (pp. 3–27). New York: Plenum.

Project MATCH Research Group. (1997). Project MATCH secondary a priori hypotheses. *Addiction, 92,* 1671–1698.

Project MATCH Research Group. (1998). Matching alcoholism treatments to client heterogeneity: Project MATCH three-year drinking outcomes. *Alcoholism: Clinical and Experimental Research, 22,* 1300–1311.

Project MATCH Research Group. (2001). *Project MATCH hypotheses: Results and causal chain analyses* (Monograph No. 8, NIH No. 01-4238). Bethesda, MD: National Institute on Alcohol Abuse and Alcoholism.

Rogers, C. (1957). The necessary and sufficient conditions for therapeutic personality change. *Journal of Consulting Psychology, 21,* 95–103.

Rollnick, S., & Miller, W. R. (1995). What is motivational interviewing? *Behavioural and Cognitive Psychotherapy, 23,* 325–334.

Saunders, B., Wilkinson, C., & Phillips, M. (1995). The impact of a brief motivational intervention with opiate users attending a methadone program. *Addiction, 90,* 415–424.

Schneider, R. J., Casey, J., & Kohn, R. (2000). Motivational versus confrontational interviewing: A comparison of substance abuse assessment practices at employee assistance programs. *Journal of Behavioral Health Services and Research, 27,* 60–74.

Stephens, R. S., Roffman, R. A., & Curtin, L. (2000). Comparison of extended versus brief treatments for marijuana use. *Journal of Consulting and Clinical Psychology, 68,* 898–908.

Swanson, A. J., Pantalon, M. V., & Cohen, K. R. (1999). Motivational interviewing and treatment adherence among psychiatric and dually-diagnosed patients. *Journal of Nervous and Mental Disease, 187,* 630–635.

Valle, S. K. (1981). Interpersonal functioning of alcoholism counselors and treatment outcome. *Journal of Studies on Alcohol, 42,* 783–790.

Van Bilsen, H. P., & Van Ernst, A. J. (1986). Heroin addiction and motivational milieu therapy. *International Journal of the Addictions, 21,* 707–713.

Wagner, C. C., & Sanchez, F. P. (2002). The role of values in motivational interviewing. In W. R. Miller & S. Rollnick (Eds.), *Motivational interviewing: Preparing people to change* (pp. 284–298). New York: Guilford Press.

Waldron, H. B., Miller, W. R., & Tonigan, J. S. (2001). Client anger as a predictor of differential response to treatment. In Project MATCH hypotheses: Results and causal chain analyses (Monograph No. 8, NIH No. 01-4238, pp. 134–148). Bethesda, MD: National Institute on Alcohol Abuse and Alcoholism.

III

COLLABORATION

INTRODUCTION: COLLABORATION

RICHARD A. RAWSON

In this part of the book, A. Thomas McLellan (chapter 10) and Deni Carise and Özge Gûrel (chapter 11) describe the need for data to address clinical and policy needs. The next two chapters (chapter 12 by Dennis McCarty and chapter 13 by Alice A. Gleghorn and Frances Cotter) frame the evolution of practice research collaboration in the field of substance abuse treatment, from older demonstration models to the current National Institute on Drug Abuse (NIDA) Clinical Trials Network (CTN) and Center for Substance Abuse Treatment (CSAT) Practice Improvement Collaboratives (PICs).

McLellan (chapter 10) is a leading substance abuse researcher with consummate sensitivity to practice issues, and he expands the discussion of data needs to the evaluation needs of every clinic. He defines the range of outcomes of substance abuse treatment to include reductions in substance abuse, improvements in health and social functioning, and reductions in threats to public health and safety. He delineates four approaches to assessing outcomes, ranging from traditional clinical tracking to more recent and managed care–driven approaches of performance indicator monitoring and quality assurance. He describes how outcomes may differ for clients in different phases of treatment and how different evaluation approaches may lead to different conclusions. He has argued in many other publications that substance abuse is a chronic illness, with challenges similar to those in other chronic illnesses. In chapter 10 he concludes that substance abuse treatment can be evaluated scientifically, just as credibly as any medical intervention.

Carise and Gûrel (chapter 11) observe the limitations of national substance abuse data sets, particularly with respect to the needs of policymakers, and describe the development of the Drug Evaluation Network System (DENS) project to address these limitations. DENS was designed to gather data for a large sample of people entering treatment, to be ongoing, accessible to participating clinics, and flexible in addressing new questions over time. DENS designed its data set in collaboration with clinical partners. Data collection was part of the assessment process, assessment write-ups supported counseling staff, data reporting replaced existing requirements, and counselors earned continuing education units for learning how to be DENS participants. Planners made extensive efforts to address policy-level needs while shaping data collection procedures that had minimum load and maximum gain for clinicians.

The building block of practice–research collaboration involves partnership between a single clinic team and a single research team, directed toward a clinical research question. In this collaboration clinicians and researchers jointly pursue treatment innovation, jointly learn about the collaborative process and build relationships, and jointly contribute to development of new knowledge. McCarty (chapter 12) describes the use of demonstration projects as an early strategy to build fundamental practice–research collaboration. The demonstration approach, now 30 years old, is a strategic policy tool. Because demonstrations are clinically focused and support applied intervention, they enable communities to address emerging substance abuse problems. By funding both treatment and evaluation, demonstrations can support promising but unproven interventions. They offer practitioners experience in providing a specific intervention, and they inform the field about how well the intervention works. Demonstrations often involved multisite collaborative models, such as the Alcohol Safety Action Program, which is funded in 35 communities. Successful demonstration projects should lead to the adoption of new interventions and to changes in policy that drive the treatment field forward. Although the logic of the demonstration project is compelling, the results are often disappointing. Collaborations supporting demonstration projects in a given community are fluid in time, treatments that have been shown to be helpful may not lead to policy change, interventions may be shown to be ineffective, and effective interventions may fare poorly because of contextual factors unrelated to the intervention itself. Many demonstration projects have not documented their successes and failures, limiting their effectiveness in supporting the next generation of demonstration efforts. One reverberating complaint about demonstrations is that, even when interventions are shown to be effective, these interventions are not widely adopted. When the demonstration funding ends, often the intervention does, too. Still, in its partial success the demonstration project set the stage for the most recent efforts to promote practice–research collaboration. These are the CSAT Practice Improvement Collaboratives (PICs) and the NIDA CTNs.

CSAT PICs (Gleghorn & Cotter, chapter 13) embody practice–research collaboration. Beginning in 1999 and currently including 11 collaboratives, PICs have in common with CTNs the federal support of practice–research collaboration and the use of these collaboratives as a base for cross-discipline training. PICs are not directly focused on clinical trial demonstrations of effectiveness; instead, they focus on identifying local treatment needs and bringing the practice–research partnership to bear on these needs. Gleghorn and Cotter describe San Francisco's PIC, offering an elegant example of this process, which includes incorporating local planning bodies, needs assessments, and forums to exchange information.

The CSAT PIC program is similar but more clinically focused than the NIDA CTN discussed in Alan I. Leshner's Foreword to this volume. The NIDA CTN began in 1999 and has been expanding and evolving rapidly (see Hanson, Leshner, & Tai, 2002). For the latest information on the CTN, readers can consult its Web site, http://165.112.78.61/CTN/Index.htm. As this is written, the CTN includes 14 research–practice "nodes." Each node involves collaboration between a research group and several clinical agency partners, and these nodes are intended to act in concert as a national network to conduct randomized clinical trials. Led by a national steering committee, practitioners and researchers identify interventions having sufficient preliminary data and treatment relevance to warrant testing in the national CTN. Each node is an ongoing practice–research collaboration, and the multisite approach has longevity beyond any single project. It creates a practice–research infrastructure through which interventions can be rapidly rolled out into multisite clinical trials. The main goal of the CTN is to test intervention effectiveness. Compared with CTN nodes, PICs are less likely to produce findings about the treatment efficacy. PICs are more likely to support treatment programs in addressing issues such as improving the cultural competence of treatment, improving management information systems, and using research to guide allocation of treatment resources. As with the CTN, the promise of the PIC remains to be realized. As recently as 15 years ago, the precursor of these, the demonstration project, was vaunted and promising. Now, with the benefit of hindsight, the value of demonstration projects has been only limited and incremental.

In the last two chapters of this part, Elisa Triffleman (chapter 14) and Vivian B. Brown (chapter 15) discuss collaboration between practice and research in clinical settings. Triffleman discusses her experience incorporating treatment for posttraumatic stress disorder in a drug treatment setting. She speaks to research concerns of recruitment and clinical concerns of how clients are treated in research, and she discusses transitioning interventions into treatment when the research ends. Triffleman expresses the same themes of equal partnership as Brown, and she applies several of the same partnership-building strategies.

We believe Brown's description of the PROTOTYPES program (chapter 16) could be required reading for both research and clinical organizations that are engaged in a practice–research partnership. PROTOTYPES is described as a living organism, with staff fully involved in programmatic change designed to better meet the needs of clients. To this point almost any program director would agree, but PROTOTYPES extends the definition of change to include the development, testing, and dissemination of new treatments so that staff see research as part of their mission and adoption of effective interventions as part of an agency's evolution.

In a U.S. Public Health Service study, conducted from 1932 to 1972, 399 African American sharecroppers were denied treatment for syphilis and deceived about the treatment they were receiving. The study, known as the Tuskegee syphilis experiment, has come to represent racism in medicine, ethical misconduct in human research, and abuse of a vulnerable population. Brown reminds readers of Tuskegee not as a roadblock but as a legacy with which practice–research partnerships must contend. She emphasizes the themes of equal ownership and partnership in practice–research endeavors, and she describes several strategies to support such a partnership. Anticipating that readers may see this partnership as a vision of leadership rather than an accomplishment, Brown includes the voice of PROTOTYPES staff as a testament to its success.

REFERENCE

Hanson, G. R., Leshner, A. I., & Tai, B. (2002, September). Putting drug abuse research to use in real life settings. *Journal of Substance Abuse Treatment, 23*(2), 69–70.

10

THE OUTCOMES MOVEMENT IN ADDICTION TREATMENT: COMMENTS AND CAUTIONS

A. THOMAS MCLELLAN

Problems of substance dependence—or addiction—produce dramatic costs to society in terms of lost productivity, social disorder, and excessive health care utilization (Rice, Kelman, & Miller, 1991). Although some segments of the public are demanding greater availability and more financing for substance dependence treatments, some individuals in government, insurance, managed care, and the public question the efficacy of these treatments and whether they are "worth it" ("Increasing Health Costs Threaten Small Business," 1997). In response to these concerns, there has been a rush to evaluate, perform quality assurance protocols, and assess outcomes. This is, of course, a highly desirable development. Because there have been significant advances in the standardization of diagnoses and in the reliable measurement of symptoms and functional status over the course of the past 10 years (American Psychiatric Association, 1994), it is now possible to

The author is a principal in the Treatment Research Institute, a nonprofit, university-affiliated firm that provides evaluation services to public and private treatment agencies. Supported by grants from NIDA, ONDCP, CSAT, and the VA.

evaluate the outcome of substance dependence treatment programs in a valid manner and without compromising ongoing treatment efforts.

At the same time, there has often been significant misapplication of evaluation designs, inappropriate measures, and illogical or inefficient methods associated with well-intentioned efforts. These poorly conceptualized or misapplied evaluation procedures not only fail to provide useful information but also may lead to inaccurate findings that could damage this developing field. It is important to offer some discussion on several important conceptual and methodological principles associated with successful and appropriate outcome evaluation efforts in this field.

The chapter is organized into three sections. First I present some suggested goals for substance dependence treatments based on an analysis of what patients, payers, and society in general expect from "effective" addiction treatment. From these perspectives it is argued that broad rehabilitation goals are pertinent and reasonable to expect from addiction treatments. These general goals go well beyond the reduction of the target symptoms of alcohol and drug use and extend to areas such as increasing employment or self-support and family and social functioning, as well as decreasing crime and the disproportionate use of health and social services. It is suggested that these general rehabilitation expectations are important not only from a public health perspective but also for the maintenance of reduced substance use in the individual patient.

I then examine differences in concept, focus, and methodology among various approaches to evaluating substance abuse treatment outcome. These approaches include quality assurance monitoring, clinical tracking, and database tracking. I describe each of these evaluation approaches in concept and include procedural comments. The conceptual and practical limitations of each approach are discussed. It is argued that some of the conflicting information regarding the effectiveness and value of addiction treatments is due to differences in the methods used in these different types of evaluations.

In the third part of the chapter I discuss addiction as a chronic illness and present the implications of this view for both treatment delivery and treatment outcome evaluation. Just as an education system should be responsible for producing broadly educated students, it is argued that an addiction treatment system should be responsible for achieving the broad rehabilitation expectations described earlier. However, just as elementary schools cannot be expected to take responsibility for the complete education of students, a detoxification/stabilization program cannot be responsible for complete rehabilitation. Instead, just as elementary schools are responsible for producing students that are well prepared for middle schools, detoxification/stabilization programs are responsible for preparing patients for successful participation in the interim and continuing care stages of rehabilitation.

Clearly, this is not a new thought or a radical reformulation of treatment. However, this conceptualization of segmented but shared clinical responsibility has not always been considered by evaluators—including myself. Thus, in the third part of this chapter I discuss three traditional stages of treatment for addiction in terms of their independent but shared clinical goals and offer some comments on evaluation models based on these stages of treatment, which might be more informative to treatment providers.

WHAT ARE REASONABLE EXPECTATIONS FOR EFFECTIVE ADDICTION TREATMENTS?

A major issue to be considered in measuring the effectiveness of substance dependence treatments is what one expects effective forms of these interventions to do. Expectations of the patient and legitimate stakeholders in the treatment form the major bases for judgments such as those regarding effectiveness or value. This is particularly complicated in the case of addictive disorders. Most illnesses or disorders affect primarily the patient and perhaps the immediate family. In contrast, addiction or substance dependence typically affects many others beyond the identified patient. Moreover, as I discuss later, these affected others are often asked to contribute in some way to the treatment of the addiction. For these reasons, many different parts of society have a right to set expectations on the judgment of effectiveness and value of substance abuse treatments. I now examine some of these expectations as a prelude to my discussion of how to measure the effectiveness of addiction treatments.

Treatment Outcome Expectations of the Patient

The expectations of the patient are clearly a primary consideration in a determination of effectiveness. Although there are exceptions, it is generally the case that addicted patients entering treatment want relief from the painful symptoms they are experiencing and that led to their admission. These symptoms are typically not only disturbing and problematic in their own right but are also preventing the patient from functioning fully in family and social relationships and may be interfering with employment and independent living. It is also true of addiction—and a few other disorders, such as hypertension and diabetes—that until the late stages of the illness, even seriously affected individuals will deny problems or symptoms. Indeed, many or even most patients entering addiction treatment have been coerced into treatment by the courts, a demanding family member, or an employer (or some combination of these). Despite these truisms regarding addiction, it is typically the case that even these patients want relief from the acute addiction-related problems that prompted the treatment admission. Thus, from the patient's perspective—even the coerced patient—there are at least two distinct sets of expectations from the outset of treatment:

1. relief from any discomfort caused by the direct effects of the substance abuse and
2. improved personal and social functioning—that is, reducing the social and personal problems that have been associated with the substance abuse.

Treatment Outcome Expectations of Others Affected by Substance Dependence

Beyond the patient, other constituents are directly or indirectly affected by the addiction problems of the patient and have legitimate expectations of their own.

Health Insurers and Managed Care Organizations

Private health insurers and public health agencies are often the primary payers for addiction treatment services. Most insurers or managed care organizations are eager for any type of addiction treatment that would reduce the disproportionate use of emergency room, general medical, and psychiatric services by substance dependent individuals. That is, these primary payers see the effectiveness of substance dependence treatment in terms of its ability to bring about subsequent reductions in use of expensive medical services.

Employers and Benefits Managers

Employers are often at least partial payers for substance dependence treatment services, through their contributions to the health insurance and the granting of medical or even disability leave for affected employees. Although employers realize that substance dependence is an important focal problem that must be addressed, their primary goal is to have their affected employees return to a productive level of work performance after treatment. Thus, employers consider effective substance dependence treatment to be that which will return employees to full productivity and minimize the employer's exposure to lawsuit and lost productivity.

Police, Probation/Parole Officers, Judges, and Child Protection Officers

Agents of the criminal justice system are also major sources of referral to, and payment for, substance dependence treatments. Current statistics indicate that as many as 60% of federal prisoners have problems of substance dependence, and as many as 80% of fatal highway accidents are due to the effects of alcohol intoxication (National Center for Addiction and Substance Abuse, 1998). Thus, for the criminal justice system the effectiveness of substance dependence treatment is measured by reductions in crime, parole and probation violations, and incarceration rates among affected individuals.

Families

Families of substance dependent individuals are major agents of referral for addicted patients entering treatment. Families are regularly called on to participate in treatment and to assist with continuing motivation for the patients. These families typically want an end to the worries, embarrassments, social disruptions, and violence that are so often associated with substance dependence. Thus, for affected family members the effectiveness of substance dependence treatment is measured in terms of family peace and safety.

Because insurers, police, families, and employers are also affected by substance dependence disorders, and because these groups are often charged directly or indirectly with paying for the treatment of addictive disorders, I argue that their expectations should form part of the judgment regarding the effectiveness of substance abuse treatments.

Suggested Outcome Domains

On the basis of the previous discussion of the patient's and society's expectations, I am arguing here that the criteria for evaluating the effectiveness of addiction treatments should be broadened to reflect these legitimate expectations. From this reasoning, I suggest three general outcome domains that appear to be relevant to the rehabilitative goals of patients and to the public health and safety goals of members of society who support addiction treatments:

1. sustained reduction in alcohol and drug use
2. sustained increases in personal health and social function
3. sustained reductions in threats to public health and safety.

Reductions in the primary symptoms (alcohol and drug use) and improved personal function (personal health and social function), the first two evaluation domains, are virtually identical with the "primary and secondary measures of effectiveness" typically used by the U.S. Food and Drug Administration to evaluate new drug or device applications in controlled clinical trials (see U.S. Food and Drug Administration, Associate Committee for Regulatory Affairs, 1980). Thus, at least in these respects, the evaluation of addiction treatments is conceptually consonant with the mainstream of thought regarding the evaluation of other forms of health care (Stewart & Ware, 1989). The final outcome dimension is much less common in the evaluation of other types of illnesses. As with some serious infectious diseases, the public is legitimately concerned with the health and safety problems produced by patients with alcohol and drug dependence.

In regard to abstinence as an outcome criterion I make a special note: For many years, addiction treatment programs conceptualized "effective treatment" as the initiation and maintenance of abstinence and, in turn, many of the earlier evaluations of treatment effectiveness reported the proportion of treated patients who had remained completely abstinent from the end of treatment to the follow-up point as the major (sometimes only) outcome criterion. The goal of complete and sustained (usually 12 months) abstinence was not selected capriciously but was based on the empirical observation that very few substance dependent individuals could return to any form of controlled use—and that many of those who were able to maintain abstinence were also functioning well in other psychosocial domains. This ideological convention has had the additional "benefit" of making outcome evaluation in substance dependence treatment very simple—in fact, too simple.

From a clinical perspective, there are problems with the abstinence criterion. To expect abstinence over a 12-month period following discharge from treatment is very close to expecting a *cure* for the illness. The available literature shows that this is not a common or expectable event among most treated samples. At least 50% of treated samples return to substance use within 6 months after treatment discharge (Holder, Longabaugh, Miller, & Rubonis, 1991; Hubbard et al., 1989). Although these results may be considered disappointing, the absence of any primary symptoms for a period of 1 year or more is a very stringent criterion of success for any illness or condition. For comparison, consider how many hypertension patients achieve normal blood pressure, continuously, for 12 months after stopping beta blocker medication.

Thus, from a clinical perspective, abstinence may be too much to ask for. Paradoxically, however, from the evaluation perspective discussed previously, *abstinence may not—by itself—be enough to ask for.* As described earlier, the patient, the public, and the payer expect reductions in the addiction-related problems of personal health, social function, and public health. Although it is often (not always) the case that abstinent individuals are better adjusted in other domains, the relationships seen between abstinence and the other important measures of psychosocial adjustment have not been robust enough to warrant the acceptance of abstinence as a proxy for the broader rehabilitation goals discussed previously. Twenty years of research in this area indicate that although abstinence is often a *necessary* condition for improvements in other health and social problems, it is typically not *sufficient* to ensure those improvements.

Are These Expectations Reasonable?

Despite the complexity and breadth of these evaluation goals, a review of the treatment evaluation literature suggests that properly structured and delivered addiction treatments can be expected to produce reductions in substance use and improve the patient's health and social function, and thereby reduce the public health and safety problems and costs associated with substance dependence (see Hubbard et al., 1989; McLellan et al., 1994; Miller & Hester, 1986). From the patient's perspective, regardless of whether these associated problems originally led to, or resulted from, the substance abuse, failure to address them concurrently with the substance dependence treatment will almost certainly lead to relapse. Thus, substance dependence treatment simply will not be worth it to a patient unless he or she gets not only symptom relief but also some assistance in resuming or initiating independent living.

From the perspective of the other affected segments of society that support substance dependence treatment, it is clear that these associated problems of unemployment, crime, overutilization of medical and social resources, and family disruption are of primary concern. Substance dependence treatment simply will not be worth it to society if it cannot play a major role in the general rehabilitation of these individuals.

METHODS FOR EVALUATING THE THREE OUTCOME DOMAINS OF ADDICTION TREATMENT

At least four methodological approaches have been used to assess whether addiction treatments are successful in achieving the three evaluation goals described previously. I now briefly describe each approach and outline its major strengths and weaknesses.

Clinical Tracking

The most commonly used method to evaluate addiction treatments in experimental and naturalistic field studies of substance abuse treatment is *clinical tracking*. Clinical-tracking evaluations begin at the time the patient enters a treatment program. In a typical procedure, randomly selected samples of patients are selected for intensive measurement throughout and after discharge from the treatment program. At each measurement point, researchers typically use questionnaires and interviews to collect data on substance use and psychosocial functioning, as well as biological samples (urine, breath, or hair analyses), to validate the self-reports. In some studies, information on treatment services received is also obtained from clients. Two of the major strengths of this approach are that (a) the procedures have been refined over time and (b) a wide variety of assessment measures with proven reliability and validity are available. In addition, no other approach to evaluating treatment effectiveness provides as complete or as detailed information on the functioning of the patients.

Unfortunately, this approach also has several major limitations. First, in order for the data to be valid, a representative sample of clients must be enrolled at treatment intake and a high follow-up rate achieved (i.e., 70%

or better). If either of these two conditions is violated, the data may not be interpretable. Second, there is usually a lengthy time period between when the study is initiated and when results are available to treatment providers and policymakers. For example, a 12-month clinical-tracking evaluation will typically require a year or more to collect admission data on patients entering the treatment to be evaluated. These patients will require 1–6 months to complete treatment and an additional 12 months for the follow-up data to be collected. This will be followed by several months of data analysis and report preparation. Thus, it can be 2–3 years before findings are made available. A third and important problem with this evaluation method is that the procedures of tracking, locating, and interviewing clients at follow-up are expensive and time consuming. Very few treatment programs or health agencies have the personnel, organization, or finances necessary to perform this type of evaluation on a continuing basis.

Database Monitoring

Given the expectations that substance abuse treatments will reduce the costs and social problems produced by addiction, another way to assess the impact of substance abuse treatment is to examine the state, city, or health organization databases that contain the expression of social problems and continued costs. There are many examples of these databases. For example, arrest and incarceration databases contain records of drug-related arrests and incarcerations. The logic here is that if addiction treatments are effective, then individuals who have been treated will not be arrested or incarcerated for drug-related crimes. Similarly, welfare or Temporary Assistance for Needy Families records, unemployment claims, and tax records can provide face-valid indications of self-support and social function. Records from hospital admissions, pharmacy records, and visits to emergency rooms and physicians can be very informative regarding the nature and amount of health care use in a sample of previously treated patients. I refer to this approach to outcome evaluation here as *database monitoring*.

The cost and efficiency advantages of a database-monitoring system are substantial. These advantages have been shown in several statewide evaluations, including in Oregon, Oklahoma, Washington, and Ohio. With good interdepartmental collaboration and the availability of technical expertise, it is possible to develop interdepartmental data transfer systems and to produce systemwide evidence of the extent to which patients treated for addiction have achieved reductions in crime, health care utilization, and social impairment. Furthermore, these databases offer an opportunity to develop good measures of costs, cost offsets, and savings. Finally, although these types of evaluations do require some technical and political skills to set up, once they are functional it is possible to perform repeated evaluations on entire populations of treated patients at very low costs.

At the same time, there are problems with this method of tracking outcomes. Again, because there is an obvious lag between the completion of treatment, the commission of the types of events that would be recorded in these databases, and the analysis of the data, these types of studies are also time consuming. There are also problems with some of the measures—particularly the primary measure of reduced substance use. For example, with the exception of readmission to substance abuse treatment, database monitoring offers no direct indication of whether former patients are still using or abusing alcohol and drugs. Furthermore, these systems typically lack treatment process information. From an analytic perspective it is difficult to compare different modalities or programs, because these systems typically do not provide enough information for "case mix" adjustment. When a sample of patients cannot be randomly assigned to the treatments of interest, any subsequent differences seen in outcomes may be due to pre-existing differences in the background characteristics, to admission problem severities of the patients compared, or to both. In clinical-tracking studies there can be adequate information to statistically adjust for case mix differences in severity in the two sets of cases. Finally, there have been concerns about the ability to maintain patient confidentiality in database-monitoring systems. For this reason—as well as the scarcity and expense of technological sophistication—there have been very few functional examples of this type of evaluation.

Performance Indicator Monitoring

Because costs, time, and clinical/management relevance are continuing problems in the monitoring of outcomes, there has been great interest in the development of faster, less expensive means of evaluating the specific effects of substance abuse treatments. Clinical managers and policymakers within the treatment field have therefore begun to look for variables that can be easily measured during treatment or at the point of discharge that have been clearly associated with (i.e., can serve as proxies for) longer term outcomes after treatment and could thereby serve as indicators of true outcomes. A more practical advantage of such measures is the opportunity to use them while the patient is in treatment as a basis for adjustments to the treatment plan and thereby improving individual care. These patient status or treatment delivery variables measured during the course of treatment have been called *performance indicators*.

These indicators have typically been developed by groups of clinicians or administrators from clinical management data in management information systems that have a face-valid or intuitive link with longer term outcomes. Some examples of performance indicators include the proportion of patients who are readmitted to inpatient care within 30 days after inpatient discharge, the proportion of patients who drop out of treatment prior to the planned discharge date, and the proportion of patients who enter outpatient care within 1 week after detoxification discharge. One additional indicator that has become a standard in all areas of health care quality monitoring is "patient satisfaction," typically measured with patient questionnaires. Because these measures can usually be collected, analyzed, and reported rapidly and inexpensively, and because they can be used in the direct management of patient care, the performance indicator approach to outcomes monitoring has had great appeal to patients, clinicians, and administrators alike. Because of their potential clinical and administrative value, performance indicator monitoring systems have already been widely adopted by treatment providers, and there is a widespread effort to build the reporting of these measures into existing clinical or management information systems.

The existing and proposed performance indicators for the substance abuse field have been useful in identifying obvious problems in the conduct of treatment, in bringing the consumer perspective into the treatment setting, and in stimulating members of the treatment field toward greater self-examination and self-evaluation. At the same time, there is some concern that these initial indicators may identify only extremely poor outcomes (e.g., malpractice) and may not be sensitive to subtle but clinically important treatment differences. In particular, although patient satisfaction is an important part of any evaluation, studies have shown that satisfaction levels are typically not well related to the other domains of outcome evaluation (McLellan & Hunkeler, 1998). Even more serious is the possibility that some of the performance indicators might be made to show *apparent* improvement through administrative action without actually changing treatment practices. For example, a program's administrators might decide not to readmit discharged patients within 1 month after treatment to give the impression of a low 1-month relapse rate.

Outcome Evaluation and Quality Assurance

There has been significant confusion between the terms *outcome evaluation* and *quality assurance* or *continuous quality improvement*. In general, outcome evaluations have taken place after discharge from treatment—or while a patient is in the later part of the continuing care stage of treatment. As described earlier, the purpose of most outcome evaluations is to address the extent to which treatment has achieved the appropriate goal expectations (e.g., sustained reductions in substance use, better social function, reduction of AIDS risk). Also as discussed previously, most clinical-tracking outcome evaluations take considerable time to complete, because measures are typically taken on many patients over the full course of the treatment period. Because of the time and expense involved in those outcome evaluations it is not appropriate to do them on all patients or even every year. Furthermore, the results of outcome evaluations should be directed to the highest levels of management to be used in deciding major aspects of treatment policy and program direction, such as whether to continue a particular program or whether an added component of care (e.g., family therapy) has met its expectations.

In contrast, most quality assurance evaluations address the extent to which the clinical and administrative procedures that have been developed as policy are being applied in the manner originally intended and whether they are achieving their procedural goals during treatment (e.g., did every patient receive a comprehensive assessment, and did that assessment lead to services and treatment components that followed logically from the assessment?). This type of evaluation is best undertaken on a regular basis (usually quarterly), especially during the initiation and development of new treatments, to ensure the fidelity or integrity of the treatment plan as originally conceived. The usual and appropriate purpose of quality assurance evaluations is to identify improper or inadequate implementation of the specific aspects of the care plan (e.g., missed treatment plans, lack of treatment progress notes, failure to monitor breathalyzer readings). Because quality assurance evaluations are more narrowly focused on elements of care as that care is being delivered, these evaluations can typically be accomplished prospectively on a small sample of patients (approximately 20–30) in 2–4 weeks, or retrospectively, through chart review, within a week or so. Results from quality assurance monitoring should not go to top management, because the results rarely require institutional or policy changes. Instead, quality assurance findings should be directed to line supervisors and middle management for the purpose of rapidly correcting problems in system implementation or to address procedural deficiencies seen (e.g., how can staff ensure that the treatment plans are completed within the first week).

As can be seen, the quality assurance component of evaluation is best conceived as a *regular, focused monitoring function directed at specific and important questions of care delivery*, the results of which will offer relatively clear guidelines for treatment supervisors to improve the care delivery procedures and services within the scope of existing policy. However, such activities do *not* address whether any of the well-accepted policies and procedures result in improved outcomes. It follows that it would be best for leaders of a treatment program to have clear evidence that the major components of their care delivery program are being implemented in the manner intended *prior to beginning an outcome evaluation*. Put differently, if there is no evidence that treatment is being delivered in the manner intended (through quality assurance monitoring), then the results of any outcome evaluation will be difficult to interpret. For example, if the outcome results show unacceptable results, are those results due to the misapplication of potentially effective procedures, or are they due to limitations in the treatment philosophy and procedures themselves? If the outcome results are positive—but the treatment has not been delivered in the manner intended—what does that mean?

Compared to What?

Regardless of the type of evaluation method used, a major question is "to what will the results be compared?" There are many possible answers here, with varying degrees of information return.

Historical Controls

One way to provide a comparison condition would be to perform, for example, the previously mentioned clinical-tracking evaluation repeatedly over several years, using the same sampling and measurement techniques. Comparisons of the results obtained across years would at least permit an evaluation of the extent to which there were differences in treatment efficacy over years—under the questionable assumption of no change in the admission severity of the patients sampled over those years.

Severity-Adjusted Comparisons

A better approach is to measure the severity of patients' problems at the start of treatment and again at follow-up; again, repeating this practice in samples of patients regularly over the course of several years. This additional step would permit a regular record of outcomes, thereby providing trend data, and would simultaneously enable the program to assess the extent to which the admission severity of the patient samples had changed over years. This second aspect of the added information is quite valuable in that it enables program staff to directly compare, over years, the outcomes of subgroups of patients "matched" for admission severity or diagnoses.

Comparisons With Other Samples

The investment of collecting additional admission information pays the dividend of providing severity-adjusted comparisons of program effectiveness over years. At the same time, when the only data that are available are those from a single program—even when those data are repeated over time and in different patient samples—it is not possible to determine whether the treatment provided in that program is better or worse than treatment (for a comparable set of patients) in another treatment program. Therefore, a still greater payoff could be achieved by using well-validated instruments that have been widely used in similar evaluations of other treatment programs and patient samples, thereby providing comparative treatment outcome information in other samples. This additional step offers the opportunity to compare the outcomes achieved by patients in the target program with the body of data that have been collected with those standard instruments on other patient samples.

More Evaluation Options Can Mean More Confusion

The availability of different assessment methodologies, and the development of reliable and valid outcome measures in all outcome domains, are positive developments in evaluation. However, more assessment options can also lead to greater confusion, particularly for individuals in public policy and administration. For example, an evaluation of a particular treatment program that focused on selected performance indicators might conclude that the program had *very good outcomes* because clients were more satisfied and were retained longer than clients in other programs. A clinical evaluator, having interviewed a sample of patients at admission to the same program and again 12 months after discharge, might conclude on the other hand that the program had *mixed outcomes*, because only 40% of the patients were abstinent after treatment, but there was a 50% reduction in medical and psychiatric symptoms. Finally, a policy analyst who used Medicaid data tapes to compare the inpatient hospital utilization rates from a sample of discharged patients from the same program, 3 years before treatment admission and 2 years after discharge, might conclude that treatment had a *very poor outcome* because there had been no decrease in health care utilization and no cost offset.

This example illustrates two points. First, these common perspectives on outcome have different expectations regarding treatment. Because of this, they measure different elements of the treatment process and the treatment results—at different points in time. Second, because of these conceptual and measurement differences it is possible that different outcome evaluations on the same program will lead to accurate (from the perspective taken) but very different conclusions. One of the important challenges for outcomes evaluation research is to better delineate the relationships among the clinical-tracking, database-monitoring, and performance indicator approaches and to determine the circumstances under which the three methodologies are likely to produce similar or dissimilar results.

THREE TREATMENT STAGES AND THEIR ROLE IN MEETING THE OVERALL REHABILITATION EXPECTATIONS OF ADDICTION TREATMENT

It should be clear that the evaluation perspective described here does not assume that any single treatment program, modality, or approach should be expected to accomplish the full range of outcome expectations described in the section titled "What Are Reasonable Expectations for 'Effective' Addiction Treatments?" This is very important. Although I argue that the *overall* goals of addiction treatment should be based on these expectations, particular types and settings of care are designed to address only a subset of the expectations and the achievement of full rehabilitation as defined previously will require integration and coordination across the separate parts.

If this is true, then any single treatment program or stage of treatment should be evaluated against the specific expectations and treatment goals that are appropriate for that segment of treatment. At the same time, because each of the different levels of care (e.g., acute care inpatient, day hospital, intensive outpatient, aftercare) for substance dependence share the overall responsibility for helping to achieve the full set of goals listed earlier, it is equally important to measure the extent to which each stage of treatment integrates its services into the overall goals of rehabilitation. This concept of *individual responsibility* for the achievement of specific interim goals—but *joint responsibility* for the integration of these separate goals toward the larger goals of rehabilitation—is described in terms of the three traditional stages of treatment.

Note that I have not discussed two other important parts of care: (a) assessment and (b) brief interventions. Assessment is critical to determine the nature, intensity, and appropriate mix of services that should be provided to a patient, but it typically occurs prior to any formal treatment. In addition, brief interventions—which are typically conducted by a physician or counselor and range from a 20-minute conversation to four 30-minute sessions—have also been shown to be very important in raising patient awareness of a problem and in encouraging motivation for change. There is an increasingly large literature on these interventions (see Fleming & Barry, 1992), but again, they typically take place outside the traditional substance abuse specialty treatment settings. Thus, in the text that follows I provide some discussion about the appropriate roles and expectations of the three usual stages of care within the substance abuse specialty treatment field.

1. *The Detoxification/Stabilization stage of care* usually (not always) occurs in an inpatient setting, is several days in duration, and is focused on ameliorating the physiological and emotional symptoms that follow recent substance use and motivating the patient to accept that there is a problem and to learn how to deal with that problem.
2. *The Intermediate stage of care* sometimes occurs in a residential setting but usually in an outpatient setting, is several weeks or months in duration, and is focused on teaching the patient new skills to cope with relapse situations and motivating him or her to develop and maintain lifestyle changes that are inconsistent with substance use.
3. *The Continuing Care stage of treatment* is 1 or more years in duration and focused on relapse prevention through continued support of positive lifestyle changes and regular monitoring of potential risk factors for return to substance use.

The Detoxification/Stabilization Stage of Treatment

Since the advent of managed care strategies in the United States, the majority of detoxification or stabilization care is rendered in an inpatient, hospital setting or a medically supported residential setting (see American Society of Addiction Medicine [2001] criteria). The goals of these acute care, detoxification/stabilization treatments, regardless of setting, follow from the admission criteria and include the medical and psychological stabilization of the patient and the development of an effective discharge plan that includes continued intermediate care. It is important that, under this framework, *rehabilitation* (as defined earlier in this chapter) *is not the goal of this stage of treatment.* Instead, this acute stage of care is charged with the preparation for the next stage of care and removal of the barriers to that level of care—specifically, the amelioration and stabilization of the medical, psychiatric, and substance use symptoms that were "out of control" and that would prevent active participation in the intermediate stage of care. Because there can be no expectation that the broader goals of rehabilitation will be achieved simply by relieving the acute physical and emotional symptoms that follow recent substance use, it is incumbent on a detoxification/stabilization program to not simply reduce physical symptoms but also to provide motivation for continuing care and active referral and engagement of patients into appropriate forms of intermediate or continuing care.

Outcome Evaluation

Given the goals just described, three specific areas are recommended both for clinical focus and as evaluation criteria:

1. stabilization of the physical and psychological symptoms of recent substance abuse
2. motivation of the patient to accept that there is a problem and that there are concrete steps that he or she can take toward solving the problem
3. transitioning the patient from the inpatient, acute care setting to the next level of care—either a residential rehabilitation site or a form of outpatient rehabilitation.

Physiological and Emotional Stabilization

Patients cannot be expected to participate in a rehabilitation program that focuses on developing a new lifestyle if there are significant physiological and emotional symptoms remaining from the discontinuation of recent alcohol and drug use. In a study of cocaine dependent veterans, Alterman, McKay, Mulvaney, and McLellan (1996) found that the single best predictor of engagement in the rehabilitation process—and, ultimately, program completion—was the presence or absence of cocaine metabolites in the urine sample submitted on admission to the rehabilitation program, signifying recent cocaine use. Of the patients without cocaine-positive urines on admission, 79% engaged in and completed the outpatient treatment, whereas only 39% of those with a positive urine sample on admission engaged and completed the outpatient treatment.

Motivation for Continuing Care

The second goal of the brief inpatient stabilization intervention is to increase motivation for continued treatment and "readiness for change" (Miller, Benefield, & Tonigan, 1993; Prochaska, DiClemente, & Norcross, 1992). This can be accomplished in both group and individual counseling sessions using the principles derived from the *motivational enhancement interviewing* protocol developed by Miller et al. (1993). Physicians, nurses, and counselors can be trained in the use of motivational enhancement techniques and can apply them during the course of the stabilization period.

Referral to and Engagement in Ongoing Care

The third part of the clinical charge for inpatient stabilization programs is to actively engage patients in the next phase of treatment—typically, outpatient rehabilitation. This can be accomplished in many ways, but the major ones include not discharging patients from detoxification on a weekend, having a counselor or member of the intended referral source (rehabilitation program) meet with the to-be-discharged patient prior to discharge, and preferred-status appointments (i.e., rapid entry) at collaborating rehabilitation programs.

Evidence of Effectiveness in the Detoxification/Stabilization Stage

Several detoxification studies have measured detoxification as 3 consecutive days of abstinence from observable withdrawal signs or symptoms (opiate or alcohol), using standardized inventories of these physical measures. Studies of amphetamine, cocaine, and marijuana stabilization have also shown that patients who are symptom free for 3 or more days from standard measures of physiological instability such as sleep disturbance, stomach and bowel upset, and irritability are stable enough to proceed with ongoing care.

It is important that, given the goals of the stabilization phase of treatment, it follows that the appropriate point at which to measure effectiveness is *1–2 weeks* after completion of the detoxification/stabilization—and not at 6–12 months, as has so often been done. "Effectiveness" evaluated solely at the time of discharge from detoxification, permits only an assessment of symptom improvement. Although acute symptom improvement is certainly important, this is not a difficult task for most contemporary inpatient substance dependence programs and is not an adequate assessment of the additional goals of integrating the patient into an appropriate level of rehabilitation care. Moreover, it is not possible to determine at the time of discharge from detoxification whether the symptomatic improvements obtained will endure the stresses of returning to the home and work environments. In contrast, an evaluation of detoxification/stabilization at an interval much beyond 2 weeks will have missed the critical points in time when the appropriate goals of integrating the patient into continued care should have been accomplished. Indeed, if a patient has entered into some form of intermediate care, any favorable results that are detected in an evaluation beyond 1 month are likely due to the direct effects of the outpatient care and cannot be automatically attributed to the inpatient component.

Thus, at approximately 2 weeks after discharge from detoxification/ stabilization, evidence of effectiveness would include the following:

- no substance use
- patient acceptance of his or her substance use problem and some motivation for change
- no or very low levels of physiological symptoms of withdrawal
- no serious psychiatric symptoms
- engagement in some form of intermediate treatment.

The Intermediate Phase of Treatment

I have called the stage of treatment that logically follows detoxification/ stabilization *intermediate care*. The types of care I am referring to are now typically called *rehabilitation programs*, but I have previously referred to *rehabilitation* (or what many call *recovery*) as the overall goal after all three stages of treatment.

As the American Society of Addiction Medicine (2001) indicated, this stage of care is appropriate for individuals who are no longer suffering from the acute physiological or emotional effects of recent substance use and who need behavioral change strategies to regain control of their urges to use substances. This intermediate stage of care may be initiated in a residential setting or an outpatient program (depending on the social supports available to the patient), *but sustained benefits require that it continue into the outpatient setting*, because life in a controlled environment does not permit patients to practice the skills necessary to prevent a relapse to substance use.

The practical goals of this stage of treatment are to *prevent a return to active substance use that would require re-detoxification or stabilization*; to assist the patient in developing control over urges to use alcohol or drugs, usually through sustaining total abstinence; and to assist the patient in attaining or regaining improved personal health and social function. As indicated previously, these improvements in lifestyle are important for maintaining sustained control over substance use.

Professional opinions vary widely regarding the underlying reasons for the loss of control over alcohol and drug use typically seen in treated patients. Genetic predispositions; acquired metabolic abnormalities; learned, negative behavioral patterns; deeply ingrained feelings of low self-worth; self-medication of underlying psychiatric or physical medical problems; character flaws; and lack of family and community support for positive function have all been suggested as mechanisms. Thus, there is an equally wide range of treatment strategies and components that have been used to correct or ameliorate these underlying problems and to provide continuing support for the targeted patient changes. Strategies have included such diverse elements as psychotropic medications to relieve "underlying psychiatric problems"; medications to relieve alcohol and drug cravings; acupuncture to correct acquired metabolic imbalances; educational seminars, films, and group sessions to correct false impressions about alcohol and drug use; group and individual counseling and therapy sessions to provide insight, guidance, and support for behavioral changes; and peer help groups (e.g., Alcoholics Anonymous [AA] and Narcotics Anonymous [NA]) to provide continued support for the behavioral changes that are important for sustaining improvement.

Clinical Objectives

Despite the diversity of settings, approaches, and procedures typically used in this stage of treatment, all have the same three goals:

1. maintain the physiological and emotional improvements that were initiated during the Detoxification/Stabilization phase, preventing the need for re-detoxification
2. enhance and sustain reductions in alcohol and drug use (most programs suggest a goal of complete abstinence)
3. teach, model, and motivate lifestyle changes that are incompatible with substance abuse and that lead to improved personal health, improved social function, and reduced threats to public health and public safety.

Evidence of Effectiveness in the Intermediate Stage

Most evaluations of the intermediate stage of substance abuse treatment should take place 6–12 months after initiation of this stage of treatment, or at least 6 months after discharge from a residential setting. At that point, evidence of effectiveness would include

- no substance use—or at least no significant return to substance abuse serious enough to require detoxification/stabilization;
- improvements in personal health and social function; and
- engagement in some form of the continuing care stage of treatment, such as regular meetings with a therapist, or community support (e.g., AA, NA), or both.

The Continuing Care Stage of Treatment

The final stage of addiction treatment has been less well specified, formalized, or studied (see McKay et al., 2000; McKay, Cacciola, McLellan, Alterman, & Wirtz, 1999) than the other stages. This may be because most formal or organized addiction treatments have been insured and delivered in some circumscribed period of time, such as 28 days. This has typically been followed by a passive referral to AA or NA but very little organized effort to retain the patient in any enduring program for monitoring and maintaining the gains that have been made. The majority of insurance programs for addiction reimburse treatment facilities for a specified or authorized period of time (measured in days), and none provide incentives for programs or patients to maintain continuous monitoring or treatments beyond 60 days. It is remarkable that despite the acknowledgment by the insurance industry that addiction is an illness requiring medically oriented treatment, there has been no acknowledgment that there is a need for continued monitoring and support for recovering patients.

It is clear from research conducted over the past 20 years that the 12-month post-treatment period—that is, the year after discharge from an organized treatment program—is a period of great vulnerability for recovering patients. As has been shown repeatedly, across a range of different types of treatments and patient populations, approximately half of treated patients (40%–60%, depending on the sample) will resume drinking or drug use in the year after discharge (Gossop, Johns, & Green, 1986; Hubbard et al., 1989; Kang, Kleinman, Woody, & Millman, 1991; McKay et al., 2000; McLellan et al., 1994; Miller & Hester, 1986). In fact, more than 60% of those who ultimately resume substance use in that year will actually begin within the first 4 months following discharge.

Clinical Objectives

Given the view that addiction is a chronic illness, it follows that the most important goal for the continuing care stage of treatment is to *prevent a return to active substance use*. Studies of effective treatments for other chronic illnesses suggest some of the following clinical objectives and strategies for the effective continuing care of addiction:

1. Monitor for early warning signs of relapse, such as
   - repeated periods of craving,
   - emotional upset,
   - loss of economic or social support, and
   - association with former drug/alcohol using friends.
2. Promote adherence to the treatment plan, including (where applicable)
   - prescribed anticraving medications and
   - attendance at AA/NA or group therapy sessions.

Virtually all treatments of chronic illnesses monitor patients after a period of intensive treatment to detect the early appearance of symptoms that will signal a recurrence of the illness and to assist the patient in continuing with the course of medications and lifestyle changes that have been recommended. Indeed, among patients treated for hypertension, asthma, and diabetes, failure to continue prescribed medications and recommended lifestyle changes are the major factors associated with relapse and retreatment (see McLellan, O'Brien, Lewis, & Kleber, 2000). In turn, among individuals treated for these three chronic illnesses, patients with low income, poor family supports, or comorbid psychiatric illness are those most likely to stop their prescribed medications and to stop the lifestyle changes that are so important to the maintenance of symptom remission (see McLellan et al., 2000). Realizing this, the physicians and nurses who are responsible for the continuing care of patients with these chronic illnesses use telephone monitoring, in-home visits, and scheduled checkup appointments on a weekly to monthly basis to support the patients and to check for the appearance of early warning signs indicating lack of adherence to the treatment plan.

Among substance abusers, research indicates that some of the major factors associated with re-addiction are found in the normal stresses of daily life. These include depression or other emotional problems, loss of family or social supports, and association with former friends and associates that are continuing to drink or use drugs. Because AA is free, omnipresent, and eminently practical in its approach, over 95% of treatment programs in the United States have incorporated referral to AA or NA into their clinical practices. Unfortunately, only about one quarter of the referred patients who attend an AA meeting go on to engage in that type of community support. Although AA and NA have been extraordinarily important to sustaining the rehabilitation of so many affected individuals, it is clear that additional options for continuing care are necessary.

Evidence of Effectiveness in the Continuing Care Stage

Because addictive disorders are chronic and relapsing, a "cure" is not now achievable in most cases. Nonetheless, there are many illnesses that cannot be cured, and yet there are effective treatments for these illnesses that arrest and contain symptoms and permit improved function. I now return to the criteria for effective substance abuse treatments that I suggested earlier. By 12–18 months after initiation of detoxification/stabilization there should be evidence of attainment of the broad rehabilitation goals discussed previously. Specifically, the Continuing Care stage of treatment can be said to be successful if the patient shows

- no substance use—or at least no significant return to substance abuse serious enough to require detoxification/stabilization,
- employment or self-support,

- fulfillment of family obligations, and
- no behaviors that could endanger others (e.g., drunk driving, sharing needles).

CONCLUSION

Perhaps the most important conclusion to be drawn from this chapter is that substance dependence *treatments can be evaluated in a scientific manner* similar to studies of pharmacological interventions or of medical devices. The importance of addiction to the public, and the dollars expended annually in attempts to treat these patients, demand evaluation. Thus, this chapter should be read as a call for more evaluation at the clinical and programmatic level; greater consideration of addiction as a chronic illness; more thinking about the appropriate clinical objectives of the particular stage of treatment being evaluated; and increased use of appropriate evaluation methods, time frames, and measurement techniques.

It is important to emphasize that this call for more evaluation is not based on skepticism or cynicism that substance dependence treatments will not be seen as effective when appropriate designs are used. Quite the opposite is true: When appropriate techniques have been applied in rigorous evaluations, the results offer heartening indications that many forms of substance dependence treatments *can* be effective, not only in reducing target symptoms but also in achieving the broader goals of rehabilitation (Hubbard et al., 1989; Institute of Medicine, 1995, 1998; McLellan et al., 2000; McLellan et al., 1994; Miller & Hester, 1986). At the same time, not all treatments are effective by any standard, and some treatment types and treatment programs are better than others (McLellan et al., 2000). Again, because of the disparity in efficacy among treatment programs, and because there are scientifically valid and clinically practical methods for outcome evaluation, it is imperative for practitioners of established treatments to begin appropriate evaluation efforts and to offer evidence of effectiveness to the public and the patients they serve.

REFERENCES

Alterman, A. I., McKay, J. R., Mulvaney, F. D., & McLellan, A. T. (1996). Prediction of attrition from day hospital treatment in lower socioeconomic cocaine dependent men. *Drug and Alcohol Dependence, 40,* 227–233.

American Psychiatric Association. (1994). *Diagnostic and statistical manual of mental disorders* (4th ed.). Washington, DC: Author.

American Society of Addiction Medicine. (2001). *Patient placement criteria for the treatment of substance-related disorders* (3rd ed.). Chevy Chase, MD: The Society for Addiction Medicine.

Fleming, M. F., & Barry, K. L. (Eds.). (1992). *Addictive disorders*. St. Louis, MO: Mosby YearBook.

Gossop, M., Johns, A., & Green, L. (1986). Opiate withdrawal: Inpatient versus outpatient programmes and preferred versus random assignment. *British Medical Journal, 293*, 103–104.

Holder, H. D., Longabaugh, R., Miller, W. R., & Rubonis, A. (1991). The cost effectiveness of treatment for alcohol problems: A first approximation. *Journal of Studies on Alcohol, 52*, 517–540.

Hubbard, R. L., Marsden, M. E., Rachal, J. V., Harwood, H. J., Cavanaugh, E. R., & Ginzburg, H. M. (1989). *Drug abuse treatment: A national study of effectiveness*. Chapel Hill: University of North Carolina Press.

Increasing health costs threaten small business. (1997, July 18). *The Wall Street Journal*, p. A12.

Institute of Medicine. (1995). *Federal regulation of methadone treatment*. Washington, DC: National Academy Press.

Institute of Medicine. (1998). *Bridging the gap: Forging new partnerships in community-based drug abuse treatment*. Washington, DC: National Academy Press.

Kang, S. Y., Kleinman, P. H., Woody, G. E., & Millman, R. B. (1991). Outcomes for cocaine abusers after once-a-week psychosocial therapy. *American Journal of Psychiatry, 148*, 630–635.

McKay, J. R., Alterman, A. I., Cacciola, J. S., Rutherford, M. R., O'Brien, C. P., & Koppenhaver, J. (2000). A comparison of group counseling vs. individualized relapse prevention aftercare following intensive outpatient treatment for cocaine dependence: Initial results. *Journal of Consulting and Clinical Psychology, 65*, 778–788.

McKay, J. R., Cacciola, J., McLellan, A. T., Alterman, A. I., & Wirtz, P. W. (1999). An initial evaluation of the psychosocial dimensions of the ASAM criteria for inpatient and day hospital substance abuse rehabilitation. *Journal of Studies on Alcohol, 58*, 239–252.

McLellan, A. T., Alterman, A. I., Metzger, D. S., Grissom, G., Woody, G. E., Luborsky, L., et al. (1994). Similarity of outcome predictors across opiate, cocaine and alcohol treatments: Role of treatment services. *Journal of Clinical and Consulting Psychology, 62*, 1141–1158.

McLellan, A. T., & Hunkeler, E. (1998). Relationships between patient satisfaction and patient performance in addiction treatment. *Psychiatric Services, 49*, 573–575.

McLellan, A. T., O'Brien, C. P., Lewis, D., & Kleber, H. D. (2000). Drug addiction as a chronic medical illness: Implications for treatment, insurance and evaluation. *Journal of the American Medical Association, 284*, 1689–1695.

Miller, W. R., Benefield, R. G., & Tonigan, J. S. (1993). Enhancing motivation for change in problem drinking: A controlled comparison of two therapist styles. *Journal of Consulting and Clinical Psychology, 61*, 455–461.

Miller, W. R., & Hester, R. K. (1986). The effectiveness of alcoholism treatment methods: What research reveals. In W. R. Miller & N. Heather (Eds.), *Treating addictive behaviors: Process of change* (pp. 241–267). New York: Plenum.

National Center for Addiction and Substance Abuse. (1998). *Behind bars: Substance abuse and America's prison population*. Unpublished report.

Prochaska, J. O., DiClemente, C. C., & Norcross, J. C. (1992). In search of how people change: Applications to addictive behaviors. *American Psychologist, 47*, 1102–1114.

Rice, D. P., Kelman, S., & Miller, L. S. (1991). Estimates of the economic costs of alcohol, drug abuse and mental illness, 1985 and 1988. *Public Health Reports, 106*, 281–292.

Stewart, R. G., & Ware, L. G. (1989). *The Medical Outcomes Study*. Santa Monica, CA: RAND.

U.S. Food and Drug Administration, Associate Committee for Regulatory Affairs. (1980). *Compliance policy guidelines*: 21 Code of Federal Regulations 310.

11

BENEFITS OF INTEGRATING TECHNOLOGY WITH TREATMENT: THE DENS PROJECT

DENI CARISE AND ÕZGE GÛREL

Although Americans spent almost $65 billion for drugs in 2000 (Office of National Drug Control Policy [ONDCP], 2002a) and more than 1 million Americans enter addiction treatments each year (ONDCP, 2002b), little is known about this population. In particular, there is no ongoing collection of descriptive information regarding such basic characteristics as demographics; types and amounts of substances used prior to treatment entry; or the nature and severity of addiction-related problems in the areas of medical health, employment, criminal activity, family relationships, or psychiatric status. The gaps created by this lack of information on substance-abusing or -dependent individuals in the U.S. treatment system, as well as a lack of standardized information at state and local levels on the treatment provided, is recognized as a problem by the ONDCP (2002c).

This gap is due, in large part, to a lack of collaborative systems between researchers and clinicians. There is no system that is beneficial to treatment programs, clinicians, and patients while also providing ongoing, timely, and useful information for policymakers or researchers. In response

181

to this information gap, and with the support of the ONDCP, we have designed and initiated the Drug Evaluation Network System (DENS). In this chapter we first review and discuss a number of clinicians' and researchers' goals in providing and evaluating substance abuse treatment. Next we present the rationale of the DENS project and one of the several studies built on the DENS platform: "Linking Assessment Technology to Improved Patient Care" (funded by a grant from The National Institute on Drug Abuse), hereafter called the "Tech Study." This project is designed to meet the goals of treatment providers and researchers and to be beneficial to both. Finally, we discuss practical implementation issues in real-world treatment settings and how treatment program staff and DENS staff have collaborated in meeting the varied needs of clinicians, treatment providers, and researchers.

Researchers and clinicians must blend their efforts to improve outcomes in substance abuse treatment. This is most effectively achieved through communication between clinical staff and researchers leading to the development of research protocols that have clinical value to treatment programs and their staff. Identifying the positive, applicable findings from these protocols, and linking the findings to the provision of services in a feasible way, would be beneficial to everyone in the field. Improving addiction treatment requires researchers, clinicians, and policymakers to establish and maintain a network of true collaboration for the benefit of the patient.

WHY INTEGRATE TECHNOLOGY AND TREATMENT? BENEFITS FOR CLINICIANS AND RESEARCHERS

Benefit of Comprehensive Information on Treatment-Seeking Individuals and Treatment Programs

Patient Information

Coexisting problems such as unemployment, crime, and mental and physical health difficulties influence the course and outcomes of treatment and are significant public health concerns in their own right. Research indicates that addiction treatment outcomes improve when patients are provided with services to meet these coexisting problems (McLellan et al., 1998). A system that includes information relevant to the multiple clinical, administrative, fiscal, evaluative, and policy questions that arise regarding the sequelae of substance dependence would be of benefit to both clinicians and researchers.

Program Information

Little information is available on what, specifically, is offered in treatment programs; the field of substance abuse has long perceived treatment delivery to occur in a "black box," with little known about exactly what happens during the delivery of treatment for substance abusers. The elucidation and quantification of the components of treatment activities will allow for the evaluation of their success and the identification of activities that are most beneficial to specific patients.

Tracking Trends

There is a need for an ongoing, nationwide, scientifically valid clinical information system that focuses on treatment programs and their patients. Early, accurate reporting on the emergence of new types of drug problems (such as current concerns regarding use of "club drugs" or the nonmedical use of Oxycontin) would allow for proactive clinical efforts. Information regarding the use of welfare, criminal justice, and mental health resources by people entering addiction treatment would allow local, state, and national policymakers as well as treatment providers to identify differences among groups of patients, programs, and communities and to plan more coordinated and efficient programs to deal with the multiple problems of substance abusers.

Benefits of a More Timely, Sensitive, and Responsive Reporting System

There has been substantial change in the characteristics of drug problems and the nature of drug treatment throughout the 1990s. In the years to come there will be an even greater need for "real-time" information about patient characteristics and their addiction-related problems to inform the individuals who plan and administrate the U.S. substance abuse treatment system.

Many research studies have provided invaluable information, but by the time the findings become available they might no longer be pertinent. For example, with an integrated system, information on the impact of a national crisis such as the terrorist attacks of September 11, 2001, could be collected at treatment programs immediately, and findings could be available in time to guide the continued efforts of both treatment providers and researchers. Without such a system, information on the impact of such a crisis would not be systematically collected in a timely fashion, and the findings would be of little use. Thus, a system that provides information on a timely basis so that corresponding modifications can be made to more effectively meet patients' needs would be beneficial.

In addition, an ongoing data collection system could establish a common ground and available resource for treatment providers and researchers. For instance, if clinicians are interested in better understanding the treatment of Hispanic men who use amphetamines with coexisting legal problems, then they will have a resource in the larger, ongoing system. Also, designing and completing a study with this population can be done in a more timely and cost-efficient manner, because the overall system would already be in place. Admission data provided by this system would make it possible to direct study participant recruitment at the programs most likely to admit the patients who are the focus of the specific area of clinical interest or outcome study, thus preventing a large, slow, costly, and fragmented effort at collecting outcome information on a general sample. As with the previous example of implementing a study after the September 11 terrorist attacks, any number of studies, large or small, could be implemented more readily and in a less costly manner if a standardized system of collecting information were in place.

Benefits of a Clinically Useful, Easily Implemented System That Streamlines Paperwork

Treatment providers want to collect information that is clinically useful and applicable to the treatment process. If such information is presented in a format that provides further insight into patients' problems and needs, such as clinically relevant reports, this data collection is more useful. A system that expedites assessment and treatment planning, and results in more time spent with patients and a more cost-efficient treatment process, will be beneficial to treatment providers, payors, and policymakers.

Easy implementation of systems is particularly necessary, because the turnover rate for substance abuse treatment personnel is estimated to be approximately 50% per year. Lack of adequate staffing and resources make clinicians' jobs even more difficult and required tasks even harder to complete.

Treatment providers will be able to work more efficiently if the reporting requirements mandated by federal, state, local, and accreditation agencies are standardized and easier to fulfill. A single system, designed through collaboration between clinicians and researchers, that integrates and captures all the required information, would overcome redundancy and allow clinicians to invest more of their time providing direct clinical care.

We have so far presented some of the benefits of integrating technology, in the form of an information or assessment system, in the substance abuse treatment and research fields. In the following section we discuss how we have worked toward achieving the benefits previously mentioned and how research and practice can be combined to create a workable, even desirable, system.

DESIGNING SUCH PROJECTS WITH EXAMPLES FROM DENS

To gather information that provides the benefits listed in a cost-efficient manner, the use of a random sample of U.S. treatment programs is necessary. To provide ease of data collection and speed of data transfer, an interactive system that is easy to implement and clinically useful is important. The system should provide information that is beneficial to clinical staff in making patient placement decisions and in planning treatment and doing administrative reporting and that is available rapidly and continuously. We now discuss some of the specific elements of DENS that were designed to meet these needs.

Meeting the Need for Comprehensive Information on Treatment-Seeking Individuals

Patient Information

The Addiction Severity Index (ASI; McLellan et al., 1992) is the primary source of patient information in DENS. The ASI gathers information on the nature, number, and severity of drug and alcohol problems and characterizes the severity of patients' medical, legal, employment, family/social, and psychiatric problems. Our decision to focus on the ASI followed more than 20 years of replicated reliability, validity, and utility evaluation of the instrument with a very wide range of substance abusers (McLellan et al., 1992; McLellan et al., 1985; McLellan, Luborsky, O'Brien, & Woody, 1980). Most of the participating treatment programs use the ASI as the intake or evaluation instrument and use the information to make clinical decisions regarding patient placement and treatment care planning.

Usefulness of Patient Information

DENS is designed to include tools for increasing the usefulness of collected data for treatment program administrators, clinicians, counselors, and policymakers. For example, program administrators can make use of data collected at their site with the four automated comparison reports generated by the DENS ASI software, such as a comparison of patients currently involved in the criminal justice system with those not involved in the criminal justice system or an automated comparison of demographics and treatment needs by gender.

Each treatment program is also given quarterly reports that compare its site-specific data to comparable programs in the DENS database (i.e., compares a methadone treatment program to all other methadone programs). These quarterly reports provide numerous comparisons of patients from all DENS participating sites. Program administration staff place a high value on these reports, which they have used to justify funding, help with accreditation proceedings, and reallocate staff. All nonidentifying data from all DENS sites are available in various formats, such as ASCII, SPSS, and SAS files. All of this information and the reports are also available on the DENS Web site listed at the end of the chapter.

The Addiction Treatment Inventory (ATI) is a standardized measure we developed as the primary source of information on "service delivery units" (Carise, McLellan, & Gifford, 2000). The ATI provides descriptive information on important structural, organizational, and service delivery aspects of the treatment programs. It was designed to be compatible with earlier surveys of treatment programs. ATI information is gathered each year and includes data on the type of facility, services and referrals provided, types of patients accepted, background of staff, and funding sources.

Gathering Information That Represents Patients Presenting for Substance Abuse Treatment

The goal of the DENS system is to represent patients who are entering substance abuse treatment across the United States, including tracking trends of patient needs and characteristics. Similarly, in many treatment programs across the country, the directors and clinicians want to achieve the same goal within their universe of patients, that is, those entering a specific clinic or group of clinics. Likewise, there is a need to collect this information at state and county levels. It is not feasible to implement a data collection system that requires regular reporting from entire populations of treatment programs at any level (national, state, county, or local); thus, we decided early on that the system will attempt to represent the most prevalent treatment modalities and sample more heavily from the areas of greatest treatment utilization. DENS collects information on patients in both alcohol and drug treatment programs that provide residential, inpatient treatment; methadone maintenance; or various levels of outpatient treatment. Thus, use of a random sample, at any level, allows participants to produce program- or policy-relevant information with the least burden.

Meeting the Need for More Timely, Sensitive, and Responsive Reporting

A significant value of the data collected through DENS is the availability of real-time information on patients entering the treatment system. DENS-participating treatment programs transfer their data biweekly via high-speed modem to the DENS (SQL Server) workstation at the Treatment Research Institute in Philadelphia, where data across the United States are received and stored.

DENS was designed with the capability to repeatedly add and change up to 35 additional questions, so specific, contemporary information can be collected, allowing emergent trends to be identified in a timely manner. The system involves a two-way transfer that permits the central system to change additional questions as the need arises. This feature of DENS keeps the information current and streamlined by asking targeted questions of administrative and clinical significance, getting answers for a desired period of time, and then discontinuing those questions in favor of other areas of interest that inevitably arise.

DENS was designed to provide the framework to fill the need for an ongoing, nationally representative data collection system that allows us to track trends in patients coming into treatment. DENS currently collects data on treatment programs and their patients at approximately 100 service delivery units. DENS provides scientifically valid clinical information that can be used to document trends in a timely manner, including early, accurate reporting on the emergence of new types of drug problems; criminal justice and mental health resources used by individuals entering addiction treatment; and so on. Just as the goal of the DENS system is to represent patients at a national level, states, counties, and treatment providers benefit from having a representative picture of the patients coming into treatment at their level.

Meeting the Need for an Ongoing, Available Framework for Other Studies: Examples From the TECH Study— Linking Assessment Technology to Improved Patient Care

One of the studies for which DENS was able to provide a framework is the one funded by the National Institute on Drug Abuse: "Linking Assessment Technology to Improved Patient Care," called the *TECH study*. The primary goal of this study is to improve patient assessment and increase the number and matches of services received in treatment by providing clinicians with relevant, reliable, and user-friendly assessment technology; the DENS ASI software; and resources and tools to aid them in treatment planning. For this purpose, with information from the United Way's "First Call for Help," we developed the DENS Resource Guide (DENS RG).

The DENS RG provides information about wraparound services (e.g., those related to employment, housing, legal, and medical) available in Philadelphia to assist clinicians in developing individualized treatment care plans that will lead to better patient needs–services matching. We have developed the DENS RG software as well as a hard copy of the RG in a binder form. Fifty counselors from 10 substance abuse treatment centers in Philadelphia are participating in the TECH study. Preliminary results show that there is (a) a better match between the needs of patients and the services they receive and (b) a higher number of services delivered to patients whose counselors received the training with the DENS RG. DENS provided the framework on which to easily build the TECH study, including providing access to treatment sites, the DENS ASI software, data collection procedures, and an established assessment training protocol.

Meeting the Needs for Easy Implementation and Clinically Relevant Information

User-Friendly DENS Software

Research and clinical staff worked together to design the DENS ASI and the RG software to help make patient assessment more comprehensive and clinically relevant and to allow for the rapid development of individualized patient treatment care plans. Programs participating in the DENS network receive a laptop computer with software that collects ASI assessment information and prints a clinically useful narrative report on each patient. Because the burden of DENS data collection was often added to treatment staff admissions personnel, the system needed to be as simple and as clinically useful as possible. The data collected ideally replace much of the program's current intake package rather than simply adding further data collection. The laptops allow the interviewer to establish good rapport with the patient by maintaining appropriate posture, eye contact, and body language, as would occur if a typical paper-and-pencil format were used. There is also a comprehensive manual that includes the intent of each question, coding conventions, and "probes." Finally, all clinicians are provided with our toll-free number to receive help from DENS staff.

Another software program designed to meet the need for easy implementation of clinically useful research studies was developed as a part of the TECH study. As mentioned earlier, we designed the DENS RG software to assist clinicians in tailoring their treatment care plans in a time-efficient and competent way. This software locates services in medical, employment, legal, family/social, and psychological areas offered at other agencies and programs in Philadelphia with the use of simple keywords and a click of a button. Information about the selected agency or program, its address, phone/fax numbers, kind of services offered, eligibility criteria, gender and ages of individuals served, languages in which services are offered, whether the facility is handicap accessible, as well as fees and transportation information are displayed and can easily be printed. We believe that the RG is a tool that will save clinicians a significant amount of time and result in increased services received and better needs–services matching.

Training of Providers to Increase the Clinical Usefulness of Data

DENS staff have provided more than 100 sessions of DENS ASI training to clinicians throughout the United States, with an average of 15 attendees at each session. Clinicians at all participating DENS and TECH study sites have been trained to administer the ASI using the DENS software. Our primary goals during training are to develop or enhance clinician skills in using the ASI for patient assessment and treatment care planning and to better learn how to make such a data collection system useful in clinical settings.

In the DENS ASI software there is a comment box in which the interviewer can type comments for every question as well as a section comment box at the end of every section. DENS software transforms the ASI data into three reports to have immediate clinical value at the time of admission. The Narrative Report is a 6- to 9-page clinical narrative suitable for use as an intake or admission summary and as a guide to initial treatment planning for each patient. Interviewer comments are integrated with the ASI data, and problem areas are ordered from most severe to least severe. The Narrative Report does not read as a stilted computer-generated program but as an integrated, comprehensive document describing the patient and the report of current problems and concerns. It is used by many providers to satisfy state requirements for an individualized intake evaluation or as the core of the biopsychosocial assessment.

The second report is the Treatment Care Plan Problem List, which lists patients' problems organized by section (e.g., medical, employment) along with a template for treatment care planning. This report helps clinicians in treatment planning by allowing them to easily prioritize the need for treatment in each of the ASI sections. A third printout, the ASI Report, is the full ASI interview printed out question by question with the corresponding answers and comments as well as graphs that represent the severity rating profiles. All three reports are easily exportable to a word processing document for editing and expanding.

Thus far we have detailed how we planned to make our data collection system, DENS, meet the needs of researchers and clinicians. In the following sections we discuss the practical implication issues that arose when implementing DENS in real-world treatment settings and, finally, how we have addressed these issues while attending to the needs of clinicians, administrators, and researchers.

"REAL-WORLD" IMPLEMENTATION ISSUES: RESEARCHER AND PROVIDER PERSPECTIVES

To address the needs of clinicians, policymakers, treatment providers, and researchers, we developed the DENS data collection system. We hope this is a substantial step toward accomplishing our goal of improving substance abuse treatment and providing national, real-time, policy-relevant information. However, various real-world implementation issues arose throughout the project, particularly regarding the recruitment of treatment programs, implementation of computerized data collection, and provision of ongoing training to clinicians to use the system accurately and fully. Researchers and treatment providers must work in collaboration to resolve problems and to develop methods of preventing the potential problems seen in the following areas.

Treatment Program Realities:
Reporting Requirements, Resources, and Staffing

Multiple Reporting Requirements

A significant concern for all treatment programs are the multiple reporting and data collection requirements from various sources (i.e., federal or state requirements, managed care and reimbursement procedures, and research protocols). Clinicians are often required to prepare multiple assessments and progress reports in specified, often overlapping formats, which is cumbersome and time consuming. As a result, clinicians spend a significant amount of time completing paperwork to meet the various requirements from federal, state, local, and accreditation agencies. This understandably serves to decrease their motivation and willingness to become a part of an additional data collection system that may require them to invest time in receiving training and in using the tools of the system.

Resources

Although over the 6 years that the DENS staff have been working with treatment programs the level of computer or assessment resources has increased, there continues to be little funding available for the expansion of technical capabilities. Because many treatment programs are not equipped to keep up with technological advancements, clinicians at these facilities are generally unfamiliar with computerized assessment and the corresponding computer technology. They have often developed other techniques of performing their tasks, mainly using paper-and-pencil forms. The result is a more difficult transition to use of new computerized systems. Some clinicians are hesitant to use computers during intake assessment, for several reasons. They may believe that their patients will be uncomfortable while being interviewed with a computerized assessment tool and may fear that some patients harbor concern for the confidentiality of the information they provide. In addition, clinicians themselves may be uncomfortable with using the computers.

Currently, when a new treatment program enrolls in DENS, it is likely that the program has a computer system and maybe some desktop PCs; however, 70% of the counselors in our current system report not having access to the Internet, and 50% report not having access to any computer. In programs where computers are available, counselors often report the need to use several software systems to fulfill requirements of the agency and state, funding sources, and accreditation agencies. Researchers without a full understanding of the multiple requirements already in place often try to impose another data collection system on treatment programs. For example, the existence of data collection systems already built into procedures at treatment programs such as the Veterans Health Information Systems and Technology

Architecture (VISTA), the system at Veterans Affairs Medical Centers, or other provider-purchased software systems lead to the problem of double data entry when getting involved in another system, causing significant time and staffing concerns. In addition, many systems are not built to be interchangeable or compatible with other systems, thus making the fulfillment of multiple needs of varying systems difficult. This highlights the need to design methods to blend different systems and make them compatible with each other at the technical and content levels to allow programs to meet reporting requirements in a more efficient way, as well as adding clinical value to the data collection process.

Staffing

In addition to the structural and organizational difficulties encountered at treatment programs, sites are also affected at the personnel level by a debilitating staff turnover rate of 50% per year on average. This leads to immense staffing pressures and understandably decreases the motivation and willingness of treatment providers and counselors to participate in yet another data collection effort requiring staff training and daily information gathering. Program directors or clinical supervisors often find it difficult to encourage employees to attend trainings because of a lack of adequate staff coverage, or financial limitations, or both. Often, scheduling and completing trainings is a tough task even if the training team is highly flexible in arranging logistics and is ready to accommodate the majority of program and clinician needs. Our experience in recruiting DENS sites has been that a motivated program director or clinical supervisor is very important in developing a team of counselors who are willing to collect information in a timely and accurate manner; however, counselors are the most important participants in these systems, and their level of involvement has a significant impact on the ability to gather this important information within real-world community-based treatment programs.

RESOLVING PRACTICAL IMPLEMENTATION ISSUES: AN EXAMPLE WITH DENS

Multiple Reporting Requirements

An example of one effort to minimize the amount of time necessary to collect information required at the treatment program is the development of a system and corresponding form to allow concurrent collection of the intake assessment and biopsychosocial data. Because most treatment programs mandate both, and the DENS intake covers most, but not all, of the items required for a biopsychosocial assessment, we developed a supplementary form for programs to enable the DENS ASI to be used as the biopsychosocial assessment. This supplementary form includes those questions required in most biopsychosocial interviews that are not covered in the ASI. Additional efforts include working with state or accreditation systems to obtain permission to allow the reports from the DENS system to fulfill state requirements or accreditation requirements such as those of the Joint Commission on Accreditation of Healthcare Organizations (JCAHO).

Resources

Many treatment programs are not adequately equipped to participate in a computerized data collection system. We provide laptops to participating sites to help address hardware problems; however, all types of computers are susceptible to technical problems, and each DENS staff member typically spends several hours per week on the telephone assisting more than 200 counselors who are using the system with a variety of computer-related difficulties, ranging from "frozen" screens to installation of new printers.

In the implementation of the DENS system we have allocated both staff and money to allow us to provide the most resources possible when working with treatment programs. We have computer systems staff, including a programmer, available to evaluate the current systems (if any) in treatment programs, increase the usefulness of our software system to fulfill other needs at the treatment program, and to integrate our system with current information system procedures. We also have training staff to provide various levels of training requested by the treatment program—not just training in DENS software but overall training in patient assessment, treatment care planning, and use of aggregate data collected, if desired by program staff. This is our effort to make participation in DENS as beneficial as possible. As mentioned, we also provide all necessary hardware and software to the treatment programs, including laptops, printers, and operating systems. In addition, we were able to budget for stipends to the treatment program or the staff to partially offset the costs of data collection. It is important for researchers to understand that when treatment programs agree to participate in any type of study or data collection effort they are allocating valuable and scarce resources to the effort, regardless of how minimal the time or resources involved may seem when compared with the benefits of the information collected. Treatment program staff want to help with data collection efforts, but their first allegiance is, and always should be, to the daily provision of services to their current patients.

When programs are using other data collection systems, we make every effort to blend the two systems or provide ample incentives to increase the benefits and make up for the extra work in implementing dual-data entry systems. We have also been flexible with our requirements in DENS, such as developing a shortened version of the ASI (ASI *Lite*) software.

Lack of Personnel

As we mentioned earlier, treatment programs often operate with limited or minimal staff, which often results in difficulty keeping staff motivated, particularly for participating in additional data collection efforts. To address this, we developed materials the counselors seem to value, such as our training binder, which contains a question-by-question ASI manual, articles, vignettes, and other information, as well as a "fast answers" manual for the DENS ASI software. We also provide continuing education credits and certificates for counselors who attend our training sessions and pass competency measures. We send quarterly reports and hold meetings with the program directors and counselors to discuss recent developments and findings. These materials can all be viewed on the DENS Web site listed at the end of this chapter.

Counselor and Patient Concerns

Some counselors expressed their concern that patients would be uncomfortable using computerized data collection, particularly with regards to confidentiality of the information. However, on the basis of our interactions with clinicians who have been using the DENS ASI software, we know that the interview flows very naturally and efficiently, especially after the administration of a couple of practice interviews. With regard to the confidentiality concern, we inform the clinicians about data transfer procedures, specifically, that when data are transferred to the central server at the Treatment Research Institute no identifying information is included. No one outside the treatment program receives identifying information about patients.

Through our pilot and expansion phase of implementing DENS, we have learned about the needs of sites, program administrators, and clinicians, and we have worked on accommodating these needs. DENS has proved to be successful not only at the implementation level but also at the maintenance level. Currently, data on more than 30,000 patients entering substance abuse treatment throughout the United States have been accumulated at the DENS central server in Philadelphia. We believe that DENS has proved to be a powerful tool in many aspects and will continue to expand to serve the needs of patients seeking treatment for substance abuse problems.

Training

It was important to provide training for clinicians on administering the ASI correctly and on using the DENS ASI software package successfully. To accommodate the difficulty in allowing all staff to attend DENS trainings, we have offered to hold trainings numerous times so that all staff interested can develop the necessary skills to participate in DENS. We are also developing a video version of the training as well as adding resources to our budget to provide stipends to programs or trainees when participation in the training takes staff away from their clinical duties to such an extent that the program suffers, or when it requires counselors to work extra shifts.

Staff Turnover

Staff turnover has posed a significant challenge to the collection of valid, consistent data. We expected some turnover and budgeted for shorter "booster" training in the following year, but the turnover rate was underestimated, and there is a need for more extensive, ongoing training and site visits. This need prompted us to develop additional, easy-to-use training manuals and "quick reference guides." The toll-free hotline continues to be available and is staffed approximately 10 hours each day.

CONCLUSION

There is a significant need for the implementation of technology in the assessment and documentation of care in substance abuse treatment programs. This will allow for the streamlining of the various reporting requirements burdening treatment providers as well as an increase in the understanding of patients' problems and the match between those problems and the services patients receive. One ongoing real-time system for collecting clinical information from individuals entering addiction treatment programs in the United States is DENS, a computer-based system that allows for rapid, standardized, clinically and policy-relevant data collection. This system has been tested in, and refined by participation from professionals at, more than 100 treatment programs. The system has been well accepted and appreciated by most programs that have participated. Furthermore, we have been able to provide rapid, clinically relevant, policy-oriented information, which has not been available to this point, that complements and enhances information from other systems and that can provide a strategic framework for the future.

DENS is currently expanding to a national, random sample of treatment programs. The DENS data can be used to track emergent phenomena (e.g., the appearance of new drug problems) and therefore address issues of immediate policy interest. DENS can also document a nationwide (or programwide) presence or increase in specific problems (e.g., new drug patterns, increased admission of welfare referrals) with a responsiveness that was previously unavailable. We hope these data will be used to inform clinicians, treatment providers, and policymakers. For example, if the DENS system had been available 10–20 years ago, it is possible that members of the scientific community could have gathered earlier information on the spread of AIDS in the substance abusing community, that policymakers could have used the information to alter funding strategies more quickly, and that clinicians could have more easily adapted treatment services to provide for the needs of substance abusers with AIDS. This is just one example of many of the use of technology to collect information in U.S. substance abuse treatment programs. Consistent with our view that this information is necessary for many purposes, the DENS reports, presentations, publications, and database will continue to be publicly available and can be accessed on the World Wide Web at http://www.densonline.org.

REFERENCES

Carise, D., McLellan, A. T., & Gifford, L. (2000). Development of a "treatment program" descriptor: The Addiction Treatment Inventory. *Substance Use and Misuse*, 35, 1797–1818.

McLellan, A. T., Hagan, T. A., Levine, M., Gould, F., Myers, K., Bencivengo, M., et al. (1998). Supplemental social services improve outcomes in public addiction treatment. *Addiction*, 93, 1489–1499.

McLellan, A. T., Kushner, H., Metzger, D., Peters, R., Grissom, G., Pettinati, H., et al. (1992). The fifth edition of the Addiction Severity Index. *Journal of Substance Abuse Treatment*, 9, 199–213.

McLellan, A. T., Luborsky, L., Cacciola, J., Griffith, J., Evans, F., Barr, H., et al. (1985). New data from the Addiction Severity Index: Reliability and validity in three centers. *Journal of Nervous and Mental Disorders*, 173, 412–422.

McLellan, A. T., Luborsky, L., O'Brien, C. P., & Woody, G. E. (1980). An improved diagnostic instrument for substance abuse patients, The Addiction Severity Index. *Journal of Nervous and Mental Diseases*, 168, 26–33.

Office of National Drug Control Policy. (2002a). *Data snapshot: Drug abuse in America, Office of National Drug Control Strategy*. Retrieved September 16, 2002, from www.whitehousedrugpolicy.gov/publications/drugfact/american_users_spend2002/index.html

Office of National Drug Control Policy. (2002b). *SAMSHA factsheet: National Household Survey on Drug Abuse, 2001*. Retrieved September 16, 2002, from www.whitehousedrugpolicy.gov/drugfact/nhsdaol.html

Office of National Drug Control Policy. (2002c). *The National Drug Control Strategy 2001 Annual Report* (p. 65). Retrieved September 16, 2002, from www.whitehousedrugpolicy.gov/policy/ndcs01strategy2001

12

ALCOHOL AND DRUG ABUSE TREATMENT DEMONSTRATIONS: DEVELOPING AND TESTING COMMUNITY INTERVENTIONS

DENNIS MCCARTY

Demonstration projects support model development, test variations and generalization, and build a platform of practice experience to guide policy and practice approaches to community problems. Research and practice are integrated to develop knowledge, deliver services, and report results that may inform policy, practice, and science (Wittman, 1982). A unique aspect of demonstration projects is that community members and stakeholders (e.g., consumers and practitioners) often participate in the creation of knowledge, and study implementation requires levels of collaboration not found in most academic-based research (Israel, Schulz, Parker, & Becker, 1998). Demonstrations illustrate the capacity of communities to contribute to and benefit from the process of testing ideas and creating knowledge (Israel et al., 1998; Stoil, Hill, Jansen, Sambrano, & Winn, 2000). The combination of

Preparation of this chapter was supported by grants from the National Institute on Drug Abuse (P50-DA-10233) and the National Institute on Alcohol Abuse and Alcoholism (R01-AA-11363).

policy, practice, and science ultimately adds to the complexity of conducting demonstrations, magnifies the challenge of systematic discovery, and may enhance the relevance and generalizability of the initiatives (Israel et al., 1998; Room, 1990).

Three active ingredients are found in most demonstrations: (a) planning, (b) implementation, and (c) evaluation (Wittman, 1982). Planning develops the project framework through an iterative articulation of needs, goals, theories, and services. Creative and innovative implementation is central to successful demonstration: Resources are allocated, staff are trained and supported, services are operationalized and delivered, and managers respond creatively to problems and barriers. Evaluation tests programmatic and theoretical hypotheses, monitors implementation, is challenged to maintain methodological rigor in a fluid environment, and reports positive and negative findings while resolving the sometimes-competing interests of different stakeholder perspectives. All of this activity occurs within the constraints of time, funding, and politics (Wittman, 1982). Projects typically receive limited authorization for time and funding in order to foster knowledge development without perpetuating services. Moreover, shifting political demands require immediate responses to critical needs but may inhibit more substantial and long-term resource commitments.

Demonstrations are authorized to document the feasibility of serving specific groups or using specific models of service delivery. They may also test the replicability and generalizability of models that appear to have potential for adoption. Ultimately, demonstrations provide examples of strategies to address specific problems that can be applied and adapted in other communities (Stoil et al., 2000). Investigators, policymakers, and practitioners therefore struggle to balance the need for action with the need to provide useful data on the quality and effectiveness of the interventions. An emphasis on study design may oversimplify complex community interventions or stress experimental control when program flexibility is required. Conversely, resource constraints and restrictions on study designs often lead to evaluations with weak statistical control and limited measurement. Demonstrations consequently provide opportunities to innovate not only in the delivery of care but also in the evaluation of services and outcomes (Gabriel, 2000; Giesbrecht & Rankin, 2000).

Demonstration programs have informed policy and practice since the beginnings of contemporary alcohol and drug abuse treatment services in the 1960s. In this chapter I review selected demonstrations, discuss linkages with research, and note the continued evolution of demonstration models. The chapter builds on the review of three demonstration initiatives included in the Institute of Medicine report on bridging practice and research in community-based drug abuse treatment: (a) The National Institute on Alcohol Abuse and Alcoholism's homeless demonstration program, (b) The National Institute on Drug Abuse's (NIDA's) HIV risk reduction programs for injection drug users, and (c) The National Institute on Alcohol Abuse and Alcoholism's prevention research replication program (Lamb, Greenlick, & McCarty, 1998).

CASES IN POINT: TREATMENT DEMONSTRATIONS

Treatment demonstrations reflect competing community needs and simultaneously address the complex and multifaceted problems of the individuals being served. Typically, treatment interventions test specified models of service delivery with explicitly defined patient populations. Treatment and intervention demonstrations have led to changes in the legal processing of inebriates and drunken drivers, enhanced services for pregnant and parenting women, evaluated service innovations, and tested changes in the organization and delivery of alcohol and drug abuse treatment.

St. Louis Detoxification and Diagnostic Evaluation Center

Chronic drunkenness offenders burdened police departments and court systems in U.S. urban centers during the 1960s (President's Commission on Law Enforcement and Administration of Justice: Task Force on Drunkenness, 1967). Court decisions and changes in state laws eventually led to the decriminalization of public inebriation for homeless individuals. The St. Louis Detoxification demonstration documented the feasibility of replacing incarceration with detoxification centers and helped catalyze the shift from drunk tanks to treatment programs.

The U.S. Department of Justice, Office of Law Enforcement Assistance (later called the Law Enforcement Assistance Administration) funded the St. Louis Metropolitan Police Department to develop and test the St. Louis Detoxification and Diagnostic Evaluation Center (a similar program was also funded in Washington, DC; St. Louis Metropolitan Police Department, 1970). A 30-bed center provided chronic inebriates with a 7-day treatment alternative to arrest, adjudication, and incarceration. The impact of the center on police and criminal justice resources allocated to drunkenness offenders was assessed, and patient outcomes were monitored. Services included medical treatment; counseling; work therapy; education; Alcoholics Anonymous meetings; and aftercare planning that addressed housing, employment, and continued treatment.

Dramatic reductions were observed in the use of police and court resources: (a) Arresting-officer time declined 50% (from 96 minutes to 48 minutes), (b) a 2-hour reduction was observed in total police time (from 190 minutes to 48 minutes), (c) drunkenness court cases declined 34%, and (d) commitments to the workhouse declined 39% (St. Louis Metropolitan Police Department, 1970). Participants also appeared to benefit. In 1967,

674 individuals had 1,120 admissions, and most (69%) had only 1 admission (St. Louis Metropolitan Police Department, 1970). The typical patient was a White (84%) man (93%) about 48 years old. Follow-up interviews with 160 men an average of 4 months after discharge reported significant improvement in 50% of the patients. The final report drew three conclusions: (a) Public inebriates benefit from treatment interventions, (b) changes in the processing of drunkenness offenders frees public safety resources for other needs, and (c) a detoxification center is a valuable resource for the community (St. Louis Metropolitan Police Department, 1970).

Although the pre–post evaluation design did not include no-treatment comparison groups, the apparently substantial impacts on public safety resources and the modest but promising evidence of patient gains generated enthusiasm for the service. The President's Commission on Law Enforcement and Administration of Justice: Task Force on Drunkenness (1967) touted the model and recommended development of community treatment services and a decriminalization of public intoxication. The St. Louis Detoxification and Diagnostic Evaluation Center illustrates the value of a well-developed demonstration program at the right moment. The relatively weak evaluation design reflects not only the state of the art at that time but also an ongoing tension between the need for programmatic development and the allocation of resources to data collection and analysis.

Alcohol Safety Action Programs

The interface of public safety, criminal justice, and rehabilitation services provided the context for another important demonstration: the Alcohol Safety Action Programs (ASAP). The Highway Safety Act of 1966 (P.L. 89-564) required a report to Congress on the effects of drinking alcohol on highway safety. The 1968 analysis, *Alcohol and Highway Safety*, concluded that alcohol consumption substantially increased the risk of highway accidents and fatalities and urged adoption of a broad array of countermeasures, including strategies to identify and treat problem drinkers (U.S. Department of Transportation, 1968). The National Highway Traffic Safety Administration initiated ASAP in 1969 and, from federal fiscal years 1970 to 1977, supported demonstrations in 35 communities at a total cost of about $88 million. Multidimensional interventions were designed to increase enforcement, improve court procedures, screen offenders for problem drinking, and provide education and rehabilitation services to drunk driving offenders (U.S. Department of Transportation, 1979a). Funded sites conducted program-level evaluation using methods and instruments outlined in the *Demonstration Project Handbook* (U.S. Department of Transportation, 1977). Evaluation activities monitored enforcement, adjudication, rehabilitation, public information, and program management components of the initiative (U.S. Department of Transportation, 1979b).

An assessment of the ASAP program located in Phoenix, Arizona, found little change in alcohol use, drinking behaviors, and social adjustment following treatment (Swenson, Struckman-Johnson, Ellingstad, Clay, & Nichols, 1981). Similarly, evaluations of 17 ASAP rehabilitation services found no evidence of impact on conviction rates (U.S. Department of Transportation, 1985) and subsequent accidents (Nichols, Weinstein, Ellingstad, & Struckman-Johnson, 1978). A subgroup analysis, however, suggested that social drinkers benefited from the intervention and were less likely to be rearrested than social drinkers who did not receive an educational service (U.S. Department of Transportation, 1985). There was no evidence that intervention services reduced rearrest rates among individuals more dependent on alcohol, that is, problem drinkers (U.S. Department of Transportation, 1985).

The ASAP model was adopted widely. The multifaceted programs enhanced enforcement, streamlined procedures for processing drinking drivers, modified sanctions available to courts, and prompted changes in state legislation. ASAPs contributed importantly to increased public awareness of the dangers associated with drinking driving. Subsequent public education and advocacy efforts by Mothers Against Drunk Driving and the Presidential Commission on Drunk Driving (1983) catalyzed continued evolution of public policies for the arrest, adjudication, and sanctioning of individuals found driving under the influence (DeJong & Hingson, 1998). Multiple offenders are now typically sentenced to incarceration, long periods of intensive treatment, or both. First offenders, on the other hand, in most jurisdictions continue to participate in ASAP-type education services. The persistence of the basic drunk driving program, in spite of the limited empirical evidence of effectiveness with more dependent drinkers, suggests that, once institutionalized, demonstration programs may experience little pressure to continue to evolve and improve.

Pregnant and Parenting Women

The potential for cocaine and crack use during pregnancy to damage fetuses and to lead to drug-affected infants received widespread attention from prosecutors, policymakers, and the public during the late 1980s and early 1990s. Medical experts responded with recommendations to develop appropriate systems of treatment for pregnant drug-using women and their children (American Medical Association, Board of Trustees, 1990; Brown, 1991; Chavkin, 1991). The "crack crisis" stimulated demands for expanded access to drug abuse treatments that met the multidimensional needs of pregnant and parenting women (Office of Inspector General, 1990; U. S. General Accounting Office, 1990, 1991). Multiple research and services demonstration projects were developed and supported by the leading federal authorities: NIDA, the Health Care Financing Administration

(HCFA), the Center for Substance Abuse Treatment (CSAT), and Center for Substance Abuse Prevention (CSAP).

Perinatal-20

NIDA initiated the Perinatal-20 Treatment Research Demonstration Program in 1989 with 10 sites and added 10 more sites in 1990. The projects were designed not only to conduct treatment research but also to expand the capacity of drug abuse treatment systems to serve pregnant and parenting women (Rahdert, 1996). Project sites implemented comprehensive services or introduced interventions in a system of care for pregnant and parenting women. Implementation barriers included community resistance to siting services; limited budgets; concerns for staff and participant safety; participant needs for housing, child care, and transportation; fragmentation of services; protection of confidentiality; and resistance to the use of comparison groups and study controls (Chasnoff, Marques, Strantz, Farrow, & Davis, 1996; Mason, 1996). Recruiting and retaining pregnant and parenting women to participate in study services proved difficult for many of the Perinatal-20 sites. Study teams modified protocols, expanded outreach, linked with other social services and health care providers, drew on the experienced clinical staff, provided transportation and child care, and worked around waiting lists (Howard & Beckwith, 1996; LaFazia et al., 1996; Lewis, Haller, Branch, & Ingersoll, 1996; Palinkas, Atkins, Noel, & Miller, 1996).

Investigators clearly struggled with many problems counselors confront daily and appear to have benefited from partnerships with experienced providers. From the published articles, however, it is less obvious that practitioners benefited from the collaboration. One of the persistent challenges in working with community treatment providers is to maintain a reciprocal and equitable relationship. It is critical that both partners continue to perceive the relationship as beneficial.

HCFA Demonstration

At least one federal analysis recommended an expansion of Medicaid benefits to include substance abuse treatment for pregnant women (U.S. General Accounting Office, 1990): HFCA initiated Demonstrations to Improve Access to Care for Pregnant Substance Abusers and supported five states (Maryland, Massachusetts, New York, South Carolina, and Washington) to test strategies for the identification and treatment of Medicaid-eligible, substance-abusing pregnant women (Howell et al., 1998). Projects provided outreach, screening for alcohol and drug abuse, substance abuse treatment, and case management to improve the health of the women and their infants and assessed the impact of increased services on total Medicaid expenditures (Howell et al., 1998). An independent evaluation concluded that it was difficult to find and engage potential substance-abusing pregnant women because they were reluctant to be identified (Howell et al., 1998). The evaluation also noted that costs for serving pregnant substance-abusing women were approximately double the expense of caring for other pregnant women in Medicaid. It is important, however, that infant birth weights were higher among women who received more services, suggesting that substance abuse treatment can contribute to improved birth outcomes (Howell et al., 1998).

HCFA authorization prohibits the use of Medicaid funds to serve individuals residing in an "institute for mental disease" (IMD). Residential services for substance abuse treatment have been classified as institute-for-mental-disease services and have been excluded from Medicaid benefits. Three of the projects (Massachusetts, New York, and Washington) received HCFA waivers to permit Medicaid reimbursement for residential services. A cost-effectiveness analysis using Addiction Severity Index interviews, birth data, Medicaid costs, and the costs of substance abuse treatment from 358 women who participated in the Massachusetts MOTHERS (Medicaid Opportunities to Help Enter Recovery Services) program suggested that the greatest cost benefits were found among participants who entered residential care (Daley, 1999; Daley et al., 2000). Decreased cost of crime was the primary source of economic benefits to society. Residential care was also associated with higher birthweights (Daley, 1999). The Massachusetts demonstration thus supported elimination of the current policy restriction that prohibits the use of residential treatment for pregnant drug-abusing women.

CSAT Initiatives

CSAT supported two demonstrations that assessed the influence of residential services when added to health, mental health, and social services for women and their children: (a) Residential Services for Women and Their Children (26 awards) and (b) Pregnant and Postpartum Women (24 awards; Dowell, Chen, Roberts, Burgdorf, & Herrell, 1999). Study sites in both programs used a standardized set of admission, discharge, and follow-up interviews. Preliminary data suggest that mental health disorders were evident among 60% of the women in the year prior to admission (Dowell et al., 1999). Women with co-occurring mental illness were less likely to complete treatment, unless they received mental health services during their substance abuse treatment (Dowell et al., 1999).

Together, the CSAT and HCFA demonstrations make a strong case for increased access to residential treatments for pregnant and parenting women. Federal Medicaid policy, however, has not changed to encourage and support the development and adoption of residential treatment models for this high-risk population with multiple problems.

NIDA's Applied Evaluation Research Portfolio

In response to the rapid spread of HIV infection among injection drug users and high-risk sexual activity among crack cocaine users, NIDA funded research demonstrations to improve engagement and retention in care and enhance delivery of drug abuse treatment services to hard-to-serve patient populations. The Applied Evaluation Research Portfolio supported 15 demonstrations beginning in 1988 and 1989 and tested treatment strategies developed in laboratory settings in community-based services (Tims, Fletcher, Inciardi, & Horton, 1997a). The demonstrations supported research-related treatment costs and, thus, increased treatment capacity; research benefited through larger samples; and the community benefited by having improved access to care (Fletcher, Inciardi, & Horton, 1994b; Fletcher, Tims, & Inciardi, 1993).

The investment in services, however, also highlighted tensions between research and practice. Investigations required control over assignment to study conditions, and counselors and programs had to follow treatment protocols, minimizing their influence on treatment planning (Fletcher et al., 1994b; Fletcher et al., 1993). Independent investigations tested strategies to enhance access to services, retain clients in care, and improve service delivery and outcomes. Treatment settings include methadone clinics, residential programs, case management strategies, day treatment models, and enhancements to outpatient services and outreach programs. Services were provided to injection drug users, offenders released from incarceration, individuals with serious mental illness, homeless men and women, and patients dependent on cocaine. Implementation in community settings meant that investigators and practitioners confronted community opposition to program siting, distractions from state budget crises that destabilized publicly funded services, and disruption caused by riots in neighboring areas and international military actions (Fletcher et al., 1994b).

Both standard care and enhanced services typically were effective and led to reductions in drug use and risk behaviors. Enhanced services were not always more effective. Innovations, however, were generally effective in increasing access to and engagement in care. A mobile methadone service retained clients who were otherwise reluctant to enter care (Brady, Besteman, & Greenfield, 1997). Clients were more likely to stay in methadone treatment when fees were eliminated and counseling was optional; moreover, admission within 24 hr improved entry to care (Maddux, 1997). The addition of tools to facilitate communication with patients and improve counselor skills led to better outcomes (Simpson, Dansereau, & Joe, 1997). Because these studies were completed in community settings, the potential for widespread application seems strong.

One of the major contributions of this demonstration is a three-volume series that provides a record of the project design (Inciardi, Tims, &

Fletcher, 1993), implementation (Fletcher, Inciardi, & Horton, 1994a), and outcomes (Tims, Inciardi, Fletcher, & Horton, 1997b). Too often demonstration projects leave incomplete histories because documentation is limited to unpublished papers or reports with limited distribution. More demonstrations should aspire to provide a systematic and complete record of design, implementation, and results that discuss problems as well as successes.

Target Cities

One of the more ambitious treatment demonstrations attempted to alter the organization and delivery of alcohol and drug abuse services in 19 cities—CSAT's (initially as the Office for Treatment Improvement) Target Cities Initiative. Treatment systems were modified with the introduction of five components designed to improve system efficiency and capacity, streamline intake, eliminate duplication, and improve flow of information on clients and system capacity (Guydish & Muck, 1999b). First, to assure broad support for system change, the initiative required a formal partnership of treatment providers, state and city substance abuse authorities, and CSAT. Second, central intake units assessed clients to determine service needs and to facilitate referrals to appropriate levels and locations of care. Automated information systems were a third required component and were intended to enhance the quality and flow of client data and to improve the identification and use of treatment capacity. Fourth, linkages with community systems for health care, criminal justice, and human services were expected to improve the integration of care and access to needed services. Finally, all projects included process and outcome evaluation components. The goal was to improve capacity without increasing cost (Guydish & Muck, 1999b). Standardization of the processes was also expected to improve the quality of assessment, referral, and treatment.

Despite efforts to assure that all stakeholders accepted the project's goals, the need for coordination and standardization was not universally recognized. Autonomous treatment programs were reluctant to relinquish control of intake and assessment processes (Guydish & Muck, 1999a). As a consequence, central intakes were difficult to develop and maintain, and cities struggled with the creation and implementation of centralized information systems (Guydish & Muck, 1999a). Changing state and local environments, moreover, complicated evaluation efforts, and few results have been reported (Guydish & Muck, 1999a). The primary summary of the Target City Demonstrations noted that system linkages were created and admission processes were enhanced; system reorganization, however, required substantial resources and infrastructure investments, and it was not clear that the benefits of the program exceeded the costs of system change (Guydish & Muck, 1999a).

DISCUSSION

Room's (1990) reflective essay on community-based demonstration projects for the prevention of alcohol problems concludes that demonstrations are challenging to implement and evaluate because the combination of change agents, community participants and interests, and investigators is inherently unstable. Stakeholders hold substantially different perspectives. Practitioners are most influential when they have a strong belief in the efficacy of the intervention. Science, conversely, encourages a skeptical view; the demand for empirical evidence is often perceived as a disbelief in the methods of practice and contributes to tension between evaluation and practice. The third set of stakeholders, community groups, tends to have little interest in the theoretical issues and tolerate the presence of interventionists and evaluators in order to access services.

The various perspectives complicate project design, delivery of services, and program assessment and, in the presence of unresolved tensions, may threaten project viability. Balancing these potential and actual tensions requires skillful project management, engagement with community politics, and creative evaluation. It is not surprising that relatively few demonstration projects successfully manage to simultaneously deliver community services, satisfy community demands, and contribute to the scientific literature. Thus, there is relatively little in the peer-reviewed literature on many demonstrations, including Target Cities and the various tests of services for pregnant and parenting women.

Room (1990) suggested that more will be learned from demonstrations when the usually unwritten saga of project processes and experiences (i.e., embarrassing mistakes, political dilemmas, and implementation conflicts) becomes a valued and expected part of the public record. The absence of careful autopsies from many demonstrations deprives investigators, practitioners, and policymakers of much that might be learned in terms of the design and management of major projects. Findings of no impact can be useful and important contributions to the science of community prevention and treatment.

Federal demonstrations have become more methodologically sophisticated. Designs are specified more carefully, and evaluation activities have become more central. Federal authorities require tighter evaluation designs and more standardization of data elements. The need to balance service delivery and knowledge creation, however, persists. The Target City communities, for example, frequently grappled with tensions between existing systems and the introduction of new coordination and referral mechanisms. In most communities, treatment programs were reluctant to cede their autonomy and to participate in centralized intake and assessment functions. Struggles between community expectations and research needs were evident in the design and implementation of services for pregnant and parenting women and drug abuse treatment services for individuals at risk of HIV infection. It was difficult to site services, communities were reluctant to participate in randomization, and requirements for data collection were often perceived as burdensome and unnecessary. In recent demonstrations, scientific rigor has been stressed perhaps at a loss of community support and subsequent institutionalization. Policy impacts have been limited: Despite evidence that residential services improve outcomes for pregnant drug-abusing women, the services remain outside the scope of Medicaid reimbursement.

All of the demonstrations illustrate the difficulty of conducting evaluations that provide unambiguous information on program impacts. Uncontrolled changes in the environment often introduce rival hypotheses for program effects. The Applied Evaluation Research Portfolio reported disruptions related to riots in nearby neighborhoods, acts of war, and state fiscal crises. The introduction of managed care complicated the implementation and interpretation of Target City Demonstrations in several communities. Development of appropriate comparison groups challenged the creativity and skill of the investigators. Treatment initiatives often encountered community resistance to program siting, the use of comparison groups, and the need for randomization. These complexities ultimately require investigators to develop more complex and skilled evaluations that engage service providers and the community. Service providers may come to recognize that investigators are allies if the results of demonstrations can be used to advocate for maintained and expanded funding.

It is noteworthy that evaluation data appear to be less important when interventions have dramatic effects. The evaluation of the St. Louis Diagnostic and Detoxification Center was unsophisticated, but the impact on police practice was so evident that a weak evaluation was sufficient to justify application of the model in other communities. Similarly, evaluation suggested that the rehabilitation aspect of ASAP was relatively ineffective for problem drinkers. The program's impact on the criminal justice system, however, was so strong that dissemination was not inhibited, and adoption was rapid.

Relationships among policy, practice, and research are always changing. Each demonstration has its own policy context. Political realities sometimes become more influential than program impacts and empirical data. In other contexts, the needs of the community drive the application of program results. Too often, the demands of science and the perspective of research dominate. Practitioners must participate assertively. The continual challenge is to find a balance that permits valid science, provides useful services, and promotes appropriate public policy. Demonstration projects will continue to provide experiential evidence and remain an important mechanism for bridging gaps between practice and research.

There is great potential for all stakeholders to benefit from participation in treatment demonstrations. Investigators must be sensitive to the complexity of contemporary community service settings and design realistic interventions that complement existing services. Evaluations must be integrated into existing administrative data collection activities with minimal additional burden on practitioners and patients. Programs and their practitioners must value the opportunities that demonstrations create. Service innovations must begin with an understanding that there are additional data collection responsibilities and requirements for adherence to protocol. Communities can appreciate the benefit of added services and simultaneously recognize that the services may be time limited.

Thirty-plus years of treatment demonstration projects have set the stage for leaps in the development of treatment technologies and the quality of drug abuse treatment research. NIDA's National Drug Abuse Treatment Clinical Trials Network (CTN) builds on the foundation of demonstrations. In the CTN, investigators partner with community treatment programs to conduct clinical trials of promising treatment innovations. The level of science is fully dependent on the ability of treatment programs and their staffs to follow study protocols and adhere to manualized services. Protocols have been altered substantially as a result of practitioner participation. As a consequence, these studies have great potential to catalyze the adoption and diffusion of treatment innovations in pharmacotherapy and behavioral techniques. The National Drug Abuse Treatment Clinical Trials Network represents a logical continuation and extension of collaborations that enhance practice, guide policy, and inform science.

REFERENCES

American Medical Association, Board of Trustees. (1990). Legal interventions during pregnancy: Court-ordered medical treatments and legal penalties for potentially harmful behavior by pregnant women. *Journal of the American Medical Association, 254,* 2663–2670.

Brady, J. V., Besteman, K. J., & Greenfield, L. (1997). Evaluating the effectiveness of mobile drug abuse treatment. In F. M. Tims, J. A. Inciardi, B. W. Fletcher, & A. M. Horton (Eds.), *The effectiveness of innovative approaches in the treatment of drug abuse* (pp. 42–58). Westport, CT: Greenwood Press.

Brown, S. S. (Ed.). (1991). *Children and parental illicit drug use: Research, clinical, and policy issues; summary of a workshop.* Washington, DC: National Academy Press.

Chasnoff, I. J., Marques, P. R., Strantz, I. H., Farrow, J., & Davis, S. (1996). Building bridges: Treatment research partnerships in the community. In E. R. Rahdert (Ed.), *Treatment for drug-exposed women and their children: Advances in research methodology* (NIDA Research Monograph 166, NIH No. 96-3632, pp. 6–21). Rockville, MD: National Institute on Drug Abuse.

Chavkin, W. (1991). Mandatory treatment for drug use during pregnancy. *Journal of the American Medical Association, 266,* 1556–1560.

Daley, M. (1999). *The cost-effectiveness of substance abuse treatment for pregnant women.* Unpublished doctoral dissertation, Brandeis University, Waltham, MA.

Daley, M., Argeriou, M., McCarty, D., Callahan, J. J., Shepard, D. S., & Williams, C. N. (2000). The costs of crime and the benefits of substance abuse treatment for pregnant women. *Journal of Substance Abuse Treatment, 19,* 445–458.

DeJong, W., & Hingson, R. (1998). Strategies to reduce driving under the influence of alcohol. *Annual Review of Public Health, 19,* 359–378.

Dowell, K., Chen, X., Roberts, T., Burgdorf, K., & Herrell, J. M. (1999, June). *Substance abuse treatment outcomes for pregnant and parenting women with co-occurring mental disorders.* Poster presented at the Substance Abuse and Mental Health Services Administration's Second National Conference on Women, Los Angeles.

Fletcher, B. W., Inciardi, J. A., & Horton, A. M. (Eds.). (1994a). *Drug abuse treatment: The implementation of innovative approaches* (Vol. 45). Westport, CT: Greenwood Press.

Fletcher, B. W., Inciardi, J. A., & Horton, A. M. (1994b). Introduction: Challenges of implementing research demonstration programs. In B. W. Fletcher, J. A. Inciardi, & A. M. Horton (Eds.), *Drug abuse treatment: The implementation of innovative approaches* (pp. ix–xvi). Westport, CT: Greenwood Press.

Fletcher, B. W., Tims, F. M., & Inciardi, J. A. (1993). Improving treatment: A program for systemic innovations. In J. A. Inciardi, F. M. Tims, & B. W. Fletcher (Eds.), *Innovative approaches in the treatment of drug abuse: Program models and strategies* (pp. xiii–xix). Westport, CT: Greenwood Press.

Gabriel, R. M. (2000). Methodological challenges in evaluating community partnerships and coalitions: Still crazy after all these years. *Journal of Community Psychology, 28,* 339–352.

Giesbrecht, N., & Rankin, J. (2000). Reducing alcohol problems through community action research projects: Contexts, strategies, implications, and challenges. *Substance Use & Misuse, 35*(1–2), 31–53.

Guydish, J., & Muck, R. (1999a). Reorganizing publicly-funded drug abuse treatment: The experience of ten target cities projects. *Journal of Psychoactive Drugs, 31,* 273–278.

Guydish, J., & Muck, R. (1999b). The challenge of managed care in drug abuse treatment. *Journal of Psychoactive Drugs, 31,* 193–195.

Howard, J., & Beckwith, L. (1996). Issues in subject recruitment and retention with pregnant and parenting substance-abusing women. In E. R. Rahdert (Ed.), *Treatment for drug-exposed women and their children: Advances in research methodology* (NIDA Research Monograph 166, NIH No. 96-3632, pp. 68–86). Rockville, MD: National Institute on Drug Abuse.

Howell, E. M., Thorton, C., Heiser, N., Chasnoff, I., Hill, I., Schwalberg, R., et al. (1998). *Pregnant women and substance abuse: Testing approaches to a complex problem* (Report No. PR97-56). Washington, DC: Mathmatica Policy Research.

Inciardi, J. A., Tims, F. M., & Fletcher, B. W. (Eds.). (1993). *Innovative approaches in the treatment of drug abuse: Program models and strategies* (Vol. 39). Westport, CT: Greenwood Press.

Israel, B. A., Schulz, A. J., Parker, E. A., & Becker, A. B. (1998). Review of community-based research: Assessing partnership approaches to improve public health. *Annual Review of Public Health, 19,* 173–202.

LaFazia, M. A., Kleyn, J., Lanz, J., Hall, T., Nyrop, K., Stark, K. D., et al. (1996). Case management: A method of addressing subject selection and recruitment issues. In E. R. Rahdert (Ed.), *Treatment for drug-exposed women and their children: Advances in research methodology* (NIDA Research Monograph No. 166, NIH No. 96-3632, pp. 52–67). Rockville, MD: National Institute on Drug Abuse.

Lamb, S., Greenlick, M. R., & McCarty, D. (1998). *Bridging the gap between practice and research: Forging partnerships with community-based drug and alcohol treatment.* Washington, DC: National Academy Press.

Lewis, R. A., Haller, D. L., Branch, D., & Ingersoll, K. S. (1996). Retention issues involving drug-abusing women in treatment research. In E. R. Rahdert (Ed.), *Treatment for drug-exposed women and their children: Advances in research methodology* (NIDA Research Monograph No. 166, NIH No. 96-3632, pp. 110–122). Rockville, MD: National Institute on Drug Abuse.

Maddux, J. F. (1997). Outcomes of innovations to improve retention on methadone. In F. M. Tims, J. A. Inciardi, B. W. Fletcher, & A. M. Horton (Eds.), *The effectiveness of innovative approaches in the treatment of drug abuse* (pp. 33–41). Westport, CT: Greenwood Press.

Mason, E. (1996). Conducting a treatment research project in a medical center-based program for chemically dependent pregnant women. In E. R. Rahdert (Ed.), *Treatment for drug-exposed women and their children: Advances in research methodology* (NIDA Research Monograph No. 166, NIH No. 96-3632, pp. 22–31). Rockville, MD: National Institute on Drug Abuse.

Nichols, J. L., Weinstein, E. B., Ellingstad, V. S., & Struckman-Johnson, D. L. (1978). The specific deterrent effect of ASAP education and rehabilitation programs. *Journal of Safety Research, 10,* 177–187.

Office of Inspector General. (1990). *Crack babies* (Report No. OEI-03-89-01540). Philadelphia: Office of Evaluation and Inspections, Office of Inspector General, U.S. Department of Health and Human Services.

Palinkas, L. A., Atkins, C. J., Noel, P., & Miller, C. (1996). Recruitment and retention of adolescent women in drug treatment research. In E. R. Rahdert (Ed.), *Treatment for drug-exposed women and their children: Advances in research methodology* (NIDA Research Monograph No. 166, NIH No. 96-3632, pp. 87–109). Rockville, MD: National Institute on Drug Abuse.

President's Commission on Law Enforcement and Administration of Justice: Task Force on Drunkenness. (1967). *Task force report: Drunkenness.* Washington, DC: U.S. Government Printing Office.

Presidential Commission on Drunk Driving. (1983). *Presidential Commission on Drunk Driving: Final report.* Washington, DC: The White House.

Rahdert, E. R. (1996). Introduction to the Perinatal-20 Treatment Research Demonstration Program. In E. R. Rahdert (Ed.), *Treatment for drug-exposed women and their children: Advances in research methodology* (NIDA Research Monograph

No. 166, NIH No. 96-3632, pp. 1–5). Rockville, MD: National Institute on Drug Abuse.

Room, R. (1990). Community action and alcohol problems: The demonstration project as an unstable mixture. In N. Giesbrecht, P. Conley, R. W. Denniston, L. Gliksman, H. Holder, A. Pederson, et al. (Eds.), *Research, action, and the community: Experiences in the prevention of alcohol and other drug problems* (OSAP Prevention Monograph No. 4, pp. 1–25). Rockville, MD: Office for Substance Abuse Prevention.

St. Louis Metropolitan Police Department. (1970). *The St. Louis Detoxification and Diagnostic Evaluation Center.* Washington, DC: Law Enforcement Assistance Administration, U.S. Department of Justice.

Simpson, D. D., Dansereau, D. F., & Joe, G. W. (1997). The DATAR project: Cognitive and behavioral enhancements to community-based treatments. In F. M. Tims, J. A. Inciardi, B. W. Fletcher, & A. M. Horton (Eds.), *The effectiveness of innovative approaches in the treatment of drug abuse* (pp. 182–203). Westport, CT: Greenwood Press.

Stoil, M. J., Hill, G. A., Jansen, M. A., Sambrano, S., & Winn, F. J. (2000). Benefits of community-based demonstration efforts: Knowledge gained in substance abuse prevention. *Journal of Community Psychology, 28,* 375–389.

Swenson, P. R., Struckman-Johnson, D. L., Ellingstad, V. S., Clay, T. R., & Nichols, J. L. (1981). Results of a longitudinal evaluation of court-mandated DWI treatment programs in Phoenix, Arizona. *Journal of Studies on Alcohol, 42,* 642–653.

Tims, F. M., Fletcher, B. W., Inciardi, J. A., & Horton, A. M. (1997a). Introduction: An overview of the Applied Evaluation Research Portfolio. In F. A. Tims, J. A. Inciardi, B. W. Fletcher, & A. M. Horton (Eds.), *The effectiveness of innovative approaches in the treatment of drug abuse* (pp. 1–13). Westport, CT: Greenwood Press.

Tims, F. M., Inciardi, J. A., Fletcher, B. W., & Horton, A. M. (Eds.). (1997b). *The effectiveness of innovative approaches in the treatment of drug abuse* (Vol. 49). Westport, CT: Greenwood Press.

U.S. Department of Transportation. (1968). *Alcohol and highway safety: A report to the Congress from the Secretary of Transportation.* Washington, DC: Author.

U.S. Department of Transportation. (1977). *Management and evaluation handbook for demonstration projects in traffic safety 1976* (DOT HS-802-196). Washington, DC: National Highway Traffic Safety Administration.

U.S. Department of Transportation. (1979a). *Alcohol safety action projects evaluation methodology and overall program impact* (DOT HS-803-896). Washington, DC: National Highway Traffic Safety Administration.

U.S. Department of Transportation. (1979b). *Results of the National Alcohol Safety Action Projects.* Washington, DC: National Highway Traffic Safety Administration.

U.S. Department of Transportation. (1985). *Alcohol and highway safety 1984: A review of the state of the knowledge* (DOT-HS-806-569). Washington, DC: National Highway Traffic Safety Administration.

U.S. General Accounting Office. (1990). *Drug-exposed infants: A generation at risk* (GAO/HRD-90-138). Washington, DC: U.S. General Accounting Office.

U.S. General Accounting Office. (1991). *The crack cocaine epidemic: Health consequences and treatment* (GAO/HRD-91-55FS). Washington, DC: U.S. General Accounting Office.

Wittman, F. (1982). Current status of research and demonstration programs in the primary prevention of alcohol problems. In National Institute on Alcohol Abuse and Alcoholism (Ed.), *Prevention, intervention and treatment: Concerns and models* (DHHS No. ADM 82-1192, Alcohol and Health Monograph No. 3, pp. 3–57). Rockville, MD: National Institute on Alcohol Abuse and Alcoholism.

13

NATIONAL AND LOCAL PERSPECTIVES ON THE CENTER FOR SUBSTANCE ABUSE TREATMENT PRACTICE/ RESEARCH COLLABORATIVE AND PRACTICE IMPROVEMENT COLLABORATIVE INITIATIVES

ALICE A. GLEGHORN AND FRANCES COTTER

To address the lack of correspondence between substance abuse treatment knowledge acquisition and field implementation, in 1999 the Center for Substance Abuse Treatment (CSAT) issued a call to award developmental projects, that is, Practice/Research Collaboratives, throughout the United States. In 2000, CSAT launched the implementation phase of this

This work was supported in part by Grants 6 KD1 TI12270-01-1 and 1 UD1 TI12623-01 from the Center for Substance Abuse Treatment (CSAT), Substance Abuse and Mental Health Services Administration (SAMHSA). Grant support does not imply endorsement by SAMHSA, CSAT, or the federal government. We thank the following individuals for their assistance with this work and for their work on the San Francisco Practice Improvement Collaborative initiative: Kathleen Adriano, Toni Rucker, Kirsten Melbye, Carmen Masson, Lisa Gutierrez, Dee-Dee Stout, Jim Sorensen, Lisa Moore, John Harcourt, Jean Oggins, Kevin McGirr, Paul Bouey, Karen Sharp, Elilta Hagos, and the San Francisco Practice/Research Collaborative Stakeholders.

program and renamed the initiative the *Practice Improvement Collaborative* (PIC) program.

The goal of the PIC program is to develop and sustain community-based collaboratives of substance abuse practitioners, researchers, policymakers, consumers, and other stakeholders in order to disseminate, implement, and evaluate the adoption of evidence-based practices that are responsive to community needs. In this chapter we describe the national program and how one local community implemented a PIC.

THE NATIONAL PIC PROGRAM

PICs share the following common characteristics:

- *Collaboratives are community based.* Each PIC serves a targeted geographic area and substance abuse treatment population within the targeted area. Collaboratives bring together community-based stakeholders that are actively engaged in substance abuse treatment, policy, education, and research activities (i.e., treatment program staff, public health administrators, and university-affiliated educators and researchers).
- *Collaboratives engage community-based providers as full partners.* Too often in the past, policymakers and researchers in the field have ignored or minimally engaged treatment providers in research and technology transfer activities. Interaction among PIC practice, research, and policy stakeholders is based on the understanding that all partners have a crucial role in developing and implementing a practice/research agenda.
- *Collaboratives are formal organizations.* The PIC network is a formal organizational structure, with a clearly articulated statement of mission, governance structure, and operating procedures. In this respect, collaboratives are distinguished from advocacy and community action groups that form to address a single issue and disband once a policy goal is achieved.

Developmental Phase Projects

CSAT awarded nine developmental phase PIC grants in 1999. These projects represented a diverse group, in terms of geographic areas served, number and type of stakeholders, and special populations targeted. Four projects were statewide (Iowa, Arizona, New York, and Oregon); another five targeted specific metropolitan areas (Tampa, Florida; New Orleans, Louisiana; Atlanta, Georgia; San Francisco, California; and Salem, Oregon–Seattle, Washington). Two of the four statewide projects—Oregon and Iowa—evolved from prior practice/research networks that had been state supported. In New York state, a recently formed provider association, the Alcoholism and Substance Abuse Providers of New York State, joined with a state agency, the Office of Alcoholism and Substance Abuse Services, to cosponsor a PIC grant. Two projects targeted specific populations: Native American youth (Salem, Oregon–Seattle, Washington) and populations with criminal justice involvement (Tampa, Florida). The other five projects targeted a diverse range of client population needs, including adolescent treatment, HIV/AIDS, co-occurring disorders, women and children.

Developmental projects recruited and engaged a broad range of community stakeholders—including policymakers, consumers, researchers, practitioners, treatment program administrators, clinical supervisors, educators, and members of the self-help community and the faith community—and from multiple service delivery systems: behavioral health, criminal justice, education, and welfare. Organizational structures established by PICs typically included a governing board; a management team; an advisory body; and multiple subcommittees, practice networks, or work groups.

Each PIC conducted a community assessment of practice/research needs that served as the basis for development of a practice/research agenda or operational plan. The task of agenda setting involved an intense process of fostering stakeholder communication, developing a shared vision and mission statement, and consensus development. Effective management of this process was a major challenge and crucial to overall project development. A broad range of network enhancement activities were conducted throughout the developmental year, including the use of Internet communication systems, conduct of focus groups, and knowledge exchange meetings and conferences. A report of the Developmental Phase PIC Program is available from CSAT and is posted on the World Wide Web at www.samhsa/csat.gov.

Implementation Phase Projects

CSAT awarded seven implementation phase PIC grants in 2000. Seven additional grants were awarded in 2001. Implementation phase projects continued to strengthen their community base of stakeholders and organizational infrastructure. The major responsibility of each PIC was to implement a locally developed practice/research agenda by conducting community-based network enhancement activities and practice improvement projects. Network enhancement activities initiated by the PICs included mentoring and clinician–researcher "in-residence" projects, "best-practices" workshops and conferences, and development of local practice improvement networks. Practice improvement projects focused on implementation of evidence-based practices in community-based organizations. Areas addressed by these projects included mental health screening, motivational interviewing, pharmacotherapy, cognitive–behavioral therapy for youth with depression and alcohol abuse, integrated treatment for offenders with co-occurring mental health and substance abuse disorders, and early intervention strategies for children of substance-abusing women. PIC grantees conducted an evaluation of the cost and effectiveness of the strategies used to implement evidence-based practices and disseminated information on successful implementation strategies to the field.

The PIC program serves as an important complement to other public and private sector practice/research initiatives described in earlier chapters of this book. Because they are community based, collaboratives are in a unique position to demonstrate how new knowledge in the field can be best disseminated and adapted at the local level.

THE SAN FRANCISCO PIC

The San Francisco PIC (SF-PIC) is an example of a PIC initiated by a county health department in collaboration with university-based researchers and publicly funded substance abuse treatment providers. Community Substance Abuse Services (CSAS) of the San Francisco Department of Public Health (DPH) was the lead agency for the SF-PIC and assumed administrative and organizational responsibility for the project. The SF-PIC was funded for a 1-year development grant and competed successfully for a 3-year implementation grant that was in progress at the time this chapter was written. In the remainder of this chapter we summarize the SF-PIC's development year accomplishments and outline planned implementation activities.

Organization

In developing the PIC, San Francisco drew on its experience facilitating community-supported initiatives such as Treatment on Demand (TOD; Guydish et al., 2000), which was developed in response to community demands and was implemented with the assistance of a community-planning group. The community-planning model followed in these endeavors involved multiple stakeholders in the design, planning, and performance of the initiative. Central to the community-planning model are the principles of inclusion and cultural competency—for example, that the planning must include representation from the communities that the policy will affect and that the planning process and resulting services must be sensitive and responsive to the diverse cultural needs of the community constituents. The initial SF-PIC stakeholder group was built from an existing collaboration of members of the TOD Planning Council, researchers involved in evaluating Treatment on Demand (the TOD Research Task Force), DPH and CSAS policymakers, and representatives of diverse substance abuse treatment programs and their clients. Both the TOD Planning Council and the PIC stakeholders reflected the racial/ethnic, gender, sexual orientation, economic status, consumer, practitioner, researcher, and policymaker diversity of the city. The community-based planning framework, based in the context of the city and county policy structure and driven by needs identified and informed by community and researchers, was a model strategy of encompassing diversity within a formal practice/research/policy partnership.

Participatory Process

The initial SF-PIC membership consisted of 11 substance abuse and prevention service providers, 10 researchers experienced in conducting substance abuse-related research, 4 members of the TOD Planning Council, 2 consumer representatives, and 6 staff members from CSAS and DPH who had developed and implemented policy and research projects. In keeping with DPH policy, all SF-PIC meetings were open to the public, and there was opportunity for public comment at each occasion. Meetings of the membership were held on a monthly basis and were facilitated by 3 cochairs, each representing policy, research, or practice interests. Decisions were reached through consensus, with divergent opinions submitted to the membership for a vote when a consensus could not be reached. Although a consensus was sometimes difficult to achieve given the diversity of the participants, CSAS had successfully facilitated a similar process with the TOD Planning Council and built on this experience to assure the SF-PIC's success.

Initial SF-PIC provider members were selected from the approximately 146 substance abuse programs funded by CSAS. Members represented a range of services (prevention, youth treatment, outreach, day treatment, outpatient, methadone, residential, and aftercare), target populations (youth, homeless, prostitutes, injection drug users, children of substance abusers, families, gay men), research experience (i.e., none, limited, extensive), and ethnic groups (i.e., Hispanic, Asian American, African American, Native American). Research members invited to participate in the SF-PIC were selected based on their interest and accomplishments in substance abuse research and included those who had worked on previous evaluation efforts with local providers, CSAS, or other health department agencies. TOD Planning Council, CSAS, and DPH members self-identified their interest in participating in this process and agreed to convey the work of the PIC back to the organizations they represented on an ongoing basis and to assist in formal presentations to local government officials.

Membership goals for the SF-PIC were to achieve a broad and diverse representation of stakeholders and to include as many interested advocates in PIC activities as possible. Therefore, ongoing attempts were made to increase the number of individuals and programs participating in PIC activities. These efforts included presentations at local provider meetings, contractor association meetings, advisory boards, community-planning councils, and statewide meetings and conferences. Through these activities, diversity representation was successfully achieved. Approximately 73 individuals attended one or more SF-PIC stakeholder meetings during the first year of the SF-PIC. On the basis of this participation, the estimated ethnic representation is as follows: 43 White Americans, 9 Hispanics, 9 Asian Americans/Pacific Islanders, 8 African Americans, 1 Native American, and 3 "other". Gay and lesbian communities are represented, as are consumers. Approximately 60% of the stakeholders are women. Providers comprise 48%, policymakers are 32%, and researchers are 30% of meeting attendance. Approximately 6% of stakeholders self-identified as consumer representatives and included individuals in recovery, clients in treatment, and clients of other substance abuse services.

SF-PIC Geographic Range

The original geographic area served by the SF-PIC was the city and county of San Francisco. Within this boundary were 146 CSAS-supported substance abuse treatment programs, more than 30 privately funded treatment providers, substance abuse treatment funded through the Veterans Affairs Medical Center in San Francisco, and a variety of substance abuse research programs affiliated with local universities and hospitals. As the SF-PIC developed, stakeholders from the wider Bay Area participated in PIC activities, including representation from four neighboring counties. In addition, SF-PIC leadership has coordinated with two statewide research organizations to inform their membership of PIC opportunities and events. As a result, the subsequent SF-PIC membership included non-CSAS-funded providers and research and service organizations outside of San Francisco. Interest from these participants expanded the ultimate boundaries of the SF-PIC to a more regional initiative over time.

Stakeholder Roles and Responsibilities

Roles and responsibilities of stakeholder members and consumers were fundamental to the committee structure and process. General SF-PIC stakeholder activities occurred under the direction of the three cochairs, whereas specific subcommittee chairs were responsible for their more focused agendas. Monthly PIC meetings were vital to continued participation of key stakeholders. Subcommittees addressed the details of specific PIC tasks and ensured member participation, responsibility, and endorsement of PIC projects. The subcommittees typically determined the key elements of projects, and those recommendations were brought before the PIC membership at monthly meetings. The general membership commented on and endorsed or revised the direction of the committee at the monthly meetings. Stakeholders who desired greater input attended subcommittee meetings and contributed to the process. Specific subcommittees formed included: Needs Assessment Implementation and Design, Knowledge Dissemination Conference, Implementation Grant Proposal, Skill Training (Knowledge Application) Activities, and Infrastructure Development Activities.

In some cases, stakeholders participated only in subcommittee functions of personal interest and did not attend the stakeholder meetings. This was more common during the implementation period, when interest groups were formed to provide more focused experiences for stakeholders concerned with a specific population or issue to collaborate on service, research, and training opportunities. For example, one interest group was formed in response to a funding opportunity for services for pregnant and postpartum women and their children. Several members of this group produced a successful grant proposal, and the entire group developed a monthly forum that alternated topics between case conferences and expert panels on priority topics (i.e., methadone maintenance during pregnancy and substance abuse treatment for women in the criminal justice system). The group also provided a venue for providers to review assessment issues and to work toward adopting a standardized instrument across provider agencies and modalities (i.e., residential, outreach, outpatient). Once achieved, this standardization would improve treatment by facilitating communications between providers when clients are transferred and reduce the burden on patients in limiting multiple formal evaluations. Additional interest groups focused on Youth, Faith and Family Support Communities and the Impact of Proposition 36 (the California Substance Abuse and Crime Prevention Act of 2000).

SF-PIC Goals

To achieve the national goal of providing the highest quality and most effective substance abuse care and prevention services to those in need, the SF-PIC used two primary strategies. The first strategy was to create opportunities for providers, researchers, and policymakers to engage in networking and exchange knowledge. The SF-PIC felt strongly that the PIC must involve all members as equal participants, as each perspective can help create a common understanding of and progress toward mutual goals. By encouraging these interactions, the SF-PIC believed that service providers would become aware of and be interested in adopting evidence-based practices, while researchers would learn of promising developments in the field and be motivated to evaluate them. By including policymakers as stakeholders, it was hoped that local policies and regulations would reflect best practices as well. Opportunities for these interactions included monthly lunchtime stakeholder meetings, subcommittee participation, knowledge dissemination conferences, skill-training workshops, and the formation of population-focused interest groups during the implementation grant period.

The second strategy built on the developing relationships to provide support for formal collaborative efforts. The grant supported specific projects that required collective involvement of all stakeholder groups during the development and implementation periods. These projects included the developmental-year needs assessment, the knowledge dissemination conferences, infrastructure development planning and implementation, the Knowledge Adoption Evaluations, the pilot studies, interest group activities, and the development of the implementation agenda. By working on these time-limited projects of general interest, the benefits of collaborative efforts were visibly demonstrated, and the groundwork was set for future endeavors that would sustain the impact of the PIC. For example, as a result of the relationships forged through the PIC activities, a number of grant proposals were written collaboratively by providers and researchers to provide needed best-practice services or to study innovative intervention strategies. Two of these projects were funded, and several more were under review at the time this chapter was written. This illustrates that PIC activities have potential to be sustained beyond the limitation of the grant period, and participants recognize and engage in the opportunities provided by the PIC.

SF-PIC Needs Assessment

A major focus of the development year was to conduct a needs assessment to identify priority issues and a practice/research agenda. This was conducted through the use of focus groups, a survey questionnaire, and PIC member input at monthly and subcommittee meetings. Nine population-specific focus groups were conducted to ascertain mutually beneficial models of collaboration between substance use researchers and providers. Associated objectives included the identification of barriers to successful collaboration, training interests, themes that might be explored in more detail in the subsequent survey, and topics that could be addressed at the knowledge dissemination conference held during the development year. The nine focus groups represented PIC core member providers, day program/case management providers, outreach/prevention providers, residential program providers, outpatient program providers, methadone maintenance/detoxification providers, program clients, researchers, and policymakers. A total of 72 individuals participated in these sessions. The ethnic distribution of participants was as follows: 53% White, 20% African American, 15% Hispanic, 7% Asian American/Pacific Islander, and 5% Native American.

Focus Group Results

Underlying much of the focus group discussion was the common appreciation among all participants of the value of research. Participants who had past experience with research/practice collaborations described successful efforts as beginning with the formulation of the research questions and ending with the final dissemination of results. Failed collaborations had not ensured equal participation in the full range of project activities, which lead to acrimony between researchers and providers. Providers noted frustration with researchers who approached them with a research concept "in hand," precluding opportunities for providers to contribute their experience and insights to the study design. One impact of this approach was lack of staff interest and investment in the project, which often resulted in questionable data. To better meet the needs and interests of providers, participants suggested being flexible in approaching the study design and developing research objectives and outcomes that were consistent with program philosophy and with the needs of clients. Of particular concern were definitions of "successful" outcomes, with knowledge of the full context of the client and program essential to understanding the achievement of an intervention.

Providers identified barriers to research participation, which included incomprehensible "academic language" used in research reports, lack of access to data collected by programs for billing information and lack of expertise to analyze such data, and absence of time to learn of new strategies or successful interventions. Providers noted that the format of many conferences, where research-based practices might be identified, is not designed to accommodate providers who have difficulty canceling client appointments for a full day. Providers suggested that a brief abstract or newsletter system could serve to keep them better informed of current issues.

Survey Methods

Drawing on themes generated from the focus group, the Needs Assessment subcommittee developed a short (20-minute) self-report survey for providers to complete. (Contact the first author [alice.a.gleghorn@sfdph.org] for a copy of this survey.) The formal needs assessment survey was sent to more than 300 substance use treatment providers in the city and county of San Francisco. This instrument included 84 questions that addressed barriers to gathering data, communication needs, training needs, experience working with researchers, and background information. A total of 164 individuals completed surveys (a response rate of approximately 55%) from the following types of programs: outpatient, residential, education/prevention, day treatment, case management/multiservice, detoxification, mental health, drop in, methadone clinics, and homeless shelters. Respondents included direct service staff (36%), program directors (29%), supervisors and administrators (27%), and executive directors (8%). White Americans comprised 44% of the respondents, African Americans and Hispanics both comprised 21%, and Asian Americans/Pacific Islanders comprised 14% of the sample.

Survey Results

Among barriers to gathering data, providers cited the lack of resources and expertise as underlying problems. They also expressed an interest in accessing data already collected by providers to fulfill county and state requirements, assistance in summarizing these data, and in sharing this information with other providers. Use of standardized assessments drew a variety of responses, and greater numbers of providers said they would use these, if they were shown to be more time efficient (i.e., through computerized assessment methods). Communication needs were focused on increasing provider access to information. Respondents expressed a strong interest in using Web-based systems and in obtaining research abstracts electronically through the Internet. The need for upgraded computer equipment and staff training in the use of this equipment were identified as well.

The highest levels of interest in general training needs were tied to current treatment models and methods. For example, provider training interest included cultural competency training to work with diverse populations (age, race/ethnicity, gender, sexual orientation), dual-diagnosis clients, and integrating psychopharmacology into treatment. Additional topics endorsed included training in reinforcement strategies for behavior change, incorporating readiness to change, increasing retention in treatment, harm reduction strategies, improving social model treatments, relapse prevention, and complementary therapies. Creating accurate and complete definitions of "success" in treatment outcomes was also stressed. Respondents also cited the need for training in research and evaluation, using standardized assessment instruments, use of databases, seeking funding for evaluation projects, and using the Internet. Most of these respondents had experience with research and expressed favorable evaluations of those experiences. Providers felt that the participation in research was beneficial to the agency, the research was relevant, and the findings were useful in agency work and in obtaining additional funding. Experiences with researchers themselves and research protocols also were positive for both staff and clients.

Discussions at the monthly PIC meetings also reviewed provider needs, although the pool of participants was much smaller than that represented by the survey and focus groups. The PIC monthly venue, and that of the Implementation Grant subcommittee, also allowed for more detailed evaluation of some of these suggestions and the exploration of other alternatives. Several primary training issues were highlighted in these discussions and included use of psychopharmacology in the treatment setting, anger management, relapse prevention, motivational interviewing, outreach strategies, harm reduction, standardized data collection, and Web-based network infrastructure development.

PIC Conference: Dissemination of Needs Assessment Results

Results from the focus groups, surveys, and PIC discussions were integrated into the agenda of the knowledge dissemination forum held on May 10, 2000, and titled "Drug Abuse Practice/Research Collaboration: Making It Work in San Francisco." This 1-day conference was advertised to all providers and researchers in San Francisco, PIC participants, and in other counties of the Bay Area. Conference presenters included provider, research, policy, and consumer representation, and 150 people attended the conference. Sessions focused on research-to-practice and practice-to-research themes and included an emphasis on topics identified through the needs assessment, including "How to Use Assessment Data to Improve Treatment," "Urgent Issues That Should Be Studied Next," and "Promising Treatment Approaches Developed Through Research." During the discussion in the "Urgent Issues" workshop several topics were identified, including cultural competence, relapse prevention, posttraumatic stress disorder, model interventions evaluated in different populations, and ascertaining barriers to treatment from client perspectives. Participants also cited the need for longitudinal studies of treatment outcomes and the development of associated follow-up strategies. In conjunction with this discussion, issues pertaining to the definition of "success" were addressed, as many providers voiced frustration with so-called *black-and-white* outcomes that are often abstinence based.

A closing session included a review of the focus group and survey assessments and a more general discussion of the future of the PIC program. Before the session adjourned, participants were asked about their interest in staff exchange placements in either provider or researcher settings. Interest in collaboration was expressed among common-interest providers and researchers. This marked the beginning of the formation of the interest groups that became part of the implementation program.

PIC Priority Issues

On the basis of the needs assessment and conference discussion, the SF-PIC defined priority issues and topics for implementation. A number of these priorities were addressed in knowledge-application and infrastructure development projects during the final phase of the development grant. For example, in response to provider interest, a series of skills workshops was developed and conducted by local experts for small groups of 20–50 participants. These sessions drew many direct service staff as they were typically offered in short (3- to 4-hour) sessions. The topics were drawn from those identified through the needs assessment. More than 220 individuals attended the first nine workshops, which were always overbooked. The workshops were so successful that the SF-PIC has made plans to repeat the series and add additional topics throughout the implementation project.

The topics of highest priority identified in the needs assessment were incorporated as key elements of the implementation proposal for the PIC program. For example, three knowledge adoption evaluation studies were proposed and focused on psychopharmacology, relapse prevention, and anger management. The proposed pilot studies focused on the development, implementation, and evaluation of infrastructure upgrades in different provider settings. This objective was consistent with provider goals for efficient standardized assessment and follow-up of clients and for enhanced access to data and Internet resources. The proposed pilot studies would initiate standardized assessment via a Web-based data collection system with provider agencies linked to a central server at the DPH. This system would give providers access to the Internet and to data analysis programs available through CSAS, allowing increased access to program data and Web resources. The infrastructure plan included the hiring of a computer support specialist to work directly with providers to identify unique needs, provide training on equipment and assessment tools, staff a helpline, and assist with using data warehouse software for analysis of program data.

In response to provider requests for training on harm reduction, a city-sponsored, 2-day conference was offered in January 2001 (Gleghorn, Rosenbaum, & Garcia, 2001). This event featured a number of sessions focused on strategies to integrate traditional and harm reduction approaches, on redefining successful outcomes in service settings, and on San Francisco's adoption of a harm reduction public health policy.

CONCLUSION

The PIC initiative marks an important step in bringing disparate members of the substance abuse community together to reach a common goal: the integration of effective, evidence-based practices into substance abuse treatment systems. The SF-PIC has been successful in developing a genuine collaboration of substance abuse providers, researchers, and policymakers to improve substance abuse services in San Francisco. The implementation projects will further expand the scope and sustainability of the PIC initiative. By encouraging the growth of these collaborative relationships this initiative has created opportunities for communities to achieve and sustain improved knowledge, practices, and outcomes in the substance abuse field.

REFERENCES

Gleghorn, A. A., Rosenbaum, M., & Garcia, B. A. (2001). Editors' introduction: Bridging the gap in San Francisco, the process of integrating harm reduction and traditional substance abuse services. *Journal of Psychoactive Drugs, 33*, 1–4.

Guydish, J., Moore, L., Gleghorn, A., Davis, T., Sears, C., & Harcourt, J. (2000). Drug abuse treatment on demand in San Francisco: Preliminary findings. *Journal of Psychoactive Drugs, 32*, 363–370.

14

ISSUES IN IMPLEMENTING POSTTRAUMATIC STRESS DISORDER TREATMENT OUTCOME RESEARCH IN COMMUNITY-BASED TREATMENT PROGRAMS

ELISA TRIFFLEMAN

A large number of substance abusers have experienced trauma and have symptoms of posttraumatic stress disorder (PTSD; American Psychiatric Association, 1994). The co-occurrence of PTSD and substance use disorders (PTSD–SUDS) has important clinical implications, although systematic treatment approaches have generally not been implemented in most clinical settings. However, addictions treatment clinicians recognize the importance and relevance of addressing psychological trauma, even when they are sometimes unsure of how to do so. In this chapter I first briefly provide information regarding the occurrence, significance, and clinical challenges associated with concurrent PTSD–SUDS and then describe an integrative,

Work on this chapter was supported by Grant R01-DA-11338 from the National Institute on Drug Abuse. I gratefully acknowledge Joan E. Zweben, Susan Sky, Joanne Bacci, Judith Martin, and the staff at the 14th Street Clinic, Oakland, CA.

227

empirically based treatment: substance dependence PTSD therapy (SDPT). I then examine issues generated by implementing PTSD–SUDS research across clinical settings both as a general and as a specialized case of the research–clinical interface. I summarize common stages of implementation, common problems of interest to clinical administrators and researchers, and the solutions generated by both clinical and research staffs. Finally, I consider the unique challenges of implementing a PTSD–SUDS related research–treatment outcome study in a clinic that had not previously hosted treatment outcome studies.

SIGNIFICANCE OF THE CO-OCCURRENCE OF PTSD AND SUDS

PTSD (American Psychiatric Association, 1994) is a widely present syndrome, affecting 9.0%–12.3% of the general community (Breslau, Davis, & Adreski, 1991; Kessler, Sonnega, Bromet, Hughes, & Nelson, 1995; Resnick, Kilpatrick, Dansky, Saunders, & Best, 1993). Substance use and substance use disorders frequently coexist with PTSD. In civilian epidemiological samples, rates of up to 43% of co-occurrence have been reported (Dansky, Saladin, Brady, Kilpatrick, & Resnick, 1995; Kessler et al., 1995). Rates of PTSD occurring in substance abusers vary from 14% to 59% (Fullilove et al., 1993; Jordan et al., 1991; Triffleman, Marmar, Delucchi, & Ronfeldt, 1995).

The clinical significance of PTSD–SUDS lies along a number of axes. First, response to standard addictions treatment is affected by PTSD–SUDS. In posttreatment follow-along studies, participants with PTSD–SUDS demonstrated shorter times to relapse (Brown, Recupero, & Stout, 1995); more treatment recidivism, although with lower treatment retention in each episode (Brown et al., 1995); and greater use of treatment services (Brown, Stout, & Mueller, 1999a). Participants with PTSD–SUDS incurred health care costs five times higher than non-PTSD substance abusers (Brown, Stout, & Mueller, 1999b). In male veterans at discharge (Ouimette, Ahrens, Moos, & Finney, 1998), at 1- and 2-year follow-ups after inpatient treatment (Ouimette, Finney, & Moos, 1999), PTSD–SUDS participants drank more, were less likely to be employed, and were more likely to be arrested than either participants with SUDS alone or those with a dual diagnosis without PTSD. Compared with a substance-use-disorders-only group, individuals with PTSD–SUDS expected fewer benefits from discontinuing substance use (Ouimette et al., 1998), whereas, compared with a PTSD-only group, women with PTSD–SUDS were less likely to have a sense of purpose, perceived fewer life opportunities, and were more likely to attempt suicide (Najavits, Weiss, & Shaw, 1999). PTSD–SUDS patients, in short, are difficult to successfully treat and may benefit less from standard addictions-only treatment.

Second, PTSD and substance use disorders are often associated with other co-occurring problems, including affective disorders, personality disorders (Rounsaville et al., 1998; Southwick, Yehuda, & Giller, 1993), lowered cardiac stress tolerance, gastrointestinal distress, the presence of pain and other health effects (Kessler et al., 1995, Shalev, Bleich, & Ursano, 1990; Wolfe, Schnurr, Brown, & Furey, 1994), and increased mortality (Bullman & Kang, 1994). PTSD is also associated with neuropsychological deficits (Bremner, 1999) and with engaging in HIV risk-taking behaviors, including IV drug use and prostitution (Stiffman, Dore, Earls, & Cunningham, 1992) and lowered CD4 counts among HIV-positive women (Kimerling, Armistead, & Forehand, 1999). Thus, the treatment of trauma and PTSD may alleviate or prevent a range of secondary problems and may improve psychosocial function. A continuing need exists for the further development of specialized treatments for PTSD–SUDS.

TREATMENT MODELS FOR PTSD–SUDS

Several clinical articles and books have examined the treatment of traumatized substance abusers (Evans & Sullivan, 1995; Hien & Levin, 1994; Miller & Guidry, 2001; Polles & Smith, 1995; Triffleman, 1998). In the Veterans Affairs health care system inpatient and outpatient units for the on-site integrated treatment of PTSD and substance dependence have developed in a limited number of locales. These programs vary with regard to treatment duration and philosophy. In the civilian treatment sector, trauma-related treatment has often meant either referral from addictions treatment to other individual or group therapy settings, which in general are physically and administratively separate from the addictions treatment facility, or to peer support, self-help, and community-based groups (e.g., rape crisis or domestic violence centers). Satel, Becker, and Dan (1993) noted that male veterans with PTSD may face serious dilemmas in attempting to affiliate with Alcoholics Anonymous. Such issues as the difficulty in surrendering one's will to a "Higher Power," by whom the PTSD patient may have felt betrayed at the moment of trauma exposure, or the feeling of being fundamentally different from others because of trauma-related guilt and estrangement, may become overwhelming obstacles to participation in 12-step programs without sufficient therapeutic preparation.

A 1- to 2-year treatment approach based on Prochaska and DiClemente's (1983) stages-of-change treatment model for male Vietnam veterans with PTSD–SUDS has been articulated by Abueg and Fairbank (1992) and by Seidel, Gusman, and Abueg (1994). The primary features of this model are (a) an early and continuing focus on symptoms of substance dependence and the need for abstinence from substances; (b) an emphasis on phases in treatment, thereby acknowledging stages of treatment readiness (Prochaska

& DiClemente, 1983) and change (McConnaughy, Prochaska, & Velicer, 1983); (c) use of cognitive approaches to combat dysfunctional patterns along with prolonged exposure for traumatic memories (Boudewyns & Hyer, 1990; Foa & Rothbaum, 1998); and (d) stress management. Thus, the patient is gradually introduced to more affectively laden material after a period of first developing a commitment to abstinence.

The principles of Abueg and Fairbank's (1992) and Seidel et al.'s (1994) model have been adapted for use in civilian methadone-maintained patients with PTSD to form Substance Dependence PTSD Therapy (SDPT; Triffleman, Carroll, & Kellogg, 1999), an outpatient cognitive–behavioral treatment that emphasizes (a) an integration of treatment techniques devised separately for drug abuse and PTSD, consistent with optimum dual-diagnosis treatment and (b) an integration of a behavioral, symptom-focused approach with an understanding of common defenses, transference and countertransference in both PTSD and SUDS, and the need for phased treatment as a means toward reducing patients' symptoms.

SDPT: AN INTEGRATED COGNITIVE–BEHAVIORAL THERAPY

SDPT is a 20-week twice-weekly individual therapy and is an adaptation and integration of cognitive–behavioral coping skills treatment for substance dependence (CBCST; Carroll, 1998; Carroll, Donovan, Hester, & Kadden, 1993) and the PTSD-specific treatment techniques of stress inoculation therapy (Meichenbaum & Cameron, 1983), in vivo systematic desensitization (Meichenbaum, 1994), and prolonged exposure (Foa & Rothbaum, 1998) in a systematic, structured, two-phase therapy. The goals of SDPT are (a) reduction of and, where possible, initiation of abstinence from, substance abuse through CBCST (Carroll, 1998; Carroll et al., 1993; Kadden et al., 1992); (b) maintenance of reduced substance use or abstinence during PTSD-focused interventions; and (c) reduction of PTSD symptom severity. SDPT is designed as a stand-alone therapy or in conjunction with substance-abuse-related medication administration (e.g., opiate agonists and antagonists, including methadone and levo-alpha-acetylmethadol [LAAM]). The first phase of SDPT (Weeks 1–12) accommodates an initial period of stabilization from recent substance use and alliance building (Wilson & Lindy, 1994) in preparation for a second, trauma-focused therapy phase. During this first phase, patients receive abstinence-focused cognitive–behavior therapy for addictions, combined with psychoeducation regarding PTSD. During the second phase (Weeks 13–20 and beyond), patients undertake the PTSD-specific interventions along with continuing therapeutic attention to drug use status and to combined trauma/drug use environmental and internal cues.

SDPT has been examined in three trials, starting with an uncontrolled N = 9 pilot trial, which suggested that SDPT was feasible and promising.

The results of a small, randomized controlled pilot study that contrasted SDPT and 12-step facilitation therapy (Triffleman, 2000) indicated that, conservatively, SDPT caused no worsening of substance use (as is often the concern about PTSD interventions) and that patients tolerated stress inoculation and *in vivo* desensitization well, with reductions in PTSD severity. The third study (the implementation of which is described next) used a components-dismantling design to contrast SDPT versus CBCST for substance dependence (Carroll, 1998; Carroll et al., 1993) to examine the impact of the PTSD-specific treatment techniques on treatment outcomes in contrast to that of manualized treatment for substance dependence alone. Results indicate that SDPT patients remained in treatment for a greater number of sessions over a longer period of time than CBCST patients and that both conditions resulted in decreased substance use and PTSD severity although SDPT appeared to confer a more stable, long-lasting reduction in PTSD severity (Triffleman, Wong, & Monnette, 2002). This is consistent with findings among non-substance-abusing samples (Foa et al., 1999; Marks, Lovell, Noshirvani, Livanou, & Thrasher, 1998). Research procedures common to all of these studies include extensive pretreatment research assessment; weekly and monthly research assessment while the patients are in treatment; and the use of part-time, doctoral-level therapists.

CLINICAL SETTINGS FOR SDPT TREATMENT TRIALS AND THE INITIATION OF PTSD–SUDS RESEARCH

Over the course of several investigations of the association among trauma, PTSD, and SUDS, both cross-sectional (Triffleman et al., 1995) and treatment outcome research (Triffleman, 2000) have been initiated in a variety of settings. Studies involving SDPT have occurred in two geographically disparate locations (New Haven, Connecticut; and Oakland, California). Participants in all of these studies have been patients in existing clinical programs, including inpatient treatment (Triffleman et al., 1995) and, for the SDPT trials, a primary cocaine abuse treatment clinic and an opiate agonist maintenance therapy (OAMT) treatment program (e.g., methadone, LAAM, and buprenorphine maintenance). Collaboration with these programs was initially necessitated as a recruitment strategy: Existing clinics have existing patients with existing needs. In the OAMT clinics, collaboration has also occurred as a research design issue, to facilitate the integration of SDPT and control therapies with the medication aspects of OAMT and so that the research therapies could be performed under these clinics' state and federal licensure and accreditation. Thus, the patients in the research treatment continued to be "owned" by the host clinic, and the therapists were considered clinic employees, informally forming a cloistered clinic-within-a-clinic.

The parent clinics for the SDPT studies have included fee-for-service, for-profit, and indigent-based nonprofit settings. In all cases, these settings were a priori "research-friendly," meaning that previous research had been conducted on a regular basis in these settings and that an understanding existed at the highest and medium levels of clinical staff that the presence of a research endeavor could have benefits for the clinic, whether in the informal interactions between research and clinic staffs, in formal training and consultation for staff, in financial benefits, or as a means of providing additional or specialized services to patients. This acceptance and understanding at the various administrative levels of the clinics then became critical to the successful outcome of the studies, as I outline further in the next section.

On a practical level, the first step toward initiating research in such settings is contact between the senior researchers and senior clinical program and administrative staff. During that initial contact, as with any initial interaction and negotiation, both sides examine content and process issues. The content issues for both parties are usually relatively similar: the focus, nature, and importance of the research study; the rationale for a specific clinical venue; what the patients will be expected to do; and the resources needed (including participants, space, and access to clinical services).

The process issues posed by both sides have proven equally critical. From the clinical side, questions may include whether the researcher respects the clinical priorities, philosophy, and pressures faced by staff; what the nature of the communication and interpersonal interactions will be between researchers and clinicians as patients become research participants; whether there is reason to trust the research team with the care and treatment of the patients; whether the researcher will satisfy other, indirect commitments to the clinic; and, as a bottom line, how the clinic or the clinic's patients will benefit from the research presence. As a general principle, the researcher's commitment to the value and importance of the research is often perceived as insufficient evidence of the need for the clinic to undertake such a collaboration, particularly if the researcher is relying on counseling staff to perform research functions, such as referring, assessing, or even treating participants. Relevance to the immediate clinical mission is a critical key to developing cooperation and has been a continuing factor in facilitating the acceptance of PTSD–SUDS research.

Equal and converse process issues face the researcher in this initial contact. Questions in the researcher's mind about the clinical system may include whether promised access to resources will be fulfilled and what barriers may exist, whether the boundary between research and clinical enterprises will be respected, and whether all relevant components of the clinical team will be reasonably supportive to the presence of the research enterprise. This last question may especially be a factor in OAMT, where clinical teams are largely composed of counselors; administrative staff; and medical, nursing, and coordinating staffs.

Even given that the clinical sites have been research friendly, it was initially a pleasant surprise to me that the proposal and initiation of trauma studies have been received over the years with few direct objections from these clinical systems. After all, one of the controversies surrounding the institution of ongoing explicit treatment for trauma exposure and PTSD within an addictions treatment context is the stereotype that clinical providers believe that discussing trauma could lead to increased substance use or other forms of decompensation among individuals who are actively addicted (Evans & Sullivan, 1995). One chief factor accounting for the acceptance of PTSD–SUDS research is that the staffs and administrators perceived that the potential benefits of such research outweighed the risks—including that the discussion of trauma and PTSD might be helpful to the patients, that it is not disruptive to the clinical enterprise, and that the clinical structure is sufficient to absorb and process responses the patients have to participating in the study. Indeed, among the participants who either are ineligible for or who choose not to enter the treatment studies, many express relief and gratitude for the opportunity to discuss their troubled lives with the research staff during the assessment process. This gratitude and desire to tell the trauma story have also been found in other studies (Newman, Walker, & Gefland, 1999). Thus, the acceptance of PTSD–SUDS research may be an example of how clinicians perceive a need, which researchers may then address.

In addition, the timing of when these PTSD–SUDS studies were begun also was a factor—in the early 1990s, when the widespread discussion of trauma became destigmatized. The latter process was itself the product of several coinciding factors over the previous 20–30 years, such as the onset of the women's movement associated with the development of informal interventions for rape and domestic violence victims, an increased influx of women into doctoral-level and other clinical mental health training programs, and the homecoming of traumatized Vietnam veterans and the controversies surrounding their treatment and eligibility for Veterans Affairs benefits. In the 1970s, many clinicians published articles regarding the treatment of rape (Metzger, 1976; Notman & Nadelson, 1976) and traumatized veterans (Haley, 1974), and researchers followed with epidemiological surveys (Centers for Disease Control, 1988; Helzer, Robins, & McEvoy, 1987) and the first treatment studies to address PTSD (Boudewyns & Hyer, 1990; Foa, Rothbaum, Riggs, & Murdock, 1991). This historical context, then, can be empowering to researchers and clinicians alike in that it provides a larger vision of direction as well as another framework for understanding just when and why projects may be acceptable.

After the initial introductory contact between researcher and senior clinical staff, the process of working together to develop an initial series of protocols and procedures begins, followed by an interactive, iterative process as time continues and necessity has dictated. The remainder of this chapter concerns highlights of areas of research–clinical interaction around PTSD–SUDS studies and the approaches to those areas.

RECRUITMENT-RELATED ISSUES

As noted earlier, participants for PTSD–SUDS studies have been recruited solely from within existing clinical populations, with the approval of the researchers' institutional review boards. This recruitment has been guided by the ethical principles of protecting patients' rights of privacy and the right to refuse or simply not participate in research in general without jeopardizing their standing in the host clinic. This meant that recruitment strategies were dependent on three basic mechanisms:

1. *Accessible presence*. This was created by, for example, stationing the research staff in a neutral spot in the clinic lobby. Research staff then offered free doughnuts and coffee to patients in exchange for filling out a brief anonymous screening questionnaire. This exchange served as the beginning of a verbal dialogue between researcher and participants regarding the nature, benefits, and risks of the study and whether the patient wished to participate further, at which time basic contact information was elicited. This recruitment mechanism occurred with the explicit permission of senior clinical staff and required their feedback regarding the acceptable physical placement of the research staff and approach to the patients.
2. *Patient-to-patient informal communications*. Once an initial cohort of patients was seen in formal research assessment, the patient-to-patient grapevine was activated. Clinic patients and their friends and relatives then spontaneously and voluntarily sought out research staff with requests to participate.
3. *Referrals from clinic counselors*. To further increase the likelihood that the patients who could most benefit from PTSD–SUDS treatment were identified and referred, clinic counselors were advised by senior clinical staff of the studies' existence and need for patient referrals. To facilitate this, presentations varying from 15 min to 60 min were made by the PI (principal investigator) or other research staff to clinical staff regarding the topic of the study, the inclusion and exclusion criteria, and the clinical intervention.

After this, and even under the best of circumstances, the willingness of counselors to refer patients to research studies varies greatly across individual staff members. Stated simply: Some counselors have referred and have done so repeatedly, and some have done so rarely or not at all. The fact and degree of this variability appeared to be independent of the content or type of research–treatment intervention and thus were not specific to PTSD–SUDS research. Counseling staff who have referred patients to a study did so for both lofty and pragmatic reasons, including understanding the potential patient benefit from participation in research assessments and treatments and the value of conveniently located, specialized therapy services that might otherwise be unavailable, especially to indigent patients. Other reasons for referral included the possibility of troubled patients perhaps achieving otherwise-unachievable clinical gains, or so that a patient might undergo systematic diagnosis. Referrals also occurred because counselors perceived doing so as a potential opportunity to divest from these difficult-to-treat and often low-functioning clients at least temporarily as well as the more general wish to reduce one's caseload. The willingness to refer did not mean that all referrals were appropriate. For example, during the SDPT trials the presence of psychosis was an exclusion criterion. Nevertheless, several participants who were psychotic were referred for assessment. At times, participants had not previously disclosed their symptoms to the counseling staff, whereas in other instances staff were not familiar with the clinical presentation of atypical psychotic symptoms.

Regardless of the reasons for or conditions of referral, counselors required individualized feedback regarding their referrals and the outcome of such referrals (see "Communication Between Research and Clinical Staff" section). As well, occasional in-service trainings conducted by the PI regarding the intellectual background of the study, the treatment techniques used, and other related issues provided support to staff who referred patients, stimulated others who otherwise might not have referred patients, and provided a general benefit to the clinic. Inasmuch as trauma and its treatment are topics of great currency in clinical treatment, such trainings also served to augment existing interest and broaden or reinforce the clinical framework that front-line staff had about traumatized individuals.

Conversely, counselors who did not refer patients to these studies may have quite legitimately believed that their relationship with their patients was primary; that their patients were too clinically fragile; or that important and beneficial therapeutic work was occurring within their relationship with their patients, including trauma-specific counseling. Alternatively, other reasons for not referring included that counselors did not share the treatment philosophy of the research intervention; felt unsure of research-based exclusion or inclusion criteria; or were in some way uncomfortable with the nature of research testing, payment for research participation, treatment protocol, or the research staff as individuals. Referrals also did not occur because counseling staff in fact knew the exclusion criteria and believed that none of their clients would be qualified. Alternatively, on a pragmatic level, referrals did not occur because the counselor needed the client contact-hours for the purposes of satisfying requirements for licensure, did not want to deal with the potential uncertainties of clients referred but not accepted into research–treatment, had too many of their referrals rejected on the basis of exclusion criteria, wished to avoid the stress of having to refill a clinical case-load lightened by referrals, and so on. As a result, although lack of referral due to uncertainties concerning eligibility requirements or other procedural matters may be amenable to outreach efforts by clinical and research staffs, the remaining reasons are based in the realities of the purposes and pressures of clinical practice and are difficult to address by even the most active re-search-based teaching, research presence, or outreach.

COMMUNICATION BETWEEN
RESEARCH AND CLINICAL STAFF

Communication between research and clinical staff has taken various forms, and because various individuals within a clinical staff benefit from different forms of communications, all are necessary. These mechanisms generally have included:

- Written notifications of and phone calls about the patient's stage in research testing, whether he or she set up or kept his or her testing appointments, whether the patient is eligible for treatment entry, and what the patient's response to an offer of treatment entry has been. This in turn requires that the patient give written consent for such releases of information, which in these studies has typically been obtained during initial pretreat-ment research assessment testing or by counseling staff before referring the patient to the research study.
- Attendance by research staff at clinical meetings where brief, clinically relevant presentations were made reviewing the progress of various patients, such as how many months into the research treatment they were, the patients' general condition, and so on.

The results of ongoing research assessments, however, are never presented and for reasons of confidentiality are not part of the clinical chart. A research presence at clinical meetings also gives the clinical staff additional opportunities to ask questions about how patients are progressing through the research testing process, how their former patients are doing in research therapy, what new studies may be recruiting for participants, and what new directions the research may take. In turn, such meetings provide a time for research staff to be made aware of changes in clinic policies and procedures, attitudes toward and past clinical experience with a given patient or group of patients, and informal communications at the level of "curbsiding" between counselor and research therapist (but not assessment) staff, thus requiring again the easy accessibility and visibility of both parties as well as bidirectional phone calls. Exchanging information about patients is, of course, contingent on receipt of participants' written permission to release this type of information.

One way in which the previously described process was systematized and streamlined was by the designation of a more senior research staff member as the liaison between the clinics and the research study. This liaison function is key in coordinating the research–clinical interface. It is not surprising that clinical staff had a variety of reactions to the designated liaison. Research staff who performed best as liaisons were those who identified at least partially or previously as clinicians and who formed informal, friendly relationships with counseling staff and program directors. Research staff who solely identified as researchers, however, tended not to curry these relationships to the same extent, and as a result the clinical staff as a whole felt less included, less involved, and therefore somewhat less likely to refer and to feel a sense of shared proprietorship in the research enterprise.

At the leadership level, the degree of contact across the research–clinical interface has varied from the occasional phone call from clinical leadership to the PI to attendance by senior research staff at biweekly clinical coordination meetings. I discuss the latter in the next section. In a process similar to that which occurs at the front-line staff level, the degree of accessibility of the PI or other senior research staff has been an important contributor to coordination and collaboration achieved in these studies.

INITIATING PTSD–SUDS TREATMENT OUTCOME RESEARCH IN A SETTING NEW TO TREATMENT RESEARCH

In one OAMT clinic (the 14th Street Clinic in Oakland, California), although cross-sectional characterization studies and longitudinal follow-along studies had frequently been conducted, a randomized, controlled treatment trial had not previously been conducted under the clinic's rubric. Certain matters, such as the need for research recruiters to be visible and accessible to the patients and the need for space for researchers to work, were similar to the needs of previous studies at the clinic and therefore required no additional special procedures or protocols—although at other clinics the need for space and its allocation may become an important indicator of the acceptability of the research protocol by clinical staff. The SDPT psychotherapy treatment trial also called for the clinic to at least temporarily "surrender" the patient to the research-based clinic-within-a-clinic for the provision of therapy; for medication-based decisions, such as methadone dosing and take-home bottle privileges; and for procedural matters, such as grounds for dismissal from the therapy. For the research team, this protocol was also unique in that methadone slot costs (i.e., the per-patient costs of the opiate agonist medication, nursing and pharmacy services, and other associated clinical and administrative costs) were covered for the patients who were in research–treatment. This therefore created a unique opportunity to develop communications processes and procedures around the flow and management of patients between the study and the clinic, which occurred in an iterative, interactive process through frequent discussions between the research and clinical teams.

The development of joint procedures occurred gradually over the course of the study's life. As discussed earlier, a liaison was designated from among the research staff to facilitate research–clinical communications on the front-line level. In addition, the PI was requested by the clinic to participate on a biweekly basis in the clinic coordinators' meetings (which included representation from nursing, the detoxification service, the medical director, and program and administration staff), to facilitate clinic team communication and the research staff, in keeping with the overall clinic culture of inclusivity on important matters. The content of the biweekly research–clinical leadership meetings varied from day-to-day matters, such as which patients were in research treatment and research staffing changes, to brainstorming about patients' attempts to split systems, through discussions of clinic policy and fee changes, and, finally, to discussions of impending new research studies and projects and the clinic's responses and suggestions about these. The result of this collaborative approach was not only a truly collegial and interactive partnership but also excellent recruitment: Of the 104 participants recruited from 14th Street Clinic and assessed for inclusion–exclusion criteria, 75% were diagnosed with lifetime PTSD, consistent with a highly PTSD-enriched sample pool, generated from the high level of interest among staff and patients alike.

DEVELOPMENT OF A JOINTLY DESIGNED METHADONE MAINTENANCE AND DOSE-TAPERING PROTOCOL

A specialized example of research–clinical coordination came with the development of an OAMT protocol, specifically designed for this study, among the clinic's medical director, the PI, and the clinic's methadone maintenance coordinator. Although the initial assumption regarding research participant recruitment was that it would be mainly patients who were stably on OAMT who come into the study, in fact it was patients who were receiving 21-day ambulatory medically supervised, methadone-based opiate detoxification—and therefore not receiving a stable methadone dose—who were more actively interested in research participation. This generated the need for in-treatment dosing guidelines along with a postresearch medically supervised tapering methadone or LAAM regimen, in the event that the patients were unable or unwilling to continue on OAMT after the treatment phase of the study ended. The PI and the clinic's medical director jointly determined that during the treatment phase of the study participants could receive a maximum daily dose of 90 mg methadone. This dosing maximum was identified on the basis of studies indicating that doses in this range are associated with improved outcomes (Strain, Bigelow, Liebson, & Stitzer, 1999). This was then followed by a 6-week supervised medical withdrawal protocol, in contrast to the typical 2-week tapering faced by any patient in financial arrears. The clinic's methadone maintenance coordinator was then charged with the responsibility of ensuring that patients who finished research treatment in good standing receive the 6-week and not the 2-week taper. This, in turn, required the research–therapists, the research–clinical liaison, and the methadone maintenance coordinator to be in close communication about the expected and actual dates of therapy termination, to ensure that dose reductions began after termination and not during therapy. Thus, medication protocol development and implementation resulted from joint discussion and approval with the intent to maximize patient outcome and comfort.

ORGANIZATIONAL DIFFERENCES BETWEEN RESEARCH AND CLINICAL STAFFING

Important "cultural" differences existed between the research and clinical teams, which were in part embodied in the differences in organizational structures between the research and the clinical staffs as well as with regard to the clinic-within-a-clinic concept. These differences in turn initially generated some confusion between the research and clinical teams. For example, during the study conducted at 14th Street Clinic, although the research therapists worked between 4 and 10 hr/week, the use of such part-time personnel was an arrangement inconsistent with existing clinic personnel structures, in which most individuals work no less than half-time. For research purposes, the use of part-timers was well within the norm for psychotherapy research trials: It provided for the therapists an opportunity for a learning experience, for the patients a uniquely focused and personalized therapy experience, and for the study an increased likelihood that the work of no single therapist could account for negative outcome findings. However, within the clinic, the use of no less than half-time counselors greatly increases the likelihood that patients are seen by their designated counselor (and thus compromises the patients' ability to avoid doing so), and senior clinic leaders are able to readily have informal, as-needed discussions with staff, thus increasing organizational cohesion.

In addition, the research therapists, although well qualified for administering SDPT and the control therapies, had no previous experience in OAMT. They were therefore not familiar with several OAMT-specific facets, including required specialized charting and the role of the counselor in recommending opiate agonist dose changes and take-home bottle privileges. Although instruction and guidance regarding these clinical and research-based administrative and medication-related matters initially occurred solely in the weekly supervision provided within the research project, clinic administrative staff felt strongly that this was insufficient to maintain the high quality level required of all clinical staff for clinic accreditation, and they were uncertain as to what actually occurred during that supervision. Therefore all therapists, immediately after being hired, were required to meet with appropriate clinical staff for an administrative orientation and an orientation to OAMT, similar to the intensive training given to standard clinic counselors. Both the research–therapy supervisor and clinic administrative staffs reviewed all charts for the appropriate records keeping. This also partially addressed the clinic staff's reservations about the part-time therapists by increasing the exposure of the clinical staff and the research therapists to one another.

PATIENT RESPONSES TO TRANSITIONS BETWEEN CLINICAL AND RESEARCH SETTINGS: ACTING OUT

Transitioning a patient from standard clinical treatment to research treatment involves a number of workaday problems. Many substance-abusing patients act out or manipulate around change, whereas traumatized individuals tend to view change as a distinct threat and may feel victimized by it. This sample of PTSD–substance abusers exhibited both traits. These dynamics surfaced in many contexts, including around the matter of fee payment. For example, the study paid for clinic slot costs, but only after a patient had been seen at least twice within a time-limited period by his or her assigned research therapist. Despite adequate warning to the contrary, patients who were just entering research–treatment whose payments to the clinic were in arrears not infrequently attempted to claim to clinical staff that the research study would pay their back fees, or that they already were eligible for an ongoing fee waiver despite not attending the two-session initial minimum. Patients who had previously departed the study treatment attempted to persuade clinical staff that their end date was later than it was or that they were entitled to additional weeks of paid treatment. When this was refused by clinical and research staffs, either or both staffs were occasionally characterized by patients as aggressive, dishonest, controlling abusers and were psychologically devalued in conversations between the patients and the counselors receiving them in return transfer and in conversation with other clinic patients.

As with all such acting out, communication between the research and clinical staffs occurred both proactively and retroactively, in the form of telephone calls and discussions at staff meetings. On a proactive basis, in addition to routine notifications regarding patients' progress through the pretreatment research assessment process, appropriate clinic staff were notified verbally and in writing when a patient formally consented to research–treatment entry and was assigned to a research therapist, when the therapist set the initial start date, and when the patient achieved the two-session minimum to trigger the methadone fee waiver. Discussion at several points between staffs, initiated by both teams, concerned the patient's prior financial status, the clinic's expectations regarding repayment of owed fees before the patient's return from the study to the clinic, and when the methadone fee waiver might start. Conversely, on return transfer, similar discussions occurred starting 1 month before the patient's expected date of research–therapy termination, in part so that the patient could then make appropriate financial arrangements for resuming payment and receive the 6-week posttreatment tapering from methadone or LAAM.

Patients in the research protocol also engaged in other types of acting out within the clinic setting while in research treatment. For example, a patient well known to the clinic for several years before he entered research treatment became bellicose in the lobby of the clinic while receiving a methadone dose. Although the patient was not explicitly threatening, his behavior was perceived as having the potential to rapidly become so. The clinic notified the research staff of the incident and strongly recommended the patient's rapid termination from the clinic, as this had been the most recent of several episodes when he had behaved in a disruptive fashion. However, the patient had also recently been diagnosed by the research psychiatrist as having a previously unrecognized psychotic disorder, which the patient had self-treated with illicit sedating substances. In addition, both the patient's research therapist and other research team members felt a strong attachment to what was seen as a patient with minimal intrapsychic organization and a trauma-related tendency to view the world as hostile. Thus, a clear split between the research and clinical teams emerged, which was resolved through discussions across all levels of both teams, resulting in an agreement that the patient could remain within both the clinic and the study protocol only if the patient agreed not to behave in this fashion again and agreed that if such behavior reoccurred, the patient would then be immediately discontinued from the clinic. This verbal contract was presented to the patient conjointly by his therapist, the senior clinical staff, and the PI. The patient agreed, and no further such acting out occurred during the study protocol. This illustrates the necessity of both communication and standard clinical judgment (presenting a consistent message across teams, setting appropriate clinical limits) in evaluating and solving such problems.

Like the problems encountered in transferring patients from the clinical to the research milieu, returning patients to the clinical milieu was also associated with problems. Given that general public awareness of PTSD and other psychiatric conditions continues to lag behind the clinical community's awareness, participation in even single-episode PTSD assessment research can be a change agent at a clinical level, with its ability to give a formal label to the participant's often very private suffering. It is for this reason that an assessment-only control condition has been used in many PTSD treatment–research studies (e.g., Foa et al., 1991). In this instance, along with the intensity of the treatment the research patients receive, the patients' changed awareness caused some difficulties on their return to standard clinical treatment. For example, although many of the research participants were referred for continuing therapy in the community as part of the research–therapy termination process, the patients mainly did not follow up on the referrals. However, on their return to clinic-based treatment as usual, the patients sometimes attempted to engage with clinical staff at a similar level of intensive contact and appeared to expect a similar level of outreach as had occurred during the research treatment period. Patients also engaged in a period of "testing" their clinic counselors, characterized by repeated mentions of their PTSD diagnosis, their trauma, or their feelings about it, with the likely purpose of establishing the counselors' reactions and whether, in fact, the counselor would also treat them for PTSD. Such behavior is not unusual among PTSD patients (Wilson & Lindy, 1994) and was also present during each patient's initial sessions with his or her research therapist. However, occurring as it did during the return from research to clinical therapy, the patients' reactions and questions generated uncertainty within the clinic counselors: Should they be fully responsive to the patients' requests and start providing primarily trauma-focused therapy, even though this is not the standard clinical counseling approach? If they do not provide trauma-related treatment, how should they address their patients' concerns? Would the lack of provision of trauma-related treatment constitute a treatment error?

Research and senior clinical staff offered support to the counselors that, indeed, administering their usual style of treatment with the patients was sufficient, given the context of treating patients in an addictions treatment milieu. Counselors were also encouraged to consider referring such patients again to outside therapy resources. In turn, planning in future research trials will include this clinical phenomenon, in that termination from the research treatment will include a transitional process of decreasing the frequency of both research assessments and therapist contacts in addition to the existing process of discussing termination on a continuous basis through the last 6 weeks (rather than the last 4 weeks) of the 20-week SDPT.

CONCLUSION

PTSD–SUDS is a relatively common form of dual diagnosis among patients with chemical addictions and one associated with a negative prognosis in standard addictions treatment. Thus, integrative treatments are necessary for improving clinical outcomes. Research studies have offered an opportunity to test new treatment models, including the SDPT model. However, from a research point of view, testing these models cannot occur in a vacuum, for practical reasons and to maintain external validity. From a clinical and administrative point of view, these studies have also served the need to address the commonly occurring but difficult clinical problem of treating trauma in actively using substance-addicted individuals. In the SDPT trials this has required active collaborations with various clinics. For researchers, clinicians, and administrators alike, these collaborations have been marked by mutual communication and coordination processes, requiring commitment to the process, time, energy, patience, and support on both sides of the research–clinical interface. Communication and coordination occurred at many different levels of both the clinical and the research organizations, thus assuring both maximum information exchange and maximum opportunity for necessary adaptations, whether in usual clinical procedures or in the research protocol. The level of understanding of the potential positive benefits of allowing research to be performed as part of the overall clinic mission, as well as the positive support for these specific research studies, together with the participation of the clinic senior administrative and medical staff from study inception to conclusion, certainly have been vital requirements for the success of this research–clinical partnership.

Although some of the processes I have discussed were in part necessitated by the nature of the population—that is, patients whose lives are frequently chaotic and who in turn sometimes generate chaos and disorganization both consciously and subconsciously (Wilson & Lindy, 1994)—many of the procedures developed are generic to establishing and maintaining a working clinical–research structure. Although this is not always an easy or automatic matter, the rewards for doing so are numerous and include improved treatment of individuals as they move from being patients to research participants and back, mutual learning, and even improved research design. Such outcomes are worthwhile.

REFERENCES

Abueg, F., & Fairbank, J. (1992). Behavioral treatment of the PTSD–substance abuser: A multidimensional stage model. In P. Saigh (Ed.), *Posttraumatic stress disorder: A behavioral approach to assessment and treatment* (pp. 111–147). New York: Pergamon Press.

American Psychiatric Association. (1994). *Diagnostic and statistical manual of mental disorders* (4th ed.). Washington, DC: Author.

Boudewyns, P., & Hyer, L. (1990). Physiological response to combat memories and preliminary treatment outcome in Vietnam veteran PTSD patients treated with direct therapeutic exposure. *Behavioural Therapy, 21*, 63–87.

Bremner, J. D. (1999). Does stress damage the brain? *Biological Psychiatry, 45*, 797–805.

Breslau, N., Davis, G., & Adreski, P. (1991). Traumatic events and posttraumatic stress disorder in an urban population of young adults. *Archives of General Psychiatry, 40*, 216–222.

Brown, P., Recupero, P., & Stout, R. (1995). PTSD substance abuse comorbidity and treatment utilization. *Addictive Behaviors, 20*, 251–254.

Brown, P., Stout, R., & Mueller, T. (1999a). Posttraumatic stress disorder and substance abuse relapse among women: A pilot study. *Psychology of Addictive Behaviors, 10*, 124–128.

Brown, P., Stout, R., & Mueller, T. (1999b). Substance use disorder and posttraumatic stress disorder comorbidity: Addiction and psychiatric treatment rates. *Psychology of Addictive Behaviors, 13*, 115–122.

Bullman, T., & Kang, H. (1994). Posttraumatic stress disorder and the risk of traumatic deaths among Vietnam veterans. *Journal of Nervous and Mental Disease, 182*, 604–610.

Carroll, K. (1998). *A cognitive–behavioral approach: Treating cocaine addiction* (NIH No. 98-4308). Rockville, MD: National Institute on Drug Abuse.

Carroll, K., Donovan, D., Hester, R., & Kadden, R. (1993). *Cognitive–behavioral coping skills program*. Unpublished manuscript.

Centers for Disease Control. (1988). Health status of Vietnam veterans: I. Psychosocial characteristics. The Centers for Disease Control Vietnam Experience Study. *JAMA, 259*, 2701–2707.

Dansky, B., Saladin, M., Brady, K., Kilpatrick, D., & Resnick, H. (1995). Prevalence of victimization and posttraumatic stress disorder among women with substance use disorders. *International Journal of Addictions, 30*, 1079–1099.

Evans, D., & Sullivan, J. (1995). *Treating addicted survivors of trauma*. New York: Guilford Press.

Foa, E., Dancu, C., Hembree, E., Jaycox, L., Meadow, E., & Street, G. (1999). A comparison of exposure therapy, stress inoculation training, and their combination for reducing posttraumatic stress disorder in female assault victims. *Journal of Consulting and Clinical Psychology, 67*, 194–200.

Foa, E., & Rothbaum, B. (1998). *Treating the trauma of rape: Cognitive–behavioral therapy for PTSD*. New York: Guilford Press.

Foa, E., Rothbaum, B., Riggs, D., & Murdock, T. (1991). Treatment of posttraumatic stress disorder in rape victims: A comparison between cognitive–behavioral procedures and counseling. *Journal of Consulting and Clinical Psychology, 59*, 715–723.

Fullilove, M., Fullilove, R., Smith, M., Winkler, K., Michael, C., Panzer, P., et al. (1993). Violence, trauma and post traumatic stress disorder among women drug users. *Journal of Traumatic Stress, 6*, 533–544.

Haley, S. (1974). When the patient reports atrocities: Specific treatment considerations of the Vietnam veteran. *Archives of General Psychiatry, 30*, 191–196.

Helzer, J. E., Robins, L. N., & McEvoy, L. (1987). Posttraumatic stress disorder in the general population: Findings from the Epidemiological Catchment Area Survey. *New England Journal of Medicine, 387*, 1630–1634.

Hien, D., & Levin, F. (1994). Trauma and trauma-related disorders for women on methadone: Prevalence and treatment considerations. *Journal of Psychoactive Drugs, 26*, 421–429.

Jordan, B., Schlenger, W., Hough, R., Kulka, R., Weiss, D., Fairbank, J., et al. (1991). Lifetime and current prevalence of specific psychiatric disorders among Vietnam veterans and controls. *Archives of General Psychiatry, 48*, 207–215.

Kadden, R., Carroll, K., Donovan, D., Cooney, N., Monti, P., Abram, D., et al. (1992). *Cognitive–behavioral coping skills therapy manual: A clinical research guide for therapists treating individuals with alcohol abuse and dependence* (DHHS No. ADM 92-1895, Vol. 3). Washington, DC: U.S. Department of Health and Human Services.

Kessler, R., Sonnega, A., Bromet, E., Hughes, M., & Nelson, C. (1995). Posttraumatic stress disorder: I. The National Comorbidity Survey. *Archives of General Psychiatry, 52*, 1048–1060.

Kimerling, R., Armistead, L., & Forehand, R. (1999). Victimization experiences and HIV infection in women: Associations with serostatus, psychological symptoms and health status. *Journal of Traumatic Stress, 12*, 41–58.

Marks, I., Lovell, K., Noshirvani, H., Livanou, M., & Thrasher, S. (1998). Treatment of posttraumatic stress disorder by exposure and/or cognitive restructuring. *Archives of General Psychiatry, 55*, 317–325.

McConnaughy, E., Prochaska, J., & Velicer, W. (1983). Stages of change in psychotherapy: Measurement and sample profiles. *Psychotherapy: Theory, Research and Practice, 20*, 368–375.

Meichenbaum, D. (1994). *A clinical handbook/practical therapist manual for assessing and treating adults with PTSD*. Waterloo, Ontario, Canada: Institute Press.

Meichenbaum, D., & Cameron, R. (1983). Stress inoculation training: Toward a general paradigm for training coping skills. In J. M. Meichenbaum (Ed.), *Stress reduction and prevention* (pp. 115–157). New York: Plenum.

Metzger, D. (1976). It is always the woman who is raped. *American Journal of Psychiatry, 133*, 405–408.

Miller, D., & Guidry, L. (2001). *Addiction and trauma recovery: Healing the body, mind, and spirit*. New York: W.W. Norton & Company.

Najavits, L., Weiss, R., & Shaw, S. (1999). A clinical profile of women with posttraumatic stress disorder and substance dependence. *Psychology of Addictive Behaviors, 13*, 98–104.

Newman, E., Walker, E., & Gefland, A. (1999). Assessing the ethical costs and benefits of trauma-focused research. *General Hospital Psychiatry, 21,* 187–196.

Notman, M., & Nadelson, C. (1976). The rape victim: Psychodynamic considerations. *American Journal of Psychiatry, 133,* 408–413.

Ouimette, P., Ahrens, C., Moos, F., & Finney, J. (1998). During treatment changes in substance abuse patients with posttraumatic stress disorder: The influence of specific interventions and program environments. *Journal of Substance Abuse Treatment, 15,* 555–564.

Ouimette, P., Finney, J., & Moos, R. (1999). Two year posttreatment functioning and coping of substance abuse patients with posttraumatic stress disorder. *Psychology of Addictive Behaviors, 13,* 105–114.

Polles, A., & Smith, P. (1995). Treatment of coexisting substance dependence and posttraumatic stress disorder. *Psychiatric Services, 46,* 729–730.

Prochaska, J., & DiClemente, C. (1983). Stages and processes of self-change of smoking: Toward an integrative model of change. *Journal of Consulting and Clinical Psychology, 51,* 390–395.

Resnick, H., Kilpatrick, D., Dansky, B., Saunders, B., & Best, C. (1993). Prevalence of civilian trauma and posttraumatic stress disorder in a representative national sample of women. *Journal of Consulting and Clinical Psychology, 61,* 984–991.

Rounsaville, B., Kranzler, H., Ball, S., Tennen, H., Poling, J., & Triffleman, E. (1998). Personality disorders in substance abusers: Relation to substance use. *Journal of Nervous and Mental Disease, 186,* 87–95.

Satel, S., Becker, B., & Dan, E. (1993). Reducing obstacles to affiliation with Alcoholics Anonymous among veterans with PTSD and alcoholism. *Hospital and Community Psychiatry, 44,* 1061–1065.

Seidel, R., Gusman, F., & Abueg, F. (1994). Theoretical and practical foundations of an inpatient post-traumatic stress disorder and alcoholism treatment program. *Psychotherapy, 31,* 67–78.

Shalev, A., Bleich, A., & Ursano, R. (1990). Posttraumatic stress disorder: Somatic comorbidity and effort tolerance. *Psychosomatics, 31,* 197–203.

Southwick, S. M., Yehuda, R., & Giller, E. L. Jr. (1993). Personality disorders in treatment-seeking combat veterans with post-traumatic stress disorder. *American Journal of Psychiatry, 150,* 1020–1023.

Stiffman, A., Dore, P., Earls, F., & Cunningham, R. (1992). The influence of mental health problems on AIDS-related risk behaviors in young adults. *Journal of Nervous and Mental Disease, 180,* 314–320.

Strain, E., Bigelow, G., Liebson, I., & Stitzer, M. (1999). Moderate vs. high-dose methadone in the treatment of opioid dependence. *JAMA, 281,* 1000–1005.

Triffleman, E. (1998). Trauma, PTSD and substance abuse. In H. Kranzler & B. Rounsaville (Eds.), *Dual diagnosis and treatment* (2nd ed., pp. 263–316). New York: Marcel Dekker.

Triffleman, E. (2000). Gender differences in a controlled pilot study of psychosocial treatments in substance dependent patients with PTSD: Design considerations and outcomes. *Alcoholism Treatment Quarterly, 18,* 113–118.

Triffleman, E., Carroll, K., & Kellogg, S. (1999). Substance dependence–posttraumatic stress disorder treatment: An integrated cognitive–behavioral approach. *Journal of Substance Abuse Treatment, 17,* 3–14.

Triffleman, E., Marmar, C., Delucchi, K., & Ronfeldt, H. (1995). Childhood trauma and posttraumatic stress disorder in substance abuse inpatients. *Journal of Nervous and Mental Disease, 183,* 172–176.

Triffleman, E., Wong, P., & Monnette, C. (2002). *A pilot comparison trial of two treatments for substance dependence and PTSD.* Manuscript submitted for publication.

Wilson, J., & Lindy, J. (Eds.). (1994). *Countertransference in the treatment of PTSD.* New York: Guilford Press.

Wolfe, J., Schnurr, P., Brown, P., & Furey, J. (1994). Posttraumatic stress disorder and war-zone exposure as correlates of perceived health in female Vietnam war veterans. *Journal of Consulting and Clinical Psychology, 62,* 1235–1240.

15

INTEGRATING RESEARCH INTO A TREATMENT PROGRAM

VIVIAN B. BROWN

The literature on bridging the gap between practice and research highlights the importance of creating and sustaining partnerships between researchers and community-based providers. In this chapter I describe a community-based program into which research has been incorporated for a long time. I begin the chapter with a discussion of the concept of equality in the partnership and describe the culture of this community-based organization, the integrative actions that have been taken to help treatment staff own the research and for the research teams to value provider input, and the steps in the development and refinement of its integrated approach.

INTRODUCTION TO PROTOTYPES, CENTERS FOR INNOVATION IN HEALTH, MENTAL HEALTH AND SOCIAL SERVICES

PROTOTYPES, Centers for Innovation in Health, Mental Health and Social Services, is a private, nonprofit, community-based organization in Los Angeles, California. It was founded in 1986 by me and Maryann Fraser, LCSW, MBA.

Mission and Services

PROTOTYPES' mission is to meet the diverse health and human service needs of women and their children who are affected by substance abuse; mental health disorders; trauma; HIV/AIDS; acute and chronic health conditions; and other life-threatening problems, including inadequate and inappropriate systems of care.

The name symbolizes the organization's mission: PROTOTYPES was designed to develop new models of care, test these models, and refine them on the basis of the research and then disseminate the results through training, technical assistance, and other multimedia activities. It was also designed to be proactive rather than reactive—to identify emerging and unmet needs in the community and, working in collaboration with others, to develop new services and new system paradigms.

PROTOTYPES began with three major components: (a) the PROTOTYPES Women's Center in Pomona, California, which was designed to be one of the first residential drug treatment programs for women dealing not only with addiction and abuse but also with mental illness and HIV/AIDS; (b) the PROTOTYPES Women and AIDS Risk Network Program, which was one of the first AIDS outreach programs specifically designed around and targeted to the needs of women and their children, funded by the National Institute on Drug Abuse;[1] and (c) training and technical assistance, which was designed to take what the PROTOTYPES staff learn and transfer that knowledge to others.

Within these three initial components, PROTOTYPES expanded its research and demonstration activities. These activities identified a number of new needs around which was eventually developed a comprehensive continuum of services. At present, PROTOTYPES has seven service divisions: (a) Substance Abuse Treatment and Prevention; (b) Community Health and HIV/AIDS Services; (c) Community Outreach, Prevention, and Intervention Services; (d) Mental Health Services; (e) Training and Technical Assistance; (f) Trauma and Domestic Violence Services; and (g) the PROTOTYPES Systems Change Center. The agency has 24 sites in Los Angeles County and Ventura County.

---

[1]The Women and AIDS Risk Network (WARN) program was a three-site project (Los Angeles; Boston; and Phoenix, Arizona). Josette Mondanaro, MD, was the Principal Investigator, and I was the Deputy Investigator.

Translating research into practice and ensuring that a continuous loop of research and evaluation was incorporated into the service delivery activities have always been important elements of PROTOTYPES' vision. From its beginnings, PROTOTYPES staff and clients have been actively involved in research—conducting, contributing, and learning from research. The staff have worked collaboratively with a number of research teams, including the Drug Abuse Research Center at the University of California, Los Angeles; The Measurement Group; the RAND Corporation; the University of Southern California; and others.

In this chapter I summarize PROTOTYPES' many experiences with research to highlight the diverse ways in which it has integrated research into its practices and its practices into research.

THE CULTURE OF THE ORGANIZATION THAT ALLOWS FOR RESEARCH-TO-PRACTICE AND PRACTICE-TO-RESEARCH RECIPROCITY

Organizational culture represents the shared beliefs and values that are reflected in traditions and habits as well as in more tangible manifestations such as stories, symbols, and products. It is the collective cognition of the organization. One of the most important values guiding PROTOTYPES has been the desirability of continual "reinvention." As Kanter (1983) stated,

> The entrepreneurial spirit producing innovation is associated with a particular way of approaching problems that I call "integrative": the willingness to move beyond received wisdom, to combine ideas from unconnected sources, to embrace change as an opportunity to test limits. (p. 27)

PROTOTYPES was also designed to be less category conscious than most health and social service agencies; for example, it does not have rigid boundaries or units based on disciplines. This design has allowed for permeable boundaries and flexibility in both program and staff development. Although the Table of Organization may reflect a traditional structure with divisions and units, in practice the organization resembles a living organism, constantly changing to meet new needs in the communities it serves.

To accomplish this, PROTOTYPES continually creates diverse staff teams that represent new and different configurations of training and life experiences, practice approaches, and cultural values. Work is done in an environment of mutual respect and multiple ties. For example, the PROTO-TYPES Women's Center was designed for women dealing with a number of co-occurring disorders, and therefore the treatment team cuts across health, mental health, and substance abuse disciplines.

Staff are empowered to bring new information and to act on new information in shaping service delivery. Staff at all levels are also assisted in understanding and conducting research. They are given what they need to identify, codify, and build judgment about emerging new tools and methods in treatment and research and to look for communities of practice where the knowledge of work practices is embedded. The staff who take action also capture, observe, and reflect on results. Thus, all staff are involved in generating information, integrating it into the big picture, making sense of it, and deciding how to act on it. They institute change, because they themselves are the learners rather than being passive recipients of someone else's learning.

PROTOTYPES has developed a research-friendly learning organization in two major ways: (a) Staff are trained to see research as part of their mission ("research-friendly" staff), and (b) best practices and innovations are woven into the organization's operations through a number of integrative actions.

Training Staff to See Research as Part of Their Mission

When PROTOTYPES was funded to enhance and evaluate its outreach services, the management staff began to train outreach staff in the "whys" and "hows" of research. PROTOTYPES management believed it was important for the staff who would be collecting data to understand that PROTOTYPES implements research endeavors to answer questions that will lead to better services for its populations and communities. Outreach staff often came to their jobs from the communities and often did not have any formal training. PROTOTYPES designed an extensive in-service training program. These staff, however, also came with an in-depth knowledge of these communities, which is recognized as an invaluable resource for the researchers with whom PROTOTYPES collaborated.

With regard to the "how" of research, staff were trained in issues of randomization, comparison groups (vs. control groups), how staff can help formulate questions, how researchers measure, what do they do with data, how it is analyzed, and how it is disseminated.

The other side of the training coin was equally important; that is, researchers had to be taught how to modify their understanding and practice of research in order to respond to the needs of service staff, clients, and the community.

Staff also met with the various teams of researchers. There are many important discussions about research being "for the agency" and not "just for the funding agencies"; about the Tuskegee syphilis experiment; and about how disenfranchised and stigmatized groups have been subjects of, but not partners in, research. Staff also discussed (alone) who talks to them with disrespect or talks down to them, who needs to learn more about the service programs, who doesn't listen, and so on. Staff are empowered to bring negative experiences with researchers to the table. Individuals who do not adapt to the culture are seen as not fitting into the work. Just as researchers and providers are committed to protecting clients from being used for research, PROTOTYPES is also committed to protecting staff from being treated in a disrespectful way by researchers.

When PROTOTYPES received funding from the National Institute on Drug Abuse and the U.S. Centers for Disease Control for research into the effectiveness of the outreach services, The Measurement Group's evaluation team met with the staff and managers to design new forms that would make existing staff tasks easier rather than adding one more form to their existing burden. This sensitivity to avoiding additional paperwork burden increased staff receptivity to participation in data collection. Among the techniques designed were scannable paper forms, often only one page long (Huba, Brown, & Melchior, 1995). This was an innovation of importance to both service providers and researchers, and the treatment and research team worked collaboratively to transfer the technology to others. The data collection tasks were experienced as not only "doable" but also intrinsically important.

When support was received from Substance Abuse and Mental Health Services Administration's Office of Treatment Improvement and the Center for Substance Abuse Treatment for research at PROTOTYPES Women's Center, the research team and management team met and then included all the center staff in helping adapt existing forms to new questions. For example, the program had designed a user-friendly form to document the 20 hours of treatment services per week required as a minimum for contract compliance. This form was adapted so it could be used for the new research with a few simple additions. Because staff were already familiar with the form, the treatment and research team knew this would ensure fewer errors than new forms would. In addition, the evaluators helped the staff learn how the new data collection forms (e.g., the Center for Epidemiologic Study—Depression Scale) that were introduced to show program outcomes might be quite useful as tools for them to use in assessing individuals' needs, progress, and outcomes.

The evaluator also joined the agency's chief executive officer in conducting quarterly case conferences with PROTOTYPES Women's Center staff, during which all data on clients were discussed, including psychosocial history, the Basic Personality Inventory, the Center for Epidemiologic Study—Depression Scale, psychiatric evaluation, counselors' perceptions, and so on. Through these meetings, staff began in a very concrete way to understand how research methodology and tools could assist them in their work. On the other side, the researchers were given a unique opportunity to see their "subjects" as real people and to understand how research findings could realistically be built into practice.

Regular use of research data to improve clinical services is an important element in successful integration. When data were analyzed, researchers and managers met with the staff to discuss possible interpretations of the results. This allowed researchers to deepen their understanding of clinical phenomena and the concerns of practitioners. This is an important part of the research–practice loop that is often left out.

Best Practices and Innovations Are Woven Into the Organization's Operations Through Integrative Actions

Training

The PROTOTYPES Training Division provides cross-training services to AOD (alcohol and other drugs) providers, HIV/AIDS providers, and mental health providers throughout Los Angeles County. As the training staff develop new curricula, they pilot the trainings with PROTOTYPES staff. Thus, training is seen as part of the culture of a learning organization. Two of the recent trainings introduced to the Los Angeles County provider network are a Hepatitis C curriculum and the chemical dependency, mental illness, and HIV/AIDS curriculum. At present, an integrated curriculum on substance abuse, mental illness, trauma, and HIV/AIDS is being developed.

As part of the training schedule, and in recognition that agency leaders require a different model of knowledge transfer, the division staff hold quarterly executive briefings. These briefings focus on emerging issues in substance abuse, HIV/AIDS, and mental health. Executive directors are invited to attend half-day sessions at which presentations are made by directors of Los Angeles County programs, researchers, and consumers. Lunch is a relaxed time for the executives to share with one another. In a community in which there are a great many turf issues and fierce competition for limited funding, these briefings allow for a "coming together" for mutual problem solving and mutual benefit.

Conferences

PROTOTYPES holds an annual skills-building conference for all substance abuse providers and researchers throughout Los Angeles County. Conference themes focus on emerging issues, for example, "women and trauma" and "integrating services." Attendance is usually approximately 350 participants.

Publications

For all research and demonstration projects, PROTOTYPES staff participate with research teams to write papers and publish findings. It is important for both service providers and researchers to understand that service staff really can enhance the interpretation of data in more relevant ways than researchers alone. One cannot conclude whether a significant result is meaningful or relevant without understanding its environmental context. When the service delivery staff are involved, the synergy that various perspectives add to the process results in a fuller, more meaningful interpretation of the data. It also leads to a more comprehensive picture of the clinical implications of the data.

Champions

The efforts embodied in staff training and staff development are significantly enhanced when leaders from the ranks of line-level staff champion the new practice. There is often a small group of staff members who are more enthusiastic and willing to try to implement a new way of doing things. Using that group as a catalyst for change in practice settings has proven to be a more effective strategy than attempting to get the entire staff to implement a change at once. Champions can assume a wide variety of activities to bring about practice change, including training peers in the new practice, assuming a quality assurance role, and acting in a supervisory capacity.

STEPS TO ACCOMPLISH AN EFFECTIVE RESEARCH–PRACTICE INTERFACE

Weaving best practices and innovations into an organization's mode of operating is not sufficient to accomplish an effective research–practice interface. In fact, the entire organizational structure and its staffing need to be conducive to integrating research and practice throughout the organization.

Organizational Structure

Commitment to Partnering

PROTOTYPES has established a new type of management. Beginning with the coleadership of the chief executive officer and the executive vice president, there is a commitment to partnering at every level in order to meet the constantly changing needs of the communities being served (Heenan & Bennis, 1999). This commitment to partnering also extends to research endeavors. Because external partners are continuously entering into the PROTOTYPES service delivery system, partnering within the organization is seen as modeling this process and enables staff to maximize resources.

Lack of Hierarchy

The organizational structure is not designed in a hierarchical fashion. There are 10 divisional directors who serve as boundary spanners across delivery systems within PROTOTYPES. This structure is seen as a "jeweled net,"[2] with numerous connections across divisions.

Staffing

Diversity

In addition to racial–ethnic–community diversity, 50% of PROTO-TYPES staff are consumers–survivors–recovering persons. In this way, the staff truly represent the populations they serve. As PROTOTYPES begins to serve new, different populations, staff stay alert to the need for increasing staff diversity.

Everyone's Perspective Is Respected

Program expansions have usually been based on input from community representatives, consumers, and staff. When a gap in services is identified, a team is formed to think through a solution. Everyone is listened to and heard.

Cross-fertilization

Some of the most exciting developments occur as one division implements a new model and it is shown to be effective. Then, staff trained in that model in that division begin to share that model with other divisions. For example, as the outreach staff demonstrated effective engagement strategies and effective strategies for helping clients enter drug treatment services (PROTOTYPES' and others), the outreach staff trained other divisional staff to implement outreach services.

Staff and Community Input Occurs on Every Level

The concept of empowerment is a key element in most effective community-based programs. Clients participate actively in their treatment planning and treatment program. Sometimes they become staff of the program. A part of their empowerment is to question why certain evaluation questions are being asked, what the data show, and how the data will be used to justify their service programs.

Cutting Across Content Areas

The managers and the board of directors of PROTOTYPES, as individuals and as a group, have a long history of work in a number of areas. This cross-cutting content expertise, along with a shared interest in responding

---

[2] I thank Charlotte Linde, PhD, for sharing the image of the jeweled net.

to clients with multiple vulnerabilities, has helped staff respect multiple perspectives and helped them respond efficiently to new issues, as they arise, for the populations served. Because managers and board members had been providing alcohol and other drug treatment services as well as mental health and trauma services for more than 30 years, with the emergence of HIV/AIDS the staff felt prepared to move quickly and expand their services to address HIV outreach, prevention, and care.

The issue of HIV/AIDS highlights the issues of crises and organizational readiness to change. When there is a crisis, such as the HIV/AIDS epidemic and the spread of crack use throughout inner cities, community providers and community-based organizations move quickly to develop programs and interventions. Under the press of an urgent need to do something to save lives and reduce community disintegration, the provider and consumer move together to intervene. It is also true that epidemiologists are often right there in the community, tracking the public health problems or crises, but the provider and consumer have usually moved in first to intervene, even if their intervention does not prove to be the most effective in the long run.

Later, researchers begin the rigorous study of the interventions and their components. Typically, the interventions studied are simplified versions of the ones in use, because research designs need to have standardized and measurable interventions. By the time the research has been conducted, the data analyzed, and reports of findings fed back to the field, the original interventions designed by the providers and consumers already have begun to change, and the research findings may not be relevant. It may be important to establish "crisis teams" of researchers, providers, and consumers who are invested in early knowledge building and application of their own innovative models as well as early adoption of others' models.

INTERVIEW

The following interview with one of PROTOTYPES' staff members, Wendy, reflects the learning culture created within the organization, for all of the staff. Wendy came into the program as an administrative assistant. A recovering drug abuser and alcoholic who has been clean and sober for 11 years, Wendy is now a deputy director, supervises 15 staff members, has helped launch a number of community initiatives, and continues to advocate for women and their families.

> *Vivian B. Brown (VBB):*   When you first heard the word "research," what did it mean to you?

> *Wendy:*   I associated it with something entirely scientific that I really didn't connect myself with. I didn't trust the scientific community. I, like many African American people, felt that

research didn't really work for poor people. I associated it with physical diseases, but when it came to community issues, you couldn't really trust researchers who came in and collected data to have it really demonstrate something real for the community. I didn't know that when we handed out evaluation forms at our groups that we were doing a type of research. It seemed like such an isolated field. I didn't realize that people like you also did research.

VBB: And now?

Wendy: Now I accept that everything is evidence based. I know that. Now I see research painting a different picture of the face of the community. So many times we are very passionate about what is needed in the community, but it's only based on passion. But I understand that funding and services need to be based on much more. The funders in Washington may not feel my passion, but they can certainly look at my data and read my material.

We would feel frustration when we felt people didn't care about what's going on in the community. But it's not that they don't care, it's that they don't know. How do we approach bureaucracies in a way that is effective? You need to come with hard facts, data, and maybe a few advocates.

In HIV/AIDS, for example, where they say African American women are disproportionately affected than the general population, we should not be doing a countywide plan or a statewide plan without taking these disparities into consideration. People like me need to understand how data can be used for you or against you. Now I know how to ask the questions.

VBB: How does it feel to be able to ask the questions?

Wendy: I feel empowered. They didn't believe I had the knowledge to ask the questions, so they initially treated me with lesser respect. But what I've learned at PROTOTYPES—over 10 years—is that my questions are legitimate. I learned to listen to what people are saying, I don't have to lash out in anger, and I can ask questions appropriately—and not be bullied. I'm willing to read the material and do all the legwork it takes to understand what the researchers did. But I've noticed often that when people are presenting their research data there are only researchers in the room. And now there's me. It took awhile for them to acknowledge me. But when a researcher in the room asked the same questions I did, they were answered. I knew I was on the right track. Now the tide has begun to change.

For years many African American people wouldn't even talk about research. The whole issue of doing testing on

African American people, like Tuskegee, kept us away. But now our not wanting to do research or be part of research has come back to bite us. There isn't [sic] enough data about African American women at risk. We need Black researchers, we need female researchers, we need researchers who live in the community. So people don't see researchers as monsters.

Research forces you to think. You find out that things are not what they appear to be. You learn how all these different variables in a community lead to disease. And now we are seeing that all organizations need to be more accountable. I think that's a good thing. There should be accountability to the community as well as the funding. That should be the foundation of how funding is decided. Did they do what they said they would do and did it make the community healthier[?] Too many times you have funding going to different programs for the wrong reasons.

You need to do your process evaluations and your outcomes evaluation, so you can see if you just stumbled your way to the end. Everyone is passionate; everyone thinks they have a good program. But did they accomplish their objectives[?] Did they have good outcomes[?] Did they implement the program in such a sloppy way, we wouldn't be able to duplicate the program[?]

VBB: What are your plans?

Wendy: I know I'm responsible and play a role. My personal mission statement and PROTOTYPES' mission statement fit. I've been at PROTOTYPES for 10 years, and in school 8 years. Everything I needed to learn and to evolve was here. I've learned to look at the big picture—to ask a lot of questions and to understand why you're doing something. That started even when I was your administrative assistant. I've been able to evolve and grow. You, and Maryann, and Ruth, and Chi, have helped me to look at what needs to be changed. And I'm willing to step up to the plate.

My major has changed from Health Sciences to Administration of Public and Nonprofit Organizations. A great master's program is where I will learn more about research. And I'm going to join the Association of Student Researchers at the university.

VBB: You'll be sitting on the new Research Advisory Panel at [the University of Southern California] for the new research project. What are you thinking about that?

Wendy: I'm excited about it, but I feel a little intimidated. All our grants have given us the opportunity to look at so many things. The landscape for delivery of services is changing. You don't have to be a researcher, but you better be able to read the research and understand it. I've read everything we've written here at PROTOTYPES. Now I understand how important it is for people—women, women of color—to get training in these areas. So [I] can sit down anywhere—in any part of the world—and say: "Here is [sic] my data. It is clean, unbiased, and it was collected uniformly." That's fun.

VBB: How did you feel about working with all the different research groups?

Wendy: I feel good about working with the different research groups. They all have their different styles, different functions. I've seen some who consider themselves a community-based evaluation company, but I don't see them as being any more community-based than the others because they try to present themselves as being something other than researchers. They try to use the language—"Hey sister, what's going on . . ."—but that's just part of a strategy to get people to answer the same questions that another researcher would ask. I think I would rather work with people who are open to asking the questions we need to ask, than with people who try to bill themselves as "well, I'm from the community so I know everything." They tend to be not as open, they tend to be a bit more patronizing, like, "well, we really know because we're African American and we're researchers and we're from the neighborhood." However, we have needed to say to them "You're wrong. Because you're African American doesn't put you in the ghetto, doesn't put you in poverty. You need to be open to everything, because there are things that you may not be asking because you think you already know the answers." If you don't respect everyone's input, you can't ask the right questions. The dynamics of the politics, poverty, race, and gender are complex and we need skilled and open-minded people to do that research.

ELEMENTS OF SUCCESSFUL COLLABORATION BETWEEN RESEARCH AND PRACTICE

Need for Evaluators Who Are "Real Partners"

One should not underestimate the magnitude of the challenges on both sides for service providers and researchers to achieve true partnerships. Although collaboration may have existed for some time, additional work is usually needed to transform it into a true partnership in which both partners offer unique contributions and complementary expertise to the venture: rigorous research methods and technical expertise on the research side and understanding of important questions and real-world problems on the provider side.

Researchers need to begin with the goals of developing therapies and treatment trials that make sense to clinicians and consumers (external validity) and that are feasible, flexible, palatable, affordable, and sustainable in real-world settings (Jensen, Hoagwood, & Trickett, 1999). Although palatability of an intervention is not an absolute requirement in every instance, such as new medical regimens for HIV/AIDS, other therapeutic factors need to be included. For example, whereas new medical–pharmacological therapies led to an increased understanding of the medical management of HIV, new psychosocial supports were needed to ensure adherence to effective medical treatments. Nonmedical providers of services understood that some clients would need interventions to correctly follow physician instructions, some clients would have concomitant emotional and behavioral problems that would need to be addressed in order for their medical therapies to be effective, and some patients might not respond medically and would need to be helped to use other therapies (Huba, Brown, Melchior, Hughes, & Panter, 2000).

From my experience, several things are key to establishing true working partnerships between researchers and service providers.

Equality of Collaboration

Researchers listen to service staff, respect their perspectives, and learn from them; likewise, service staff listen to researchers, respect their perspectives, and learn from them. To facilitate this process, meetings to decide on research questions and on methods for collecting data (e.g., fax-in forms that were developed in collaboration) are held on a regular basis. Research questions need to be relevant to and useful for the provider in order for there to be buy-in for the research. It is also helpful for the research team to present a list of potential instruments to program staff, explain the strengths and weaknesses of each, and then allow program staff to choose.

It is important to establish ongoing meetings to share data as they are collected and analyzed so that staff can assist in the interpretation of the data. If there are barriers related to the collection of data, staff may generate solutions.

Other mechanisms for sharing data and perspectives include joint training workshops by teams of researchers and providers, community-based research briefings, and forums for promising practices.

It is also important for there to be an ongoing mechanism and support for joint publications. Although it is extremely valuable for the research team to write articles for research journals, many of the providers read other types of journals and learn about promising practices through trainings and meetings with colleagues. Therefore, if the partners write joint publications and adapt them to a wide variety of formats, there is a greater likelihood of adoption of the research findings.

Staff Ownership of the Research

When service staff participate in writing the grant proposals they develop a sense of ownership and are more likely to support project implementation as designed. Service staff can participate in the planning meetings for the grant proposal, can assist in writing clinical sections, can participate in focus groups that give input for needs assessments, and so on. Time is set aside at the beginning of research projects to discuss why the data are wanted and how the data will inform practice. I noted earlier that program staff also help formulate the research questions.

When data are analyzed, provider staff can present findings to the community. In this context, "community" includes the therapeutic community, the community studied, the community of providers, and other community-based organizations. In addition, service staff can recommend changes in practice that are based on the data.

Mechanisms for Dissemination

Often, research fundamentally redefines a technology, a service, an intervention process. In order for this new knowledge to move into practice, the provider community must experience it in a way that demonstrates its effectiveness and its possibilities. This process involves both partners: research and provider staff. Joint presentations given locally and nationally, joint articles published in a wide variety of formats, and joint training workshops can help in the dissemination. The research team needs to be able to communicate which elements are critical to the program effectiveness and which elements can be reinvented by the providers. The provider team needs to be able to communicate what struggles they went through in implementing the new practice, what "fit" for them, and how they will use the new practice in their agency.

It is also important for the partners to develop multimedia formats to present the results. These could include program manuals and protocols, videotapes, and a Web site.

PROTOTYPES staff have also learned that both clinical staff and evaluation staff not only bring valuable skills to the practice–research collaboration but also develop valuable skills as a result of that partnership (Huba et al., 2000). For example, program staff learn how "objective" or "outside" observers come up with questions about how the program works and the ways in which its effectiveness can be demonstrated. They begin to understand how ongoing data collection can provide the feedback necessary to improve the quality of the program as well as the outcomes for individual clients. They learn how to collect information that will allow them to justify expanding the program to offer other needed services. Finally, they can help the evaluation staff identify gaps in the evaluation design that are occurring because the data collection methods or design are not sensitive to important program outcomes.

Conversely, evaluation staff learn how to understand the ongoing treatment protocols for clients. Within the context of these treatment protocols, individual client treatment plans, and program goals, the evaluation staff can come to view program success for individual clients in a broader way. They can learn that success is a continuous process rather than a simple outcome captured by a few data indicators. Evaluation staff can also begin to understand the importance of treatment team approaches that stress the synergistic effects of different kinds of services for different kinds of clients. They learn about the burdens of data collection on both the clients and the program staff, and they realize that it may be desirable to reduce that burden by eliminating redundant or secondary data items. Finally, evaluation staff can help the clinical staff understand the general patterns of services in the program, including possible treatment gaps, emerging client needs, or unanticipated outcomes of program and policy decisions.

CHANGES THAT STILL NEED TO BE IMPLEMENTED

Issues of Culture

There is still much to be done to ensure that evaluations are culturally competent.

Ethnic Diversity in Contract Evaluation Staff

Although a number of the research–evaluation teams with which I have worked have had staff who were ethnically diverse, not all of the teams met even this minimal step. Because PROTOTYPES' staff and clients are ethnically and racially diverse, it is important that the evaluation teams represent the same balance. However, this diversity does not ensure that the evaluation team will be culturally competent. For that step, it might be important to ask that the evaluation team participate in cultural diversity trainings.

Culturally Competent Instruments

Although much has been done to move toward more culturally and linguistically appropriate measures, there is still more to accomplish. In Los Angeles County there is an attempt to develop materials and instruments in nine core languages: English, Spanish, Chinese, Vietnamese, Cambodian,

Armenian, Korean, Russian, and Farsi. This would be an important goal for all evaluation instruments (i.e., to have measures that are developed in the core languages of that site).

Strengths vs. Deficit Models

There is a need to request that evaluators use more strengths-based evaluation models rather than reliance on only problem or deficit-based models.

The fields (i.e., substance abuse, mental health, and HIV/AIDS) are not only about the study of pathology, weakness, and damage but also the study of strengths, optimism, and hope (Rapp, 1998; Seligman & Csikszentmihalyi, 2000). Providers and researchers need to work together to develop new research that will identify the unique strengths in individuals, families, and communities and to determine how these strengths can be mobilized to build better lives for their clients.

REFERENCES

Heenan, D. A., & Bennis, W. (1999). *Co-leaders*. New York: Wiley.

Huba, G. J., Brown, V. B., & Melchior, L. A. (1995). Fax-in forms as a technology for evaluating community projects: An example of HIV risk reduction. *Educational and Psychological Measurements, 55*, 75–83.

Huba, G. J., Brown, V. B., Melchior, L. A., Hughes, C., & Panter, A. T. (2000). Conceptual issues in implementing and using evaluation in the "real world" setting of a community-based organization for HIV/AIDS Services. *Drugs and Society, 16*(1–2), 31–54.

Jensen, P. S., Hoagwood, K., & Trickett, E. J. (1999). Ivory towers or earthen trenches? Community collaborations to foster real-world research. *Applied Developmental Science, 3*, 206–212.

Kanter, R. M. (1983). *The change masters*. New York: Simon & Schuster.

Rapp, C. A. (1998). *The strengths model*. New York: Oxford University Press.

Seligman, M. E. P., & Csikszentmihalyi, M. (2000). Positive psychology: An introduction. *American Psychologist, 55*, 5–14.

IV

IMPLICATIONS

INTRODUCTION: IMPLICATIONS

JAMES L. SORENSEN

This part provides perspective on the problems addressed by this volume and uses this book as a lens to view the future. In chapter 16 Thomas E. Backer points out that the drug abuse field is not alone in experiencing a substantial gap between research and practice. He reviews forces that are converging to open new avenues for integrating research and practice. Backer presents science-based principles for dissemination and how they can be applied to drug abuse treatment. By applying strategic dissemination methods to the drug abuse treatment field, substance abuse treatment professionals can make it easier to disseminate information between research and treatment.

In the final chapter, the coeditors, led by Joseph Guydish, make policy recommendations based on the preceding chapters. This chapter provides specific recommendations for practice, research, and policy in coping with the problems of drug abuse. We suggest several avenues for future research, including development of a research program on understudied interventions that are thought to be effective and a research plan to investigate and compare techniques for disseminating information to the field. We contend that solutions to the problem of research–practice separation will need to come from within those communities and that policymakers can promote this mobilization. This chapter and the book conclude by emphasizing that long-lasting solutions involve more than merely meeting requirements for collaboration; rather, enduring changes will evolve over time with trust-building experiences and involve a new generation of staff who have been trained to respect both treatment and research.

16

SCIENCE-BASED STRATEGIC APPROACHES TO DISSEMINATION

Thomas E. Backer

> There has been a widespread reluctance to aggressively assemble, analyze and disseminate what is, in fact, known. . . . Leaving local initiatives to painstakingly make these discoveries on their own, or to never make them at all, has been a wasteful process and will interfere with further progress in spreading these initiatives. . . . Most wasteful of all has been the absence of well-funded, concerted attempts to learn systematically from current experience and to disseminate that learning to those responsible for community-change initiatives, to those who make relevant policy in the private and public sector, and to the general public. (Schorr, 1997, p. 370)

Many currently available, science-based drug abuse treatment approaches are not yet widely used by community-based treatment agencies, yet, if effectively disseminated, these research-based technologies have the potential to improve the quality and impact of treatment services, especially in a time of tight resources and increasing demand.

In all areas of health and human services there is a substantial gap between research and practice. This has been documented for various types of drug abuse treatment programs, such as those for methadone maintenance (D'Aunno, Folz-Murphy, & Lin, 1999; D'Aunno & Vaughn, 1995; Etheridge, Craddock, Dunteman, & Hubbard, 1995; Higgins, Budney, Bickel, & Badger, 1994; McLellan et al., 1994; Silverman et al., 1996; Simpson, Joe, & Brown, 1997; Widman et al., 1997). It is equally true for science-validated drug abuse prevention methods (Backer, 2000b). Examinations in virtually every other field of education, social service, and community development reveal similar types of gaps, as the opening quote by social and public policy analyst Lisbeth Schorr makes clear.

Lamb, Greenlick, and McCarty's (1998) study, which was conducted for the Institute of Medicine, identified some important dimensions of this gap specific to drug abuse treatment: structural barriers, such as regulations constraining what treatment approaches may be used in publicly funded programs, financial barriers, insufficient training and education of practitioners to implement new practices, and inadequate attention by researchers to the complex challenges of dissemination. Research-based dissemination strategies from various fields can help identify and close these and other gaps. Such methods have been well discussed in the drug abuse literature (Backer, 1991; Backer, David, & Soucy, 1995; B. Brown, 1998) but often are not used to maximum impact.

SCIENCE-BASED PRINCIPLES OF DISSEMINATION

Dissemination of innovations in any field is inherently a social phenomenon, influenced by the real and perceived characteristics of the innovation (including the cultural beliefs and prejudices of particular groups—such as drug abuse treatment counselors or their clients), the methods by which dissemination occurs, and the organizational or community environment in which the effort to introduce the innovation occurs (Rogers, 1995). More than 80 years of empirical study about how to promote dissemination of innovations, leading to change at the individual, organizational, and community levels, has confirmed four basic principles that underlie successful dissemination efforts (this literature has been summarized by Backer, 1991, and Backer et al., 1995):

1. *User-friendly communication.* Information about the innovation and its relevance to potential adopters must be communicated effectively, in user-friendly, easily accessible formats.
2. *User-friendly evaluation.* Evidence must be available indicating that the innovation is effective, works better than available alternatives, and doesn't have significant side effects; this information must also be communicated effectively to potential adopters.

3. *Resource adequacy*. Sufficient human and financial resources must be available to implement the innovation effectively in new settings.
4. *Addressing the complex human dynamics of change*. Potential adopters must be able to handle the human dynamics of change associated with innovation adoption, by rewarding change activities and involving those who will have to live with change in designing how the innovation will be implemented and by helping adopters overcome their fears, resistances, and anxieties.

These fundamental principles have been confirmed in research specific to drug abuse treatment. For example, Sorensen et al. (1988) demonstrated through a 6-year empirical study funded by the National Institute on Drug Abuse (NIDA) that site visits and conferences are more effective than print materials and other traditional forms of education in promoting dissemination of innovations in drug abuse treatment facilities; their impact is enhanced through creating lively partnerships with state drug abuse authorities (Lipton & Appel, 1984).

Treatment-focused dissemination efforts must also address the perspectives typical of treatment personnel. For instance, Backer, Brown, and Howard (1994) highlighted the importance of constructing dissemination efforts for treatment personnel that respect their personal experiences with addiction. V. B. Brown and Backer (1988) identified a number of active–directive teaching methods that drug abuse personnel prefer for learning about new technologies.

Shortfalls between knowledge and action in the adoption of worthwhile treatment innovations occur for reasons quite similar to those that make it difficult to change individual behavior related to substance abuse or other types of health-related behavior. Incentives to change; resistance to change; and many other technological, organizational, and human factors significantly influence the outcome of efforts to change behavior. This is true whether the behavior is avoidance of street drugs by a recovering cocaine user or adoption of a new treatment technology by a community-based program for heroin addicts.

PRACTICAL DISSEMINATION STRATEGIES DERIVED FROM THESE PRINCIPLES

The complexity of change needed to successfully introduce an improved drug abuse treatment method into one or more treatment settings and communities suggests that scientists, practitioners, and community leaders need to work together in disseminating science-based drug abuse treatment strategies to the treatment field. The four science-based principles for effective dissemination just cited provide a conceptual base from which to design such collaborative interventions, but the knowledge base also provides some more specific strategies for dissemination, which I present here with some briefly stated current examples.

1. *Interpersonal contact.* To get an innovation used in new settings, there needs to be direct, personal contact between those who will be adopting the innovation and its developers or others with direct knowledge about the innovation. For instance, in November 2000, NIDA and the Robert Wood Johnson Foundation (along with local sponsors) cosponsored a conference in Los Angeles, "Blending Clinical Practice and Research: Forging Partnerships to Enhance Drug Addiction Treatment," which brought together some 800 researchers and practitioners to discuss these issues face to face over several days (this is in contrast to most professional conferences, which draw only one audience or the other). A similar conference—"Common Ground, Common Language, Common Goals: Bringing Substance Abuse Practice and Research Together"—was held in April 2001 (also in Los Angeles), cosponsored by the Robert Wood Johnson Foundation; the University of California, Los Angeles's (UCLA's) Integrated Substance Abuse Programs; and the Center for Substance Abuse Treatment (CSAT). Both conferences appeared to be successful in promoting an exchange between drug abuse researchers and practitioners about issues in dissemination (M. Douglas Anglin, personal communication, May 16, 2002).

2. *Potential user involvement.* Everyone who will have to live with the results of the change that adopting an innovation requires needs to be involved in planning and implementing the adoption effort. Inclusion of all players is needed, both to get a range of suggestions for how to undertake the adoption effectively and to facilitate "felt ownership" of the new program or activity (thus decreasing resistance to change). For example, Richard Rawson at the UCLA Integrated Substance Abuse Programs helped to organize a consortium of researchers and practitioners who have worked for several years on the dissemination issues specific to drug abuse treatment in south central Los Angeles, including those related to African American culture (M. Douglas Anglin, personal communication, May 16, 2002).

3. *Planning and conceptual foresight.* A well-developed strategic plan for how an innovation will be adopted in a new setting,

including attention to possible implementation problems and how they will be addressed, is essential to meet the challenges of innovation adoption and sustained change. Part of the work of the south central Los Angeles consortium just mentioned has been to create such plans for disseminating and implementing science-based treatment programs in this community.

4. *Outside consultation on the change process.* Consultation can provide conceptual and practical assistance in designing the adoption/change effort efficiently and can offer useful objectivity about the likelihood of success, costs, possible side effects, and so on. PROTOTYPES, a comprehensive service program for drug-abusing women and their children in southern California that includes several residential treatment facilities (see chapter 15), organized a Systems Change Center that has identified science-based treatment strategies (targeting multiply vulnerable women) and now regularly brings in consultants who can help PROTOTYPES and its community partners wrestle with the complex issues of getting these programs implemented (Vivian B. Brown, personal communication, May 16, 2002).

5. *User-oriented transformation of information.* That which is known about an innovation needs to be translated into language potential users can understand readily—abbreviated so that attention spans are not exceeded and are made to concentrate on the key issues of "Does it work?" and "How can I replicate it in my setting?" The Drug Abuse Treatment Outcome Study Web site (http://www.datos.org), for instance, presents findings from this comprehensive research program in interactive-friendly formats not only for scientists but also for students, treatment counselors, and the general public. Practitioner-oriented videos on science-based treatment methods created by NIDA and CSAT serve as good examples of user-oriented transformation; so do print and online documents such as CSAT's Treatment Improvement Protocols and Technical Assistance Publications (M. Douglas Anglin, personal communication, May 16, 2002).

6. *Individual and organizational championship.* An innovation's chances for successful adoption are much greater if influential potential adopters ("opinion leaders") and organizational or community leaders express enthusiasm for its adoption. Championship can also be provided by what Rogers (1995) referred to as "change agents"—individuals who are actively involved in promoting the process of dissemination itself. The ongoing efforts to introduce levo-alpha-aceytlmethadol (LAAM) into treatment programs for heroin addicts contain many examples

of both positive and negative championship. Treatment program administrators often have resisted efforts to disseminate this science-based treatment innovation because they fear that its administration will be burdensome or that their counselors or clients will resist because of inaccurate but widespread misbeliefs about LAAM (Rawson, Hasson, Huber, McCann, & Ling, 1998). On the other hand, one clinic director successfully forced a switch to LAAM after his clinic was raided by the police because clients were selling their methadone on the street, and his "championship" ultimately proved effective (M. Douglas Anglin, personal communication, May 16, 2002).

Drug abuse researchers and their collaborators in communities (practitioners, clients, and community leaders) can explore together how these six practical strategies might be applied for a particular treatment innovation in a particular setting. For additional inspiration they can also look beyond methods already validated by the science on dissemination and beyond the drug abuse treatment field itself.

NEW AREAS FOR EXPLORATION

In addition to the science-based principles and strategies just presented, there are some emerging areas of science and community practice that could open new avenues for closing the gap between research and practice in the drug abuse treatment field.

- There is a growing knowledge base about how to create and sustain *partnerships* to promote effective dissemination and create change (Backer & Norman, 1998, 2000)—such as the researcher–practitioner partnerships emphasized in Lamb et al.'s (1998) study.
- The increased availability of *capacity-building* services and grant programs for nonprofit organizations (Backer, 2000a) provides opportunities for nonprofit drug abuse treatment agencies to strengthen their human, physical, and technological infrastructures in ways that make adopting new programs easier and their sustained success more likely.
- Recent behavioral and management science research offers a range of strategies for assessing and increasing the *readiness* of groups, organizations, and communities to participate in change (such as introduction of a new drug abuse treatment method); other research examines the opposite end of the adoption

spectrum, looking at ways to increase the *sustainability* of innovations, such as through early planning for long-term financing and ability to adjust to changing external circumstances.

- Dissemination strategies are being developed and tested in *other fields*—such as drug abuse prevention (Backer, 2000b), the larger field of health care (Sechrest, Backer, Rogers, Campbell, & Grady, 1994), the corporate world (Howard & Backer, 1998), and the work of private foundations (Backer, 1995, Backer & Bare, 1999)—that can themselves be transferred to encourage similar efforts in drug abuse treatment.

- The transition to *managed health care* in drug abuse treatment opens new options for financing and service systems change that could support dissemination of innovative treatment programs.

- Drug abuse research, such as that sponsored by NIDA, is concentrating increasingly on *applied research* methods that can be used to test and refine the application of evidence-based principles of dissemination to drug abuse treatment (e.g., clinical trials research, services research, and a new program focused directly on dissemination).

PARTNERSHIP STRATEGIES

Lamb et al. (1998) especially highlighted the critical importance to dissemination of creating and sustaining partnerships between researchers and community-based providers. They assessed a number of models for partnership in substance abuse research that have been tried in geographic areas (e.g., Iowa and the Navajo Nation), identified roles that funders of research and services can take to stimulate such partnerships both directly and indirectly, and addressed some of the challenges to making partnerships work (e.g., they seldom work if treatment agencies want to collaborate on research simply to obtain funds for expanding clinical services).

Lamb et al. (1998) also urged drug abuse research funders (such as NIDA) to look beyond substance abuse for learnings about how to create research–treatment partnerships. They give as an example of such "cross-fertilization" the National Cancer Institute's Community Clinical Oncology Program.

An even larger perspective, on which Lamb et al.'s (1998) report touched but did not treat centrally, is to address the fundamental question of "What factors in its development and operation maximize the chances that a partnership will be successful over time?" Increasing evidence from research studies in substance abuse (Backer & Rogers, 1993), health care (Kreuter & Lezin, 1998), and many other fields (Backer & Norman, 1998, 2000) make it clear that creating and sustaining partnerships is a complex process and that many partnerships fail.

For instance, in a recent study of multicultural coalitions in California (Backer & Norman, 1998), two of the most common threats to long-term sustainability of these partnerships were the failure to (a) address the frequent occurrence of burnout and departure of a coalition's charismatic leaders and (b) handle underlying racial and ethnic stereotypes within the leadership group of the coalition. Research-based innovations in substance abuse treatment need to be analyzed and custom tailored to fit different racial and ethnic groups (Alegria et al., 1994) as well as other special groups, such as people with disabilities (Backer & Newman, 1995), whose communities will be part of the partnerships.

Other evidence about factors that encourage partnership success comes from a recent study of collaboration strategies used by foundations with their nonprofit grantees, including drug abuse agencies (Backer, 1999). This study concluded that funders need to provide training and technical assistance to grantees about the basic process of building and sustaining a partnership. They also need to issue clear guidelines for how a partnership should be set up and direct resources to sustain the collaboration process itself; it is not cost free.

Encouraging a well-crafted infrastructure to support partnerships among researchers and community treatment programs also is imperative. Two examples of infrastructure from related health service fields might be explored for their relevance to substance abuse treatment:

1. *San Francisco Bay Area HIV/AIDS Prevention and Evaluation Initiative.* This multiyear initiative brings together community-based AIDS prevention agencies; evaluation researchers from the University of California, San Francisco; and a consortium of 17 foundations for a team effort to develop, implement, and empirically evaluate AIDS prevention interventions. An evaluation of the initiative suggests that this three-way infrastructure works, but that its partnerships take time and are expensive, and that careful selection of partners and honest discussion among them help improve the quality of partnership (Northern California Grantmakers AIDS Task Force, 1998).

2. *Substance Abuse and Mental Health Services Administration (SAMHSA) Community Action Grant Program.* This funding initiative makes up to $300,000 of federal funding available to plan and then implement a systems change intervention that will bring a validated innovation (including those in substance abuse treatment) into community practice. It begins by initiating a large-scale community planning process, with careful attention to issues of community readiness. Out of this

planning phase a partnership is formed to take responsibility for implementing the innovation. (For more information on this program, consult the funding agency's Web site: http://www.samhsa.gov.)

Such carefully designed, systems-level interventions are especially helpful when difficult innovations are being implemented, for example, those that face an unusual amount of either community resistance or professional skepticism. Methadone maintenance and LAAM (also discussed briefly earlier) are two research-based innovations in drug abuse treatment that seem to fit this profile, and they are discussed in chapter 7 of this volume.

Finally, the longer term success of dissemination transfer in drug abuse treatment will in part be dependent on introducing preservice (i.e., university-based) as well as in-service training on these strategies for drug abuse treatment personnel and for drug abuse researchers. This can be done through universities; through professional associations, such as the College on Problems of Drug Dependence; and through programs offered directly by NIDA or other funders.

NONPROFIT ORGANIZATIONAL CAPACITY BUILDING

Capacity building to strengthen the staff and infrastructure of community-based nonprofit organizations can significantly increase the chances of successful operation (Backer, 2000a). An increasing number of American communities have capacity-building services available to local nonprofits, supported primarily by private foundations. These include technical assistance on uses of technology for information management, building community partnerships, working with boards of directors, managing confidential information, fund raising, and so on. I (Backer, 2000a) identified a number of these programs, many of which provide comprehensive, assessment-based interventions that could also help nonprofits become more capable of addressing planned change efforts, such as those needed to identify, implement, and sustain an innovation.

Awareness of and direct contact with these capacity-building resources has yet to filter down to specific-focus nonprofits, such as the many nonprofit drug abuse treatment facilities in the United States. Yet research on dissemination suggests strongly that one main reason organizations fail to engage—or at least fail to engage successfully—in significant change based on innovations in practice they have identified is that they are too fragile, too disorganized, and too much preoccupied with day-to-day survival matters to engage strategically in change efforts. More systematic access by drug abuse treatment facilities to nonprofit capacity-building resources could help meet this challenge.

Capacity-building efforts are part of a national system for improving nonprofit management, including the ability to innovate and to respond to the demands of systems change. Elements of this system include 83 graduate-level nonprofit management training programs in universities, many additional undergraduate programs, more than 300 management service providers (community-based organizations that offer capacity-building services), and national and state associations ranging from state nonprofit associations to the national Alliance for Nonprofit Management.

READINESS AND SUSTAINABILITY

Oetting et al. (1995) emphasized that substance abuse innovations often fail not because they are inadequate but because communities are not ready to accept and implement them effectively. Therefore, assessing readiness, and intervening with communities to enhance readiness for the kinds of changes required by an important innovation such as a drug abuse treatment program, are action steps that can greatly increase the actual effectiveness of these programs. For instance, even the very best science-based treatment program may fail to get implemented if it encounters low readiness on the basis of not in my backyard resistance from the community. If community residents' fears about physical dangers or drops in property values are responded to effectively, then readiness for change can be increased.

Oetting et al. (1995) proposed a nine-stage model of community readiness for substance abuse programming. I (Backer, 1995) reviewed the larger literature in behavioral and management sciences on readiness for change and its implications for the drug abuse field. Kumpfer, Whiteside, and Wandersman (1997) developed a model of readiness assessment and enhancement specific to the substance abuse prevention field; most of its elements also could be used successfully by treatment agencies.

Sustainability of innovations is an issue that has been little explored in substance abuse or other fields, yet it is clear from both research and the "wisdom of practice" that many innovations do not last over time (Backer & Rogers, 1999), and if they do not, then the investment in dissemination strategy that led to adoption of these innovations may be largely wasted.

The existing empirical literature is mostly based on case studies. Glaser and Backer (1977, 1980) conducted two intensive investigations, both of which used case studies based on site visits of long-lasting, successful innovations (a program evaluation method and a community-based mental health service model). The results indicated that key factors in long-term sustainability were (a) adaptation of the innovation due to changing community circumstances or service needs and (b) availability early in the life cycle of technical assistance on enhancing long-term survival strategies.

In the drug abuse field, Gager and Elias (1997) tested a resiliency model for helping substance abuse programs survive in high-risk environments, using interventions focused on the resiliency factors similar to those found in children who thrive in high-risk environments. Goodman, McLeRoy, Steckler, & Hoyle (1993) described several efforts to develop measures of sustainability for health promotion programs. Studies such as these could readily be used to develop guidance for drug abuse treatment facilities about how to promote sustainability of innovations they adopt.

DISSEMINATION STRATEGIES FROM OTHER FIELDS

Expertise and methods of dissemination in other fields may be applied to improving such efforts in the drug abuse treatment field. Some of these applications include the following.

Applications From Drug Abuse Prevention

Strategies for implementing prevention innovations in high-risk environments (Gager & Elias, 1997), already discussed, are an example. This work suggests that evidence-based innovations can succeed even in challenging environments (troubled school districts in this case) but that strategically designed implementation is the key: linking the innovation to the mission and operations of school districts and schools, making programs visible and part of the culture, and having programs carried out by well-trained personnel using well-crafted materials. Approaches to diagnosing and enhancing organizational and community readiness, and a number of other dissemination-related strategies, all have been developed in the prevention environment and could be readily adapted to the treatment field.

Dissemination infrastructure in drug abuse prevention (see also Backer & Rogers, 1999) may also be reviewed both for its learning value and for some possible direct use to communicate treatment innovations. The on-line information systems of Join Together, a project funded by the Robert Wood Johnson Foundation, is just one prominent example. (For more information, visit the Join Together Web site at http://www.jointogether.org.)

NIDA funded Danya International and the Human Interaction Research Institute to develop an "action community" for promoting drug abuse prevention research dissemination. After issuing a publication summarizing innovations in a particular area—environmental approaches to substance abuse prevention—this effort's dissemination phase involves developing and operating an interactive Web site specially targeted to support the action community and providing funding support to four communities to implement environmental innovations, using the Web site and technical assistance to support their efforts. (For more information, visit http://www.danya.com.)

Applications From Health Care

Examples of dissemination strategies from the field of general health care include (a) computer-based decision support systems for new medical technologies, (b) communications about innovations disseminated through local opinion leaders in the medical community, (c) informal study groups for medical practitioners, and (d) site-based education in doctors' offices based on successful approaches developed by pharmaceutical companies (Bero et al., 1998; Davis, Thomson, Oxman, & Haynes, 1995; Greco & Eisenberg, 1993; Hunt et al., 1998; Oxman et al., 1995; Soumerai & Avorn, 1990; Soumerai et al., 1998). A review of literature by the VERDICT program (1998a), described further later in the chapter, summarizes the scientific evidence supporting the value of each of these approaches. In another VERDICT review (1998b), guidelines also were given for evaluating and understanding systematic reviews as a part of dissemination. The drug abuse treatment field also could take advantage of many of these programs now that they have been created by foundation and other sponsors.

Applications From the Corporate World

"Best-practices" systems (Howard & Backer, 1998) provide one example. Corporations such as Hewlett-Packard, Arthur Anderson, and Chevron have created computer networks with extensive best-practices databanks. These interactive systems (many of which are based in Lotus Notes software) permit employees worldwide to exchange information and opinions about best practices in a large number of subject fields. Some of these systems are quite extensive; for instance, Arthur Anderson's best-practices system has an annual budget of $8 million for research alone (Howard & Backer, 1998). Best-practices systems also are being developed with increasing frequency in the nonprofit world (Backer & Bare, 1999).

Commercial consumer information systems also can be explored both for direct use and possible adaptation in the drug abuse treatment field. For instance, Medscape is an Internet startup company that provides free weekly online updates in summary form of the latest medical research and practice worldwide (see http://www.medscape.com). A searchable database is available for individuals who want the full text of articles or other details. Its membership includes more than 130,000 physicians and 150,000 laypersons. WebMD (http://www.webmd.com) is a similar consumer-oriented service with a large number of users. These systems already include information on drug abuse treatment research but could be modified to address dissemination issues more directly. Even more helpful would be a Web site specifically oriented to providing information on science-based treatment to practitioners, clients, and the public.

Applications From the Work of Foundations

Philanthropic organizations have developed several innovative programs, such as the Kaiser Family Foundation's approaches to creating health policy change through targeted dissemination of information to both policymakers and the general public, or the Dana Foundation's integrated system for promoting application of brain research findings (Backer, 1995). Another example, from the best-practices systems alluded to earlier, is the Robert Wood Johnson Foundation's Closed Grant Report System, which provides online access to well-written, concise summaries of final reports from the foundation's many grant projects, including a number of substance abuse projects (Backer, 1999). This system is accessible to both foundation staff and the public.

MANAGED CARE AND SERVICE SYSTEMS CHANGE

As drug abuse treatment evolves in a managed care environment, there are some advantages for future dissemination efforts. One is that the cost containment ethic of managed care can often overcome the traditional resistance to change such as that just described, *if* there is research evidence on cost advantage. Moreover, dissemination efforts in drug abuse treatment can through managed care systems be tied more directly to parallel efforts in the larger health care system (Sechrest et al., 1994).

The U.S. Department of Veteran's Affairs' VERDICT research brief (1998a) on this topic contains much from which professionals in the drug abuse field can learn—and much that can be used to convince skeptics within drug abuse treatment, because it comes from controlled studies in the medical field. For instance, in nine controlled trials, printed materials were found to have no significant effect in promoting actual change in clinical practice. Six randomized, controlled studies showed that traditional continuing medical education activities similarly had no impact on clinical practice change. Thus, the VERDICT brief concluded that the two most commonly endorsed approaches to disseminating new medical knowledge simply don't work—if actual practice change is the criterion. There is no reason to believe that drug abuse treatment is any different.

On the other hand, there is growing evidence in medical technology transfer that practice change does happen if there are changes in financing strategies; what is paid for tends to get used (Sechrest et al., 1994). The evolution of managed care may also afford new opportunities for testing and using this principle in drug abuse treatment, in part through collaborations with managed care organizations. The managed care initiatives of both CSAT and the Center for Substance Abuse Prevention may provide helpful input on this topic (see SAMHSA's Web site, http://www.samhsa.gov, for more information).

Dissemination of drug abuse treatment innovations may also succeed by exploring applications that involve service systems integration, given the high rate of people with multiple vulnerabilities in the public system (Backer & Howard, 1998). Impact may be increased by developing dissemination strategies that attend to the larger context of ongoing change in communities and health care. *Information fatigue syndrome*, a new field of medical research, is just one sign that too much change can affect the capacity of a system to absorb a new technology, regardless of its merits or evidence of efficacy (Backer, 1998).

NIDA'S FUTURE RESEARCH PORTFOLIO

In the end, NIDA and other funders of research have a responsibility to address the issues of dissemination raised here through funding more research about how this complex process works in drug abuse treatment. I have suggested a good number of outside-the-box approaches in this chapter, but their application to widespread systems change in drug abuse treatment can be confirmed only through good research. Here are three examples:

1. NIDA's clinical trials program can address the issues of dissemination, perhaps using as an analogy CSAT's recently funded seven-site methamphetamine treatment research program, whose coordinating center is based at UCLA's Integrated Substance Abuse Programs. The coordinating center will explore dissemination approaches that can be woven into the research effort from its beginning.
2. NIDA's services research program can address issues of research–treatment provider partnership, within the larger frame of service systems change.
3. NIDA's own dissemination research program can examine new frontiers—such as the transfer of approaches from other health and social service fields, as discussed here. The power of the Internet in this realm also needs to be studied, with some of the themes identified by recent NIDA-sponsored projects, such as the Danya effort, mentioned earlier. It also can look at existing NIDA efforts, which seem to have been successful but have not been empirically evaluated.

NIDA's 1997 publication, *Preventing Drug Use Among Children and Adolescents*, is a prime example of a more user-friendly publication and one that has been extremely popular in the field. According to Susan David at NIDA (personal communication, October 6, 1998), it has been distributed to more than 200,000 people and institutions—amidst much favorable reaction—or *buzz*, to use the Hollywood term. It is a success, but it is a limited success at this point, because no evaluation has been done of its effectiveness, and there is no strategically designed community campaign to extend its impact. Technology transfer research could help to address some of these unmet needs and provide confirmation that such an approach ought to be used more frequently in the future.

A modest first step, to help mobilize these new forces for promoting more effective dissemination of drug abuse treatment innovations, would be to gather together both treatment practitioners and scientists for a brainstorming conference that also would include representatives from each of the "other worlds" just mentioned. Ideas for further action generated from this conference could be pursued using existing funding sources (NIDA, SAMHSA, and foundations interested in substance abuse issues, such as the Robert Wood Johnson Foundation). Fundamental to the success of this or any other effort to close the research–practice gap is the creation of a truly equal partnership between researchers and practitioners, with two-way communication to identify challenges and opportunities related to effective dissemination.

REFERENCES

Alegria, M., Amaro, H., Backer, T. E., Diaz, E., Faruque, S., Mata, A. G., et al. (1994). *Policy report: AIDS and drug abuse research and technology transfer in Hispanic communities*. Rockville, MD: National Institute on Drug Abuse.

Backer, T. E. (1991). *Drug abuse technology transfer*. Rockville, MD: National Institute on Drug Abuse.

Backer, T. E. (1995). Assessing and enhancing readiness for change: Implications for technology transfer. In T. E. Backer, S. L. David, & G. Soucy (Eds.), *Reviewing the behavioral science knowledge base on technology transfer* (pp. 21–41). Rockville, MD: National Institute on Drug Abuse.

Backer, T. E. (1998). Dissemination in a time of great change. *Science Communication, 20*, 142–147.

Backer, T. E. (1999). *Innovation in context: New foundation approaches to evaluation, collaboration and best practices*. Northridge, CA: Human Interaction Research Institute.

Backer, T. E. (2000a). *Strengthening nonprofits: Capacity-building and philanthropy*. Encino, CA: Human Interaction Research Institute.

Backer, T. E. (2000b). The failure of success: Challenges of disseminating effective substance abuse prevention programs. *Journal of Community Psychology, 28*, 363–373.

Backer, T. E., & Bare, J. (1999, November–December). Scanning the environment for philanthropic best practice systems. *Foundation News and Commentary, 40*, 25–28.

Backer, T. E., Brown, B. S., & Howard, E. A. (1994). *Evaluating drug abuse technology transfer: An analytic review*. Los Angeles: Human Interaction Research Institute

Backer, T. E., David, S. L., & Soucy, G. (1995). *Reviewing the behavioral science knowledge base on technology transfer*. Rockville, MD: National Institute on Drug Abuse.

Backer, T. E., & Howard, E. A. (1998). *Integrated service systems for women with multiple vulnerabilities*. Culver City, CA: PROTOTYPES Systems Change Center.

Backer, T. E., & Newman, S. S. (1995). Organizational linkage and information dissemination: Strategies to integrate the substance abuse and disability fields. *Rehabilitation Counseling Bulletin, 38,* 93–107.

Backer, T. E., & Norman, A. J. (1998). *Best practices in multicultural coalitions: Phase I report to The California Endowment*. Northridge, CA: Human Interaction Research Institute.

Backer, T. E., & Norman, A. J. (2000). Partnerships and community change. *California Politics and Policy,* 39–41.

Backer, T. E., & Rogers, E. M. (Eds.). (1993). *Organizational aspects of health communication campaigns*. Newbury Park, CA: Sage.

Backer, T. E., & Rogers, E. M. (1999). *Briefing paper: State-of-the-art review on dissemination research and dissemination partnerships*. Encino, CA: Human Interaction Research Institute.

Bero, L. A., et al. (1998). Closing the gap between research and practice: An overview of systematic reviews of interventions to promote the implementation of research findings. *British Medical Journal, 317,* 465–468.

Brown, B. (1998). Making a difference: Is journal publication enough? *Contemporary Drug Issues, 13,* 117–132.

Brown, V. B., & Backer, T. E. (1988). The substance abusing mentally ill patient: Challenges for professional education and training. *Psychosocial Rehabilitation Journal, 10,* 14–19.

D'Aunno, T., Folz-Murphy, N., & Lin, X. (1999). Changes in methadone treatment practices, 1988–1995. *American Journal of Drug and Alcohol Abuse, 25,* 681–699.

D'Aunno, T., & Vaughn, T. E. (1995). The organizational analysis of service patterns in outpatient drug abuse treatment units. *Journal of Substance Abuse Treatment, 7,* 27–42.

Davis, D. A., Thomson, M. A., Oxman, A. D., & Haynes, R. B. (1995). Changing physician performance: A systematic review of the effect of continuing medical education strategies. *Journal of the American Medical Association, 274,* 700–705.

Etheridge, R. M., Craddock, S. G., Dunteman, G. H., & Hubbard, R. L. (1995). Treatment services in two national studies of community-based drug treatment programs. *Journal of Substance Abuse Treatment, 7,* 9–26.

Gager, P. J., & Elias, M. J. (1997). Implementing prevention programs in high-risk environments: Application of the resiliency paradigm. *American Journal of Orthopsychiatry, 67,* 363–373.

Glaser, E. M., & Backer, T. E. (1977). Innovation redefined: Durability and local adaptation. *Evaluation, 4*, 131–135.

Glaser, E. M., & Backer, T. E. (1980). Durability of innovations: How Goal Attainment Scaling programs fare over time. *Community Mental Health Journal, 16*, 130–143.

Goodman, R. M., McLeRoy, K. R., Steckler, A., & Hoyle, R. H. (1993). Development of level of institutionalization scales for health promotion programs. *Health Education Quarterly, 20*, 161–178.

Greco, P. J., & Eisenberg, J. M. (1993). Changing physicians' practice. *New England Journal of Medicine, 319*, 1271–1273.

Higgins, S. T., Budney, A. J., Bickel, W. K., & Badger, G. J. (1994). Incentives improve outcome in patient behavioral treatment of cocaine dependence. *Archives of General Psychiatry, 51*, 568–576.

Howard, E. A., & Backer, T. E. (1998). *Private sector best practice systems: An overview.* Northridge, CA: Human Interaction Research Institute.

Hunt, D. L., et al. (1998). Effects of computer-based decision support systems on physician performance and patient outcomes. *Journal of the American Medical Association, 280*, 1339–1346.

Kreuter, M., & Lezin, N. (1998). *Are consortia/collaboratives effective in changing health status and health systems?* Paper presented at the Health 2000 conference, Atlanta, GA.

Kumpfer, K. L., Whiteside, H. O., & Wandersman, A. (1997). *Community readiness for drug abuse prevention: Issues, tips and tools.* Rockville, MD: National Institute on Drug Abuse.

Lamb, S., Greenlick, M., & McCarty, D. (1998). *Bridging the gap between practice and research: Forging partnerships with community-based drug and alcohol treatment.* Washington, DC: National Academy Press.

Lipton, D. S., & Appel, P. (1984). The state perspective. In F. M. Tims & J. Ludford (Eds.), *Research analysis and utilization system* (NIDA Research Monograph Series No. 51). Rockville, MD: National Institute on Drug Abuse.

McLellan, A. T., Alterman, A. I., Metzger, D. S., Grissom, G. R., Woody, G. E., Luborsky, L., et al. (1994). Similarity of outcome predictors across opiate, cocaine and alcohol treatments: Role of treatment services. *Journal of Consulting and Clinical Psychology, 62*, 1141–1158.

National Institute on Drug Abuse. (1997). *Preventing drug use among children and adolescents: A research-based guide.* Rockville, MD: Author.

Northern California Grantmakers AIDS Task Force. (1998). *San Francisco Bay Area HIV/AIDS Prevention and Evaluation Initiative: Lessons for funders, nonprofits and evaluators.* San Francisco: Author.

Oetting, E. R., Donnermeyer, J. F., Plested, B. A., Edwards, R. W., Kelly, K., & Beauvais, F. (1995). Assessing community readiness for prevention. *International Journal of the Addictions, 30*, 659–683.

Oxman, A. D., et al. (1995). No magic bullet: A systematic review of 102 trials of interventions to improve professional practice. *Journal of the Canadian Medical Association, 153,* 1423–1431.

Rawson, R., Hasson, A., Huber, A., McCann, M., & Ling, W. (1998). A three year progress report on the implementation of LAAM in the United States. *Addiction, 93,* 533–540.

Rogers, E. M. (1995). *Diffusion of innovations.* New York: Free Press.

Schorr, L. (1997). *Common purpose.* New York: Simon & Schuster.

Sechrest, L., Backer, T. E., Rogers, E. M., Campbell, T. F., & Grady, M. L. (Eds.). (1994). *Effective dissemination of clinical and health information.* Rockville, MD: Agency for Health Care Policy and Research.

Silverman, K., Higgins, H. T., Brooner, R. K., Montoya, I. D., Cone, E. J., Schuster, C. R., et al. (1996). Sustained cocaine abstinence in methadone maintenance patients through voucher-based reinforcement therapy. *Archives of General Psychiatry, 53,* 409–415.

Simpson, D. D., Joe, G. W., & Brown, B. (1997). Treatment retention and follow-up outcomes in the Drug Abuse Treatment Outcome Study (DATOS). *Psychology of Addictive Behaviors, 11,* 294–307.

Sorensen, J. L., Hall, S. M., Loeb, P., Allen, T., Glaser, E. M., & Greenberg, P. D. (1988). Dissemination of a job seekers' workshop to drug treatment programs. *Behavior Therapy, 19,* 143–155.

Soumerai, S. B., & Avorn, J. A. (1990). Principles of education outreach ("academic detailing") to improve clinical decision-making. *Journal of the American Medical Association, 263,* 549–556.

Soumerai, S. B., et al. (1998). Effect of local medical opinion leaders on quality of care for acute myocardial infarction: A randomized controlled study. *Journal of the American Medical Association, 279,* 358–363.

VERDICT Brief Biannual Newsletter. (1998a, Fall). San Antonio, TX: VA Center of Excellence in San Antonio and Charleston.

VERDICT Brief Biannual Newsletter. (1998b, Spring). San Antonio, TX: VA Center of Excellence in San Antonio and Charleston.

Widman, M., Platt, J. J., Marlowe, D., Lidz, V., Mathis, D. A., & Metzger, D. S. (1997). Patterns of service use and treatment involvement of methadone maintenance patients. *Journal of Substance Abuse Treatment, 14,* 29–35.

17

CONCLUSION: RECOMMENDATIONS FOR PRACTICE–RESEARCH COLLABORATION

JOSEPH GUYDISH, JAMES L. SORENSEN, RICHARD A. RAWSON, AND JOAN E. ZWEBEN

Research efforts are too often and too far removed from the clinical and service needs of practice, and practice too often fails to adopt, or is too slow to adopt, innovations shown to be effective. Where the 1998 Institute of Medicine report left off, by noting the general failure of collaboration between research and practice in substance abuse (Lamb, Greenlick, & McCarty, 1998), this volume picks up. The chapters in this volume represent a collection of voices, of practitioners and researchers, each recounting their experience in bridging the gap between research and practice. They tell the story, at least as old as methadone and therapeutic communities (TCs), of successes and failures in practice–research collaboration.

This volume reflects the support of numerous organizations and individuals. Organizations that provided support for this chapter include the National Institutes of Health (Grants P50DA09253, R01DA08753, R01DA11344, R01DA12221, and R01DA14470) and the Substance Abuse and Mental Health Services Administration (Center for Substance Abuse Treatment Task Order 282-98-0026).

In this chapter we draw out of these stories a series of recommendations to support a greater synergy between practice and research; to accelerate the adoption of innovations in treatment; and to more effectively address the personal, social, and financial costs of substance abuse. In framing these recommendations we relied mainly on the material presented in the preceding chapters, with attention to recurring themes and to issues with overarching importance. We incorporated our own experiences in the collaborative enterprise based on collective discussion among the editors. We offer eight recommendations and, within some of these, further recommendations that amplify or offer detail to the main theme.

RECOMMENDATIONS

1. Recognize That Practice–Research Collaboration Is an Evolving Process

One of the driving themes in the assembled chapters is that the elements of the practice–research collaboration are evolving. These elements include the interventions themselves, the federal strategies applied to support collaboration, and the readiness and suitability of practice and research partners. Interventions develop along a course from more academically focused to more practice focused, as in the case of relapse prevention and motivational interviewing (chapters 8 and 9), or from a practice focus to incorporating a research focus, as in the case of needle exchange programs (NEPs; see chapter 5). The questions posed in a practice–research collaboration also change over time, as described by George De Leon (chapter 2), from the general question of whether an intervention works to progressively specific questions such as who is best served, what are the effective ingredients, and whether the intervention can be extended to other populations. Federal strategies designed to support practice–research collaboration are also changing, as described in Part III, from single-site to multisite collaborations and from one-time demonstrations to ongoing collaborations that can address changing service and research over a longer term. The focus of investigation is also evolving. The Clinical Trials Network (CTN) provides a venue for randomized clinical trials of intervention effectiveness on a national scale, whereas the Practice Research Collaborative/Practice Improvement Collaborative (PRC/PIC) model supports communities and agencies in addressing needs identified at the local level. Critical questions evoked by these models include, for the CTN, what determines when an intervention is sufficiently established to warrant a multisite clinical trial and, for both the CTN and PRC/PIC approaches, how innovative interventions, policies, or procedures can be most rapidly incorporated into practice. In this context of evolution and development individual practice and research partners may be more or less able to participate productively in the collaborative effort.

1a. In seeking a clinical partner, researchers may find it is rewarding to seek clinics that have an established service history and stable funding.

Just as organizations need enough resources to attempt innovations (Rogers, 1995), drug treatment programs need to have stabilized their basic clinical operations before they can take on research. Simpson (2001) referred to this concept as having enough "organizational slack" to adopt innovations. Programs with a service and funding history are better positioned to focus institutional energy on the practice–research collaboration. Treatment programs in early implementation or survival stages may be weaker partners in collaboration, as their main energy is needed to provide service and garner funding.

1b. Clinical partners may find it is rewarding to seek researchers with lasting links to the community, such as a history of working in clinical settings and of supporting both services and research.

Likewise, clinics contemplating a practice–research partnership can consider the community history and dedication of research partners. Building long-term relationships with researchers contributes to better collaborative projects.

2. Develop Partnership, Joint Ownership, and Collaborative Leadership

The chapters in this volume offer different perspectives on partnership in the practice–research collaboration. Elisa Triffleman (chapter 14) speaks to the partnership of a single study conducted in a single clinic in which the collaborating partners simultaneously balance treatment and research integrity. Vivian B. Brown (chapter 15) describes partnership from the viewpoint of a clinic director, where the clinic participates in multiple projects over time so that research collaboration is a process rather than an event. Dennis M. Donovan (chapter 8) and George De Leon (chapter 2) refer to a broader practice–research partnership at the level of the intervention, which informs and drives a specific line of research—for example, research related to TCs or relapse prevention. PRC/PICs (Alice A. Gleghorn and Frances Cotter, chapter 13) reflect systemwide partnerships in which multiple clinics and research teams collaborate on a range of community-identified needs. Multisite demonstration projects (Dennis McCarty, chapter 12) and clinical trials require collaboration not only among clinicians and researchers in a single site but also among researchers and clinicians from different sites and in this way multiply the challenges of effective collaboration. Yet however narrowly or broadly the partnership is construed, the fundamentals of effective collaboration are the same.

2a. Involve stakeholders as early as possible in project planning.

The earlier the involvement of all partners, the greater their input into the project plan, and the greater their investment in seeing the plan successfully implemented.

2b. Collaborating partners need to develop, support, and maintain ownership of the practice–research partnership.

Ownership within a clinic setting can include not only staff directly involved in the project but also more general staff ownership of the practice–research process (chapter 15). In PRC/PICs (chapter 13), ownership refers to many stakeholders both within and across community systems, such as drug abuse treatment, criminal justice, and health services. Holly Hagan, Don C. Des Jarlais, and David Purchase (chapter 5) remind readers how ownership by consumers can support collaboration. Although discussions of partnership and ownership typically focus on clinical partners in the collaborative effort, the same issues apply to research teams, particularly in the context of multisite studies. Here, the ownership of local site research teams, no less than the ownership of local site clinical teams, must be developed and maintained.

2c. In collaborative projects, leadership works best when it is equal and shared.

Chapter 15 describes this most clearly, but chapter 13 describes shared leadership in a community-based PRC/PIC. There are, of course, many situations in which a partner with special expertise takes the lead. For example, in a practice–research partnership the community clinic may lead a proposal to the Substance Abuse and Mental Health Services Administration, whereas the university-based researcher may lead a proposal to the National Institutes of Health. Shared, equal leadership is an ideal that, in reality, comes with many options.

2d. Effective collaboration includes ongoing meetings or conferences involving all partners.

These forums promote partnership through information exchange, shaping research to be clinically relevant, and shaping clinical practice to accommodate research activities. These forums erode the cultural differences between practitioners and researchers (discussed in chapter 1) by bringing the experiential knowledge base of practitioners to researchers and the scientific knowledge base of researchers to clinicians in the field.

2e. Support collaboration in the grant application and review process.

Applicants may be encouraged, in the Request for Application or Guidelines for Applicants, to demonstrate in the application that practitioners, researchers, policymakers, and consumer representatives were involved in project planning. We advocate that these constituencies be represented in the makeup of the application review groups and, further, that a history of effective collaboration be incorporated into scoring criteria.

3. Focus on Adoption of Useful Interventions

The substance abuse treatment field has been slow to adopt evidence-based practices, yet this slowness is common in other fields (Thomas E. Backer, chapter 16). In writing about intervention adoption, Rogers (1995) described "innovators" who are leaders in the field but who are also advocates of a specific intervention. Innovators develop, launch, promote, and guide the application of new interventions. Interventions grow through the work of "early adopters" who implement, replicate, and refine the work of innovators and bring the intervention into the mainstream. Innovators and early adopters work in a context where the intervention itself is maturing, research is often evolving from an advocacy focus to an outcomes-oriented focus, and the nature of practice–research collaboration is also evolving. This was exemplified by the role of Jerome Jaffe in the early efforts to move methadone into the U.S. treatment system (Walter Ling, Richard A. Rawson, and M. Douglas Anglin, chapter 7).

The development of drug courts also demonstrates these issues (Elizabeth Piper Deschenes et al., chapter 6). Drug court innovators were judges and other criminal justice and treatment specialists who were less concerned about outcomes than about their ineffectiveness in addressing the revolving door of drug-involved offenders and who were looking for a less drastic alternative to incarceration for this population. The development and growth of drug courts were driven by good policy reasons unrelated to research. Early research was focused on process and advocacy, designed to gather descriptive information and to support the drug court movement.

The questions raised for intervention adoption include when to implement outcome research for innovative interventions; when federal funders should come in and what requirements they impose; and what sort of data are needed before an intervention is ready to move onto multisite clinical trials. To people working in the field, federal funders may sometimes appear as laggards, yet accumulation of evidence of promise may take a long time. The Center for Substance Abuse Treatment (CSAT) has been addressing these issues through the development of Treatment Improvement Protocols (TIPS) and by promoting full partnerships rather than having research dictate what interventions should be adopted. An ongoing discussion and dynamic in PRC/PICs is whether the organization is research led or practitioner led. In the evolution of our own thinking, and consistent with the Institute of Medicine report (Lamb et al., 1998), the collaboration can be redefined not in terms of practice–research but in terms of practice–research–policy.

4. Collaborate With Policymakers

The chapters in this volume do not directly represent the voice of policymakers, but the importance of policy is evident, even if not separately articulated. Ling et al. (chapter 7) comment that levo-alpha-aceytlmethadol was killed by regulations, and we observe in chapter 1 that buprenorphine may face similar regulatory problems. Contingency management is another example of where an innovative intervention has been limited by restrictions on use of treatment funds. The demonstration of the Target Cities model (chapter 12) was likewise hampered in communities because, although designed to improve treatment infrastructure, the demonstration program offered only limited funding for treatment itself. In cases such as these, controversy between the scientific and treatment communities may play into the hands of regulators, and the field as a whole loses effectiveness in moving interventions into application sooner, or at all.

4a. Link funding initiatives to evidence-based treatments.

Much treatment funding comes with specific guidelines and restrictions as to how it can be used and for what kinds of treatment. Such *categorical funding* is a policy tool used to emphasize specific treatments or intervention for specific populations and, in this way, funnels funds where policy leadership has identified pressing and unmet needs. Categorical funding can also be a top-down approach in which funders directly encourage providers to use specific interventions. At the same time, categorical funding limits the use of treatment funds and sometimes steers funding away from local needs and away from innovative interventions. To the degree that categorical funding is necessary, application guidelines can emphasize the need to use empirically supported treatments that are in line with National Institute on Drug Abuse research-validated treatments (National Institute on Drug Abuse, 1999) or the CSAT TIPS. This may allow practitioners greater flexibility while supporting implementation of evidence-based treatments and increasing emphasis on research in the field.

4b. In the immediacy of policy decisions, researchers can provide partial information rather than no information.

From the viewpoint of practice and policy, the work of research exists on a timeline that is unencumbered by many real-world pressures. A randomized clinical trial of almost any treatment intervention needs at least 1 year for startup, 1 year for recruitment, and 1 year before follow-up data are completed and analyzed. Findings thus begin to emerge at least 3 years after the start of the project, by which time the initial study question may have lost relevance because of changing drug use patterns. Practitioners and policymakers have no luxury of time as they develop treatment strategies and policies to meet rapidly changing needs. Researchers can be more responsive to real world problems, considering the trade-offs between the scientific integrity of lengthy blinded trials and immediate policy and practice needs and, in every event, can bring findings to the field as soon as possible.

Demonstration projects, if well done, address these issues by balancing the demands of research and practice. Yet McCarty (chapter 12) found that findings were sometimes not published and, even when they were published, often had limited policy effects. Policy experts can question the role of federal demonstration projects and how much they should be emphasized. If the demonstration approach is effective at the federal level, this approach may be passed down to state or local levels. This may make demonstration efforts more responsive to local practice and policy needs, as states may be able to act more quickly and locally. As McCarty acknowledges, CTN and PRC/PIC models are now setting the stage for leaps in the development of treatment technology and in the quality of drug abuse treatment research.

5. Practice–Research Collaborations Work Best When They Support the Costs of Clinic Participation

In many studies where research comes into community settings, researchers are willing to pay only for the limited costs of data collection. The clinical partner is often not involved in budget planning, and research teams have been historically naive about the cost of setting up a research project in a treatment setting. When program directors and staff take the time to work with researchers, they are not doing other revenue-generating activities, so research activities represent costs to the program. Researchers working with clinical agencies can become educated about the complexity of substance abuse treatment financing and understand that clinics need reimbursement for all of the costs associated with research participation. A strength of the demonstration model (chapter 12) is that such projects usually include substantial funding for both treatment and research activities.

6. Make Full Use of the Potential for Both Dissemination and Training

6a. Use practice dissemination and research dissemination strategies to support intervention adoption.

When researchers consider *dissemination* they mean publication of research findings in scientific journals. This is driven by the requirements of the academic culture, in which much research originates, and by research funders who use publication as a barometer of the success of research projects. When clinicians consider dissemination they mean the development of tools, such as workbooks and training modules, that support them in meeting the needs of day-to-day practice.

Above and beyond the fundamentals of partnership, ownership, and leadership, Ling et al. discuss in chapter 7 the role of champions, and Donovan describes in chapter 8 the role of translators in moving research-based interventions into practice. Other interventions—such as acupuncture, self-help, NEP, and TCs—can have high clinical appeal and gain widespread application with less reliance on research champions or translators. This is not to say that these interventions did not have champions—such as Dave Purchase in the case of NEPs—but only that the role of research was a secondary factor in their adoption. The success of these interventions was supported by efforts to create national organizations and annual conferences directed primarily to clinicians and practitioners, as seen most clearly in Deschenes et al.'s discussion in chapter 6 of drug courts. Even in the case of drug courts, which represent one of the boldest practice-based innovations in the field of substance abuse treatment in recent years, Deschenes et al. note the general failure of dissemination in scientific journals. Although interventions benefit from practice-focused dissemination through professional organizations, standards, and trainings, these clearly are necessary but not sufficient to support intervention adoption. McLellan (chapter 10) points out that different evaluation approaches may lead to different conclusions. Funders and policymakers eventually will require compelling evidence of effectiveness and will ask for published scientific studies.

6b. Provide training and certification credits for clinicians involved in practice–research collaborations.

Every practice–research collaboration is a laboratory in which researchers and clinicians are learning how to improve substance abuse treatment. Recent and innovative laboratories include the development of national data systems, such as the Drug Evaluation Network System, the PRC/PICs, and the CTN. In these laboratories a new generation of practitioners and researchers is being trained, yet the value of collaboration is often more tangible for research teams that will garner funding, recognition, and publications. Deni Carise and Õzge Gûrel comment in chapter 11 on the tangible gains for clinicians and suggest that clinicians involved in practice–research collaboration can gain continuing education units (CEUs) for their participation. The broader application of this tool, providing CEUs for clinicians involved in collaborations, is a viable but underused strategy for bringing added value to clinicians. PRC/PICs, the CTN, and every practice–research collaboration may be strengthened by finding ways to offer clinician CEUs in the context of the collaboration, possibly by working with CSAT addiction technology transfer centers and with state drug abuse treatment accrediting bodies.

7. Increase Understanding of Intervention Dissemination and Adoption

The history of demonstration projects includes examples where practice–research collaborations succeeded in implementing, and demonstrating the effectiveness of, an intervention but failed in disseminating findings and supporting intervention adoption. Improving practice–research collaboration indirectly promotes adoption but, like the CTN and PRC/PIC approaches, does not directly address how effective interventions become part of current practice.

We recommend that every practice–research collaborative effort undertake, as part of its agenda, the study of dissemination and intervention adoption. Such work can reflect on treatment outcome studies in which one treatment is compared to another but can also reflect on efforts to change, improve, or modify practices within clinics and within treatment systems. The general questions are whether the efforts of the practice–research collaboration did or did not lead to change in the treatment system and, if not, what the barriers to change were. With respect to multisite clinical trials, such as those operating under the aegis of the CTN, we recommend that every clinical trial incorporate a study of intervention adoption once the clinical trial has ended. The field needs to know not only whether one treatment is more effective than another but also whether the more effective intervention was adopted, in whole or in part, in the clinics that participated in the trial. Where interventions were adopted, did they diffuse into the broader host treatment system? Where they were not adopted, what were the barriers to adoption?

8. Develop a Practice–Research Collaboration Agenda in Single-State Agencies, in National Organizations, and in their State Affiliate Organizations

Models of practice–research collaboration described in Part III of this volume (e.g., demonstrations, CTNs, PRC/PICs) reflect federal leadership. Yet there are other levels of leadership in the substance abuse treatment field. These include single-state agencies responsible for substance abuse treatment, county-level substance abuse treatment offices, private health care providers involved in substance abuse treatment, and national organizations such as the American Society for Addiction Medicine and the National Association of State Alcohol and Drug Abuse Directors.

To support federal leadership, and to strengthen state and local leadership in this area, we recommend that these agencies review current policies with respect to research, establishment of evidence-based practices, and dissemination and adoption of effective interventions. These agencies can, by including practice, research, and policy representatives in their membership and leadership bodies, and by including these issues in national meetings and other forums, support and guide practice research collaborations within their jurisdiction.

CONCLUSION

Some of these recommendations are broad, such as recognizing that collaborative efforts occur in a multifaceted, complex, and evolving process (Recommendation 1) and asking partners to revisit the fundamentals of effective collaboration (Recommendation 2). Promoting collaboration is not an end in itself but a means to more rapid study and adoption of effective treatments (Recommendation 3), and the field of substance abuse treatment will be strengthened by greater inclusion of and dialogue with policymakers (Recommendation 4). The remaining recommendations reflect on the costs of clinic involvement in research, the need to pursue both practice and research dissemination strategies, investment in the issues of intervention adoption, and drawing state and national organizations into the arena of practice research collaboration.

Developing practice–research collaboration in substance abuse treatment is a vital objective, yet it is not the main goal. The main goal is to transform the treatment and research systems, and their associated policy and funding networks, so that new treatments are tested and effective treatments are adopted. This will institutionalize the search for more effective treatments and accelerate the pace for bringing effective treatments into widespread use. Achievement of this goal will increase reliance on evidence-based practices and, in turn, will ensure that the most effective treatments are available for people who use drugs and for their families and communities. Improving practice–research collaboration brings us nearer to the achievement of this goal.

REFERENCES

Lamb, S., Greenlick, M. R., & McCarty, D. (Eds.). (1998). *Bridging the gap between practice and research: Forging partnerships with community-based drug and alcohol treatment*. Washington, DC: National Academy Press.

National Institute on Drug Abuse. (1999). *Principles of drug addiction treatment* (NIH Publication No. 99-4180). Rockville, MD: Author.

Rogers, E. M. (1995). *Diffusion of innovations* (4th ed.). New York: Free Press.

Simpson, D. D. (2001). Modeling treatment process and outcomes. *Addiction, 96,* 207–211.

AUTHOR INDEX

Numbers in italics refer to the listings in the reference sections.

Yarmolinsky, A., 110, *119*
Yehuda, R., 229, *246*

Zadelhoff, A. W., 71, *82*
Ziegenfuss, J. T., *31*

Ziff, D. C., 141, *148*
Zuckoff, A., 143, *148*
Zweben, A., 65, *69*
Zweben, J., *227*
Zywiak, W. H., 132, *136*

SUBJECT INDEX

for participation in practice–research collaboration, 294

Championship
  and dissemination, 273–274
  for new practice (PROTOTYPES), 255

Change
  human dynamics of, 271
  in practice, 281

Change agents, 273

Changing the Conversation (CSAT), xii

Chevron, best-practices databanks of, 280

Child protection officers, outcome expectations of, 160

Chinese medicine, acupuncture within framework of, 38–39

Clearinghouses, on drug courts, 91

Client-centered therapy, and motivational interviewing, 139

Client self-efficacy, in motivational interviewing, 141

Client-treatment matching, and therapeutic communities, 21–22

Clinical assessment, and therapeutic communities, 21, 25

Clinical partner, with established history and funding, 289

Clinical practice, integration of self-help into, 65–67

Clinical tracking, as evaluation method, 163–164

Clinical Trials Networks (CTNs), xviii–xix, 208, 288, 293, 294
  and adoption, 295
  and PICs, 155
  Web site of, 155

Cocaine, number of users of, 39

Cocaine addiction
  auricular acupuncture for, 39–40, 42
    (*see also* Acupuncture, auricular)
  and financial incentives for abstaining, 3–4, 8
  and Matrix model, 129

Cocaine Alternative Treatment Study (CATS), 42–43

Cocaine Anonymous, 57, 60

Cognitive–behavioral coping skills treatment (CBCST), 230, 231

Cognitive–behavioral therapy, 26
  for relapse prevention, 127
  in Matrix model, 128

SDPT as, 230–231

Cognitive impairment, and acupuncture treatment, 50

Collaboration
  equality of, 261–262
  See also Practice–research collaboration

Collaboration strategies, 276

Collaborative leadership, 289–291

Collaborative project(s)
  through Practice Improvement Collaboratives, xii–xiii
  Tacoma Syringe Exchange as, 81
    (*see also* Tacoma Syringe Exchange)

College on Problems of Drug Dependence, 277

"Common Ground, Common Language, Common Goals: Bringing Substance Abuse Practice and Research Together" (conference), 272

Communication
  between research and clinical staff, 28, 29, 236–237, 238, 241–242
  user-friendly, 270

Communication between technology and treatment. *See* Technology-treatment information system

Community-based demonstration projects. *See* Demonstration projects

Community-based providers, and PICs, 214

Community Clinical Oncology Program, National Cancer Institute, 275

Community as method, 18. *See also* Therapeutic community(ies)

Community readiness for substance abuse programming, 278

Comparisons with other programs, in outcome evaluations, 168

Conceptual foresight, as dissemination strategy, 272–273

Conferences, by PROTOTYPES, 254

Confidentiality
  in database-monitoring systems, 165
  and DENS, 193
  and drug courts, 95

Confrontational approach vs. motivational interviewing, 141, 144, 146

Consultation, and dissemination, 273

Consumer information systems, 280

Context of treatment, 51

and acupuncture research, 51–52

Contingency contracting, 26

Continuing Care stage of treatment, 170, 175–177

Continuing education units (CEUs) for participation in practice–research collaboration, 294

Continuous quality improvement, 166

Contract evaluation staff, ethnic diversity in, 263

Co-occurrence of PTSD and SUDS. *See* PTSD–SUDS co-occurrence

Coping skills training group (CST), and acupuncture, 43–44, 46–47, 49, 50

Coping style, and acupuncture treatment, 50

Corporate world, dissemination strategies from, 280

Counselor and patient concerns, and DENS, 193

Counselors, researchers' culture different from, 7

"Crack crisis," and pregnant or parenting women, 201

Criminal justice settings
motivational interviewing in, 146
substance abuse treatment programs in, 86

CSAP. *See* Center for Substance Abuse Prevention

CSAT. *See* Center for Substance Abuse Treatment

CTNs. *See* Clinical Trials Networks

Culturally competent instruments, 263–264

Daley, Dennis, 106, 127

Dana Foundation, 281

Danya International, 279

Database monitoring, as evaluation method, 164–165

Data collection system, Web based (as SF-PIC goal), 224

Data sets (databases)
on drug courts, 94
national need for, 154

Data systems, 28, 280, 294. *See also* Clinical Trials Networks; Drug Evaluation Network System; PRC/PICs

David, Susan, 282–283

Decisions, seemingly irrelevant, 125

Deficits vs. strength models, 264

"Defining Drug Courts: The Key Components" (Department of Justice), 89

Demonstration Project Handbook (Department of Transportation), 200

Demonstration projects, 154–155, 197–199, 206–207
multisite, 289
research and practice balanced in, 293
stakeholders' various perspectives on, 206
treatment demonstrations, 207–208
Alcohol Safety Action Programs (ASAP), 154, 200–201
for pregnant and parenting women, 201–205, 206–207
St. Louis Detoxification and Diagnostic Evaluation Center, 199–200
and Target Cities Initiative, 205, 206, 207

Denial
substance-abuse practitioners in, xxi
and 12-step program, 59
See also Responsibility for abstinence violation

DENS. *See* Drug Evaluation Network System

DENS Resource Guide (DENS RG), 187, 188

Des Jarlais, Don, 75, 76, 78

Detoxification, of heroin addicts, 108–109

Detoxification/stabilization stage of care, 170–173

Diffusion of new knowledge
lack of understanding of, xiii
See also Dissemination

Disease models, vs. behavioral models, 126

Dissemination
and capacity building, 277–278
making use of, 293–294
mechanisms for, 262–263
of motivational interviewing, 145–147
need for, 269
partnership strategies for, 274, 275–277
and research–practice integration, 29
from St. Louis Diagnostic and Detoxification Center, 207
science-based principles of, 270–271
practical strategies derived from, 271–274

through scientific journals, 7
strategies for, 91
    from other fields, 270, 275, 279–281
understanding of, 294–295
See also Research–practice links
Dole, V. P., 109, 110
Drinkers
    motivational interviewing for, 142–143
    See also Alcohol abuse
Drug abuse
    costs of, 4, 181
    and motivational interviewing, 145
    TC view of, 18
    See also Substance abuse
"Drug Abuse Practice/Research
        Collaboration: Making It Work in
        San Francisco" (conference), 223
Drug abuse prevention
    dissemination infrastructure in, 279
    See also Relapse prevention
Drug Abuse Research Center, University
        of California Los Angeles, 251
Drug Abuse Treatment Outcome Study
        Web site, The, 273
Drug Court Clearinghouse and Technical
        Assistance Project and drug court
        evaluation, 90
Drug Court Programs Office (DCPO), 15,
        88, 89, 90, 91, 92, 97, 98
Drug Court Publications Resource Guide
        (Tauber, Snavely, and Wilkosz),
        95
Drug courts, 5, 15–16, 86, 87
    costs incurred or averted by, 98
    emergence and development of, 87–89
    innovators in, 291
    research on, 13, 15–16,89–95, 97
        measuring impact of, 95–97
        recommendations for future
            partnerships in, 97–98
    standards for, 89
Drug Courts Standards Committee, 89
Drug Court Training and Technical
        Assistance Project, 89
Drug Enforcement Administration,
        and acceptance of methadone
        maintenance, 117
Drug Evaluation Network System
        (DENS), 154, 182, 184–89,
        194–195, 294
    implementation issues for, 189
        counselor and patient concerns, 193

multiple reporting requirements,
        190, 191–192
    personnel lack, 193
    resources, 190–191, 192
    staff turnover, 194
    training, 193–194
software for, 188
and TECH study, 187–188
training for, 188–189, 193–194
Web site of, 193, 195
Drug users, as subjects vs. participants, 72

Early adopters, 291
Effectiveness
    evidence of in continuing care stage,
        176–177
    as outcome criterion, 172–173
    vs. retention, 20
Emotional stabilization, in outcome
        evaluation, 171–172
Emotions Anonymous, 56
Empathy, in motivational interviewing,
        140, 141
Employers, outcome expectations of, 160
Equality, of collaboration, 261
Evaluation
    of demonstration projects, 198, 208
    of drug courts, 89–92, 95
    misapplication of, 158
    and outcome evaluation vs. quality
        assurance, 166–167
    of relapse-prevention approaches,
        130–132
    of treatment outcomes, 157–158, 177
        comparisons of, 168
        confusions from options in, 169
        domains of, 161–162
        and expectations, 159–163,
            169–170
        methods of, 163–166
        vs. quality assurance, 166–167
        in relapse-prevention approaches,
            130–132
        and three stages of treatment,
            170–177
    user-friendly, 270
    See also Outcome evaluation
Evaluation staff, 263
    ethnic diversity in, 263
Evidence-based practices or treatments,
        291, 292, 296

Information
    and time pressures, 292–293
    user-oriented transformation of, 273
Information fatigue syndrome, 282
Information system integrating technology
        and treatment. *See* Technology-
        treatment information system
Infrastructure, for support of partnerships
        among researchers and community
        treatment programs, 276
Injection drug users (IDUs), harm
        reduction approach for, 71–72
Innovators, 291
Institute of Medicine (IOM), *Bridging the
        Gap Between Practice and Research*,
        xi, xviii, 4, 198, 270, 287
Institute for Social Research, 94
Integrated Substance Abuse Treatment
        Programs, UCLA, 272, 282
Intermediate stage of care, 170, 173–174
*International Working Group on AIDS and
        IV Drug Use* newsletter, 73
Internet, and dissemination, 282
Interpersonal contact, as dissemination
        strategy, 272
Interpersonal situations, high risk, 123.
        See also High-risk situations
Interventions, time needed for adoption
        of, xiv
Interview
    motivational, 141–142
    with PROTOTYPE staff member
        (Wendy), 257–260
Iowa, PICs in, 214, 215

Jaffe, Jerome, 105, 109–110, 111, 113,
        114, 291
Joint Commission on Accreditation
        of Healthcare Organizations
        (JCAHO), 192
Joint ownership, 289–291
Judges, outcome expectations of, 160
Junkiebonden, Amsterdam, 71

Kaiser Family Foundation, 281

LAAM (levo-alpha-acetylmethadol),
        105, 107–108, 110–112, 113–115,
        116–117

difficulties in introducing, 273–274,
        277
    and Jaffe, 109–110
    lessons and recommendations on,
        115–116
    and PTSD–SUDS study, 239
    as research product, 5
    and SDPT, 230, 231
Labeling Assessment Study, 112
Languages(s)
    developing diversity of, 263–264
    of Matrix model, 129
    vernaculars of researcher vs. clinician,
        29
    See also Communication
Leadership, collaborative, 289–291
"Linking Assessment Technology to
        Improved Patient Care," 182.
        See also TECH Study
Local governments, in drug courts, 90
Los Angeles, needle exchange program
        in, 72

Managed care organizations
    and detoxification or stabilization care,
        171
    and dissemination efforts, 275, 281–282
    outcome expectations of, 160
    and Target City Demonstrations, 207
Marlatt, G. Alan, 106, 122, 127, 134, 143
Marlatt's model of relapse prevention,
        123–125
    investigations of, 132, 133
    and other approaches, 127
Matrix model of treatment for cocaine
        dependence, 128–130
    outcome evaluation on, 130–132
    refinement of, 132
Measurement Center, The, 251
Medicaid, and residential treatment
        models for pregnant/parenting
        women, 203
Medscape, 280
Mental health services, in therapeutic
        communities, 23
Mentor courts, for drug courts
        practitioners, 91–92
Methadone, 108–109
    increase in dosage of, 6
Methadone detoxification and
        maintenance, 26

Methadone maintenance, 105, 107–110,
112–113, 116–117
in acupuncture study, 46–47
as difficult to implement, 277
lessons and recommendations on,
115–116
limitations of, 111
with motivational interviewing, 143
in NIDA demonstration, 204
in PTSD–SUDS study, 238–239
and SDPT, 230, 231
in U.S. vs. rest of world, 110
Methods for evaluating treatment
outcomes
clinical tracking, 163–164
database monitoring, 164–165
performance indicator monitoring,
165–166
MI. *See* Motivational interviewing
Miami, Florida, drug court in, 88
Minority groups, and motivational
interviewing, 144
Model program or policy, use of research
in, 97
Moderation Management (MM), 57,
63–64
Nine-Step Program of, 63
MOTHERS (Medicaid Opportunities to
Help Enter Recovery Services),
203
Mothers Against Drunk Driving, 201
Motivation
for continuing care, 172
and therapeutic communities, 25
Motivational enhancement therapy, 143
Motivational interviewing (MI), 26, 105,
106, 139, 147–148
assumptions underlying, 139–140
dissemination of, 145–147
and evolution of practice–research
collaboration, 288
four foundational principles of, 140–141
and stabilization intervention, 172
strategies in, 141–142
studies on use of for drug abuse,
142–145
Moyers, Bill, 6
Multicultural coalitions, in California, 276
Multiple reporting requirements, as
DENS implementation issue, 190,
191–192
Multisite demonstration projects, 289

NADA. *See* National Acupuncture
Detoxification Association
protocol
Naloxone, 117
Naltrexone, 117
Narcotics Anonymous, 55, 57, 60
referral to, 175, 176
as strategy, 174
Narrative Report, in DENS ASI, 189
National Acupuncture Detoxification
Association (NADA) protocol,
39–40
and acupuncture counselors, 48
National Association of Drug Court
Professionals (NADCP), 89, 98
and evaluation of drug courts, 90
and mentor courts, 92
National Association of State Alcohol
and Drug Abuse Directors, 295
National Cancer Institute, Community
Clinical Oncology Program of,
275
National Development and Research
Institutes, Inc., Center for
Therapeutic Community
Research at, 25
National Drug Abuse Treatment Clinical
Trials Network. *See* Clinical Trials
Networks
National Drug Court Evaluation Program,
90
National Drug Court Institute (NDCI),
91
and drug court evaluation, 90, 92
National Highway Traffic Safety
Administration, 200
National Household Survey on Drug
Abuse, 39
National Institute on Alcohol Abuse and
Alcoholism, 132
homeless demonstration program of,
198
prevention research replication program
of, 199
National Institute on Drug Abuse
(NIDA)
Applied Evaluation Research Portfolio
of, 204–205, 207
and brainstorming conference, 283
Clinical Trials Network of, xviii–xix,
155, 208, 288, 293, 294, 295
conference sponsored by, 272

Danya International funded by, 279
and disconnect between science and
practice, xvii–xviii
and disconnect between science and
public perception, xvii
dissemination study funded by, 271
and drug court evaluation, 90
future research portfolio of, 282–283
HIV risk reduction programs of,
198–199
Human Interaction Research Institute
funded by, 279
IOM study sponsored by, xi
and LAAM, 111, 114–115
Medications Development Division of,
112
and opiate dependence treatment, 105
Perinatal-20 program of, 202
practitioner-oriented videos of, 273
*Preventing Drug Use Among Children and
Adolescents* of, 282
and PROTOTYPES, 253
and research-treatment partnerships,
275
and studies on therapeutic community's
efficacy, 28
support from, xxii
TC initiatives of, 31
transfer-strategy programs of, 277
treatment-approaches booklet of, 5
National Institute of Justice, and drug
court evaluation, 90
National Institutes of Health, xiv, 117
National Treatment Plan Initiative, xii
NDCI. *See* National Drug Court Institute
NDCI Review, 91
Needle exchange programs (NEPs), 15
in Amsterdam, 71, 73
and evolution of practice–research
collaboration, 288
and research, 13, 15, 72
Tacoma Syringe Exchange, 72–82
Needs assessment, of SF-PIC, 220
Networking, in self-help groups, 67
Neurobehavioral approach, Matrix model
as, 129
New Haven, Connecticut
needle exchange in, 79
SDPT studies in, 231
New Life Acceptance Program, 61–62, 67
New Mexico, drug-court evaluation in, 94
New Orleans, PICs in, 214–215

New York State
drug-court evaluation in, 94
PICs in, 214, 215
NIDA. *See* National Institute on Drug
Abuse
"NIDA Clinical Toolbox," xviii
Nixon, Richard, 105, 109, 116
Nonprofit management, and capacity
building, 277–278

Oakland, California, OAMT clinic in,
231, 237–238, 239
OAMT protocol, in PTSD–SUDS study,
238, 239, 240
Office of Alcoholism and Substance Abuse
Services, 215
Office of National Drug Control Policy, on
unmet demand for drug treatment,
4
Ohio
database-monitoring system in, 164
drug-court evaluation in, 94
Oklahoma, database-monitoring system
in, 164
Omnibus Crime Control Act (1994), 88
Opiate agonist maintenance therapy
(OAMT) treatment programs, in
Oakland clinic, 231, 237–238
Opioid dependence treatment. *See*
LAAM; Methadone maintenance
Oregon
database-monitoring system in, 164
PICs in, 214, 215
Organizational slack, 289
Organizational structure, at
PROTOTYPES, 255–256
Organizations, levels of, 295
Outcome(s), black-and-white, 223
Outcome evaluation, 157–158, 177
comparisons of, 168
confusion from options in, 169
domains of, 161–162
and expectations, 159–163
and particular types of care, 169–170
as varying with various perspectives,
169
methods of
clinical tracking, 163–164
database monitoring, 164–165
performance indicator monitoring,
165–166

and Addiction Technology Transfer
Centers, xix
as blending, xvii–xviii
changeableness of, 207
and Clinical Trials Network (CTN),
xviii–xix
in conventional vs. therapeutic-
community fields, 26
cultural issues for, 263–264
and narrow views of parties involved,
xxi
at PROTOTPES, 251–252, 262–263
and cross-area experience, 256–257
and integrative actions, 254–255
interview on (Wendy), 257–260
and organizational structure, 255–256
and staffing, 256
and staff training, 252–254
in PTSD–SUDS research, 232–234, 243
and communication between research
and clinical staff, 236–237, 238,
241–242
and differences in organizational
cultures, 239–240
and methadone maintenance/dose-
tapering protocol, 238–239
recruitment-related issues in,
234–236
and transitioning of patients,
240–242
in relapse prevention, 125–130,
132–133
and strength vs. deficit models, 264
and therapeutic communities
(reciprocity), 13, 21–22, 25–26,
26, 30–31
and varying interests of stakeholders,
206
See also Dissemination; Practice–
research collaboration
Research–practice utilization model, and
therapeutic communities, 28–29
Research strategies, "deconstructive" and
"enhancive," 30
Residential Services for Women and Their
Children, 203
Resource adequacy, and dissemination,
271
Resources, as DENS implementation issue,
190–191, 192
Responsibility for abstinence violation,
124

Responsibility for achievement of goals,
individual and joint, 170
Retention
and drug courts, 87, 96
vs. effectiveness, 20
and therapeutic communities, 20, 21, 28
Reward program, for abstaining from
cocaine, 3–4, 8
Rituals, of self-help groups, 67
Robert Wood Johnson Foundation, 272,
283
Closed Grant Report System of, 281
Rogerian approach, and motivational
interviewing, 139–140
Role playing, to desensitize anxiety, 66
Room, R., 206
Roxanne Pharmaceuticals, 114

Saint Louis Detoxification and Diagnostic
Evaluation Center, 199–200
Salem, Oregon—Seattle, Washington,
PICs in, 215
SAMHSA. See Substance Abuse
and Mental Health Services
Administration
San Francisco, needle exchange program
in, 72
San Francisco Bay Area HIV/AIDS
Prevention and Evaluation
Initiative, 276
San Francisco PIC (SF-PIC), 215,
216–224
Santa Cruz, New Mexico, needle
exchange program in, 72
SAODAP (Special Action Office for Drug
Abuse Prevention), 110, 111, 113
SAODAP Cooperative Study, 111
Schorr, Lisbeth, 270
Science
vs. ideology, 6
and practice, xvii
See also Research; Research–practice
links
Scientific journals, 7
clinicians distant from, 7, 16
SDPT. See Substance Dependence PTSD
Therapy
Secular Organizations for Sobriety (SOS),
56, 57
"social safety net" of, 67
Seemingly irrelevant decisions, 125

and veterans with PTSD, 229
  See also Self-help groups
"Twin Epidemics of Substance Use and
    HIV, The" (National Commission
    on AIDS report) 79

University of California Los Angeles
  Drug Abuse Research Center at, 251
  Integrated Substance Abuse Treatment
    Programs of, 272, 282
University of Southern California, 251
  Research Advisory Panel at, 259
U.S. Centers for Disease Control. *See*
    Centers for Disease Control, U.S.
U.S. Department of Justice, Office of Law
    Enforcement Assistance (later
    Law Enforcement Assistance
    Administration), 199
U.S. Department of Veterans' Affairs,
    VERDICT research brief of, 281
Useful interventions, focus on, 291
User involvement, as dissemination
    strategy, 272
U.S. General Accounting Office (GAO),
    and needle exchange, 79
U.S. Public Health Service, Tuskegee
    syphilis experiment of, 156

VERDICT program, 280, 281
Veteran Affairs Cooperative Study, 111
Veterans' Affairs Department, VERDICT
    research brief of, 281
Veterans Affairs health care system,
    treatment of PTSD and substance

dependence in, 229
Vietnam veterans
  and need to address heroin problem,
    109, 117
  with PTSD–SUDS, 229–230, 233
Vouchers, to reward abstinence, 8

Wall, The (in Matrix model), 129
Washington, DC, detoxification program
    in, 199
Washington State, database-monitoring
    system in, 164
Web-based data collection system, as SF-
    PIC objective, 224
Web sites
  for consumer information systems, 280
  for CTN, 155
  for Danya International, 279
  for DENS, 193, 195
  for Drug Abuse Treatment Outcome
    Study, 273
  for PIC program, 215
  for SAMHSA, 277, 282
Wendy (interviewee at PROTOTYPES),
    257–260
Whysner study, 112
Women for Sobriety (WFS), 56, 57, 61
  ritual of, 67
Working Alliance Inventory, 42
Working the program, in AA, 64–65
Workshops, on drug courts, 91–92

Yale Medical School, acupuncture
    research at, 42–47

ABOUT THE EDITORS

James L. Sorensen, PhD, is a professor of psychiatry at the University of California, San Francisco. With support from the National Institute on Drug Abuse and the American Foundation for AIDS Research, he has developed and evaluated numerous innovative treatment approaches. He has coauthored *A Family Like Yours: Breaking the Patterns of Drug Abuse* (with G. Bernal) and *Preventing AIDS in Drug Users and Their Sexual Partners* (with L. Wermuth, D. Gibson, K.-H. Choi, J. Guydish, and S. Batki) and has authored more than 170 professional publications. He is a member of the board of the College on Problems of Drug Dependence and has served on the boards of American Psychological Association (APA) Divisions 50 (Addictions) and 28 (Psychopharmacology and Substance Abuse), where he is president-elect.

Richard A. Rawson, PhD, is the associate director of the University of California at Los Angeles Integrated Substance Abuse Programs. During the past decade, he has worked with the U.S. State Department on large substance abuse research and treatment projects. He has published two books, 15 book chapters, and more than 100 professional papers and has conducted more than 1,000 workshops, paper presentations, and training sessions.

Joseph Guydish, PhD, is an associate adjunct professor of medicine and health policy at the University of California, San Francisco. He has led several studies funded by the National Institute on Drug Abuse and the Center for Substance Abuse Treatment. He has served on various local, state, and national committees related to substance abuse treatment, most recently as scientific advisor on a California statewide evaluation of drug courts.

Joan E. Zweben, PhD, is a clinical psychologist and APA Fellow. She is a clinical professor of psychiatry at the School of Medicine, University of California, San Francisco. She is the founder and executive director of the 14th Street Clinic and Medical Group and the East Bay Community Recovery Project. Her books include *Treating Patients With Alcohol and Drug Problems: An Integrated Approach* (with R. Margolis) and *The Alcohol and Drug Wildcard: Substance Abuse and Psychiatric Disorders in People With HIV Disease* (with P. Denning). She has published more than 55 articles or book chapters and has edited 14 monographs on treating addiction.